TO FEED THIS WORLD———————————————————

W9-BPN-504

STERLING WORTMAN · RALPH W. CUMMINGS, JR.

TO FEED THIS WORLD

The challenge
and the strategy

THE JOHNS HOPKINS UNIVERSITY PRESS · BALTIMORE AND LONDON

Copyright © 1978 by The Johns Hopkins University Press
All rights reserved. No part of this book may be reproduced or
transmitted in any form or by any means, electronic or mechanical, including photocopying, recording, xerography, or any
information storage and retrieval system, without permission in
writing from the publisher. Manufactured in the United States
of America.

The Johns Hopkins University Press, Baltimore, Maryland 21218
The Johns Hopkins Press Ltd., London

Originally published, 1978
Second printing, 1979

Johns Hopkins paperback edition, 1978
Second printing, 1979
Third printing, 1979

Library of Congress Catalog Card Number 78–8478
ISBN 0–8018–2136–3 (hardcover)
ISBN 0–8018–2137–1 (paperback)

Library of Congress Cataloging in Publication data will be
found on the last printed page of this book.

To our families

for their support and understanding

CONTENTS

The challenge

Implications for the assistance community

PREFACE

A DILEMMA faces those attempting to increase world food supplies and to alleviate poverty and suffering.

The increasingly critical nature of the world food-poverty-population situation must be plainly stated; local, national, and international authorities must somehow be mobilized for quick action. Yet description of the crisis so often leads to despair—to an attitude, exacerbated by superficial coverage of the subject by some of the mass media and by some individual writers, that the situation may already be hopeless.

Contrarily, attempts to describe the growing world capabilities to deal with the problems are shouted down by pessimists. Or, more critically, descriptions of new technological capabilities sometimes lead the public to the mistaken belief that the food problem will be overcome without serious additional efforts; that human and financial resources can be directed to other concerns.

Let us be clear on these points. The world food situation is alarming, but increased food production is only a part of the solution.

All nations—wealthy or poor, agrarian or industrialized—must work more effectively to increase agricultural production, decrease population growth rates, and promote widespread improvements of incomes in developing countries. We believe that a vigorous campaign must begin quicky—not in the mid 1980s or 1990s, but now. Failure to do so could result in much greater suffering in low-income countries plus substantial penalties for the industrial nations. Moreover, a magnificent opportunity —possibly a once-in-history opportunity—to deal with this global threat may be missed.

For millions of rural families, and for scores of nations in distress, quick and effective action is especially important. Food is an individual family problem, and it is not enough for a nation simply to produce more. Each family needs to be able to produce or earn access to its food supply.

xi

We believe that new world capabilities offer a firm basis for hope that world hunger and the associated poverty can be alleviated. Not quickly. Not in a year. Perhaps not in a decade. Certainly not without interruptions, for progress will depend in large part on actions of individual national governments, and these vary in interest and in resources. But those poorer nations with the will to do so should be able to make rapid progress. The tide could be turned in the next decade if they implement appropriate domestic policies, if they launch sound programs, and if they receive adequate technical and financial assistance.

These new capabilities have for the most part emerged since the early 1960s. They have been described piecemeal. Some of the few people centrally involved in trying to feed people remind us that they generally have been too busy to put more books on the shelves. Consequently, literature on accelerated development of agriculture is fragmented and dominated by the writings of observers, not participants, and is often based on third-hand information.

It is not enough to say that world capabilities allow a solution and leave it at that. Success in overcoming the food-poverty-population problem will not result from past accomplishments, important as they have been. Rather, progress will depend on actions taken now and in the immediate future. We feel that most of the needed steps are understood or can be learned quickly; that the elements of the solution can now be fitted together through the concerted and sustained actions of many governments, institutions, and individuals.

We appear to be at a point in dealing with the world food situation similar to that which the U.S. reached around 1960, when the decision was made to put a man on the moon in a decade: the achievement of the goal is technically feasible; many elements of a successful approach are known; it is likely that the many additional problems can be solved as they occur; and the time is propitious to embark on a far-reaching effort. There is one major difference: we dare not fail to make the effort on the food-poverty-population problem, and we dare not delay in that effort. The nature and the existence of civilization are at stake.

What do we hope to accomplish in this book?

First, for authorities of the developing countries and those who assist them, we seek to point out the approaches to rapid agricultural development that seem most promising in light of recent experience, the new resources that can be exploited, and some pitfalls that can be avoided.

Second, accelerated agricultural development involves a process of economic participation which seems to many to be even more difficult and painful to achieve than political enfranchisement. Most countries have powerful minorities who perceive the kind of change we describe as being inimical to their own interest and therefore to the national interest. That need not be. We wish to demonstrate that economic and social justice, as well as prosperity, is in the long-run interest of most, if not all, elements of society, and we hope that this message gets through.

Third, since we believe that the future welfare of developed countries depends heavily on concurrent advances in the well-being of people elsewhere, we wish to present arguments for the immediate strengthening of technical assistance efforts and for increases in financial aid through existing international banks and bilateral agencies.

Fourth, for those studying or writing on the subject, we wish to provide our best explanations for some misunderstood aspects of agriculture and the evidence on which our explanations are based, together with some references to writings of others which might be useful in future coverage of events as they unfold.

Fifth, to our colleagues in the biological sciences, in economics, and in other disciplines, we want to suggest some new opportunities to make our professional contributions more effective and to allow scientists to lead a world effort to improve the lot of mankind. The gap between what we have learned and what is applied in the countryside remains enormous. We must go beyond "research" and "model-building" to apply the fruits of this work in actual practice—to focus on the missing links between perceived potential and actual performance.

Sixth, we wish to reassure the public that progress has been made in dealing with the food-poverty-population problem, that there is a realistic basis for hope, and that this is a time for action, not despair.

Seventh, we hope to direct more attention and debate to strategies for action, rather than to a continuation of superficial descriptions of the food problem.

The materials presented are based on the work of many individuals and institutions. It would be impossible to name them all. In particular, this report has been prepared from the vantage point of individuals associated with The Rockefeller Foundation and the International Agricultural Development Service. We have been privileged to have many opportunities to exchange views with knowledgeable persons working on agricultural development from developing and developed countries, from the international banks, from bilateral assistance agencies, from the Ford Foundation, Canada's International Development Research Centre, FAO, and the United Nations Development Programme, from universities, from the international agricultural research institutes, and from many corporations. At a meeting held at Airlie House, Virginia in June 1977, major components of the strategy discussed in Chapters 10 through 14 were debated by 70 agricultural authorities with expertise in the biological sciences and social sciences and experience in planning, administration, and implementation of commodity production programs, defined-area campaigns, and organization of services in a range of countries throughout the low-income world. Much of what we have learned has been distilled from such exchanges. We credit them for that in this report which is correct, accepting for ourselves blame for errors of fact or interpretation. We wish to express our special appreciation to Steven Breth, who did so much to make this book readable, particularly for the nonspecialist. Support from The Rockefeller Foundation and the Lilly Endowment made this book possible.

We cannot claim to be equally knowledgeable about all aspects of agricultural development. For example, we have more experience in Asia and Latin America, and therefore know more about the people and conditions in these regions, than in Africa and the Mideast. We have been closer to developments in crops than in animals. We place an especially high premium on the role of technology and the importance of research, but only if it is organized to reach and benefit great numbers of rural people. Perhaps other biases also enter our treatment of agricultural development. We acknowledge these personal or professional shortcomings and ask that the reader bear them in mind. However, we believe that the principles discussed apply to all aspects of agriculture, whether crop or animal oriented, and to most, if not all, regions of the world.

It was tempting to prepare, or to attempt to prepare, a scholarly work on this subject. But, aside from the fact that we might not have been equal to such a task, the future of agricultural development and its benefits to man are really in the hands of nonscientists, even nonagriculturists. The political, commercial, and financial authorities, with proper advice from informed agriculturists, will make the key decisions on which agriculture's future contribution will depend. This book, then, has been prepared for such nonspecialists, rather than for the agricultural specialist.

The task ahead is great and complex, involving the synchronization of efforts of many institutions in each country and requiring decisions to change by millions of farmers. And agricultural development is not a panacea for the troubles of mankind. As Carlos P. Romulo of the Philippines reminds us, "A stimulated agriculture does not decrease the number of problems for governments. But the nature of the problems changes, and in the process people and nations benefit. What nation would not exchange the problems of static production for those of lively progress?"

We hope the material we present in this volume will hasten change.

STERLING WORTMAN
RALPH W. CUMMINGS, JR.

Overview of the food-poverty-population problem

Introduction

THAT THE WORLD food situation today is serious, even precarious, is well established. That world population was only 2,000 million in 1930, reached 3,000 million in 1960, and now stands at over 4,000 million is a fact. That man's numbers will reach 6,000 million or more during the next 25 years is a near certainty. That food deficits in many countries are reaching dangerous levels is well documented. That hundreds of millions of people in several scores of nations still live in abject poverty, plagued by hunger or malnutrition, is undeniable.

The complexity and magnitude of the task notwithstanding, for the first time in history it is now possible for many governments to act against *both* hunger and poverty. A decade ago—or probably even 5 years ago— success would not have been possible for most countries. In making this assertion, we are quite mindful of the words of U.S. President Truman in the now-famous "Point Four" of his 1949 inaugural address:

Fourth, we must embark on a bold new program for making the benefits of our scientific advances and industrial progress available for the improvement and growth of underdeveloped areas.

More than half the people of the world are living in conditions approaching misery. Their food is inadequate, they are victims of disease. Their economic life is primitive and stagnant. Their poverty is a handicap and a threat, both to them and to more prosperous areas.

For the first time in history, humanity possesses the knowledge and the skill to relieve the suffering of these people.

One may ask, then, why it is any more realistic to claim today that governments could successfully attack hunger and poverty than it was three decades ago. There are good reasons, and a strategy for action is emerging. But to understand the strategy, one must understand the nature of the problem.

The three eras of agricultural development

For as long as man has inhabited the earth, securing adequate food supplies has been one of his primary preoccupations. Over thousands of years, people have practiced subsistence or traditional agriculture. First, there were the hunters and gatherers of food; then, as groups took up sedentary farming, there began the long and slow process of the evolution of countless systems of crop and animal production, many of which persist today. Those traditional farming systems comprise only man, his animals, his seed, and his land. There is little need for involvement of government or industry, or cooperation with others outside the community. The productivity of such systems is largely limited by fertility of the soil and characteristics of climate.

As populations have burgeoned, particularly in recent decades, land-holdings have been divided and subdivided among heirs so that in many of the more populous nations, farms are tiny by North American standards. For example, in Nepal, a nation of some 12 million people, 92 percent of the farms are under 3 hectares in size. In parts of Indonesia, the average holding is less than one-half hectare. Land is so dear that terraces have been carved into the hillsides from bottom to top, at great expense in human labor, causing serious erosion problems.

The evolution, over thousands of years, of traditional farming systems —which the great bulk of the world's farmers still use today—constitutes a *first era* of agricultural development.

A *second era* of agricultural development—science based and industry supported—has largely occurred in this century. During the past 75 years we have witnessed an agricultural revolution in which the now-industrial nations pioneered and excelled. That revolution has been characterized by the creation, by genetic manipulation, of more efficient crop varieties and animal strains; the development and use of chemical fertilizers and of science-based means to control diseases and insect pests; the development of agribusiness; the expansion of road networks, power grids, and use of farm machinery; the development of means of mass communication of information; and of course the ever greater skill of farm entrepreneurs in intensified agriculture. Rising economic demand for goods and services has spurred this remarkable era of ever higher yields per unit of area, time, or investment. Science and industry have provided the building blocks for today's advanced agricultural systems, but let us not forget the role of the farm producer in the equally sophisticated task of putting together for the individual farm all the components of productive and profitable systems. Nor should we forget that the agricultural revolution of this century, triggered by the rediscovery in 1900 of Mendel's laws of genetics, has spanned three-fourths of a century.

We are now entering a *third era*, the era of accelerated, forced-pace agricultural and rural development efforts. Scores of nations in serious difficulty are looking for ways to increase food production and incomes and raise living standards among the rural masses, not in 50 or 75 years, but in 10 or 15. There is no time to lose. The incentives for action are becoming clear: they involve urgent matters of political stability and national security, as well as economics.

First, government leaders are increasingly aware that, unless they take steps to develop their rural areas through widespread involvement of the rural poor, they will likely face unrest, violence, even revolution. With advances in mass communication and transportation, long-neglected people are recognizing that a relatively small fraction of the citizenry is enjoying the comforts of life. Yet they see little hope for themselves or for their children. They are responsive to any ideology which will offer to them those things they hold most important: food, clothing, health care, education, security—and hope.

Second, with the recent (1973–74) disappearance of large crop surpluses in the U.S. and other countries and the resulting high prices, governments have learned that they can no longer count on continuing access to the cheap sources of food which enabled them to keep food costs low in their urban areas while neglect of their agricultural areas and people persisted. High food costs in international markets, which require substantial outlays of scarce foreign exchange, have for the first time forced some governments, for security reasons, to worry about increasing the productivity of their long-neglected small farms.

Third, governments are learning they can substantially expand their domestic markets for products of urban industry by extending science-based, market-oriented agricultural production systems among great masses of rural people. As farm families have access to greater disposable income through increased agricultural profits, they become purchasers of goods and services. Employment rises not only on farms but especially in rural trade centers.

This third era of agricultural development must involve concerted efforts to move into the countryside more aggressively and systematically with roads and power systems, with supply of inputs and arrangements for the marketing of agricultural products. Moreover, scientists must work directly in rural areas to create the more highly productive, more profitable farming systems which will contribute to the primary ingredient for rural development: increased income for large numbers of farm families.

Decreased rates of population growth must be achieved wherever necessary; otherwise there can be no long-term solution to the food-poverty-population problem. Economic development should contribute to the lowering of population growth rates, and successful efforts to get agricultural production up in the developing countries is central to economic development. Agricultural development efforts buy time for slowing population growth, and that time must be used wisely.

The task ahead

We must not underestimate either the complexity of the task ahead or the dedication to the efforts required. In mid-1975 the world population was about 4,000 million. About 2,000 million people will be added by the year 2000, about two-thirds of them in already heavily populated nations.

Before World War II, Latin America, Africa, and Asia were net exporters of grain—the staple food of most populations. By 1950 they had become net importers of about 5 million tons a year. By 1960 their net deficit had climbed to 19 million tons and by 1973 to around 47 million tons. Their combined deficit for 1976 was about 60 million tons. Unless the trend in production in developing market-economy countries improves, world production of cereals by 1985 is projected to fall short of demand by 100–200 million tons.

It is important to understand the nature and diversity of the countries where the problems of hunger and poverty are or will likely become most severe.

- *Most developing countries are extremely poor.* While in 1975 the per person gross national product was US$7,060 in the U.S., $6,650 in Canada, and $2,620 in the U.S.S.R., there were 61 countries with per capita gross national products of less than $500 and 36 with GNPs of less than $250. The nations in difficulty are terribly poor, and, generally speaking, income levels among the masses of the rural people are well below the average in each of those countries.
- *Many nations are small.* In 1976 there were 161 nations or geopolitical entities with substantial local autonomy, and 105 had populations of less than 10 million (78 had populations of 5 million or less and, of these, 34 had fewer than 1 million).
- *Many nations are newly independent.* Of the 43 nations considered by the United Nations as "least developed" or "most seriously affected" by the recent economic crisis, 36 have become independent since 1945 and 29 of these since 1960.

The newer, smaller, poorer countries face most of the problems of the larger, older, developing countries. In addition, they have severe problems in gaining access to trade, financial and technical assistance, and knowledge.

As colonial systems have weakened, the cutting of political ties with major industrial nations has frequently been accompanied by a loss of assured markets for exports or assured sources of needed imports. New trade relationships must be worked out with the industrialized countries. Foreign commercial investment in local agricultural enterprises has generally become less attractive because of local opposition to management of domestic enterprises by foreign personnel. Each small entity finds itself jostling with a great number of other small entities for technical and financial assistance. The developing countries face serious difficulties in attempting to fit the vast new array of potential assistance to their particular needs.

Most of the newly independent nations were left with limited scientific or managerial capability to improve food production. In general, the colonial powers had done much to develop export crops and animal species destined for sale abroad. While the developing nations are dotted with centers for research on coffee, cacao, rubber, or jute, until a few years ago one could find few centers for work on wheat, maize, rice, the food legumes, the root crops, the vegetables, or other food crops. The basic food crops were neglected. It should be recalled, however, that in 1930 the world population was only 2,000 million, or half that of 1975; there was not the same population pressure on the land that exists today in most countries, and, until a few decades ago, the increasing food needs of those countries could be met by cultivating more land. But that option is disappearing—or is already gone.

Small nations, whether they are newly independent or not, cannot expect to have the full range of scientific and other professional services required in all fields important to their development. They must usually rely heavily on external help.

In the governments of most low-income countries, the persons in authority are military men, lawyers, businessmen, physicians, engineers, economists, or religious leaders. Few understand agriculture or the technology and science which underlie it.

Given the complexity and urgency of the task ahead, one can rightly ask, Is there any hope? The answer is yes, the world does have the capabilities, and the reasons why need to be understood. To a large degree, these capabilities have come into being during the past decade.

The basis for hope

The basis for hope rests on several factors. The world's leaders are becoming more aware of the problem. The physical resource base, particularly arable land and water, can permit a substantial increase in the intensity of cropping in most countries. Steps have been taken to begin to produce the crop strains and related technologies required to increase agricultural production in the tropics and subtropics, where most developing countries are. Fertilizers have become available in sufficient quantities and at low enough cost to allow their use to be extended to the food crops in the low-income countries. International assistance mechanisms exist which can provide funds and technical counsel for development efforts. Most of these efforts can be financed on a loan basis because investment in agriculture is at least as profitable as investment in airlines, manufacturing, or housing. It has been demonstrated that the developing countries can, if they will, successfully promote agricultural and rural development. It has been shown that the farmers will shift to new systems if these prove sufficiently productive and profitable. The will of governments to take action is growing. These factors, combined with the tremendous scope for increasing food-crop production in most developing countries, represent the basis for the statement that for the first time in history we now have an opportunity to deal effectively with the problem.

The strategy

A prime concern of the government of any nation, if that government is to remain in power, is provision of the fundamental requirements of its citizenry. Among those requirements are security, an adequate food supply, and the means for an improved standard of living. Central to progress in all poorer agrarian countries is increased productivity and prosperity of the rural areas.

In agrarian nations it is the many farmers with tiny landholdings, often in remote areas, plus those people on the coasts who depend upon near-shore fisheries and aquaculture[1] for a livelihood, who produce the bulk of the food supplies. Usually, raising the productivity and income of these rural dwellers—among the poorest of the poor—requires new high-yielding, science-based crop and animal production systems tailored to the unique combination of soil, climatic, biological, and economic conditions of each locality.

In short, the agricultural revolution which has undergirded the economic advances of the industrialized nations must be extended quickly and systematically to all areas of the poorer agrarian countries.

SOURCES OF RURAL WEALTH

There are several possible sources of increased wealth in rural areas, including agriculture, extractive industries (for example, mining, oil

---

[1] Culture and husbandry of aquatic plants and animals in fresh or brackish water.

production), manufacturing, tourism, public works, and activities financed by entities external to the locality (extension, education, and health programs). Each, in essence, involves the production of goods and services for sale to, or financed by, people outside the area. Local people may then use the money earned for increased consumption of goods and services produced in the area or elsewhere, for reinvestment in production enterprises, or for savings.

The income multiplier. To the extent that increased income circulates locally in payment for goods and services—to the food seller, the bank, the shoe-repair shop, or laborers—that wealth has a "multiplier" effect on employment and standard of living. A unit of currency brought in may pass through several hands. Those seeking to improve the well-being of people in particular regions should try to exploit all possible sources of significantly increased wealth, but special attention should be given to the contribution of each activity to "multiplier" effects.

The role of agriculture. Agriculture has several characteristics which make it particularly attractive for increasing rural incomes. It is the activity in which most rural people, either directly or indirectly, are already involved. Because a high proportion of the rural income of farm families is spent locally, it has a high potential multiplier effect. Numerous agricultural industries can be established to supply production inputs such as seeds, tractors, implements, and fertilizers, and to process products. Finally opportunities that would permit significant increases in agricultural productivity already exist.

TWO SIDES OF THE FOOD PROBLEM

Increasing farm production to meet the needs of the rural family is important. But one objective of agricultural development must be to allow individual families to produce a surplus for sale so that the total output of a locality exceeds total local requirements and permits sales in urban centers, other rural regions, or in international markets. Inputs required for higher productivity must be purchased and markets for products must be established. In short, traditional farmers must be brought into the market economy. In this way they will become purchasers of larger amounts of goods and services, contributing not only to the vitality of enterprises in the rural trade centers (through the multiplier effect), but also to the expansion of domestic markets for products of urban industry.

As increasing numbers of traditional or subsistence farms are brought into the market economy, they will require a range of services similar to those of other small businesses. Many of these services—input supply and marketing—can often be supplied most efficiently by private enterprise.

Some, including development of improved farming systems and development of nonhybrid crop varieties, must be provided by government since private industry usually cannot recapture investments in such activities.

When we speak of the world food problem, we often tend to oversimplify it. The immediate problem to be attacked is low agricultural productivity and lack of employment of great masses of rural people.

Clearly there are two sides to the food problem: one is to increase production; the second is to create purchasing power among the hungry. The effort to increase crop and animal production on the hundreds of millions of family farms around the world gets at both sides of the equation. It is the only approach which does.

TARGETING ON THE SMALL FARMER

Agricultural development is commonly organized to achieve local or nationwide gains in the production of particular commodities, or of many commodities in particular regions of countries. Goals are often expressed in terms of tonnages to be achieved or hectares to be covered in a given time. Such goals may be appropriate under some circumstances. But if such are the goals, agencies cannot be blamed for concentrating on the better agricultural regions or working with large farmers, because those are the quickest and least expensive ways to achieve output or area-coverage goals. Until recently, there have been few direct attempts to help large numbers of *small* farmers to increase productivity and incomes, with numbers of farmers to be benefited as the goal. If such farmer-participation goals are not clearly stated, agencies will not undertake the difficult task of working with numerous small farmers, and they will continue to be by-passed. Contrarily, if efforts are aimed at the small farmers, all farmers will benefit, for the educated farm operators with large holdings are generally quick to adopt any advances which increase farm profitability. By casting the development net to involve small farmers, most farmers will benefit.

MEETING REQUIREMENTS FOR FARMER PARTICIPATION

Experience in many countries demonstrates that farmers will shift to more productive and profitable agricultural systems *if they can*. This applies to the relatively uneducated producer with small holdings as well as to those well-educated entrepreneurs with large farms. To enable farmers to participate in the market economy, a number of requirements must be met simultaneously. First, productive and profitable combinations of technology must be available. Second, the farmer must be instructed in their use. Third, necessary inputs (seed, fertilizer, pesticides, vaccines and feed supplements for animals) and credit must be available when and where the farmer needs them and at a price that allows a profit. Fourth, there must be markets for farm produce.

If any of these four requirements is lacking, farmers will not switch to more productive practices. Government efforts in the past have often centered on individual components such as supply of credit, or of seed, or extension services, with disappointing production results. Such failures usually stem from remaining weaknesses in the system, quite often in the technological component, or from markets or supply points that are too distant from farms, or from prices to farmers that are too low to allow a reasonable profit. Usually the fault for failure is not the farmer's; it lies in the design or execution of programs, including policy components.

AGRARIAN TRANSFORMATION

In many countries the institutional structure of agriculture, particularly the land tenure situation, is not conducive to developing a productive agriculture built on small farms, individually or collectively managed. Land tenure largely determines who benefits from increases in productivity. It influences the amount of the farmer's production by determining when he gets access to new technologies, including the necessary inputs, and how much of the production he is able to retain. It shapes the distribution of employment opportunities in the agricultural sector. It influences the rural person's income and status in the community.

In some countries, governments are distributing state-held lands. And some individuals and corporations are beginning to divest themselves of extensive landholdings—some doing so, they say, while they still can. In other countries, however, land reform may be required.

Distribution of land in itself will not lead to higher productivity unless the four requirements listed earlier also are met. Often these conditions do not exist and results of land reform programs remain disappointing.

Programs to increase the productivity and profitability of agriculture need not wait for land reform; many subsistence farms, or those with limited sales, could, through provision of necessary services (including supply of technology), produce larger surpluses than they do now—and without undue delay. However, in the absence of effective agrarian reform the results will never reach full potential in terms of either production or income distribution. This concept of a high density of farms owned and operated by families is broad enough to embrace independent farm units in a free-enterprise system, farm federations, cooperatives, and even the communes of the People's Republic of China (Chapter 11).

APPROACHES TO ACCELERATED AGRICULTURAL DEVELOPMENT

Development of agriculture and rural areas has taken many forms. Most offer some benefits and most have significant limitations. None alone is adequate.

New institutions have been established and existing ones—planning agencies, research and extension organizations, universities or colleges and schools of agriculture, credit banks, supply and marketing organizations, farmer groups (including cooperatives)—have been strengthened with varying degrees of success. All are important, and such efforts must continue. If national progress is to be greatly accelerated, however, such institutions, and others public and private, must become directly involved in development programs, making concerted efforts in each farming district. Their contributions to development, rather than their own growth and prosperity as institutions, must be the measure of success. This will often require substantial modifications in their goals, their organizational structures, the qualifications of their staff, the arrangements for integration of their efforts, and their reward systems.

The most dramatic advances of recent decades have involved *commodity production programs*. In the developing countries there have been many instances of success—particularly with plantation or export crops—involving synchronization of production, research, and marketing. More recently there have been successes with basic food crops such as wheat in India, Mexico, Pakistan, and Turkey; rice in Colombia, India, Pakistan, and the Philippines; and maize in Kenya.

Another tactic now being widely employed is *defined-area campaigns* to achieve widespread gains in the productivity and incomes of rural people. In a particular locality this approach may be limited to intensive efforts to increase the productivity and profitability of one or a few commodities, or it may encompass comprehensive attempts to improve agriculture, education, housing, and health care, as well as to provide nonfarm sources of employment, through "integrated development." Defined-area development builds understanding of a rural community— its resources, the aspirations and activities of the people, its problems, and its potentials—and permits subsequent changes in the community to be measured. The ability of public and private agencies to cooperate can be determined, and weaknesses can be corrected. Innovations can be tested, and errors minimized, prior to wider-scale application. Moreover, such defined-area programs allow staff, through work with farmers and others, to become skilled in the solution of farm-level problems.

Successful efforts to force the pace of agricultural development must involve simultaneous provision of all necessary services, locality by locality—roads, markets, prices, input supply, and research. This will require *reorientation and synchronization* of the activities of diverse government agencies and of private industries, and decentralization of marketing and supply systems. To be effective at local levels, synchronization or coordination must occur at every level of government, including the top levels of ministries. A number of nations are seeking mechanisms by which to facilitate such synchronization.

The most comprehensive and desirable approach to accelerated development is a *combination* of commodity-oriented and defined-area efforts, supplemented by the strengthening of relevant institutions and attention to synchronization of the many services required for the success of either approach. It is important to note that the most effective way to improve institutions is to involve them in purposeful, fast-moving development efforts. The alternative of building institutions with the expectation that somehow they will later contribute to rapid development generally has been disappointing. While staff members may be well educated, they will lack the competence which only prior experience in development programs can provide.

Before national, comprehensive, accelerated agricultural development programs begin, long-term (15- to 20-year) goals should be established. This will provide the framework for shorter-term (say, 5-year) plans. At best, agricultural development is slow and involves large numbers of biological and social variables. It is important that such efforts be made in the right direction. Long-term goals cannot be precise, for no one can foresee all problems and potentials with clarity. Much planning must be based on the judgment of knowledgeable individuals, bolstered by experimental evidence to the extent possible. This will require the joint efforts of political leaders, planners, businessmen, industrialists, and persons of vision in the various agricultural specialties.

Obstacles to overcome

One might wish that accelerated agricultural development were a simple matter that men of vision, authority, and good will could with confidence set in motion at once. Sometimes, unusual opportunities do occur, as when India launched the High-Yielding Varieties Program in 1964, when the Philippines started its "Masagana 99" campaign, or when Turkey intensified wheat production in her coastal areas (Chapter 8). Similar opportunities no doubt will continue to arise, but isolated instances will be insufficient. Rather, governments must establish long-range national goals and create mechanisms and conditions for broad and rapid change in desired directions. They must place responsibility in the hands of individuals prepared to achieve ambitious targets, and then sustain long-term efforts. And international assistance agencies must support enlightened governments in such endeavors.

The wide range of barriers to the acceleration so urgently needed in so many countries must be surmounted.

• Not all national governments have the will to invest in agricultural development. The high financial returns to investment in agriculture

Three nonsolutions

Three often-mentioned "solutions" are important but do not address the basic causes of the world food problem. First, increased production in North America and by surplus-producers elsewhere will not contribute directly to the solution of the *world* food problem. Poor countries can ill afford to pay for food imports. Moreover, their deficits are growing so fast that neither North America nor others can possibly afford to provide free or subsidized food on the scale which soon will be required if developing countries are unable to speed agricultural development.

Second, large-scale mechanized crop production in most of the densely populated developing countries is not a practical solution to their food problem so long as the hungry have no way of getting more money to buy food. Moreover, large-scale mechanized farming generally is less productive per hectare than is "gardening," which can be practiced on small farms with abundant labor supply. Mechanized agricultural systems raise productivity per man-year and are highly productive otherwise, but most poor countries need labor-intensive systems.

Third, production of synthetic foods, single-cell protein, or other manufactured food products is not an answer to the world food problem. Here again the hungry have no means by which to pay for food of any kind, and such items are too expensive for free distribution on the scale which would be required.

often are not made known to national authorities in language they understand. Moreover, food aid—food sold at concessional rates or donated—is often used for continuing support of governments which neglect their rural problems.

- Development efforts are often fragmented. Responsibilities are divided among ministries or among departments within ministries. Capital and technical assistance is often provided through a series of scattered and uncoordinated projects.
- Individuals in developing countries who are attracted to agricultural development programs often are poorly trained and do not have farm-level experience.
- Too few of the technical assistance personnel from the developed countries are experienced in planning and implementing programs to accelerate agricultural development.
- Conservatism predominates among scientists in both the developing and developed countries. Disciplinary rather than problem-solving orientations persist. Laboratory work is of higher prestige than farm-level research and action programs. In-service training receives minor attention.
- The literature on agricultural development is often only remotely relevant to the problems that program practitioners must face.

A new level of effort required

The task ahead is vast and complex. It requires concerted work by individuals of considerable scientific and managerial ability—at least equivalent to those of the research and development efforts undergirding space programs.

The creation of new crop varieties and associated cropping systems will require, both at international centers and in national research programs, capable plant breeders, agronomists, soil specialists, plant pathologists, entomologists, animal scientists, biochemists, and economists, to name a few. They must tailor the crops and cropping systems to the ecological, climatic, and soil conditions of every season of every region of every country.

Decentralized systems must be devised to supply the inputs, fertilizers, pesticides, water, and credit to large numbers of farmers at low cost, and these must be established in a hurry. There must be improved marketing systems, including arrangements for the purchase, transport, processing, and sale of farm products. Industry must be involved in preservation, storage, supply of quality seed, and many other aspects of modern market-oriented agricultural systems.

In each country attention must be given to means of involving every relevant institution—public and private—in direct efforts to lift productivity, incomes, and living standards in rural areas. This calls for individuals who understand how national systems can be synchronized to achieve maximum progress at lowest cost.

The old idea that the U.S. or other countries could transfer agricultural know-how to other countries wholesale is a myth. Much technology, of course, is transferable. However, the idea that industrial countries could simply send farmers or extension specialists to the poor countries to show them how to farm, and thereby raise yields, has now been set aside. Such farmers and extension agents generally are highly competent people, but most of the temperate-climate farming practices in which they are skilled simply will not work in developing countries. The reason is that such prerequisites as efficient crop varieties, disease and insect-control practices, and means of preventing animal diseases are not yet available. The sophistication of the efforts required must not be underestimated.

Where responsibility rests

Every government must be responsible for the food supply of its own people and for the development of its rural areas. Only the individual government can determine amounts to be imported or produced locally.

Only the government can set the policies, strengthen the institutions, and reach the farmers and other rural people. Outside agencies can assist, as they must wherever governments are committed to rural progress and outside help is welcomed, but that is all they can do.

Summary

The challenge of increased food production is urgent for all. A primary component of the solution to the world food problem is for poor countries to get crop and animal production up, and to do so on hundreds of millions of small farms. But production of food in itself is not enough. The hungry have no money, and until their purchasing power is increased, giving them access to food as well as other necessities, there can be no solution to the world food problem.

In discussing strategies for advances in rural areas, one must remember that increasing agricultural productivity and prosperity in the countryside is not a panacea for the economic and social problems of a nation. But rural progress will be crucial to the general development of most nations. Those responsible nationally for establishing goals, allocating resources, and implementing programs of work must achieve a balance among the many competing demands upon national resources. Our appeal is not for exclusive attention to agriculture, for that would be naive; rather, it is for greater investment in agriculture and other means of increasing the productivity of rural dwellers, and for substantially improved effectiveness of efforts already under way.

For the first time in history the world now appears to have the capability of dealing effectively with the difficult problems of hunger and poverty. The future of any nation is clearly entwined with that of nations elsewhere. Clearly the wisdom of choices in the immediate future will markedly affect the nature of the world in which the next generations will live. And, while the food-poverty-population problem is massive and complex and will be extremely difficult and time-consuming to resolve, the existence of new capabilities provides a magnificent opportunity, perhaps a fleeting one, to deal with it effectively—if governments have the wisdom and the will to act.

The challenge

The ominous food deficits

Introduction

In MID-1975 the world population was 4,000 million and growing at 1.8 percent a year. At that rate it would double in 38 years, with 900 million people being added by 1985 (Table 2.1). Almost half the world's population lives in the developing market economies,[1] where the annual population growth rate is currently 2.7 percent and will double in 26 years. These low-income countries have the most acute food problem. The purpose of this chapter is to describe the changing pattern of food production over recent decades and to review projections into the future.

World food output: Rising, erratic

For both the developed and less-developed countries, world food output has been rising approximately 3 percent per year over the past 20 years (Fig. 2.1). On the average, the 3,800 million people in the world in 1973 had over 20 percent more to eat per person than did the world's 2,700 million people in 1954. The upward trend has not been smooth for either the developed or the developing countries; during this period, total food production fell below the previous year's level three times in developed countries and twice in developing countries. Per capita food production of the developing countries failed to increase over the previous year in 9 of these 19 years.

[1] The terms "developing countries," "developing market economies," "less-developed countries," and "low-income countries" are generally interchangeable. They refer to the market-oriented countries, *excluding* Canada, the U.S., those in Western Europe, Israel, South Africa, Japan, Australia, and New Zealand. The countries in Eastern Europe, the U.S.S.R., and communist countries of Asia (some of which have low per capita incomes) are termed "centrally planned economies."

Sources of production data

The primary sources of information on world agricultural production are the Food and Agriculture Organization (FAO) and the U.S. Department of Agriculture (USDA). Other systems maintained by individual countries, international organizations, or the private sector use FAO or USDA data as their prime sources or produce data limited to their specific needs.

FAO data generally are based on information supplied by the member governments, whose own purposes may be served by inflating or deflating figures. Until institution of its early warning system, which gives a qualitative although not quantitative evaluation, FAO data were not very timely. The USDA also depends on sources in each nation, but these data are evaluated by its overseas network of agricultural attachés and are analyzed by USDA specialists in Washington, D.C.

These weaknesses notwithstanding, these data are the most accurate available indicators of past trends and the current situation. Constant efforts are being made by FAO and the USDA to improve the information published.

Fig. 2.1. Food production and population in developed and less-developed countries

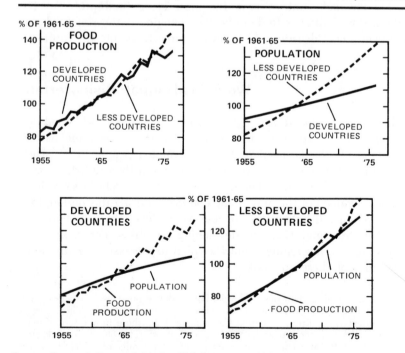

Source: Economic Research Service, U.S. Department of Agriculture.

Table 2.1. World population data by region, 1976 estimates

Region	No. of countries	Population (millions)		Growth rate(%)[a]	Doubling time (yrs.)[b]
		1976	1985		
Africa					
Northern	6	100	140	2.6	27
Western	16	120	155	2.6	27
Eastern	15	117	149	2.8	25
Middle	9	47	52	2.4	29
Southern	5	29	34	2.7	26
Total	51	413	530	—	—
Asia					
Southwest	16	87	121	2.9	24
Middle South	10	851	1,137	2.2	32
Southeast	11	327	434	2.4	29
East	8	1,023	1,182	1.7	41
Total	45	2,288	2,874	—	—
Americas					
North	2	239	263	0.8	87
Middle	7	81	112	3.4	20
Caribbean	12	27	36	2.1	33
South					
Tropical	9	178	236	2.9	24
Temperate	3	39	51	1.5	46
Total	33	564	689	—	—
Europe	27	476	515	0.6	116
U.S.S.R.	1	257	287	0.9	77
Oceania	4	22	27	1.8	38
World	161	4,020	4,933	1.8	38

Source: Population Reference Bureau, *1976 World Population Data Sheet*.
[a] Based on population changes during part or all of the period since 1970.
[b] Assuming that present rate continues over that period.

Developing countries: Production gains offset by population increases

While the population in the developed countries has been rising at only 1 percent per year, that of the developing countries has been climbing by about 2.5 percent per year, largely offsetting gains in farm output. Consequently, food production *per person* in the developing countries has been rising extremely slowly.[2]

[2] One bit of evidence of the increasing availability of food in the developing countries is that life expectancy at birth has increased from approximately 35–40 years in 1950 to 52 years in 1970–75—an increase of almost 40 percent.

This pattern has held for all developing regions except Africa (Fig. 2.2), where there was a decline in output in the 1970s caused in part by prolonged drought, especially in the Sahel.[3] High rates of population growth have severely limited needed increases in food availability in Mexico, Central America, and tropical South America. Economic policies have generally been unfavorable to farmers. Food output per person in South Asia has varied greatly, particularly because of drought in India and Pakistan in 1965–67 and in 1972. Changes in governments have introduced other instabilities throughout Asia.

An equally discouraging picture emerges from a closer look at the performance of individual countries. The Preparatory Committee of the World Food Conference estimated in 1974 that during 1953–71 food production in 24 developing countries (out of 71 studied) with a combined population of over 350 million failed to keep pace with population growth, and that food production in 17 more developing countries with a combined population of almost 1,000 million failed to equal the growth of domestic demand. An analysis carried out by the International Agricultural Development Service indicated that the annual percentage change in cereal production (1961–65 average compared with 1972–74 average) failed to exceed the increase in population in 52 of the 110

[3] Many of the estimates of population and food production in Africa, however, are based on very inadequate data and may not be as reliable as those of other regions.

Fig. 2.2. Food production per capita in less-developed countries

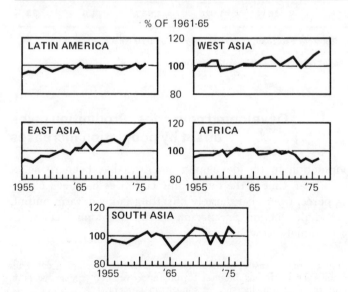

Source: Economic Research Service, U.S. Department of Agriculture.

Table 2.2. Comparison of total per capita meat consumption in selected countries, 1961–65 and 1972–74 (averages, in kilograms)

Country	Average 1961–65	Average 1972–74	Country	Average 1961–65	Average 1972–74
Belgium-Luxembourg	51	70	Canada	65	73
Denmark	58	63	U.S.A.	76	84
France	57	63			
West Germany	54	66	Mexico	16	20
Italy	27	45	Venezuela	23	26
Netherlands	44	50			
Austria	55	64	Bulgaria	29	39
Finland	35	47	Czechoslovakia	46	58
Greece	26	41	Hungary	34	49
Spain	22	34	Poland	36	49
Sweden	46	48	Yugoslavia	28	35
Switzerland	51	62	U.S.S.R.	31	43

Source: U.S. Department of Agriculture, *1974 Per Capita Meat Consumption Levels Reported by 48 Countries.*

countries and geopolitical entities for which data were available; the proportion is much higher when one compares the rate of food production increase with change in demand.

Developed countries:
Agricultural gains and affluence

Food production per person has increased significantly in the developed world, where population growth has averaged only 1 percent per year.

The Soviet Union and Eastern Europe have produced the largest percentage per capita increases. However, both were recovering from abnormally depressed conditions following the end of World War II. Production in Canada and the U.S. at times has been held back deliberately because of bothersome surpluses. Production in Canada, the U.S.S.R., and Australia has been characterized by recurrent fluctuations attributable to weather.

Steadily rising incomes have resulted in a rapidly rising demand for livestock products in the developed countries (Table 2.2). The relatively low grain prices in these countries have made it economical to feed cereals to livestock. Since several kilograms of grain produce a kilogram of livestock product, grain consumption in the developed countries is high. In 1969–71 it was 529 kilograms per person (in large part animal feed), versus 175 kilograms per person in the less-developed countries, where most grain is consumed directly as human food.

Net effect: Shifting food supply/
demand balances

There has been a significant shift in the balance of supply and demand for food among regions of the world. Between 1934–38 and 1973, Latin America, Eastern Europe and the U.S.S.R.,[4] Africa, and Asia changed from net exporters of grain to importers, requiring increasingly large amounts (Table 2.3). In contrast, North America during this period shifted from a slight export to a dominant export position—from an average 5 million tons of grain exported in 1934–38 to 94 million tons exported in 1975. Oceania slightly increased its net exports during this period.

Many developing countries do not have the financial resources to purchase enough grain from the developed countries to supplement their own production.[5] As a result, 462 million people, according to FAO, had an insufficient supply of calories and protein[6] in 1970—that is, 16 percent of the world population, excluding Asian centrally planned economies. Of that total, 434 million, or 94 percent, were in developing regions (Table 2.4). The accuracy of such estimates is controversial, but they suggest the magnitude and location of the problem.

[4] For 1963 through 1974, according to D. Gale Johnson, approximately 80 percent of the variability or fluctuations in world imports of wheat were due to variations in the imports of the Soviet Union.
[5] The bulk of grain trade goes on among *developed* countries. Some—for example Japan—are more dependent on imports for their basic food and feed supplies than most low-income countries. The U.S.'s major export customers are still Europe, Japan, and the U.S.S.R.
[6] Deficiencies of vitamin A (resulting in xerophthalmia, a form of blindness), iodine (resulting in goiter), iron/folate (resulting in anemia), and vitamin D (resulting in rickets) also constitute serious health problems in many developing countries.

Table 2.3.   The changing pattern of world grain exports

Region	Exports (million tons)[a]					
	1934–38	1948–52	1960	1966	1973[b]	1975[b]
North America	5	23	39	59	88	94
Latin America	9	1	0	5	−4	−3
Western Europe	−24	−22	−25	−27	−21	−17
Eastern Europe & U.S.S.R.	5	—	0	−4	−27	−25
Africa	1	0	−2	−7	−4	−10
Asia	2	−6	−17	−34	−39	−47
Australia & New Zealand	3	3	6	8	7	8

Sources: Lester Brown and Erik Eckholm, *By Bread Alone*; Lester Brown, *The Politics and Responsibility of the North American Breadbasket.*
[a] Minus sign indicates net imports.
[b] Fiscal year.

Table 2.4. Estimated number of people with insufficient protein/energy supply, 1970

Region	Population (millions)	People with insufficient supply	
		(%)	(millions)
Developed regions[a]	1,070	3	28
Developing regions[b]	1,750	25	434
Latin America	280	13	36
Far East	1,020	30	301
Near East	170	18	30
Africa	280	25	67
World[b]	2,820	16	462

Source: United Nations, *Assessment: Present Food Situation and Dimensions and Causes of Hunger and Malnutrition in the World.*
[a] Includes 33 major countries located primarily in Europe and North America plus Australia, Israel, Japan, New Zealand, South Africa, and the U.S.S.R.
[b] Excluding Asian centrally planned economies—the People's Republic of China, the Democratic People's Republic of Korea, Mongolia, and the Democratic Republic of Vietnam.

Recent events

Events since 1965 dramatically underscore the interdependence of nations, and particularly the vulnerability of the developing world to the changing balance of supply and demand.

1965–72

Drought in India and Pakistan occurred in 1965/66 and again in 1966/67, severely depressing total grain output and causing starvation. Substantial emergency shipments of grain were made, largely on a concessional basis. World grain stocks fell from 156 million tons (about 16 percent of world production) in July 1965 to 129 million tons in July 1966 (Table 2.5).

The world did respond, at least temporarily, to the challenge of a continued world food shortage. Some developing countries began to push agricultural production. Fertilizer factories were built. Grain exporting countries expanded output.

From 1967 to 1971 output of food grains (rice and wheat) rose substantially. The "green revolution" began in Asia. World stocks of grain rapidly built up to an all-time high of over 200 million tons by July 1969.

As a result of this brief period of visible and widely publicized progress, significant changes in thought and action occurred. The worry of the mid-1960s about impending world food disasters turned to belief by some observers that the world food problem finally was being brought under control. Low prices of food and feed grains—because of lack of demand for human food—stimulated use of large quantities to feed live-

Table 2.5. Total world grain stocks at beginning of crop year: 1960/61–1977/78 (million tons)[a]

(July–June)	Wheat	Coarse grains	Rice	Total	Total stocks as proportion of apparent consumption
1960/61	76.8	89.9	3.0	169.7	0.20
1961/62	79.9	99.3	2.7	181.9	0.21
1962/63	67.8	84.5	2.2	154.5	0.18
1963/64	73.3	82.3	2.1	157.7	0.18
1964/65	64.7	85.6	2.3	152.6	0.17
1965/66	74.8	78.8	2.8	156.5	0.16
1966/67	56.6	62.0	10.2	128.8	0.13
1967/68	80.5	66.3	8.7	155.4	0.15
1968/69	84.5	77.4	11.9	173.8	0.17
1969/70	109.6	81.1	15.0	205.7	0.19
1970/71	96.5	74.5	17.7	188.7	0.17
1971/72	74.8	58.4	8.7	151.8	0.13
1972/73	79.7	74.1	15.9	167.7	0.14
1973/74	59.7	57.4	11.2	128.3	0.10
1974/75	69.1	56.2	12.5	137.8	0.11
1975/76	62.8	52.4	12.0	127.0	0.10
1976/77	59.6	52.2	18.0	129.8	0.10
1977/78	98.1	71.4	15.6	185.1	0.13

Sources: International Food Policy Research Institute, *Current Food Policy Indicators*; U.S. Department of Agriculture, *World Grain Situation: Crop and Trade Developments*.
[a] Includes estimates for U.S.S.R. but not for China.

stock. The major grain exporting nations (U.S., Canada, Australia, and Argentina) again reduced area planted. Between 1968 and 1970, wheat area in these nations fell from 50 million to 33 million hectares, and annual grain output dropped more than 20 million tons (offset somewhat by expansion of grain output in the U.S.S.R., some European countries, and Japan). World stocks, mostly held by the U.S., Canada, Australia, and Argentina, were reduced to about 150 million tons by July 1971— down over 50 million tons from the 1969 high point. Low crop and fertilizer prices and cutbacks in area planted caused a slowdown in construction of fertilizer factories. High levels of food aid continued—at about US$1,300 million annually, of which in 1972 the U.S. contributed products worth nearly $1,000 million.

Meanwhile, only a few of the developing nations, mostly in Asia, had initiated serious efforts to increase their own agricultural production. Apathy toward development of agriculture still prevailed in most governments—in both developed and less-developed nations—and in most assistance agencies as late as 1972.

1972/73

The world was jolted again by the events of 1972/73 (Table 2.6). World grain production fell 35 million tons below the previous year. Shortfalls occurred simultaneously in such widely dispersed regions as North America, the U.S.S.R., and Asia. Although total food production had declined for developed countries as a group in 1961 and 1969, this was the first time since 1954 that it had declined on a global basis. The U.S.S.R. unexpectedly entered the world market to make large grain purchases, quietly buying 30 million tons at low prices rather than slaughtering livestock as it had previously done when faced with domestic grain production shortfalls. Governments in many of the European and centrally planned countries kept their own domestic grain prices steady, thereby protecting their economies from effects of rising world prices. Prices in world trade rose rapidly, returning in real terms to levels of the late 1940s or early 1950s (Fig. 2.3). Food stocks held by the traditional exporting countries, including the U.S., were drawn down to below 130 million tons, the lowest level in 20 years, with the exception of 1966/67 (the period of the Indian drought).

1973–75

World food production was generally good in 1973/74 except in Africa and the Mideast. Prices, however, did not decline to previous levels and food stocks held by major exporting nations were not rebuilt.

Then the energy crisis occurred. High petroleum prices plus high prices for foodgrains and fertilizers reduced the foreign exchange reserves of many developing countries to dangerously low levels. The World Bank estimated that the cost of the 1974 volume of oil imports of the less-developed countries increased over the previous year by US$10,000 million, or 15 percent of their total import bill and 40 percent of their entire net inflow of capital. Furthermore, the low-income countries were hurt disproportionately in the allocation of scarce production supplies such as chemical fertilizers and pesticides.

In spite of these difficulties, there was hope that 1974/75 production would be great enough to replenish world grain stocks. With a few exceptions—notably India, Bangladesh, Sri Lanka, and several nations in Central America—the developing countries did a surprisingly effective job of obtaining enough fertilizer for their major food crops, although at a heavy foreign exchange cost. The U.S. attempted to expand food production by releasing the last of its land previously set aside. Early production forecasts—some made before crops were planted—were very favorable. However, weather intervened to reduce this optimism. Excellent weather early in the U.S. planting season was followed by heavy

Table 2.6. Cereal production in selected countries, 1972/73–1976/77

Commodity and country	Production (million tons)				
	1972/73	1973/74	1974/75	1975/76	1976/77
Wheat					
Canada	14.5	16.2	13.3[a]	17.1	23.6
Australia	6.6[a]	12.0	11.4[a]	12.0	11.8[a]
Argentina	6.9	6.6[a]	6.0[a]	8.6	11.0
Western Europe	51.3	50.8[a]	56.7	48.5[a]	51.1
U.S.S.R.	86.0[a]	109.8	83.9[a]	66.2[a]	96.9
Eastern Europe	30.7	31.5	34.0	28.5[a]	34.5
India	26.4	24.7[a]	21.8[a]	24.1	28.8
U.S.	42.1[a]	46.6	48.5	57.8	58.3
Others	79.8	73.6[a]	80.5	86.3	97.3
Total	343.2[a]	371.6	356.0[a]	349.9[a]	413.4
Coarse grains					
Canada	20.9[a]	20.4[a]	17.4[a]	20.0	21.3
Australia	3.7[a]	4.7	4.5[a]	5.6	5.0[a]
Argentina	16.0	17.9	13.8[a]	12.4[a]	17.0
S. Africa	4.5[a]	11.9	9.7[a]	7.7[a]	10.1
Thailand	1.4[a]	2.5	2.7	3.3	3.0[a]
Brazil	14.6[a]	16.9	16.9	18.5	19.4
Western Europe	81.6	84.1	85.1	81.5[a]	72.9[a]
U.S.S.R.	72.5[a]	101.0	99.7[a]	65.8[a]	115.0
Eastern Europe	56.7	55.7[a]	57.3	59.4	59.4
U.S.	182.1[a]	186.8	150.9[a]	184.4	192.7
Others	148.8[a]	158.8	162.8	175.6	176.5
Total	602.7[a]	660.7	620.8[a]	634.4	692.3
Rice[b]					
Bangladesh	15.1	17.9	17.1[a]	19.2	17.7[a]
Burma	7.4[a]	8.6	8.6	9.2	9.3
India	58.9[a]	66.1	59.4[a]	73.2	64.2[a]
Indonesia	19.4	21.5	22.5	22.3[a]	23.3
Japan	14.9	15.2	15.4	16.5	14.7[a]
Korea	5.5[a]	5.9	6.2	6.5	7.2
Pakistan	3.4	3.7	3.5[a]	3.9	4.0
China	109.4[a]	113.0	127.5	126.5[a]	125.5[a]
Thailand	12.2[a]	14.4	14.5	15.2	15.8
Brazil	6.6	6.5[a]	7.0	8.5	8.0[a]
U.S.	3.9	4.2	5.1	5.8	5.3[a]
Others	46.4[a]	47.9	49.0	51.8	51.4[a]
Total	303.1[a]	324.6	337.7	360.3	348.2[a]
Total food- and feedgrains	1,249.2[a]	1,356.9	1,314.5[a]	1,343.6	1,453.9

Source: U.S. Department of Agriculture, *World Grain Situation: Crop and Trade Developments.*
[a] Decline in production from previous year.
[b] Data are for calendar year; e.g., 1976/77 represents 1977.

rains in May and June across the maize area and up to the spring wheat area, while the Southwest stayed dry, thereby reducing grain and soybean plantings below farmers' early plans and cutting into prospective yields as well. Rains sharply curtailed Canadian spring wheat plantings. In Eastern Europe a wet spring and summer followed a dry winter. On the Indian subcontinent the usually reliable winter and spring rains were sparse. The summer monsoon started late and was never very strong in northern India. Widespread flooding occurred in eastern India and Bangladesh. There were reports of drought in China. Drought affected the Argentine wheat crop. A hurricane devastated Honduras, and the same storm, in combination with an early frost in the higher altitudes, seriously hurt the Mexican maize crop. Finally and most significantly, the U.S. Midwest experienced its worst summer drought since the 1930s. This was followed by an early and severe frost. Western Europe had an exceptionally wet fall, which badly interfered with harvesting.

As a result, the 1974/75 world wheat and feedgrain harvests were

Fig. 2.3. World export prices of selected commodities, 1948–77

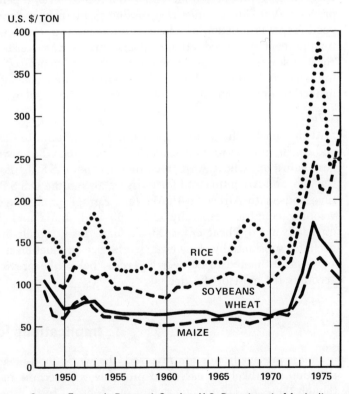

Source: Economic Research Service, U.S. Department of Agriculture.

below 1973/74 levels. Total foodgrain production in 1974/75 was over 3 percent below the previous year and only a little above the level 3 years earlier—but population had grown by 250 million over these 3 years. World wheat production was down over 4 percent (with significant declines in the U.S.S.R., Canada, Argentina, and India) and feedgrain production was down by over 6 percent (with the major decline occurring in the U.S., and with production in Canada, Argentina, and South Africa suffering also), while rice production was 4 percent above 1973/74 levels (although India had a large decline). Severe food shortages occurred in Bangladesh, India, and, in spite of the resumption of rains in the Sahel, in several countries of Africa.

Reduced economic growth prospects and rising prices in the developed countries slowed the demand for meat and therefore the commercial demand for feedgrains. However, world food reserve stocks were drawn below even the uncomfortably low 1973 levels. Many countries were severely pressed to get the food they required to meet minimal needs.

1975/76

Fortunately food production improved in most developing countries in 1975/76. Rice production increased to a record level, 6 percent above the previous year. Most major rice producers in the developing world had good crops. Production of wheat also increased in the developing world, by 9 percent, and production of coarse grains was over 6 percent above 1974/75 levels, although the world picture was depressed by disappointing harvests in the U.S.S.R. and Eastern Europe. Total grain stocks remained at approximately the same levels as the previous year.

1976/77

At the time of this writing, preliminary data indicate that world wheat and coarse grains production reached a new record in 1976/77. The biggest gains for wheat were recorded in the U.S.S.R., Eastern Europe, Canada, and Argentina and for coarse grains in the U.S.S.R., U.S., Argentina, and South Africa (with Western Europe producing less). The developing countries generally did well, with India and Turkey having especially good wheat crops. Stocks have been rebuilt and prices have declined substantially. However, world rice production in calendar year 1977 was estimated to be over 3 percent below the previous year; India accounts for most of the decline.

Implications for the future

Unless present trends are reversed, the world food-poverty-population situation is unlikely to ease, and probably will become much worse. Although there are encouraging signs of declining birth rates in some low-income countries (Fig. 2.4), population growth in the low-income countries averages 2.35 percent annually and is not expected to fall below 2 percent until after the end of the century. The United Nations medium variant projects a population for the low-income regions of 3,600 million in the year 2000, over 1,600 million above the 1975 level.

Income trends are more difficult to predict. Assuming a continuation of the 1965–73 economic growth rates in most countries, with a sharp upward adjustment in the economic growth rates of members of the Organization of Petroleum Exporting Countries (OPEC) to reflect higher oil revenues since 1973, real per capita incomes in the developing market economies are expected to increase at 3 percent per year. If the higher oil prices continue to disrupt the economies of the non-OPEC countries, as well as reduce their exports to industrial countries, which have more

Fig. 2.4. Changes in crude birth rates in selected countries, 1965–74

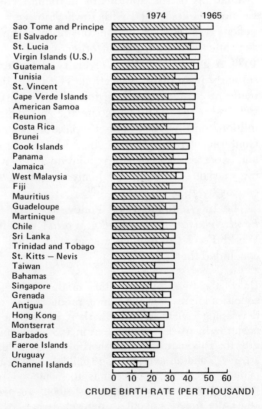

CRUDE BIRTH RATE (PER THOUSAND)

Source: James W. Brackett and R. T. Ravenholt, *World Fertility, 1976: An Analysis of Data Sources and Trends.*

slowly expanding economies, the average increased per capita income growth of developing countries might be almost halved. In either case three disturbing facts stand out:

- The developing countries are not likely to gain much on the industrialized countries in levels of per capita income.
- Among the developing countries there is considerable variation in economic performance, with some countries even having declining standards of living.
- Within the developing countries, as in industrial countries, not all people share the gains of development equally. Even in countries that have rapidly growing average incomes, much of the population is not benefiting. In other words, the ability of many people in the low-income countries to purchase foodgrains is expected to remain low.

Based on projected population and income growth, future global food production has been projected to increase at various rates depending on evaluations of the abilities of particular countries to accelerate output. Economists associated with Iowa State University (U.S.) have projected deficits of almost 35 million tons of wheat and rye, over 5 million tons of rice, and 15 million tons of other grains for the developing countries by 1985. A group from the University of California (U.S.) has presented a similarly pessimistic projection. The U.S. Department of Agriculture has made projections based on four different assumptions regarding production and demand and has come out with deficits ranging from 15.8 to 71.6 million tons in 1985. The Preparatory Committee of the World Food Conference projected that, based on past food production growth rates and expected increases in population and per capita incomes, the developing market economies are likely to have a deficit of 73 million tons of cereals by 1985.

The International Food Policy Research Institute (IFPRI) (*Meeting Food Needs in a Developing World*) reexamined the projections of the World Food Conference a year and a half after they were made and concluded that,

Unless the trend of production in the DME (developing market economy) countries improves in the future, production of cereals, the major food in most developing countries, will fall short of meeting food demand in food deficit countries by 95–108 million tons in 1985/86 depending on the rate of economic growth. This compares with shortfalls of 45 million tons in the food crisis year, 1974/75, and an average of 28 million tons in the relatively good production period, 1969/71. Asia accounts for some 50 percent of the total projected deficits, North Africa/Middle East about 20 percent, and sub-Saharan Africa and Latin America about 15 percent each.

They further note that during 1967–74, the growth rate of cereal production in the developing market-economy countries slowed to 1.7 percent annually. While IFPRI recognizes that this is too brief a period on which to base reliable projections, maintenance of this performance could mean that cereal production in 1985/86 would "fall short an additional 100 million tons, doubling the cereal deficit to about 200 million tons," an amount which could be unmanageable physically or financially. About half of the deficit is expected to occur in the low-income, food-deficit countries—those with per capita incomes of less than $200—where 60 percent of the developing market economies' population is located. Many of these areas, including India, Bangladesh, Nigeria, and sub-Saharan Africa, probably will not have the financial resources to provide for imports, so they must produce for their own needs. One-third of the expected deficit is projected to occur in the high-income developing market-economy countries, including the North Africa/Mideast OPEC countries, Venezuela, Taiwan, and South Korea, but these countries will probably have the capacity to generate sufficient foreign exchange to meet their import needs. An intermediate group of countries, including Mexico and Egypt, containing about 20 percent of the population of developing market economies, faces the problem that very high increases in demand are outstripping what would otherwise be an acceptable rate of food production increase—3 percent annually. While their immediate needs may be less urgent than some others, they still have serious problems.

To put the projections into perspective, it should be emphasized that they are based on the assumption that political and economic choices regarding development will not change but that population will continue to grow. In other words, they state what might happen if present trends continue during the next decade.

What if these projections are wrong? Some contend that these projections of larger deficits are incorrect, that the assumptions on which they are based are unsound. Some argue that the proportion of total world production represented by projected deficits for a decade hence is not large and that the world can handle the problem; that is, that interpretations of the data are wrong.

Even if the projections are in error, the urgent need to alleviate the poverty and improve the diet and standard of living of great numbers of the poor in the developing countries remains, as does the need to promote economic and social progress.

In the final analysis, these trends are projected, not inevitable; positive action can be taken. This thesis will be developed in greater detail in later chapters.

Projected food deficits

In 1977 the International Food Policy Research Institute (*Food Needs of Developing Countries*) calculated food supply and demand data on individual low-income countries to the year 1990. Its conclusions were not reassuring:

- Longer-term food prospects in food-deficit countries with developing market economies remain unfavorable, despite good crops in some recent years. Under the conditions assumed in the IFPRI study, production of staple food crops in these countries would fall short of demand in 1990 by 120–145 million tons. This is over three times the shortfall of 37 million tons in 1975, a relatively good production year.
- The core of the food problem is the low-income, food-deficit countries in which the per capita GNP in 1973 was less than US$300. These countries have almost two-thirds of the total population of the developing market economies. Their food deficit is projected to rise from 12 million tons in 1975 to 70–85 million tons by 1990. Just to maintain consumption at the 1975 per capita level would require 35 million tons more than projected production would provide.

Prospects for some low-income countries are as follows:

Country	1975 Deficit (million tons)	1975 % of consumption	Projections for 1990 Deficit (million tons)	Projections for 1990 % of consumption
India	1.4	1	17.6–21.9	10–12
Nigeria	0.4	2	17.1–20.5	35–39
Bangladesh	1.0	7	6.4–8.0	30–35
Indonesia	2.1	8	6.0–7.7	14–17
Egypt	3.7	35	4.9	32
Sahel Group	0.4	9	3.2–3.5	44–46
Ethiopia	0.1	2	2.1–2.3	26–28
Burma	(0.4)[a]	(7)[a]	1.9–2.4	21–25
Philippines	0.3	4	1.4–1.7	11–13
Afghanistan	—	—	1.3–1.5	19–22

[a] Surplus.

Summary

Four conclusions stand out in this analysis of recent food production.

First, in spite of substantial increases in world food production, food-grain availability per person is still alarmingly low, especially in the developing countries. Carryover stocks in some recent years have not been large.

Second, year-to-year variations in agricultural production in a few countries can result in wide swings in food availability and price. The free-market countries are vulnerable to quiet purchases by centrally planned economies. Many of the developing countries do not have adequate foreign exchange to make the purchases necessary to supplement their own production, especially during periods of world shortages. The interdependent world is very vulnerable to the consequences of poor harvests.

Third, unless significant changes occur, the world food-poverty-population situation is likely to become significantly worse in the next decade; the growing deficits are ominous.

Fourth, these developments are causing food-importing nations, rich or poor, to seek ways to bring sources of food supply under national control, for reasons of national security; some governments fear that failure to meet the food needs of their populations could cause them to be replaced, in some cases by force.

References

INTRODUCTION
Population Reference Bureau. *1976 World Population Data Sheet.* Washington, D.C.: Population Reference Bureau, 1976.
U.S. Department of Agriculture, Economic Research Service. *The World Food Situation and Prospects to 1985.* Foreign Agricultural Economic Report No. 98. Washington, D.C.: U.S. Department of Agriculture, December 1974.
U.S. Office of Technology Assessment. *Food Information Systems: Summary and Analysis.* Washington, D.C.: U.S. Government Printing Office, August 1976.

DEVELOPING COUNTRIES: PRODUCTION GAINS OFFSET BY POPULATION INCREASES
Johnson, D. Gale. *World Food Problems and Prospects.* Washington, D.C.: American Enterprise Institute for Public Policy Research, 1975.
U.S. Department of Agriculture, Foreign Agricultural Service. *1974 Per Capita Meat Consumption Levels Reported by 48 Countries.* Foreign Agriculture Circular FLM 2–76. Washington, D.C.: U.S. Department of Agriculture, February 1976.

NET EFFECT: SHIFTING FOOD SUPPLY/DEMAND BALANCES
Brown, Lester R. *The Politics and Responsibility of the North American Breadbasket.* Worldwatch Paper No. 2. Washington, D.C.: Worldwatch Institute, October 1975.
Brown, Lester R., and Eckholm, Erik. *By Bread Alone.* New York: Praeger, 1974.
Johnson, D. Gale. *World Food Problems and Prospects.* Washington, D.C.: American Enterprise Institute for Public Policy Research, 1975.
United Nations, Economic and Social Council, Preparatory Committee of the World Food Conference, 2nd Session. *Assessment: Present Food Situation and Dimensions and Causes of Hunger and Malnutrition in the World* (E/CONF. 65/PREP/6), May 8, 1974.

RECENT EVENTS
International Food Policy Research Institute. *Current Food Policy Indicators.* PI/7. Washington, D.C.: International Food Policy Research Institute, February 1977.
U.S. Department of Agriculture, Foreign Agricultural Service. *World Grain Situation: Crop and Trade Developments.* Foreign Agriculture Circular FG 23–77. Washington, D.C.: U.S. Department of Agriculture, November 11, 1977.

IMPLICATIONS FOR THE FUTURE
Blakeslee, Leroy L.; Heady, Earl O.; and Farmingham, Charles F. *World Food Production, Demand, and Trade.* Ames: Iowa State University Press, 1973.

Brackett, James W., and Ravenholt, R. T. *World Fertility, 1976: An Analysis of Data Sources and Trends.* Population Reports, Series J, No. 12. Washington, D.C.: George Washington University Medical Center, November 1976.

University of California. *A Hungry World: The Challenge to Agriculture.* Berkeley: University of California, Division of Agricultural Sciences, July 1974.

International Food Policy Research Institute. *Food Needs of Developing Countries: Projections of Production and Consumption to 1990.* Research Report No. 3. Washington, D.C.: International Food Policy Research Institute, December 1977.

International Food Policy Research Institute. *Meeting Food Needs in the Developing World: The Location and Magnitude of the Task in the Next Decade.* Research Report No. 1. Washington, D.C.: International Food Policy Research Institute, February 1976.

United Nations, Department of Economic and Social Affairs, Population Division. *Selected World Demographic Indicators by Countries, 1950–2000* (ESA/P/WP.55), May 28, 1975.

United Nations, Economic and Social Council, Preparatory Committee of the World Food Conference, 2nd session. *Assessment: Present Food Situation and Dimensions and Causes of Hunger and Malnutrition in the World* (E/CONF. 65/PREP/6), May 8, 1974.

U.S. Department of Agriculture, Economic Research Service. *The World Food Situation and Prospects to 1985.* Foreign Agricultural Economic Report No. 98. Washington, D.C.: U.S. Department of Agriculture, December 1974.

From evolution to revolution in agriculture

Introduction

AGRICULTURE is complex and easily misunderstood. It is a way of life to some; a business, a profession, a science, a sector of the economy, to others. To urban consumers it may simply be—via the supermarket—the source of most of their food supplies. In reality it is all of these things. Because agriculture is essential to the lives of all human beings, because it is imperative that food supplies be increased to meet the needs of growing populations, and because more productive and profitable farming can contribute to the higher standards of living sought so widely, the nature of agriculture and the requirements for its improvement need desperately —and quickly—to be more widely understood.

The purposes of this chapter are, first, to describe the transformation from subsistence agriculture to intensive agriculture, from poverty to relative prosperity in rural areas, and, second, to define some terms and introduce concepts relevant to this process.

The origins of agriculture

Early man was a gatherer and a hunter of food. He was forced to spend most of his efforts securing meals; there was little time for other pursuits.

Early civilizations flourished where food supplies, plant or animal, were naturally abundant. As animals were domesticated, they were herded from one grazing area to another or, later, used to provide power for tilling soil, pumping water, or transporting man and his goods. As man learned to manage crops and animals, agriculture in some places became sedentary—that is, farms were established. And, if fertility of the soil and other factors were favorable, such farms became relatively perma-

Fig. 3.1. Areas where plants were domesticated

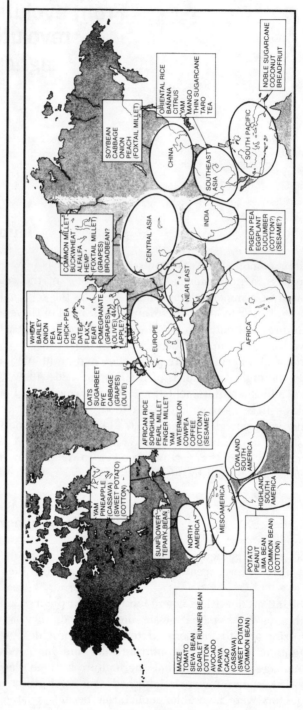

NORTH AMERICA
SUNFLOWER
TEPARY BEAN

YAM
PINEAPPLE
(CASSAVA)
(SWEET POTATO)
(COTTON)

MAIZE
TOMATO
SIEVA BEAN
SCARLET RUNNER BEAN
COTTON
AVOCADO
PAPAYA
CACAO
(CASSAVA)
(SWEET POTATO)
(COMMON BEAN)

MESOAMERICA

LOWLAND
SOUTH
AMERICA

HIGHLAND
SOUTH
AMERICA

POTATO
PEANUT
LIMA BEAN
(COMMON BEAN)
(COTTON)

OATS
SUGARBEET
RYE
CABBAGE
(GRAPES)
(OLIVE)

WHEAT
BARLEY
ONION
PEA
LENTIL
CHICK-PEA
FIG
DATE
FLAX
PEAR
POMEGRANATE
(GRAPES)
(OLIVE)
(APPLE?)

EUROPE

NEAR EAST

AFRICA

AFRICAN RICE
SORGHUM
PEARL MILLET
FINGER MILLET
YAM
WATERMELON
COWPEA
COFFEE
(COTTON?)
(SESAME?)

COMMON MILLET
BUCKWHEAT
ALFALFA
HEMP
(FOXTAIL MILLET)
(GRAPES)
BROADBEAN?

CENTRAL ASIA

SOYBEAN
CABBAGE
ONION
PEACH
(FOXTAIL MILLET)

CHINA

SOUTHEAST
ASIA

INDIA

PIGEON PEA
EGGPLANT
CUCUMBER
(COTTON?)
(SESAME?)

ORIENTAL RICE
BANANA
CITRUS
YAM
MANGO
THIN SUGARCANE
TARO
TEA

SOUTH PACIFIC

NOBLE SUGARCANE
COCONUT
BREADFRUIT

Source: From Jack R. Harlan, "The Plants and Animals That Nourish Man." Copyright © 1976 by Scientific American, Inc. All rights reserved.

nent. Where soil fertility was exhausted by a few years of cropping, "shifting cultivation" became the norm. Farmers cut or burned vegetation, planted their crops for a few years, and then moved to a new location to repeat the process.

Nascent civilizations were based upon crop and animal species as diverse as the regions in which people settled. In the highland areas of Latin America, maize and beans constituted the basic foods, supplemented by the potato in the Andes. In the temperate regions of the Mideast, the principal crops were wheat and barley. In parts of Africa, sorghum and millets were important. In the humid tropics of Asia, rice was the basic food.

The world's early farmers discovered a number of ways in which production of crops could be stabilized or improved. Water could be carried to the crops from streams, ponds, or wells, or diverted to crop lands by ditches (irrigation). Where water was on occasion excessive, drainage systems were built. It was discovered that turning under vegetation or applying animal or human wastes to crop land (fertilization) would improve crop performance. In areas of sparse rainfall, land was rested between crops to allow moisture to accumulate in the soil: these were the first systems of "fallow." Rotation of crops from one season to the next on the same plot of land was in some areas found to be beneficial, though undoubtedly the reasons for it (improved soil fertility or soil structure and the control of weeds, diseases, and insect pests) were not understood.

We now know that for each crop species, there were one or more "centers of origin" where many early types evolved (Fig. 3.1). Scientists still seek out centers of genetic diversity in their quest for plant strains having resistance to specific diseases or insect pests, unusual capabilities to extract nutrients or water from soils, or other characteristics of potential value in modern plant breeding programs.

The earliest farmers were the first plant breeders, at least in the sense that they selected and saved the seeds from the plants in their fields that seemed to perform best or to have characteristics of taste, color, texture, or ease of handling that were valued. They also practiced selection in their animal populations, saving those which were more docile, or stronger, or relatively free of diseases or defects.

This early selection by farmers of plant and animal strains in many regions contributed to a diversity of types, superimposing variation on that caused by natural crossing among wild relatives and "natural selection" in new places following dispersion of seed by wind, water, or birds, or following migrations of animals.

As man migrated and settled new areas, he generally took with him the crops on which he had come to depend. And in each of the new areas the crop varieties were forced to become adapted, through natural selection augmented by farmer selection, to a new combination of soil properties, rainfall and temperature patterns, and daylengths. Moreover, resistance was built up to disease organisms or insect pests peculiar to each new location.

With the discovery of the Americas, a vast and continuing exchange of crop and animal strains began between the Old World and the New.

As the crop and animal strains became adapted to the conditions of specific new environments, totally new "varieties" or breeds evolved, each specifically adapted to one of the multitude of specific sets of environmental conditions. From this worldwide process, spanning thousands of years, there arose today's great diversity of plant and animal germ plasm, a diversity which will be important in the development of improved types of the future, and which must be collected, preserved, and evaluated without delay.

First era: Emergence of traditional farming systems

Wherever man settled, there emerged systems of "traditional" farming suited to the ecological conditions of particular localities. All of these farming systems had one set of factors in common: the farmer had at his disposal his land, the climate, his seed, his own labor, his domestic animals, and the knowledge and wisdom accumulated during the generations of farming by his ancestors. These were the only "factors of production," regardless of the location or nature of the farming system. As T. W. Schultz points out: "Farming based wholly upon the kinds of factors of production that have been used by farmers for generations can be called traditional agriculture, and a country dependent upon traditional agriculture is inevitably poor."

Until the beginning of this century, virtually all of the world's family farms—even in the presently developed countries—were still largely of this traditional type. Even now, a substantial part of agriculture in the low-income countries is of the traditional or subsistence sort. This emergence of traditional agriculture might be called the "first era" of agricultural development.

PRODUCTION PRACTICES

For the most part, crop varieties available to the traditional farmer consist of those that have survived because of their ability to produce dependable but modest yields on soils of relatively low fertility and with minimum management. In times past, land generally was not a limiting factor. Cultivated plants were widely spaced to maximize yield per plant (rather than per hectare) and to facilitate harvesting by hand. Wide spacing allowed plants to draw nutrients and moisture from a large volume of soil.

Normally the traditional farmer could do little to improve yield by changing varieties. He could select and save the better types with modest gains in performance. Occasionally, he could replace one of his own varieties with another in his locality which in some respect was superior. The opportunities, however, were limited and yields rose slowly.

Protection against the ravages of insect pests and diseases could be gained only by replacing susceptible types with more resistant ones, by altering dates of planting to escape severe attacks, or by crop rotation.

Power was generally limited to the labor of the farmer and his family, supplemented by help from neighbors and, in some more advanced systems, by animals. Limited farm power restricted the farmer's options with regard to depth of plowing, amount of cultivation, and transport of himself and his goods. It also restricted the total land area that the family could dominate and the timing of farming operations. This in turn limited the income (mostly "in kind") that the farmer could derive from his land.

These constraints on traditional farmers of centuries past still limit the productivity and income of innumerable subsistence farmers today. But land per person is much more scarce, for man's numbers have burgeoned.

REMOTENESS AND ITS IMPACT

In traditional farming systems farm products are consumed, sold, or traded for services or other products within the farmers' community. Products are infrequently exchanged with distant markets. Hence, there are few ways to raise prosperity in the rural areas, and rural markets for products of urban industry develop slowly. When a farm or farming system yields little more than is needed to sustain the farm family, it is often labeled "subsistence" farming. Generally, the terms "*traditional*" and "*subsistence*" can be used interchangeably.

The remoteness of traditional farmers is a major problem in poor countries. Without motorized vehicles, farmers usually can travel or transport goods only within a very small area.

THE ROLE OF LIVESTOCK

A frequently misunderstood aspect of agriculture is the role of livestock in the farming system. Recently, for example, there has been a clamor in the developed nations for reductions in meat consumption and a questioning of the desirability of undertaking research on animal production in the tropics and subtropics.

Farm animals are, however, a buffer between man and his variable food supply. When farmers produce crop surpluses, they can invest them in farm animals. The investment pays off when the animals are later consumed or marketed for cash.

Farm animals are also "extenders" of food supplies. In traditional farming systems, animals are generally fed materials which otherwise would not be consumed by humans. Ruminant animals (cattle, sheep, goats, buffalo) can harvest grasses and other forage materials and convert them to meat or milk for human consumption. Their digestive system, which includes a microbiological fermentation stage, allows them to break down coarse, fibrous plant material in ways that monogastric animals like swine, poultry, and man cannot.

In some remote areas farmers feed grain or other plant materials to animals in order to market crops indirectly. When farms are remote, it is too costly to haul bulky vegetative materials to market. Instead, crops can be fed to animals which later can be driven to market—self-transported.

Animals have many other uses. Their hides and hair are made into clothing and blankets. Their dung is used for both fuel and fertilizer. In many countries they are the principal source of supplementary farm power.

Finally, animal products are important because of their contributions to the quality of man's diet. Meat, milk, and eggs are high in protein, and small amounts can contribute importantly to human health, particularly for people who otherwise would subsist largely on starchy foods.

In traditional, sedentary ranching systems, in which the productivity of pastures is relatively low, a farmer may require many hectares to maintain a relatively small herd of animals. Total income from such ranches may be meager, despite their size; these large-area farm operations in reality are small when gauged by value of output or amount of net income.

THE RATIONALITY OF FARMERS

The fact that traditional farmers have little education does not mean that they are unintelligent. For a long time the general belief persisted that the farmer was so concerned with noneconomic objectives that he was not motivated by profits—in other words, that he was not economically rational in his decision-making. While the farmer, especially the small farmer, operates under numerous constraints which limit his action, the evidence is now overwhelming that within his environment even the traditional farmer is an economically rational operator. As one poor farmer in the Puebla Project in Mexico put it: "When you don't have an education, you have to use your head." One challenge to policymakers is to understand the environment in which the farmer operates and the incentives to which he responds.

RISK

The traditional farmer, operating efficiently but at low levels of productivity, has evolved many ways to minimize risks. Farmers whose output barely meets their needs must be cautious. With little wealth to fall back on, one year of failure could mean disaster. A benefit of fragmented landholdings, brought on by subdividing inheritances over many generations, has been the scattering of the family's farming area so that its entire crop is less likely to be ruined by an isolated climatic misfortune at attack of pests or diseases. The traditional farmer tends to grow many crops together rather than practice monocropping. And, as noted earlier, animals provide insurance against crop failures.

The implications are clear. When changes in farm practices are proposed, the effects on farmers' risk must be carefully assessed.

SEASONALITY OF WORK

Demand for farm labor from month to month is uneven. It usually peaks at the planting and harvesting times of the principal crops. Farm people generally organize their time shrewdly. In their choice of crops, their arrangements for swapping labor with neighbors, their maintenance of animals, and their involvement in off-farm work, they are likely to be influenced by the need to spread workloads. T. W. Schultz points out that, contrary to the belief of some investigators, farmers usually are as efficient in allocating their labor as they are in using other limited resources.

Those introducing new farming systems must weigh the effects of recommended changes on the demand for labor; however, the true impact of a system is unlikely to be clear until it is tried in a large pilot area.

PRODUCTION SYSTEMS

The importance of risk and the need to allocate labor effectively during the cropping season influence the production systems which traditional farmers employ. Monoculture (single-crop farming) is less common than mixed culture in traditional farming. One reason is the need to spread risks (pests or diseases that attack one crop may not affect the others). Also, mixed cropping can spread labor requirements so resources are used more effectively. Animals, too, are often integral to the production systems in developing countries, providing a buffer between the farmer and his variable food supply. Farm animals feed on what otherwise would be waste products, but in periods of ample crop production their browsings may be supplemented with surplus grain. In periods of crop shortage, on the other hand, animals may be eaten as food. Overall, then, they make more complete use of total farm resources.

Programs which focus on a single crop often meet resistance because they fail to take account of the system of which proposed technological components are a part.

SUSPICION OF OUTSIDERS

The rationality of farmers is reflected in a common reluctance to join into groups and to take advice from government or other organizations. Traditional farming is relatively simple by modern standards. Since the system involves only man, his land, his seeds, his animals, and the climate, there is little need for intervention in the farmer's affairs by either government or private industry. Moreover, the traditional farmer often does not desire such intervention. He judges, by experience, that he is better off to trust his own resources than to rely on cooperative, often unreliable action with others, which introduces new risks. Furthermore, his experience with government often has been in payment of taxes or other actions which, to his mind, have not contributed to his well-being.

ACCEPTANCE OF CHANGE

Yet traditional farmers do welcome change and are willing to work hard—as most already do—if real gains are likely.

In the Philippines a respected Filipino leader was asked in the early 1960s if he thought that farmers with small holdings would double their rice output if they were provided with opportunities to do so. He replied that he doubted that they would; that instead they would double their yield on one-half of their area, which would allow them to spend more time "going to cockfights and scratching their bellies." He was wrong. When appropriate high-yielding rice varieties and accompanying technology were introduced, the Filipino farmers who could, lost little time in putting them fully to use.

W. David Hopper ("Investments in Agriculture: The Essential for Payoff") summarizes the status of the traditional farmer well when he states:

I have long ago lost tolerance with the argument that the farmer—his stubborn resistance to change, his fixation on tradition, his low aspiration—is the major constraint holding development in check. It is just not true. There are cultural differences in work habits and in the desire for leisure, but I know of no country where highly productive and profitable technology that is tested and proven is available to cultivators, along with the requisites for its use, and yet languishes unadopted because farmers are traditional. No farmer has followed his "age-old methods for thousands of years." If a program to extend changed practices fails to evoke a rural response, one should scrutinize the program and its staff and look to the productivity of the so-called changed practices, but one should not condemn the farmer—he acts in his own best interests, and these are obviously not being served.

ESCAPE FROM POVERTY

Even though the traditional farmer may use the resources at his disposal efficiently, those resources generally are meager. Subsistence agriculture and inadequate landholdings condemn the farm family to abject poverty without hope for a better life. Raising the income of farm families must involve higher productivity and income per hectare, an increase in the size of landholdings, an increase in both productivity and size of farm, or off-farm employment.

Those who deny traditional farmers the opportunity to improve their income by use of improved farming systems or by increasing farm size, or by obtaining other employment, are in effect keeping rural people shackled to a risky and hopeless system.

Second era: Science and industry fuel a revolution

Scientific advances, primarily in the 20th century, have revolutionized agriculture, permitting quantum jumps in productivity of crops and farm animals wherever such advances have been applied systematically. The contributions of science and industry to high yields have resulted in a "second era" of agricultural development.

To understand the forces that permit high crop and animal yields, it may be helpful to review some of the advances that have overcome the constraints that characterize traditional agriculture and to consider the nature of intensive (or modern) agriculture.

CROP IMPROVEMENT: BIOLOGICAL ENGINEERING

In 1900 the rediscovery of Mendel's laws of inheritance provided a basis for the development of the field of genetics, which in turn led to revolutionary advances in plant and animal breeding. While man's selection of superior strains over the previous centuries accounted for substantial plant and animal improvement, entirely new dimensions were added as scientific advances occurred in genetics, chemistry, physics, physiology, pathology, entomology, mathematics, and other fields.

Scientists have learned to design and systematically develop plants[1] that are efficient in converting high levels of applied nutrients (fertilizers)

[1] This topic is described in more detail in Chapter 7.

to the products desired. In cereal crops such as rice, wheat, and barley, plant types have been devised that are short, stiff-stemmed, with narrow, erect, dark-green leaves. These new types efficiently convert nutrients, water, and energy to carbohydrates in the form of grain.[2] Similar advances have occurred with maize and sorghum in temperate areas, and now are prospects for the tropics and subtropics.

By the 1920s, techniques of production of maize hybrids were developed. This process was attractive to private industry, especially in the U.S., resulting in an upsurge in development of superior hybrids and the competitive marketing of seed of highest quality.[3] By the 1950s, sorghum hybrids were appearing in quantity. Major advances through breeding, including development of hybrids, have occured with many other grain, forage, and vegetable crops. Even breeding techniques for fruit and forest trees have been improved.

As a result of advances in other fields, plant breeders can now tailor varieties to particular cropping systems of specific regions, and incorporate particular characteristics desired by consumers or required for processing. With reduced sensitivity of daylength and temperature variations, new crop varieties (especially wheat and rice) have far greater ranges of adaptation than their precursors.[4] Ways have been found to improve the nutritional quality of plants, to make harvest more convenient, and to increase tolerance to deficiencies or excesses of chemical components of soils. Plant pathologists and entomologists have identified the essential life cycle characteristics of many major disease organisms and insect pests. In cooperation with plant breeders, they have identified genetic mechanisms for plant resistance to specific organisms and found ways to incorporate that resistance into high-yielding types of plants.

SOILS AND FERTILIZERS

The nature of soils is increasingly understood, and substantial progress has been made in characterizing and mapping them. Plant and soil scientists have learned plants' symptoms of deficiency or excess of many nutrients, mineral elements, and chemical compounds. Some of the important interactions are understood. Means of correcting soil acidity or alkalinity are known, as are techniques for improving soil structure. Scientists now are able to determine the combinations of fertilizers and soil

[2] Traditional varieties tend to be tall and leafy, and when grown with high rates of nitrogen fertilization the tendency is accentuated—that is, a relatively large part of the additional carbohydrate the plant produces is deposited in the leaves and other vegetative parts of the plant; little goes to the grain.
[3] See Chapter 8 for more details.
[4] The flowering mechanism, hence the mechanism which initiates production of grain or fruit, in photoperiod-sensitive varieties is controlled by daylength—that is, when the daylight period reaches a certain length, the plant is induced to flower, beginning its reproductive process.

amendments required to make most soils productive, though the specific combinations required for specific crops in specific seasons must be determined in the field for each locality.

A major factor contributing to the agricultural revolution has been the increased availability and use of chemical fertilizers. According to FAO, world fertilizer consumption (excluding the People's Republic of China) rose gradually from 2 million tons at the beginning of this century (total for nitrogen, phosphoric acid, and potash) to 4 million tons just before World War I, to 9 million tons in 1938–39. Set back slightly during the years of World War II, consumption in 1945 was 7 million tons. Since then usage has increased steeply, to 21 million tons in 1955, 41 million tons in 1965, and about 90 million tons in the mid-1970s. Real costs per unit of nutrient have diminished with advances in engineering and marketing.

Since fertilizer is a purchased input, it normally can be used only in a cash market system. Consequently, before the 1960s, limited supplies in low-income countries were primarily used on high-value cash crops such as cotton, tobacco, and vegetables, or on tropical plantation (export) crops. As fertilizer costs fell and as scientists developed crop varieties that could convert high levels of fertilizer to harvestable product, the use of fertilizers naturally spread to the lower-value food crops, and even forage and pasture crops, especially in the developed countries. The use of fertilizers on wheat in Mexico in the 1950s, and on wheat and rice in Asia in the 1960s—the "green revolution"—was promoted by development of high-yielding wheat and rice varieties and by related technology.

PLANT PROTECTION

While built-in varietal resistance to specific strains of organisms is a primary means of limiting losses due to disease, an increasing array of chemicals is available for preventing loss from both disease and insect pests. The limitations on their safety and use are reasonably well known. Coupled with the scientists' ever improving knowledge of destructive organisms, these compounds have contributed greatly to today's high yields, especially when used in combination with improved varieties, fertilizers, and irrigation, where necessary.

Like fertilizers, most chemical compounds are relatively costly, so their use has generally been limited to the higher-value cash crops. When yields of the cereal grains are high, however, the use of chemicals— fungicides, insecticides, herbicides—can pay handsomely. That they are increasingly used wherever yields are high is evidence not only of their profitability but of the necessity for their use.

The farmer is no longer limited in protection of his crop to the age-old systems of crop rotation, selection of date of planting, or choice of indigenous variety.

IRRIGATION

Irrigation is an ancient art, and the many elaborate systems of canals for water transfer are reminders of the great capabilities of past civilizations. Many old systems have been extended and countless new ones constructed, particularly with the development of heavy machines to move earth, bore wells, lay pipe, and pump water. Controlled use of explosives permits construction in situations which would have been difficult if not impossible to exploit using human and animal power. Water application is being managed more and more knowledgeably to maximize plant production.

NEW POWER SOURCES

During this century many new sources of power have given farmers options that did not exist under traditional systems. Extension of electrical grids and elaboration of systems for distributing petroleum products have permitted the installation of tube wells or pumps along streams or rivers, greatly extending areas under irrigation. A growing array of farm implements permits land leveling, drainage, preparation of a proper seedbed, precision placement of seed and fertilizers, application of plant protectants, rapid harvest, crop drying and processing, and transport. Soils can be worked more rapidly and to greater depths. In Asia, where the water buffalo often cannot develop enough power to pull an implement through hardened soil, use of tractors permits the planting and cultivation of crops during the highly productive dry season.

TRANSPORT, PROCESSING, AND STORAGE

For a farmer to participate in intensive agriculture, he must be able to obtain seed, fertilizer, and other materials and to market his products within the range of his mobility. Distribution of inputs and purchase of produce in each locality become necessary. Construction of roads or arrangements for transport clearly are of high priority, but they have little effect on productivity if other factors, such as improved technology, incentive prices at markets, and instruction of farmers, remain lacking.

Most agricultural products are perishable; even cereal grains must be dried to allow them to be stored for a reasonable time without deterioration. In many climates, particularly when crops are harvested during the monsoon period, supplemental drying facilities are needed. Highly perishable crops, like vegetables and fruits, must be moved quickly to market to avert spoilage; if volumes are great and distances are long, refrigerated trucks, railway cars, or ships are needed to carry the produce to the consumer. Milk, one of the most perishable of commodities, must be cooled quickly in the milking sheds and kept refrigerated until it is consumed.

Scientists and engineers have created a range of devices which help the farmer harvest, process, market, and store his produce. They have collaborated in the design and construction of efficient factories for purposes as diverse as sugar refining, fruit and vegetable canning, quick freezing of fruits, vegetables, and pastries, conversion of perishable products such as potatoes to dry powders with a long shelf life, and production of nutritionally balanced rations for animals.

INTENSIVE AGRICULTURE, MODERN AGRICULTURE, AND EFFICIENCY

One confusing aspect of the literature on development is that key concepts are often understood differently; the debates sometimes focus on definitions of concepts rather than the concepts themselves.

Extensive versus intensive agriculture. As we have noted, gains in output today must come increasingly from intensification of agriculture; that is, by raising crop and animal yields per unit of area per unit of time (Fig. 3.2). Intensification could occur in diverse ways:

- *Raising yields per hectare per crop without lengthening the growing period.* This is the conventional concept of intensification; that is, increasing the yield of a 120-day crop from, say, 6,000 kg/ha to 8,000 kg/ha. In parts of some nations in Asia today, wheat and rice yields are double or triple what they were 3 or 4 years ago on the same farms. This is intensified crop production.
- *Increasing crop yields per hectare per day.* To improve production per hectare per day, growth periods of crops are being shortened. For example, production of a 6,000 kg/ha crop in 90 days (67 kilograms per hectare per day) is more intensive than production of 6,000 kg/ha in 120 days (50 kilograms per hectare per day). A shorter growing period for a first rice crop will, in some tropical areas, permit cultivation of a second or third crop, whose yield more than makes up for any reduced production from the first crop. In the Philippines many farmers grow only a single crop of rice, during the rainy season, and the good producer harvests around 4,000 kg/ha of grain using a variety that matures in 150–160 days. But scientists at the International Rice Research Institute, using varieties of shorter duration (110–125 days), have managed to get three crops a year, with a total yield of about 20,000 kilograms of grain per hectare per year. A total of four crops per year, producing 30,000 kilograms per hectare per year or more, is in sight. This is intensified crop production.
- *Increasing the off-take from cattle herds.* If by increasing the productivity of pastures or improving the diets of animals in other ways, less time is required to bring animals to market weight, intensification has occurred. Increasing the calving percentage, or by any other means in-

creasing the number of kilograms of beef that can be harvested per hectare, would constitute a move toward intensification. Other useful indicators are rates of gain in animal weight per unit of feed, increases in annual egg production per hen, or increases in kilograms of milk produced per day or per year per cow.

* *Shifting from less valuable to more valuable crops on the same farm or land.* If, for example, a subsistence farmer can raise the yield of a basic food crop such as maize, and then reduce the area in maize in order to grow a more profitable vegetable or industrial crop, that would be a move toward intensification.
* *Devising diversified farming schemes to include crop and animal pro-*

Fig. 3.2. Intensification of farming: Current rice yields in selected Asian countries compared to the historical growth of rice yields in Japan (solid line)

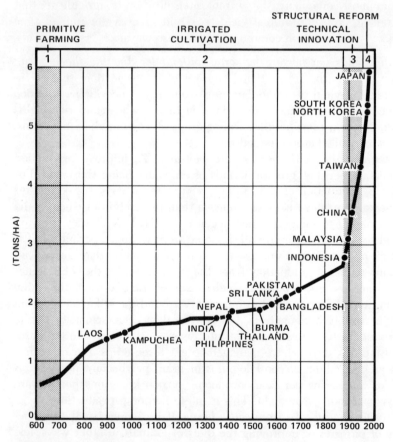

Source: From W. David Hopper, "The Development of Agriculture in Developing Countries." Copyright © 1976 by Scientific American, Inc. All rights reserved.

Yield per unit of time

Frequently, yields of crops in different countries are compared without mention of the length of the growing season in each location. This can be a misleading measure of productivity if the lengths of the growing seasons differ and if other crops are grown on the same land, taking advantage of the shortened growing season of the main crop. A better comparison would be on a kilogram-per-hectare-per-day basis.

duction and fuller use of by-products of crops. If a maize grower also raises cattle, he can feed them the stalks and leaves and return the manure to the fields—making his system more intensive if the total productivity of the farm operation increases. In Taiwan, rice farmers with small holdings have begun to produce mushrooms as part of the farm enterprise, using rice straw as a part of the material on which mushrooms are grown and thereby increasing output of the farm.

Thus, intensification of agriculture can be viewed in several different ways: to the farmer, intensification means greater production and income per hectare per year from his farm enterprise; to the scientist concerned with efficiency in the use of nutrients, energy, and water, it involves an increase in output per hectare per day; to national and international policymakers, useful indices would include national average yields of crops, average number of eggs per hen per year, kilograms of milk per cow per year, or kilograms of beef marketed per animal unit or per hectare.

Intensive versus "modern" farming. In recent years there have been repeated admonitions that nations should "modernize their agriculture." But viewpoints also vary widely on what constitutes modernization.

In the industrialized nations the degree of modernization is often gauged not only by yields attained but also by *output per unit of human time.* Thus, in affluent countries, degree of mechanization or even of farmer convenience becomes an important criterion. Some machinery, however, does little more than replace human labor and therefore is not directly related to "intensification" of production (in the sense of increased yields per unit of land area per unit of time).

To the extent that machinery permits precision placement of fertilizers and seed, or irrigation, or supply of water to animals, or distribution of animal wastes on fields, mechanization contributes importantly to higher yield. Other forms of mechanization may be irrelevant to yield but do permit a farmer to cultivate a greater area and may increase his total income.

Mechanization is not the only approach to modernization. A rice crop of record yield level is modern whether produced on 1 hectare by a farmer using hand methods or animal power or on a highly mechanized farm of larger proportions. *Use of high-yielding varieties coupled with high levels of fertilizer application and appropriate plant protectants is modern regardless of the tools used in the process.*

Efficiency. Viewpoints on "efficiency" also vary greatly. In large part, the problem is due to confusion in the use of physical and economic criteria. In a country where labor is scarce and land is relatively plentiful, the goal may be to maximize output per man rather than output per hectare. In a country where land is scarce and labor is relatively abundant, the goal is more likely to be to maximize output per hectare.[5] To contend that Japanese agriculture is more efficient than U.S. agriculture because yields per hectare are higher in Japan would be misleading. Similarly, to contend that U.S. agriculture is more efficient than Japanese agriculture because labor productivity is higher in the U.S. would be equally erroneous. The basic rule is to maximize the profits of the total enterprise; that is, to maximize the return to the scarcest factor. In most areas of the U.S. the scarce factor is labor, and labor productivity (yield per person) is maximized. Most farmers in Southeast Asia have small landholdings. To them an efficient system is one that allows them to obtain maximum productivity and income per hectare. They opt for labor-intensive systems, and the development of such systems should be encouraged in that part of the world.[6] In arid areas of Africa or Latin America, on the other hand, where population is not so dense, extensive systems such as open-range grazing may be the most efficient ways to use resources. The valid measure of efficiency is a standardized comparison of returns to the enterprise rather than to a single factor.

EVIDENCE OF THE REVOLUTIONARY GAINS

During the two decades ending in 1969–71, world output of grain nearly doubled—a compound average annual rate of increase of 3 percent (Table 3.1). The developed and the developing market economies, however, have achieved their food production increases in different ways.

During this period, production in the developed countries climbed 63

---

[5] In 1973, on U.S. rice farms, an average of less than 20 man-hours of labor per hectare was used in rice production. In many Asian countries, requirements range from 900 to 2,000 man-hours per hectare.

[6] An "extreme" case of labor-intensive agriculture is East Java, where workers pick the leaves from apple trees to simulate a dormancy period, a condition which would be caused by cold weather in temperate climates.

Table 3.1. Contribution of area and yield to increase in world grain production, 1948–71 and 1960–71

Region	Grain production (million tons) 1948–50	1969–71	Annual change (%)	Change (%) 1948–71 Area	Yield	1960–71 Area	Yield
Western Europe	72	137	3.1	3	97	−3	103
Eastern Europe & U.S.S.R.	107	230	3.7	11	89	3	97
North America	162	244	2.0	−50	150	−35	135
Latin America	31	69	3.9	69	31	57	43
Near East	22	42	3.0	78	22	36	64
Far East	135	249	2.9	50	50	42	58
Africa	28	52	2.9	48	52	43	57
China	104	202	3.2	28	72	21	79
Oceania	7	15	3.7	73	27	118	−18
World	669	1,238	3.0	28	72	20	80

Source: "Sources of Growth in World Agricultural Production," *World Agriculture.*

percent.[7] Almost all of this increase was due to higher yields; the area planted to grain crops expanded little. In the U.S., there was surplus production—that is, more was being produced than could be sold for cash at existing prices. Large amounts of surplus stocks were given to countries in need or were sold at concessional prices. A substantial portion of U.S. crop land was taken out of production. Consequently, the failure to expand was not caused by an inability to expand.[8]

The developing countries did better: total grain production rose 78 percent. This increase was due almost equally to expansion in area planted and to improvement in yields. With the passage of time, higher proportions of output growth are increasingly accounted for by improvements in yield (Table 3.1).

The "green revolution" is a limited extension of the general agricultural revolution to food crops in the developing countries.[9] That term may be excessive, but there is no doubt that the new wheat and rice varieties have had a substantial impact on yields in several Asian countries (Fig. 3.3). The new varieties are now sown on a large proportion of the wheat and rice areas of many countries in Asia (Fig. 3.4). Associated with the adoption of new varieties have been significant increases in the use of chemical fertilizers and in the attention paid to water management and

[7] We are using USDA data from *The World Food Situation and Prospects to 1985.*
[8] The experiences with maize in the U.S. and rice in Japan are described in Chapter 8.
[9] The experiences of Mexico, India, Kenya, Turkey, Colombia, and the Philippines are described in Chapter 8.

to the other practices that are essential for intensifying agricultural production.

While much has been written about wheat and rice, progress has also been made with other crops (Table 3.2). Recent gains in the yield of sorghum (primarily in the developed countries thus far) have been

Fig. 3.3.   Trends in wheat and rice yields

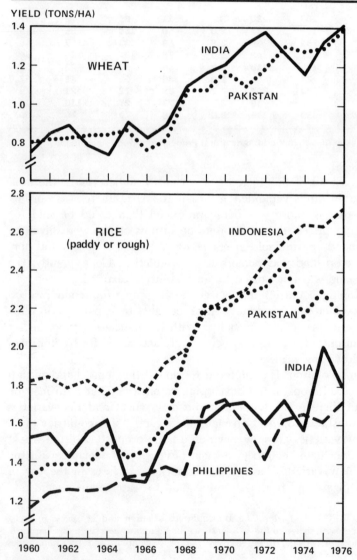

Source: Dana G. Dalrymple, *Measuring the Green Revolution: The Impact of Research on Wheat and Rice Production.*

particularly great with the advent of hybrids. Barley is important as a food crop in some countries, but a substantial portion is used for malting and for livestock feed.

Impressive as these gains in output have been, they are not adequate for future needs.

Fig. 3.4. Proportion of total wheat and rice area planted to high-yielding varieties

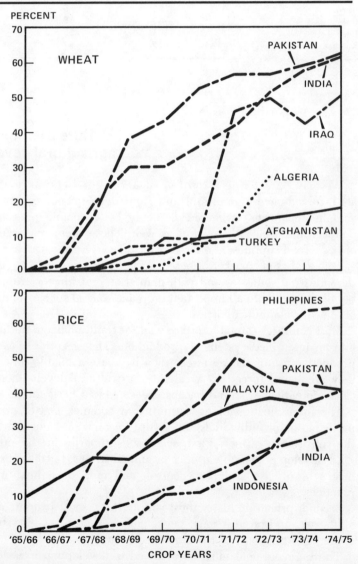

Source: Dana G. Dalrymple, *Development and Spread of High Yielding Varieties of Wheat and Rice in the Less Developed Nations.*

Table 3.2. Changes in world cereal crop area, yield, and production, 1948–71

Crop	Change (%)		
	Area	Yield	Production
Wheat	28	58	103
Rice	33	42	88
Maize	22	61	97
Sorghum	40	107	191
Barley	52	65	152
Oats	−41	58	−7
Rye	−51	65	−20
All cereals	17	57	85

Source: "The Green Evolution," Ceres.

Third era: Accelerated agricultural development

We may be entering a *third* great agricultural era, an era of accelerated, forced-pace agricultural and rural development campaigns in developing countries, triggered not only by economic pressures but by political and security pressures as well. Those pressures—security, costs of basic food supplies, and rural restlessness—were discussed in Chapter 1. Science-based, market-oriented agricultural systems, so successful in the industrial countries and with plantation crops in the tropics, must be rapidly extended to all important crop and animal species in most regions of most developing countries.

Most countries cannot afford to wait for traditional agriculture to evolve into an intensified system of production. The scientific means to make productive use of the resources they have are available now. Therefore, they are being forced to accelerate agricultural development both because potentials exist and because needs cannot be ignored.

The intensification of agriculture is a complex matter, requiring the participation of individuals and institutions not previously involved with the subsistence farmer. First, scientists, primarily in the public sector, must develop new crop varieties or animal strains, fertilizer-use practices, means of disease and pest control, and crop or animal management practices.

Second, private industry must supply the essential inputs at a reasonable price, and often it must participate in the processing, storage, marketing, and transport of the harvested product.

Third, government must be involved in developing markets, establishing price policies, organizing and supporting research, extension, and education, and arranging the supply of inputs either by business or by public agencies.

While in traditional agriculture the farmer and his family essentially controlled the whole—but limited—production system, in market-oriented agriculture scientists, industry, and government interact closely. If any one of the three fails in its contributions, intensification fails.

References

THE ORIGINS OF AGRICULTURE

Harlan, Jack R. "Our Vanishing Genetic Resources." *Science* 188 (1975): 618–621.

Harlan, Jack R. "The Plants and Animals That Nourish Man." *Scientific American* 235 (September 1976): 88–97.

Rasmussen, Wayne D. "Experiment or Starve: The Early Settlers." In *That We May Eat: The 1975 Yearbook of Agriculture.* Washington, D.C.: U.S. Department of Agriculture, 1975.

FIRST ERA: EMERGENCE OF TRADITIONAL FARMING SYSTEMS

Dalrymple, Dana G. *Survey of Multiple Cropping in Less Developed Nations.* Foreign Economic Development Report No. 12. Washington, D.C.: U.S. Department of Agriculture, October 1971.

Hopper, W. David. "Investments in Agriculture: The Essential for Payoff." In *Strategy for the Conquest of Hunger.* New York: Rockefeller Foundation, 1968.

Kao, C. H. C.; Anschel, K. R.; and Eicher, C. K. "Disguised Unemployment in Agriculture: A Survey." In *Agriculture and Economic Development,* edited by E. Eicher and L. Witt. New York: McGraw-Hill, 1964.

Lele, Uma J. *The Design of Rural Development.* Baltimore: Johns Hopkins University Press for the World Bank, 1975.

Loomis, Robert S. "Agricultural Systems." *Scientific American* 235 (September 1976): 98–105.

Oshima, Harry T. "Seasonality and Underemployment in Monsoon Asia." *Philippine Economic Journal* 10 (1971): 63–97.

Paarlberg, Donald. "Food for More People and Better Nutrition." In *Overcoming World Hunger,* edited by Clifford M. Hardin. Englewood Cliffs, N.J.: Prentice-Hall, 1969.

Rockefeller Foundation. *The Role of Animals in the World Food Situation.* Working Paper. New York: Rockefeller Foundation, December 1975.

Schultz, T. W. *Transforming Traditional Agriculture.* New Haven, Conn.: Yale University Press, 1964.

Wharton, Clifton R., Jr. "Risk, Uncertainty, and the Subsistence Farmer: Technological Innovation and Resistance to Change in the Context of Survival." In *Studies in Economic Anthropology,* edited by George Dalton. Washington, D.C.: American Anthropological Association, 1971.

Wharton, Clifton R., Jr. "Subsistence Agriculture: Concepts and Scope." In *Subsistence Agriculture and Economic Development,* edited by Clifton R. Wharton, Jr. Chicago: Aldine, 1969.

SECOND ERA: SCIENCE AND INDUSTRY FUEL A REVOLUTION

Dalrymple, Dana G. *Development and Spread of High Yielding Varieties of Wheat and Rice in the Less Developed Nations.* Foreign Agricultural Economic Report No. 95, 5th ed. Washington, D.C.: U.S. Department of Agriculture, August 1976.

Dalrymple, Dana G. *Measuring the Green Revolution: The Impact of Research on Wheat and Rice Production.* Foreign Agricultural Economic Report No. 106. Washington, D.C.: U.S. Department of Agriculture in Cooperation with U.S. Agency for International Development, July 1975.

Gough, Paul. "Natural Enemies Used to Fight Insect Ravages." In *That We May Eat: The 1975 Yearbook of Agriculture*. Washington, D.C.: U.S. Department of Agriculture, 1975.

"The Green Evolution." *Ceres* (January–February 1972): 11.

Harpstead, Dale D. "Man-Molded Cereal: Hybrid Corn's Story." In *That We May Eat: The 1975 Yearbook of Agriculture*. Washington, D.C.: U.S. Department of Agriculture, 1975.

Hopper, W. David. "The Development of Agriculture in Developing Countries." *Scientific American* 235 (September 1976): 196–205.

Horsfall, James G. "The Fire Brigade Stops a Raging Corn Epidemic." In *That We May Eat: The 1975 Yearbook of Agriculture*. Washington, D.C.: U.S. Department of Agriculture, 1975.

Mangelsdorf, Paul C. "Hybrid Corn." *Scientific American* 185 (August 1951): 39–47.

Pound, Glenn S. "Plant Disease Toll Is Cut with Resistant Varieties." In *That We May Eat: The 1975 Yearbook of Agriculture*. Washington, D.C.: U.S. Department of Agriculture, 1975.

Sanchez, P.A., and Buol, S. W. "Soils of the Tropics and the World Food Crisis." *Science* 188 (1975): 598–603.

"Sources of Growth in World Agricultural Production." *World Agriculture* 22 (1973): 7–9.

U.S. Department of Agriculture, Economic Research Service. *The World Food Situation and Prospects to 1985*. Foreign Agricultural Economic Report No. 98. Washington, D.C.: U.S. Department of Agriculture, December 1974.

Wortman, Sterling. "The Technological Basis for Intensified Agriculture." In *Agricultural Development: Proceedings of a Conference*. New York: Rockefeller Foundation, 1969.

CHAPTER 4

A world perspective: Adequacy of physical resources

Introduction

MANY FACTORS contribute to the production of agricultural commodities. Oxygen, carbon dioxide, and sunlight are in abundant supply and have no economic cost. However, other essential physical resources such as land, water, some nutrients, and some forms of energy are limited and occasionally are nonrenewable. Man controls how and to what degree the physical resource base is used in agriculture. These resources and their management cost money. Therefore, it is important to understand what is known (and not known) about the limitations on future agricultural growth imposed by each category of resources and to appreciate what can be done to relieve these limitations.

The purposes of this chapter are two. First, we will review the adequacy of the physical resource base to support increased conventional crop and animal production. Second, we will briefly explore two additional means of increasing the available food supply: fisheries and aquaculture, and reducing waste.

Crop and animal production

Crops and animals produced on farms or grazing lands provide the major source of food for humankind, It appears unlikely that these conventional commodities will be replaced by synthetic foods to any great extent in the decades immediately ahead; therefore, the seriousness of constraints on expansion of production from conventional agriculture must be understood.

ARABLE LAND

Calculations of the amount of potentially arable land in the world are highly speculative. The usual procedure is to identify those areas in which the physical, chemical, and biological properties of soils, the temperature patterns, and the amount and distribution of rainfall would support crop production with existing technology. Soils already under cultivation are included, as are those which could be put into production, some after clearing or irrigation and drainage. By comparing the amount of land already under cultivation in each region of the world with that which could in time be cultivated, the potential for expansion of crop lands can be estimated.

In one comprehensive exercise using this methodology, the U.S. President's Science Advisory Committee (PSAC) in 1967 estimated that there are over 13,000 million hectares of ice-free land in the world, of which 3,200 million hectares, or 24 percent, were at that time considered to be potentially arable (Table 4.1). Of these potentially arable lands, 1,400 million hectares, or 44 percent, were already under cultivation—that is, under crops, temporary fallow, temporary meadows, market and kitchen gardens, fruit trees, vines, shrubs, and rubber plantations. About 350 million hectares, or 11 percent of the total potentially arable land, would require irrigation to produce one crop. On the remaining 2,800 million hectares, at least one crop could be grown without irrigation.[1]

Multiple cropping—the more intensive use of land by growing several crops a year through the use of short-season varieties, intercropping, and relay cropping—has immediate potential for extending the effective land base in densely populated areas. Over a considerable region PSAC estimated that without additional irrigation multiple cropping could increase the gross cropped area (the cultivated area times the number of crops) to 4,000 million hectares annually, about three times the land presently classified as cultivated.

---

[1] Using similar methodologies, both FAO and Iowa State University (U.S.) reached similar conclusions. In its "Indicative World Plan," FAO found that only 45 percent of the 1,100 million hectares in Africa south of the Sahara, Asia and the Far East, Latin America, and Northwest Africa was actually being used for crops. The Iowa State study estimated that 3,200 million hectares of land in the world could be used to grow food crops and raise livestock but that only 1,400 million hectares were then being used.

Roger Revelle, the principal analyst in the land-use exercise for the PSAC study, published new calculations, based on a somewhat different methodology, giving slightly different results. He concluded that the gross potential area which can be cropped without irrigation is 3,200 million hectares, over twice the amount presently cultivated. In addition, he identified 500 million hectares in the humid tropics as having soil, temperature, and rainfall conditions that would permit triple cropping (that is, a gross area of 1,500 million hectares), but for which in his opinion "no technology is currently available for high-yielding agriculture on a large scale."

Table 4.1.   Estimated amounts of cultivated land by region versus potentially arable land, 1965[a]

Region	Area (million hectares)				Cultivated land	
	Total	Potentially arable	Cultivated	Potentially arable, not cultivated	As % of area potentially arable	Per person (hectares)
Africa	3,019	732	158	574	22	0.5
Asia	2,736	627	518	109	83	0.3
Australia & New Zealand	822	154	16	138	10	1.2
Europe	478	174	154	20	88	0.4
North America	2,108	465	239	226	51	0.9
South America	1,752	679	77	602	11	0.4
U.S.S.R.	2,234	356	227	129	64	1.0
World	13,148	3,189	1,388	1,801	44	0.4

Source: U.S. President's Science Advisory Committee, *The World Food Problem*.
[a] "Cultivated area" is called by FAO "arable land and land under permanent crops." It includes land under crops, temporary fallow, temporary meadows for mowing or pasture, market and kitchen gardens, fruit trees, vines, shrubs, and rubber plantations. Within this definition there are said to be wide variations among reporting countries. The land actually harvested during any particular year is about one-half to two-thirds of the total cultivated land.
   Potentially arable land includes soils considered to be cultivated and acceptably productive of food crops adapted to the environment. Some soils will need irrigation, drainage, stone removal, clearing of trees, or other measures, the cost of which would not be excessive in relation to anticipated returns. Agricultural technology equivalent to average U.S. agricultural technology is assumed. All arable land has potential for grazing and, where not too dry, for forestry too.
   Nonarable land with grazing potential includes soils with severe limitations for growing crops requiring tillage, but with at least some potential for grazing. Where not too dry, all of these soils have potential for forestry too.
   Nonarable land without grazing potential includes land (roads, cities, etc.) not available for cropping or grazing, and soils which without extreme reclamation measures have insignificant potential for crop production and grazing.

Furthermore, it estimated that an additional 3,600 million hectares, 27 percent of the ice-free land of the earth, had some grazing potential, even though it was not potentially arable.

IRRIGATION

Water is probably the most limiting physical factor in extending cultivated area. The total amount of water on our planet is constant. While it cannot be increased or diminished, more can be done to move water in the air, on the earth's surface, or underground to areas where it would have higher economic value. In addition, more efficient use can be made of existing water.

Fourteen percent of the agricultural land in the world was under irrigation in 1970 (Table 4.2). Attempts to estimate the world potential

Table 4.2. Cultivated and irrigated land by country or region, 1970

Country or Region	Land (million ha)			Irrigated land (%)	No. of persons per irrigated hectare
	Cultivated		Irrigated		
Europe	145.0		12.3	8.5	37.6
EEC[a]		52.4	5.4	10.2	46.6
Eastern Europe		46.0	2.7	5.8	38.9
U.S.S.R.	232.6		11.1	4.8	21.9
North America	236.1		16.2	6.9	14.0
U.S.		192.3	15.4	8.2	13.3
Canada		43.8	0.4	0.8	60.0
Oceania	47.0		1.6	3.4	11.9
Australia & New Zealand		45.4	1.6	3.5	9.4
Asia	463.0		145.7	31.5	14.1
Japan		5.4	2.6	48.2	39.2
China		111.2	76.0	68.3	10.0
India		164.6	27.5	16.7	19.5
Indonesia		18.0	6.8	37.8	17.1
Latin America	118.9		10.4	8.8	27.2
Mexico		23.8	4.2	17.6	12.1
Brazil		29.8	0.5	1.6	202.2
Africa	214.0		6.3	3.0	54.3
World	1,457.0		203.6	14.0	17.8

Source: University of California, *A Hungry World: The Challenge to Agriculture.*
[a] European Economic Community.

for new irrigation development, like estimates of potential arable area, are highly speculative. Nevertheless, rough estimates of irrigation potential can be made by considering the amount of potentially arable land in different geographic areas having deficiencies of precipitation during all or part of the year, together with the estimated groundwater supplies and river runoff in the same regions.

The amount of river runoff presently used for irrigation is only about 4 percent of the total available. However, the potential for future development, while great, is limited by the uneven distribution of runoff among regions of the world and within different climatic zones of each region. For example, about a third of the total runoff is in South America, which has less than 15 percent of the earth's land area. Africa, which has 23 percent of the land, has only 12 percent of the runoff. Runoff in Southwest Asia, North Africa, Mexico, the southwestern U.S., temperate South America, and Australia is less than 5 percent of the total, yet these regions comprise 25 percent of the world's land area. As a result of the uneven distribution of runoff, only a third of the land considered potentially arable by means of irrigation could actually be irrigated.

In general, surface water resources have received much more attention in the past than have groundwater resources, knowledge of which is relatively limited.

These methodological problems notwithstanding, the PSAC study estimated that the gross cropped area of the world could be increased by 2,600 million hectares if irrigation water could be made available for two or three crops per year. The gross cropped area of the earth could thus be extended to 6,600 million hectares.

In all regions the potentially high production levels permitted by modern crop technology demand that new irrigation systems be built to much higher performance standards than in the past. In particular, systems must permit delivery of water to farms when it is required by crops. Moreover, development of cropping systems should be initiated along with the construction of dams and canals for new irrigated areas. There is a critical need for coordinated application of technology and expertise to use of water for farm production. This will require teamwork among agronomists, irrigation engineers, social scientists, and others, including the farmers who use the water.

CLIMATE

Since the early decades of this century, global average annual temperatures have been relatively warm, rising to a maximum in the 1940s.[2] From the 1940s to the present, there has apparently been a cooling trend in the northern hemisphere at latitudes of 55°N and above. Even in that region, however, average annual temperatures are still higher than the averages for the past several centuries.

It is not certain that the temperature decline in the northern hemisphere will continue; it may halt or reverse. Even if the average global temperature were to decrease steadily over the next 20 years, it is unlikely that it would drop as much as 1°C. Temperature change itself is not known to be a serious climatic threat to food production. However, there is a possibility that, associated with the temperature changes, weather variability could increase. If such variability increases the fluctuation of precipitation, it could affect agricultural production.

There appears to be a consensus that climatic variability—region by region and from year to year in particular regions—is and will continue to be large, resulting in substantial variability in crop yields. Whether or not the high-latitude cooling trend continues, increased climatic variability could result in some of the following conditions, which would vary in severity from region to region:

[2] *Climate* refers to the *average* weather conditions of a place over a long period of years; *weather* refers to the condition of the atmosphere (temperature, moisture, sunlight) at a particular place and time.

- changes in seasonal and geographical distribution of precipitation;
- occasionally shorter crop-growing seasons in higher latitudes; and
- cooler temperatures during crop-growing seasons in some years.

Some climatic changes would be beneficial to agriculture and others would be detrimental, but the net effect for the whole world, or for any particular region, or for any particular time, is not known.

Growing world population and demand for food are placing increasing stress on crop production systems. Therefore, it is important that the agricultural science community be well informed about the possibility of greater future climatic fluctuations. In addition to irrigation, which was just mentioned, there are three possible responses to this problem. One is through agricultural research, a second is improved weather prediction, and the third is weather modifications.[3]

Agricultural research. Current agronomic testing techniques are designed to take into account substantial year-to-year and place-to-place variations in climatic factors. Thus it appears that agricultural research methods would allow probable future changes or fluctuations to be accommodated with reasonable ease. Nevertheless, agricultural scientists could profitably increase investigations in several areas. Possible increases in variability of the length of growing seasons, the amount and distribution of rainfall, and the effects of temperature should be considered on a region-by-region basis, together with implications for research and testing strategies. Attention should be given to ways to increase the capacity of agricultural systems to adjust to climatic fluctuations or anomalies. The adequacy of research on stability of yield should be reviewed from the standpoint of possibly greater climatic fluctuations in the future. Of particular importance are better crop tolerance to drought, tolerance to saline soils, and more efficient use of water, which will be in diminishing supply in some regions regardless of future climatic patterns. Seeds of fast-maturing crop varieties will be especially useful for years in which growing seasons are unexpectedly shortened by failure of early rains or by unfavorable temperatures at normal planting times. Research strategies must be developed to improve crop, soil, and water management policies and practices for nonirrigated farming and grazing. These include water collection, storage, and conservation techniques, as well as breeding plants for improved efficiency in water uptake.

Weather prediction. In recent years the prospects for weather prediction have become brighter, partly because of the use of weather satellites

[3] A fourth response, although limited in application, is controlled-environment agriculture.

and fast electronic computers. With the help of weather satellites, man is for the first time able to obtain a global picture of the weather. The use of electronic computers will enable greater amounts of information to be analyzed, thus permitting more reliable long-range forecasts.

While some optimism about weather prediction is justified, the same cannot be asserted about forecasts of changes in climate. Causes of the ice ages—dramatic events of the past—are apparently still unknown. It is hardly possible to say whether the somewhat colder temperatures in the recent past are a fluctuation or the beginning of a trend.

Weather modification. While weather prediction is a partially successful practice, the status of weather modification is much less clear. Progress has been limited. Cloud seeding can apparently produce rainfall in some situations.[4] There is evidence that hail suppression works. Techniques for dispersing cold fog are used at many large airports. It has been demonstrated that hurricane velocity can be reduced with certain kinds of treatment, although at the possible cost of widening the base of the hurricane. If perfected and used responsibly, weather modification could result in more efficient availability of rain water. However, the potential conflicts which may arise from these practices deserve substantial study.

ENVIRONMENT

Agriculture in both developed and low-income countries is generating environmental stress in some places.

Wind and water erosion, loss of vegetative cover, desertification, and destruction of soil fertility are occurring in areas where land is relatively abundant as well as in areas where population pressure is high. Over the past few years, human and livestock populations along the sub-Saharan fringe have increased rapidly. This has resulted in overgrazing and denudation of the land, a major reason why the Sahara Desert is estimated to be edging southward in some places by several kilometers per year. Erosion is reducing arable land in the Indian subcontinent, the Mideast, the Caribbean, Central America, and the Andean countries. Clearing land to plant more crops in the Himalayan foothills has contributed to increased flooding in India and Pakistan. Cutting trees on slopes in Java has rapidly increased silting in the irrigation channels so vital to Indonesia's agriculture. Slash and burn techniques in South America are exposing large areas to deterioration and soil erosion. Towns are ex-

---

[4] In fact, cloud seeding does not have an unassailable reputation. The correlation between the effort and the effect is so poor that it takes years of careful statistical study to prove that attempts at modification are responsible for altered precipitation.

panding and new highways are being built. Several million hectares of actual or potentially cultivated land are being ruined for agriculture each year in the developing countries for these reasons.

In more intensively cultivated areas, it is alleged that heavy use of chemical fertilizers ruins the soils; that the use of pesticides necessary for high yields in many circumstances leads to contamination of food chains with toxic substances and even to deaths of animals and humans; that construction of irrigation systems, if improperly designed, leads to new health problems, to salinization of soils, or other difficulties; and that replacement of diverse native varieties by relatively few genetically uniform strains not only increases vulnerability of crops to wide-scale attack by disease organisms or insect pests, but could displace the indigenous varieties which have value as future breeding materials and which must be preserved.

While intensification of agriculture probably has degraded land in some areas, leveling, irrigation, drainage, and careful management of fields has probably resulted in a net improvement of most of the agricultural lands involved. Land values have generally increased, making reinvestment in maintenance or improvement of agricultural areas a more attractive proposition. The Morrow plots at the University of Illinois (U.S.), continuously cropped and monitored for over a hundred years under various levels of fertilizer, provide evidence that chemical fertilizers under proper management will not "burn out" the soil. In fact, some of the worst environmental abuse is occurring under traditional, not intensive, agriculture. The spread of the Sahara Desert and soil erosion and flooding in Asia, partially due to overgrazing or deforestation, are evidence of the heavy price often paid when traditional agriculture is asked to attempt to sustain increasing numbers of people.

These problems have received attention in major national research programs and international institutions. However, the chief environmental problems of rural areas of developing countries are associated with abject poverty—poor housing, lack of sanitary facilities, impure water supplies, inadequate diets and hunger, to name a few—which, to be overcome, requires an increase in the incomes of people. Views on "environment" differ greatly in affluent and impoverished societies, a point seemingly better understood by the poor than by the affluent.

REGIONAL LAND AND WATER AVAILABILITY

Global data on land have little value except to establish a perspective from which to examine practical possibilities for increasing cropped area in specific locations.

It is in Asia that the potential for expanding cultivated land is most limited. The amount of land per capita is very small (Table 4.3). Moreover, much of Asia's potentially arable land is already under cultivation.

Table 4.3. Estimated agricultural land per capita in the most densely populated
Asian and Mideastern nations, early 1970s

Country	Hectares per capita	Country	Hectares per capita	Country	Hectares per capita
Mideast		Southeast Asia		Far East	
Egypt	0.08	Vietnam (North)	0.10	Japan	0.05
Lebanon	0.12	Indonesia	0.15	Taiwan	0.06
Jordan	0.60	Vietnam (South)	0.16	South Korea	0.07
South Asia		Philippines	0.23	China	0.13
Bangladesh	0.13	Malaysia	0.32		
Sri Lanka	0.19	Thailand	0.32		
Nepal	0.19	Cambodia	0.33		
India	0.30	Laos	0.57		
Pakistan	0.40	Burma	0.69		

Source: International Bank for Reconstruction and Development, *Land Reform*.

If we subtract potentially arable land area where the supply of water is so limited that not even a single four-month growing season is possible, little excess of potentially net arable land remains over that actually cultivated. To increase food supplies in Asia, therefore, either yields per hectare must be increased or gross cropped area must be enlarged through double or triple cropping. Expanded irrigation will be a major tool in raising yields and increasing gross cropped area.

The possibilities for developing new irrigation resources, like the possibilities for bringing new lands into cultivation, differ considerably from one region of Asia to another. By the end of the century, surface water resources may be nearly fully exploited in Taiwan, Korea, and in the Indus basin of Pakistan. However, in eastern India and Bangladesh, the rivers have been only partially harnessed for irrigation and much more could be accomplished. Progress often depends on the undertaking of major works to regulate and control the flow of large rivers. Ground-water potential is reportedly great in South Asia. Comprehensive water resource development on the Ganges, the Bhramaputra, and their tributaries could have immense impact on the agriculture of India and Bangladesh.

North Africa and the Mideast are similar to Asia: people are crowded into the relatively small areas where there is water. Surface water is, or soon will be, a limiting factor for irrigation development, but some additional groundwater supplies may be used.

The nations of the Sahel and some others have large areas where rainfall is low and erratic. In these areas the challenge is to manage the land so that available resources are not overused and consequently improve rather than deteriorate.

In sub-Saharan Africa, only a small fraction of the potentially arable land is in use. Water availability poses relatively few limitations, especially in West Africa. While land pressure in Africa is seemingly less severe, the problems are no less real. In much of the area the land is very fragile. The lives of many people depend on the use of large areas for grazing or shifting cultivation. Efforts to develop improved varieties and practices for food crops of the area are very recent. It will take years of research on soils, climate, crop varieties, and farming systems before these areas can be expected to make major contributions to the world's food supply. Trypanosomiasis and East Coast fever limit the use of cattle for food or power in much of the area. River blindness, a serious disease, limits human activity in parts of West Africa.

In Latin America the physical resources in most countries are adequate to permit a substantial increase in food output over the next several decades. In Central America the often rugged terrain limits cultivation, however. There are great areas of potentially arable land which are yet to be brought under cultivation in South America.[5] Many large rivers have been only partially harnessed for irrigation. In some areas on the western coast of South America, however, water resources will soon be developed nearly to their potential. The same is true for the drier parts of Mexico.

Europe, like Asia, has little additional land which can be brought under cultivation, and land available per person is not great. However, the nations of Europe have very intensive agricultural production. Many of them now have crop yields which rank among the highest in the world.

In North America (U.S. and Canada) in 1965, an estimated 226 million hectares suitable for cultivation were not used for that purpose; this was an amount about equal to that already under the plow.[6]

In summary, there clearly is great potential for expansion of cultivated area in some developing parts of the world. However, underutilized lands are not evenly distributed. Most of these areas are distant from population centers. More intensive use of these resources will require investments in roads, inducements to people to settle in the areas,[7] provision

[5] Michael Nelson's *The Development of Tropical Lands* gives an excellent review of recent land settlement schemes in tropical Latin America.
[6] Experience in 1973, when the U.S. attempted to bring land back into production, suggests that much farmland classified as suitable for field crops or being withheld from such use could not actually be easily returned to crop production.
[7] The PSAC report listed the range of costs (in 1967 U.S. dollars) of agricultural development of new areas based on then recent experience to be between $225 per hectare for a settlement scheme in Guatemala, including infrastructure, to $2,400 per hectare in Kenya for irrigation development, excluding associated infrastructural costs. The FAO used an estimate of an average of over $370 per hectare for land settlement in its World Food Conference document. It estimated that the total cost for land development, rising to 6–7 million hectares per year, would add up to $30,000 million through 1985.

of irrigation or drainage,[8] organization of social services, and much new research.

FERTILIZER

Substantial amounts of nutrients are supplied by nature. Worldwide, biological nitrogen fixation in the soil is estimated to total 90 million tons annually: 35 million tons in legume crops, 9 million tons in nonlegume food crops, and 45 million tons in permanent meadows and grasslands. As much as another 45 million tons of atmospheric nitrogen are estimated to be fixed annually by lightning, by the action of ozone, and by combustion, including forest fires, and part of this nitrogen is deposited on the earth's agricultural lands. Nutrients are returned to soils by decomposition of vegetative and animal matter and are moved from place to place by irrigation water and runoff. These amounts by themselves, while valuable, are not adequate to support present levels of production, let alone the higher levels of production needed in the future. Therefore, chemical fertilizers will remain essential to improvement of agricultural production.

Chemical fertilizer consumption is still quite small in most developing countries. Average use in the developing countries of Africa (5 kg/ha) is about one-seventeenth of that in the U.S. (85 kg/ha) and one-fortieth of that of Western Europe (192 kg/ha); average dosages in developing Asia (20 kg/ha) and developing Latin America (30 kg/ha) also are low (Table 4.4). Moreover, in these developing regions, a high proportion of the fertilizer is used on export crops. There is considerable scope for increasing basic food-crop yields in the developing countries through higher fertilizer applications. Forecasts indicate that additional production of nitrogen, phosphates, and potash of 4–6 million tons of nutrients per year will be required to meet expected demand over the next few years.

Some of the increase can be achieved through more effective use of fertilizer-plant capacities. For example, in developing countries in Asia, with the exception of operations in South Korea, Taiwan, and Indonesia, factory production has averaged only 60 percent of rated capacity. These inefficiencies relate to inadequate electric power, inefficient design, equipment failure and lack of spare parts, improper maintenance, inadequate supplies of raw materials or improper raw materials for a specific plant, problems with scheduling and planning for delivery, and difficulties with management and labor—problems which are not easily resolved. Produc-

[8] The improvement and expansion of irrigation will require substantial capital investment. The World Food Conference Preparatory Committee estimated that renovation of 46 million hectares of existing irrigated area would cost US$21,000 million; irrigating an additional 23 million hectares by 1985 would cost $38,000 million.

Table 4.4.   Fertilizer consumption per hectare, 1972/73[a]

Over 200 kg/ha		25–50 kg/ha (cont.)	
Developed nations		**Developing nations**	
Netherlands	France	Brazil	Algeria
Belgium	Czechoslovakia	China	Mexico
Germany, West	United Kingdom	Peru	Guatemala
Switzerland	Denmark	Kenya	Honduras
Japan	Austria	Chile	Indonesia
Germany, East	Poland	Vietnam (North)	Nicaragua
Ireland	New Zealand	Uruguay	Panama
Norway			
Developing nations			
Korea (South)		**0–25 kg/ha**	
100–200 kg/ha		**Developed nations**	
		Canada	
		Developing nations	
Developed nations		Turkey	Burma
Hungary	Bulgaria	Bangladesh	Saudi Arabia
Sweden	Italy	Pakistan	Iraq
Finland		Morocco	Cameroon
Developing nations		Philippines	Afghanistan
Korea (North)	Egypt	India	Uganda
Israel	El Salvador	Venezuela	Khmer Republic
Lebanon	Trinidad and	Thailand	Tanzania
Albania	Tobago	Iran	Ghana
		Nepal	Ethiopia
50–100 kg/ha		Ecuador	Mali
		Syria	Haiti
		Tunisia	Nigeria
Developed nations		Sudan	Zaire
Greece	Spain	Mozambique	Yemen (North)
Yugoslavia	Romania	Madagascar	Upper Volta
U.S.	Portugal	Bolivia	Burundi
Developing nations		Angola	Jordan
Dominican Republic	Costa Rica	Laos	Central African
Cuba	Colombia	Argentina	Rep.
Rhodesia	Malaysia	Chad	Congo
Vietnam (South)	Sri Lanka	Benin	Guinea
South Africa	Jamaica	Ivory Coast	Lesotho
		Liberia	Libya
25–50 kg/ha		Malawi	Rwanda
		Senegal	Sierra Leone
		Somalia	Togo
Developed nations		Zambia	Paraguay
Australia		Indonesia	Papua-New Guinea
U.S.S.R.			

Source: FAO, *Annual Fertilizer Review, 1973.*
[a] Fertilizer as NPK; based on total arable land; includes all countries with over 1 million population in 1973. Figures for the Netherlands, West Germany, East Germany, France, the U.K., and Denmark are somewhat misleading because much of this fertilizer is used on pasture land and not on crop land.

Organic fertilizers

Organic fertilizers, including both decomposed vegetative matter and animal excrement, have served as important sources of plant nutrients for centuries. They still serve this role in many countries, especially China. However, composting, distribution to fields, and incorporation into the soil involve costs, sometimes large in proportion to the amount of nutrient received. In countries which are short of other fuels, animal dung (excrement) often has a higher value when used for cooking or heating. For these reasons, the supplies of organic materials for fertilizer use are not adequate to satisfy requirements. R. Glen Anderson, in "Grain Production Potentials in Developing Countries: World Implications," has observed that, "in 1975, in addition to the organic fertilizers used, about 47 million tons of chemical nitrogen were used. A calculation of the size of the dung pile required to equal this amount in nitrogen tonnage gives a figure of 3,200 million tons or enough to build a road 117 meters wide and 2 meters deep around the earth at the equator! Further, it would require the collection of droppings from twice as many animals as we now have."

Use of chemical fertilizers has expanded because they are economical. Generally speaking, the growing plant does not distinguish between, say, urea and decomposed organic matter as a source of nitrogen.

Organic materials should continue to be used wherever feasible. However, they have no inherent advantage over chemical fertilizers when the latter are used under proper management. Even China, for these reasons, is investing heavily in large chemical fertilizer factories.

tion costs increase sharply as operating levels drop below 80 percent of capacity.[9] When high operating costs are combined with higher raw materials costs, the effect on cost of fertilizer produced can be serious.[10] If efficiency of fertilizer plants in developing countries could be brought up to levels achieved elsewhere, over a million tons of additional nitrogen (an increase of 10 percent) would be available, given present production facilities.

However, a large part of additional fertilizer production must be supplied through construction of new manufacturing plants. Construction

[9] Harre, Livingston, and Shields estimate that in a modern 1,000-ton/day plant, the cost of urea increases from about US$42/ton (assuming a natural gas cost of $0.20/cubic standard foot) at 100 percent capacity to $60/ton at 60 percent capacity. To illustrate the economies of scale of the 1,000-ton/day plant, a 200-ton/day plant, by contrast, produces nitrogen at $79/ton or more at 100 percent capacity.

[10] Using conservative assumptions, M. S. Rao of the International Development Research Centre in Canada has estimated that in the developing countries a tripling of crude petroleum prices would increase the selling price of urea by at least 40 percent. In practice, since capacity and many other factors influence cost, there is no simple relationship between the price of petroleum-based inputs and that of urea.

and operation of fertilizer plants entail huge investments.[11] Based on calculations made in 1974, a 1,000-ton/day ammonia plant and a corresponding 1,667-ton/day urea plant (urea is 46 percent nitrogen) required an investment of over US$100 million, excluding land costs. The investment costs were higher for plants based on naphtha ($110 million at 1975 prices), heavy oil ($119 million), or coal ($147 million). A 600-ton/day diammonium phosphate (16–46–0) complex required an investment of almost $50 million. Construction costs have inflated steeply. A natural gas urea plant designed in 1974 for completion in early 1977 required more than 50 percent more total capital investment than a similar complex completed in early 1974.

Other factors that are likely to limit new-plant expansion include shortages of qualified engineers, shortages of capacity for building the specialized equipment needed in fertilizer plants, and the high price and uncertain availability of raw materials such as natural gas, naphtha, and phosphate rock. These factors will greatly influence future fertilizer supply. They must be overcome.

Policy considerations, often misguided, limit growth in demand for fertilizers. National efforts to be self-sufficient can lead to prohibition of imports as a means of supporting existing, more expensive, local fertilizer production. This, in turn, makes fertilizer more expensive, hence less attractive for farmers to apply (especially given controlled, low agricultural product prices).

Availability of raw materials is not expected to pose major problems in the expansion of production of nitrogen fertilizers. Although the principal feedstocks—natural gas, naphtha, heavy oil, and coal—are in heavy demand for generating power, heating buildings, running vehicles, and manufacturing petrochemicals, constantly expanding world supplies appear to be adequate for fertilizer manufacture, at least until the end of the century.

There are no substitutes for phosphate rock from which phosphate fertilizers can be produced with existing technology in the quantity required (over 100 million tons a year) to sustain world agricultural production. However, phosphate rock is available in large quantities in several areas—the U.S., the U.S.S.R., and North Africa (Table 4.5). Shortages of sulfur (used in the manufacture of phosphatic fertilizers), one of the most plentiful minerals, should be overcome because of price incentives and new mining technologies now in the development stage.

Potash, the third major fertilizer, is mined directly. Abundant deposits

[11] Raymond Ewell estimates that US$100 billion would be required between 1975/76 and 1985/86 to finance fertilizer production plants, raw materials, production facilities, transportation and storage, and distribution facilities needed to satisfy demand.

Table 4.5. World phosphate rock resources (million tons)

Region	Known reserves[a]	% of total	Other resources[b]	Total resources	% of total
U.S.	2,300	14	4,100	6,400	8
U.S.S.R.	700	4	2,900	3,600	5
Africa	11,600	72	49,000	60,600	80
Morocco	9,100[c]	57	45,400	54,400	71
Spanish Sahara	1,500[d]	9	1,800	3,400	4
Tunisia	500	3	1,400	1,800	2
Other	600	4	400	1,000	1
Asia	300	2	1,800	2,100	3
Australia	900	6	1,800	2,700	4
Other	200	1	500	700	1
World	16,100	—	60,000	76,100	—

Source: Richard Reidinger, *World Fertilizer Review and Prospects to 1980/81.*
[a] Estimated recoverable reserves at 1974 price levels.
[b] Includes reserves recoverable at higher prices, with improved technology, etc.
[c] Reserves may be as high as 36,000 million tons.
[d] Reserves may be as high as 9,000 million tons.

are located in Canada (Table 4.6). Canadian government policy toward development of this resource is the major factor determining its availability.

OTHER AGRICULTURAL CHEMICALS

Although less widely publicized than fertilizer problems, shortages of other agricultural chemicals may have even more serious short-run effects on food production in the low-income countries. As use of fertilizer rises, herbicides are increasingly being used to control weeds. Lush plant growth often provides a favorable environment for pests and pathogens. Before the World Food Conference, surveys carried out by UNIDO/FAO

Table 4.6. World potash resources (million tons of K_2O)

Region	Known reserves	% of total	Other resources[a]	Total resources[b]
Canada	4,300	43	62,600	67,100
East Germany	2,400	25	2,400	4,900
West Germany	1,600	15	1,600	3,300
U.S.S.R.	700	7	900	1,600
Israel & Jordan	200	2	900	1,100
U.S.	200	2	200	400
Other	200	2	400	600
World	10,000	—	69,100	79,000

Source: Richard Reidinger, *World Fertilizer Review and Prospects to 1980/81.*
[a] Recoverable at higher prices or with improved technology.
[b] World potash production capacity was estimated at 29.8 million tons (K_2O basis) in 1975/76.

in 14 developing countries in Asia indicated that pesticide requirements would increase by about 3.5 times in the region between 1974 and 1982. For some of the same economic reasons as those that apply to fertilizer—but in addition because of rising pressures from environmentalists and regulatory agencies—the production of herbicides, pesticides, and other agricultural chemicals recently has been barely adequate for current demands, and some believe the production of such products is in jeopardy. The long-run answer is to breed crop varieties having broad resistance to disease and insects, and to develop more selective control measures. In the short run, however, some compromise must be reached between the conflicting objectives of environmental protection and food production, for the livelihood of millions of people is at stake.

ENERGY

One result of rising energy prices has been increased attention to the importance of energy in modern agriculture. For example, it has been calculated that the U.S. food and fiber sector, a highly complex and interrelated system, uses almost 13 percent of the total energy expended in the nation. Pimentel et al. and Steinhart and Steinhart make a convincing argument that the efficiency of energy conversion to food may be decreasing in the U.S.

A large part of energy use is accounted for in processing, distribution, and consumption (Table 4.7). Less than half of the energy use in the U.S. food and fiber sector occurs during farm production and in the manufacture of major inputs. Nevertheless, energy use in production is substantial. Fertilizer is generally applied at high levels, and additional dosages of chemical fertilizers give progressively lower incremental yield increases. Agricultural production is becoming more mechanized, and drying and processing are being used more extensively. Economic incentives have produced this situation, and energy use at current levels has generally been profitable in U.S. agriculture.

Table 4.7. Distribution of energy use in the U.S. food and fiber sector

Activity	Percent		Activity	Percent	
Input manufacturing	19.8		Farm production	22.5	
Prepared feed		2.1	Crops		16.4
Animal and marine fats			Livestock		6.2
and oils		0.7	Farm family living	11.9	
Fertilizer		11.9	Food and kindred-product		
Farm machinery		0.7	processing	27.9	
Pesticides		0.2	Marketing and distribution	17.9	
Petroleum		4.2			
			Total	100.0	

Source: USDA, *The U.S. Food and Fiber Sector: Energy Use and Outlook.*

Energy use is also surprisingly high in rural areas of low-income countries. The primary reason is found in the types of energy sources used and the ways in which they are used.

Arjun Makhijani and Alan Poole observe that

wood is the poor man's oil. . . . Together with wood, animal dung and crop residues, human and animal labor provide the barest of energy necessities for 50 to 60 percent of the world's population who live in the villages and small towns of Asia, Africa, and Latin America. . . . The commonly held notion that energy use in the underdeveloped countries is far below that in the industrialized nations is based only on the use of commercial fuels, such as oil, coal, and hydropower. The energy characteristic that is typical of poverty is not so much low per capita energy use—though that is part of it—but the relatively small amount of *useful work* that is obtained from it.

Crop yields are quite low. The result is that subsistence agriculture can use as much or more energy to produce a given unit of food; that is, it can be more inefficient than U.S. commercialized agriculture. However, subsistence agriculture is based on supposedly renewable forms of energy, while *nonrenewable* forms of energy—which are the issue in the "energy crisis"—play an important role in many intensified agricultural production systems.

High-yield agriculture does not necessarily require high levels of energy from nonrenewable sources. In many developing countries, particularly in Asia, labor is abundant. In these countries, multiple cropping or "gardening" techniques, which require low levels of fossil fuel input, have been developed successfully. Moreover, in many parts of the world, draft animals still provide adequately for agricultural needs.

Still, energy is an important input in all agricultural systems, and fossil-fuel energy will become increasingly important in future agricultural development efforts. Development of new land can require heavy equipment for clearing and shaping. Higher dosages of fertilizer must be used. Irrigation with electric or diesel pumps must be used in many countries, especially in Asia, to provide adequate water during the nonmonsoon periods.[12] Peak labor demands, producing serious bottlenecks in production in many areas, can be reduced or eliminated by selective mechanization of those agricultural operations that cause it. In the Philippines (as in Japan and Taiwan previously), the hand tractor is rapidly replacing the water buffalo as the major source of farm power. Four-wheel tractors are a significant source of farm power in the wheat areas of India and Pakistan. There are already over 100,000 large tractors in Turkey. Fuel

[12] India had almost 300,000 diesel pumps in 1965. At normal growth rates, the current number could be 600,000–750,000, each capable of irrigating an average of 10 hectares. Eastern India and Bangladesh also make extensive use of low-lift pumps for irrigation from rivers.

is used to generate electricity to dry crops, to transport crops, and to do other jobs. And, no less important, fuel is used to move commodities from surplus to deficit countries of the world.

While the availability of nonrenewable energy will not necessarily limit future food production efforts, rapidly rising petroleum prices do introduce at least short-run problems in the plans for many developing countries, if for no other reason than that they place yet another demand on their limited financial resources. The search for more energy-efficient food systems is being intensified. More effective use of fertilizers through split application and slow release of nutrients, higher labor intensities, and drying methods using waste materials for fuel are all being explored. Incentives and disincentives are being explored to shift energy use away from sources that are especially scarce. New ways to increase energy in low-income areas with bio-gas (heat-induced decomposition of manure) or fast-growing trees, such as eucalyptus, are being tried.

Fisheries and aquaculture

The important potential contribution of aquatic proteins to world human nutrition appears to be poorly understood. Some observers note that the world fish catch has been leveling off in recent years after a period of rapid growth and infer that this resource cannot realistically be considered as a major additional contributor to food supply. Others argue that doubling the world capture-fisheries' harvest of aquatic animals— that is, fish caught by hooks or nets—and increasing aquacultural pro-

Fig. 4.1. Production and potential of the world's oceans, 1970

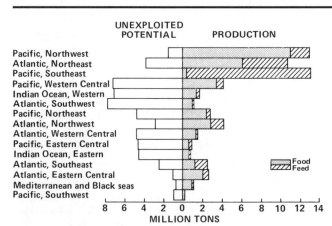

Source: M. A. Robinson and Adele Crispoldi, "Trends in World Fisheries." Reprinted by permission of *Oceanus Magazine*, Woods Hole Oceanographic Institution.

Table 4.8. World trends in production of aquatic foods by class, 1961–72
(thousand tons)

Year	Fresh-water and diad-romous	Marine	Molluscs and crus-taceans	Aquatic mammals	Misc.	Aquatic plants	Total
1961	6,960	32,190	3,520	—	200	690	43,560
1962	6,090	34,040	3,770	—	240	790	44,930
1963	6,570	34,920	4,150	—	220	690	46,550
1964	7,580	39,540	3,900	—	270	580	51,870
1965	8,560	39,600	4,140	—	240	650	53,190
1966	9,240	42,950	4,290	10	140	680	57,310
1967	9,020	45,930	4,540	—	150	830	60,470
1968	9,310	48,670	4,960	—	130	850	63,920
1969	9,790	47,190	4,750	10	100	770	62,610
1970	11,260	52,360	4,890	10	130	870	69,580
1971	11,830	51,920	4,900	10	120	920	69,690
1972	11,900	47,000	4,900	—	100	900	64,800

Source: United Nations, World Food Conference, The World Food Problem: Proposals for National and International Action.

duction tenfold could be achieved before the end of the century. Most agree that, as yet, there are few adequate plans, and few significant commitments by countries, to realize the potentials, whatever they are.

At present, fish provide 14 percent of world consumption of animal protein. This percentage varies from less than 1 percent in some land-locked countries to more than 60 percent in some coastal developing countries, particularly in Southeast Asia, where both capture-fisheries and aquaculture are important. Fortunately, many countries that depend heavily on fisheries and aquaculture also possess significant potential to increase production.

The world yield of all aquatic foods is about 65 million tons per year (Table 4.8). The potential world harvest of presently consumed species is estimated at about double this amount (Fig. 4.1). It might be even higher if species now used for fish meal, such as menhaden and Peruvian anchovy, were used for food rather than for production of fertilizers. However, at the present rate of growth of consumption, the demand for fish could surpass the production capacity of the world's oceans and lakes well before the end of the century.

A total yield several times in excess of 100 million tons may be possible if harvesting turns to less familiar types of marine animals. An example is squid, which is heavily fished in a few areas but almost unexploited in others. Other examples are the krill of the Antarctic and the lantern fish of warmer oceans. Large-scale harvesting and marketing of these less familiar species present serious technological problems.

The total Peruvian fish catch (which is 90 percent anchovies) reached a high of 12.3 million tons in 1970, dropped to 1.8 million tons in 1973, and slowly climbed back to 3.9 million tons in 1976. In 1977, large-scale fishing was permitted for only a few weeks. This phenomenon demonstrates the caution necessary in estimating potential ocean yield. Many species are now fully exploited or overexploited. Management is needed to maintain catches of the conventional species.

Wild aquatic species have traditionally been considered a common-property resource, belonging to no one until they have been harvested. The only significant recent change in this policy has been the declared expansion of the distances from shoreline (to 200 miles) within which the aquatic resources belong to the inhabitants of specific countries. Until international understandings are reached on rights in national as well as international waters, improvements in management do not appear likely. Open-sea pollution is becoming alarming and is an additional reason why more attention is being given to aquaculture.

World production from aquaculture is approximately 6 million tons per year, or less than 10 percent of the yield from capture fisheries. The potential for significantly increasing production from aquaculture is promising. In many parts of the world, particularly Asia, aquatic organisms have been successfully cultured for centuries. In these countries, herbivorous species such as mullet and milkfish are cultured in brackish-water ponds. Naturally occurring feeds are used to increase the net production of human food at relatively low costs. If methods are developed for routine production of juveniles of these species (seed production), the extent of coastal wetlands devoted to aquaculture could be greatly increased. For example, according to FAO estimates, Indonesia possesses 6 million hectares of coastal wetlands which could be converted to fish farms. There are over 400 million hectares of coastal wetlands in the world.

Aquaculture can be labor intensive, with production of up to 25 tons per hectare per year with relatively low feed and energy use; or it can be capital intensive, with high financial and energy requirements. For example, milkfish production in the Philippines is about 6 tons per hectare per year and has the potential of increasing tenfold with improved techniques. Aquaculture of salmon and trout, which combines culture in enclosures with "ocean ranching," in which fish go to sea to forage and grow, then return "home" to coastal waters to spawn, already is approaching 1,000 tons per hectare per year in Oregon (U.S.). In Japan, a combination of sophisticated technology plus traditional know-how has led to a highly productive oyster-culture industry. All Japanese oysters are cultured "off bottom," usually suspended from rafts. Yields average about 20 metric tons (shells excluded) per hectare per year, and occasionally exceed 400 tons per hectare per year. Following World War II, Taiwan developed a highly successful intensive aquaculture based particularly on true eel, which is stocked at levels reaching 160,000 per hectare.

There is a direct link between aquaculture and capture fisheries. In Southeast Asia, for example, pond production of mullet and milkfish depends on obtaining a supply-of juveniles from natural stocks. As aquaculture expands, more and more juveniles are taken and natural fishing is imperiled. Consequently, a large and dependable supply of cultured "seed" stock is essential for increased aquaculture production.

Aquatic foods can be used in many ways. They can be eaten fresh; they can be preserved by technologies ranging from simple salting or sun drying to blast freezing or processing into meals; or aquatic proteins can be combined with vegetable carbohydrates and proteins. New aquatic food technologies, such as minced-flesh machines, can turn aquatic animals not culturally acceptable in their natural forms into new, acceptable products.

To realize the potential of aquatic foods requires better understanding of the life processes of the most important species, and improvement in the technology of both aquaculture and capture fisheries. The less-developed nations especially need better methods for pond and estuarine-enclosure forms of aquaculture and improved, low-cost fisheries techniques. The infrastructure to service aquatic food production also needs drastic improvement, and extension services and manpower training are clear requirements.

Most needed, however, is commitment to the goal of maximizing aquatic food production. With clear and forceful national policies, backed by a relatively modest commitment of resources, aquatic protein production can achieve a vital role in world food production. Lead times for developing living aquatic resources are necessarily long; early commitment and action are needed to achieve timely results.[13]

Waste

Despite numerous studies, data on food waste are rarely reliable. Waste occurs at every stage, from the time a crop emerges from the ground until its eventual use as food, feed, or industrial product. There is loss at the farm, in market channels, in storage, and in food preparation and consumption. Estimates of waste in storage range from 5 to 10 percent in the U.S. In developing countries, waste in storage could average as

---

[13] The International Center for Living Aquatic Resources Management has been established in the Philippines. Its purpose is to strengthen and coordinate the science base for understanding aquatic species and their management, to train manpower at all levels, and to strengthen the development of infrastructure such as credit, delivery of information, marketing, and processing.

Table 4.9 Loss of certain commodities during storage in selected countries

Commodity	Estimated loss (%)	Major cause	Period of storage (months)	Country
Legumes	9.3	Insects	12	Ghana
	50–100	Insects	12	Upper Volta
	10	Insects	6	Nigeria
	50	Insects	12	South Africa
	50	Insects	12	Tanzania
Beans	38–69	Insects	6	Uganda
	3.6	Insects	4	Zambia
	80.7	Insects	12	Zambia
	35–44	Insects	12	Uganda
Wheat	34	Insects	24	Nigeria
	8.3	Pests	12	India
	3.0	Insects	12	U.S.
Grain	20–50	Rodents & rats	12	Somalia
Food Grain	20	Pests	12	India
Maize	0.5	Insects	12	U.S.
	30–50	Insects	5	Dahomey, Togo
	45–75	Insects	7	Uganda
	90–100	Insects	12	Zambia
Sorghum	3.4	Insects	12	U.S.
	11–88	Insects	26	N. Nigeria
Rice	5	Insects	12	Japan
	1.5	Insects	12	U.S.

Source: Agricultural Research Policy Advisory Committee, *Research to Meet U.S. and World Food Needs.*

much as 25 percent (Table 4.9). Additional waste due to rot, insects, rodents, birds, and other pests may total at least this amount (Table 4.10). But in many countries, farm animals serve as scavengers, consuming lost, unused, spoiled, or surplus food, thus sponging up the otherwise "wasted" resource and storing it in animal tissue to be consumed later. The pig is an especially efficient scavenger in many developing countries. In modern agricultural societies, the scavenger role of animals has nearly disappeared.

There is also a great deal of waste of food from the seas. Fish are thrown back as "trash" by vessels fishing for other species, especially by shrimp fleets. Large losses after catching result from improper handling, preservation, and storage.

Regardless of the accuracy of estimates, it is agreed that the waste is sizable. Improved methods of storage which are low-cost and economical should be developed for small farmers. Reduction of waste in processing can increase fish yields. Reducing losses could be one means of substantially increasing the food available to people.

Table 4.10. Losses of potential crop production by region

Region	Value (million US$)		Losses (%) due to:			Loss as % of potential value	Value of lost production (million US$)
	Actual	Potential	Insect pests	Diseases	Weeds		
North & Central America	24,392	34,229	9.4	11.3	8.0	28.7	9,837
South America	9,276	13,837	10.0	15.2	7.8	33.0	4,561
Europe	35,842	47,769	5.1	13.1	6.8	25.0	11,927
Africa	10,843	18,578	13.0	12.9	15.7	41.6	7,735
Asia	35,715	63,005	20.7	11.3	11.3	43.3	27,290
Oceania	1,231	1,707	7.0	12.6	8.3	27.9	476
U.S.S.R. & China	20,140	28,661	10.5	9.1	10.1	29.7	8,521
World	137,439	207,786	12.3	11.8	9.7	33.8	70,347

Source: Agricultural Research Policy Advisory Committee, *Research to Meet U.S. and World Food Needs.*

The growing knowledge base

Physical resources are of limited value unless the knowledge exists to utilize them effectively. This knowledge consists of two basic types. The first involves the scientific base required to exploit the physical resources. The second relates to organizational requirements that would permit gains to be widespread and to be sustained.

W. D. Hopper speaks to the issue as follows:

The relevant question for mankind, however, may not be one about investment return. It may rather be: What is the long-run cost of not initiating now a program of investing in man's future food supply? Water-resource development has a long gestation time before it yields benefits, and so do many other elements of agricultural modernization. Political leaders in both the rich and the poor countries have a short time horizon; they focus on immediate concerns. Yet future food supplies depend not on the application of more fertilizer to existing fields this year or next but on a joint and shared commitment by the developed and the developing countries to the long-term and expensive development of the world's untapped farm resources.

It is important to recognize that the world's food problem does not arise from any physical limitation on potential output or any danger of unduly stressing the "environment." The limitations on abundance are to be found in the social and political structures of nations and in the economic relations among them. The unexploited global food resource is there, between Cancer and Capricorn. The successful husbandry of that resource depends on the will and the actions of men.

Over the past two decades, and especially in the last few years, much progress has been made in raising the questions, mobilizing the money, and establishing the institutions and the research programs to provide these answers. Chapters 5, 6, and 7 will review this progress in more detail.

Concluding comments

The evidence clearly indicates that the overall physical potential exists on earth to feed a vastly larger population than now lives here. Estimates of the carrying capacity of the earth have ranged as high as 76,000 million people, based on a minimum subsistence diet of 2,500 kilocalories per person per day. Providing an "adequate" diet, including high-quality protein (protein with the balanced content of amino acids required by human beings and all other warm-blooded animals except cattle and related ruminants) and "protective" foods such as fruits and vegetables, or the equivalent of 4,000–5,000 kilocalories per person per day, the potential gross cropped area of the world is estimated (by Revelle) to be sufficient for 38,000–48,000 million people—over 10 times the present human population of the earth. Even in India, for example, which is often cited as one of the more hopeless cases by the professional pessimists, the Indo-Gangetic Plain with its abundant sunlight and water resources and deep, rich soils is estimated to be capable of producing many times the amount of food currently being grown.

Despite this encouraging world potential, it must be reemphasized that the resources of individual countries vary widely. Each country has its own special responsibility to assure food supplies to its people, and many of the deficit countries have the physical potential to produce much more, if they will make the necessary effort. However, the longer serious efforts are delayed by governments, the greater will be the pressure of man on land, the dilution of financial resources, the neglect of food crops, and the desperate plight of the small farmers. While some problems loom large, inaction can only make them worse.

References

CROP AND ANIMAL PRODUCTION

Anderson, R. Glenn. *Grain Production Potentials in Developing Countries: World Implications*. Translations and Reprints No. 20. Mexico City: Centro Internacional de Mejoramiento de Maiz y Trigo, 1976.

Bene, J. G.; Beall, H. W.; and Cote, A. *Trees, Food, and People: Land Management in the Tropics*. Ottawa: International Development Research Centre, 1977.

Blakeslee, Leroy L.; Heady, Earl O.; and Farmingham, Charles F. *World Food Production, Demand, and Trade*. Ames: Iowa State University Press, 1973.

University of California. *A Hungry World: The Challenge to Agriculture.* Berkeley: University of California, Division of Agricultural Sciences, July 1974.

Crosson, Pierre R., and Frederick, Kenneth D. *The World Food Situation: Resource and Environmental Issues in the Developing Countries and in the United States,* forthcoming.

Eckholm, Erik P. *Losing Ground.* New York: Norton, 1976.

Ewell, Raymond. "Fertilizer Industry World Plan of Action." Paper presented at the UNIDO's Second General Conference, March 1975, Lima, Peru. Mimeographed.

Food and Agriculture Organization. *Annual Fertilizer Review, 1973.* Rome: Food and Agriculture Organization, 1974.

Food and Agriculture Organization. *Provisional Indicative World Plan for Agricultural Development.* 2 vols, plus regional studies. Rome: Food and Agriculture Organization, 1970.

Ford Foundation. *Exploring Energy Choices.* New York: Ford Foundation, 1974.

Harre, E. A.; Livingston, Owen W.; and Shields, John T. *World Fertilizer Market Review and Outlook.* Bulletin Y–70. Muscle Shoals, Ala.: National Fertilizer Development Center, Tennessee Valley Authority, March 1974.

International Bank for Reconstruction and Development. *Land Reform.* Sector Policy Paper. Washington, D.C.: World Bank, May 1975.

Makhijani, Arjun, and Poole, Alan. *Energy and Agriculture in the Third World.* Cambridge, Mass.: Ballinger, 1975.

National Academy of Sciences. *Climate and Food: Climatic Fluctuation and U.S. Agricultural Production.* Washington, D.C.: National Academy of Sciences, 1976.

Nelson, Michael. *The Development of Tropical Lands: Policy Issues in Latin America.* Baltimore: Johns Hopkins University Press for Resources for the Future, 1973.

Pimentel, David; Hurd, L. E.; Bellotti, A. C.; Forster, M. J.; Oka, I. N.; Sholes, O. D.; and Whitman, R. J. "Food Production and the Energy Crisis." *Science* 182 (1973): 443–449.

Reidinger, Richard. *World Fertilizer Review and Prospects to 1980/81.* Foreign Agricultural Economic Report No. 115. Washington, D.C.: U.S. Department of Agriculture, February 1976.

Revelle, Roger. "The Resources Available for Agriculture." *Scientific American* 235 (September 1976): 164–78.

Rockefeller Foundation. *Climate Change, Food Production, and Interstate Conflict.* Working Paper. New York: Rockefeller Foundation, February 1976.

Steinhart, John S., and Steinhart, C. E. "Energy Use in the U.S. Food System." *Science* 184 (1974): 307–16.

United Nations, World Food Conference. *The World Food Problem: Proposals for National and International Action. Item 9 of the Provisional Agenda, United Nations World Food Conference,* Rome (E/CONF. 65/4), August 1974.

U.S. Department of Agriculture, Economic Research Service. *The U.S. Food and Fiber Sector: Energy Use and Outlook.* Washington, D.C.: U.S. Government Printing Office, 1974.

U.S. President's Science Advisory Committee. *The World Food Problem.* Vol. 2: *Report of the Panel on the World Food Supply.* Washington, D.C.: U.S. Government Printing Office, May 1967.

FISHERIES AND AQUACULTURE

Agricultural Research Policy Advisory Committee. *Research to Meet U.S. and World Food Needs: Report of a Working Conference Sponsored by the Agricultural Research Policy Advisory Committee.* Vol. 1. Kansas City, Mo.: Agricultural Research Policy Advisory Committee, 1975.

International Center for Marine Resource Development. *Prospects for Fisheries Development Assistance.* Marine Technical Report Series No. 19. Kingston: University of Rhode Island, 1974.

Robinson, M. A., and Crispoldi, Adele. "Trends in World Fisheries." *Oceanus* 18 (Winter 1975): 23–29.

United Nations, World Food Conference. *The World Food Problem: Proposals for*

National and International Action. Item 9 of the Provisional Agenda, United Nations World Food Conference, Rome (E/CONF. 65/4), August 1974.

WASTE

Agricultural Research Policy Advisory Committee. *Research to Meet U.S. and World Food Needs: Report of a Working Conference Sponsored by the Agricultural Research Policy Advisory Committee.* Vol. 1. Kansas City, Mo.: Agricultural Research Policy Advisory Committee, 1975.

Araullo, E. V.; de Padua, D. B.; and Graham, Michael, eds. *Rice Postharvest Technology.* Ottawa: International Development Research Centre, 1976.

Breth, Steven. "Asian Farmers Can Adopt Guatemala's Low-Cost Metal Silos." *Modern Agriculture & Industry—Asia,* April 1976, p. 10.

THE GROWING KNOWLEDGE BASE

Hopper, W. David. "The Development of Agriculture in Developing Countries." *Scientific American* 235 (September 1976): 196–205.

CONCLUDING COMMENTS

Hopper, W. David. *To Conquer Hunger: Opportunity and Political Will.* Lecture delivered at Michigan State University, May 16, 1975. Ottawa: International Development Research Centre, 1975.

Revelle, Roger. *Population and Resources.* Research Paper No. 5. Cambridge, Mass.: Harvard University, Center for Population Studies, July 1974.

Decade
of awakening

Introduction

THE YEARS 1965–74 might be called "The Decade of Awakening" in relation to the world food-poverty-population problem. The last years of this decade were marked by an upsurge in serious studies of the problem, an evolution of strategies, and a marshaling of resources and talents. A growing debate, a battle for ideas, has swirled around such questions as:

- Was Malthus correct when he argued in 1789 that human populations, which tend to increase exponentially, would overtake the world's capability to produce food, which tends to increase linearly? And is the confrontation near at hand?
- Could food needs continue to be met by expansion or improvement of conventional agriculture—by more extensive plantings or grazing, or by raising yields per hectare of crops and livestock products—or would a solution, if there is one, involve primarily nonconventional food supplies such as single-cell protein, leaf protein, or synthetic foods?
- Could less-developed countries, with their shortages of trained personnel, their bureaucracies, their low per capita incomes, and their high levels of illiteracy, hope to increase agricultural productivity fast enough to meet the needs of their burgeoning populations?
- Should nations such as the U.S., Australia, and Canada, with their capacities to produce food surpluses, continue to provide food aid to countries that suffer periodic deficits, or should the less-developed countries be required to provide for their own needs?
- If improvement of conventional agriculture is a principal solution, can it be attempted on the hundreds of millions of small, subsistence farms of the developing countries? Or is that an uneconomical approach, a system of welfare agriculture, destined to fail because of the conservatism, apathy, or incompetence of uneducated peasants?

• Is investment in industrial rather than agricultural development the primary pathway to general economic progress—the quickest route to modernization and employment of large numbers of people?

These questions have been put into stark perspective in books and papers written over the last decade by such authors as Lester Brown, Paul Erlich, Georg Borgstrom, Garrett Hardin, and William, Elizabeth, and Paul Paddock. They dramatize the seriousness of the problem and are generally doubtful that adequate solutions can be found. Some therefore argue that drastic steps must be taken to contain the crisis. "Triage" and "lifeboat ethics" have been proposed.[1] At another extreme, Roger Revelle has been consistently optimistic about the future of the world's ability to feed itself.

A review of in-depth studies, in contrast to the more popular writings of the period, indicates that a remarkable degree of understanding of the nature and seriousness of the problem and what might be done about it has emerged recently. The purpose of this chapter is to review these studies and indicate the points of widespread agreement.

The nature and seriousness of the problem understood

The food-poverty-population problem justifies concern, even alarm. But the problem is not new. The world's food supply and demand have been in close balance throughout recorded history. The Bible refers often to famine. A crisis atmosphere similar to today's existed during the late 1700s, when Malthus wrote his famous book *An Essay On the Principle of Population*. At the turn of the 20th century, Sir William Crookes (according to Blakeslee, Heady, and Farmingham, *World Food Production, Demand, and Trade*), in his presidential address to the British Association for the Advancement of Science, projected a bleak future for the U.S., which now accounts for 40–50 percent of the world's wheat exports:

there remains no uncultivated prairie land in the United States suitable for wheat growing. The virgin land has been rapidly absorbed, until at present there is no land left for wheat without reducing the area for maize, hay, and other necessary crops. It is almost certain that within a generation the ever

---

[1] These policies, using analogies to the treatment of wounded on battlefields or the allocation of seats on a single lifeboat to passengers of a sinking ship, suggest that low-income countries that have the fewest prospects (how this decision is reached is unclear) to improve their food-population-poverty situation should be denied outside assistance and abandoned so that more assistance can be focused on the countries that have better prospects of survival.

Major reviews of the world food situation

1957

The Next 100 Years, by Harrison Brown, James Bonner, and John Weir. An analysis of the relationships among world population, food production, natural resources, and knowledge generation. Three chapters deal directly with factors affecting food production.

1963

Strategy for the Conquest of Hunger, by J. George Harrar. Selected papers by the president of The Rockefeller Foundation on the 20th anniversary of the foundation's agricultural sciences program. An updated edition of Dr. Harrar's papers was published in 1967 under the title *Strategy toward the Conquest of Hunger.*

Man, Land, and Food, by Lester R. Brown. An analysis of grain production, trade, and per capita availability, with projections to the year 2000.

1964

Agricultural Sciences for the Developing Countries, edited by Albert H. Moseman. One of the first attempts by the agricultural science community to review the role of agricultural science and technology in accelerating economic progress in developing nations. Papers are organized under the following topics: characteristics of agricultural systems in emerging nations; research to devise and adapt innovations; education and development of human resources; and establishing indigenous institutions to serve advancing agriculture.

No Easy Harvest: The Dilemma of Agriculture in Underdeveloped Countries, by Max F. Millikan and David Hapgood. Summary of a workshop, involving 44 world authorities, held to examine the prospects for increasing agricultural production in low-income countries, with particular emphasis on policies which could promote faster growth. A remarkably well-balanced presentation deserving study today.

1965

Changes in Agriculture in 26 Developing Nations, 1948–1963, by the Economic Research Service, U.S. Department of Agriculture. Analysis of agricultural production change in selected developing countries.

Increasing World Food Output: Problems and Prospects, by Lester R. Brown. Study of possibilities and prospects for increasing yields, with particular emphasis on the less-developed regions.

World Food and Population Supplies, 1980, published by the American Society of Agronomy. Contains papers by Lester Brown, Frank W. Notestein, Nevin S. Scrimshaw, and Kenneth L. Bachman dealing with the world food situation and prospects for meeting needs.

1966

Prospects of the World Food Supply, published by the National Academy of Sciences. A collection of papers on the responsibilities of government (David Bell); the roles of international agencies (J. Burke Knapp); economic requirements (Theodore W. Schultz); population and food supplies (Roger

Revelle); nutrition (Nevin S. Scrimshaw); animal health (W. R. Pritchard); genetic potentials for increasing yields of food crops and animals (P. C. Mangelsdorf); pest, pathogen, and weed control (E. C. Stakman); and fertilizers (Frank W. Parker and Lewis B. Nelson).

1967
The World Food Problem, by the U.S. President's Science Advisory Committee. A three-volume report of recommendations and supporting data prepared by 12 subpanels which examined population and nutritional demands; trends in trade; crop production; animal production; increasing high-quality protein; manufactured inputs; water and land; tropical soil and climates; production incentives for farmers; marketing, processing, and distribution of food products; transportation; research and education; and financial methods, sources, and requirements.

1968
Strategy for the Conquest of Hunger, published by The Rockefeller Foundation. A collection of 13 papers by authorities from 10 nations on three themes: "The Experience of Nations"; "The University as an Instrument of Agricultural Development"; and "Accelerating Agricultural Output."

1969
Overcoming World Hunger, edited by Clifford M. Hardin. A collection of papers which served as background reading for a national American Assembly program. Topics covered are "Population Growth and Its Control" (Frank W. Notestein); "Food for More People and Better Nutrition" (Don Paarlberg); "Expanding Food Production in Hungry Nations" (J. George Harrar and Sterling Wortman); and "Hope for the Hungry: Fulfillment or Frustration" (David E. Bell, Lowell S. Hardin, and F. F. Hill).
Agricultural Development, published by The Rockefeller Foundation. Proceedings, including background papers and the summary statement, of a conference sponsored by The Rockefeller Foundation at Bellagio, Italy. Participants included heads of major international assistance agencies—the so-called Bellagio Group—which was instrumental in forming the Consultative Group for International Agricultural Research.

increasing population of the United States will consume all the wheat grown within its borders, and will be driven to import and . . . scramble for a lion's share of the wheat crop of the world.

The early 1920s (following World War I), the late 1940s and early 1950s (following World War II), and the mid-1960s (during the droughts on the Indian subcontinent) were periods of similar world concern.

These earlier warnings notwithstanding, the quickening tempo of attempts to understand the food-poverty-population problem in recent years is revealed by the number of major studies, symposia, and reviews which have appeared.

1970
Provisional Indicative World Plan for Agricultural Development: Summary and Main Conclusions, published by FAO. Includes three major sections: The Challenge of 1985—the Key Problems for Agriculture; Policies for the Achievement of the Strategic Objectives; and Summary and Conclusions. First issued as a working paper for the 15th session of the FAO Conference.

1974
A Hungry World: The Challenge to Agriculture, published by the University of California. A comprehensive report by a knowledgeable University of California task force. The short-range and long-range demands on food supplies and U.S. ability to meet them are examined. Rich in data.
The World Food Situation and Prospects to 1985, published by the U.S. Department of Agriculture. "Designed to provide a comprehensive analysis of the factors which influenced food production, consumption and trade in the two decades prior to 1972, the causes for the turbulent development of 1972–74, and the main factors which will shape developments in the next decade."
Assessment: Present Food Situation and Dimensions and Causes of Hunger and Malnutrition in the World, published by the United Nations. A preliminary assessment of the present food situation and future outlook, prepared for the Preparatory Committee of the World Food Conference, 2nd session.

1976
Scientific American, September 1976. Entitled "Food and Agriculture," the entire issue is devoted to analysis of the world food situation, with special attention to the role of science.

1977
World Food and Nutrition Study: The Potential Contributions of Research, published by National Research Council, National Academy of Sciences. An assessment of how U.S. research and development capabilities can be applied to meeting world food and nutrition needs.

FOOD SUPPLY BALANCES

In 1963 the U.S. Department of Agriculture published an imaginative set of data which still deserve attention. In *Man, Land, and Food*, Lester Brown reported food supply projections (not predictions) to the year 2000 assuming modest gains (10 percent from 1960 to 1980, plus another 10 percent from 1980 to 2000) in consumption (Table 5.1). He assumed that world population in 2000 would be 6,300 million, the medium estimate of the 1958 U.N. projections.

In a paper prepared in 1968, Don Paarlberg referred to Brown's book as both "pioneering" and "still reasonably indicative of the basic situa-

Table 5.1.   Projected total annual grain production, net trade, and per capita availability by the year 2000[a]

Region	Production (million tons)		Imports[b] (million tons)		Grain available (kg/person)	
	1957/61	2000	1957/61	2000	1957/61	2000
North America	204	375	−34	−94	883	900
Western Europe	85	176	23	34	364	500
Eastern Europe & U.S.S.R.	180	325	—	4	542	625
Oceania	8	21	−4	−12	294	310
Latin America	42	140	−1	7	207	248
Africa	38	100	1	6	171	205
Asia	353	1,014	12	54	230	276
Developed nations	476	897	−15	−68	550	644
Developing nations	433	1,253	15	68	222	265
Free World	574	1,374	−3	−19	304	324
Communist Bloc	336	776	3	19	348	380

Source: Lester R. Brown, *Man, Land, and Food.*
[a] Assuming a 10 percent gain in per capita availability from 1960 to 1980 and another 10 percent increase by the year 2000.
[b] Negative figures are exports.

tion." Paarlberg drew attention to two major implications: (1) For Latin America, grain production would need to be tripled by the year 2000, and still some imports would be required. (2) Exports from developed to developing countries would need to more than quadruple (from 15 to 68 million tons), even if developing countries were to triple grain output (from 433 to 1,253 miilion tons). Other projected changes included massive grain transfers to Asia, increased imports by Europe, and a tripling of exports from North America. Paarlberg cautioned that "the studies are more clearly an estimate of need than a prediction of supplies that will be forthcoming. In fact, the procedures have generally been to estimate need based on certain criteria and then to compute the volume of production required to meet this need. Commonly, those who read these projections impute to them greater reliability than do those who make the analyses."

THE GROWING DEFICITS IN DEVELOPING NATIONS

In 1966 doubts became widespread about the future ability of poor agrarian nations to feed themselves and about the capacity of other nations to cover their deficits. In *Symposium on Research in Agriculture*, published in 1966 by the U.S. Department of Agriculture (USDA) and the National Academy of Sciences, Dorothy H. Jacobson, Assistant Secretary of Agriculture, made revealing, and typical, comments about the situation. She projected a very rapid increase in the food aid needs of the developing countries and indicated that U.S. output could rise rapidly within a 5-year period if then-idle lands were put back into use, but she also suggested that, if three assumptions[2] on which the data were based were valid, *food aid needs would exceed the productive capacity of the U.S. before 1985* (Fig. 5.1).

Data such as these were instrumental in causing government officials as well as academics to realize that unless developing countries increased their own food output, their deficits could become so large within two or three decades that they would exceed the production capacity of developed nations. And, given the inability of many developing nations to pay for imports, the cost of donations or concessional sales would be staggering.

But Mrs. Jacobson also noted that a USDA study of agricultural pro-

[2] That food production in 66 aid-recipient nations would continue to increase at 2.6 percent a year, as in the past; that the population in these countries would increase at the rate of the U.N.'s medium projection; and that the per capita consumption of food in these countries would increase slightly over the years as a result of slightly rising incomes.

Fig. 5.1. Availability of all U.S. grains for food aid and the food aid needs of 66 developing nations, 1965–85 (projections made in 1966)

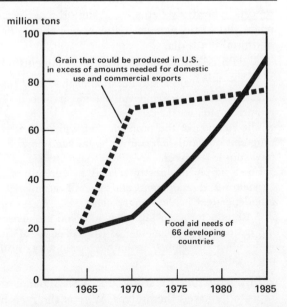

Source: Dorothy H. Jacobson, "Our Mission Abroad—Opportunities to Aid Developing Countries."

duction of 26 developing nations revealed that 12 had each increased output by 4 percent or more per year over a 15-year period; and that the average annual increase of these 12 nations was over 5 percent. She stated:

Some of them were tropical, and some were temperate. Some had high levels of literacy and some very low. Less than half of them had new land that they could put under cultivation, but more than half had to do it by increasing yields.

Out of a variety of factors, there was only one factor that they all had in common: A sufficient national determination to improve their agricultural production, to give that effort priority, to adopt policies directed toward that end, whatever the varying policies that might have been called for in each particular circumstance.

Two ideas were beginning to emerge: first, developing nations would need to increase their own output; and, second, given the will, they could do so.

THE PSAC REPORT

In 1966 a fresh study of the world food situation was started in the U.S. by the President's Science Advisory Committee (PSAC). Under the leadership of a medical scientist, Ivan L. Bennett, Jr., and an agricultural scientist, H. F. Robinson, a panel of 125 scientists worked nearly a year to bring together information on the problem and workable approaches to its solution and to make recommendations. Its major findings were published in 1967 in a 127-page summary, backed up by two volumes of reports. The study had special importance because it appeared at a time when the world was very concerned about the second consecutive year of drought in India.

The PSAC summary lists four basic conclusions:

1. The scale, severity, and duration of the world food problem are so great that a massive, long-range, innovative effort unprecedented in human history will be required to master it.
2. The solution of the problem that will exist after about 1985 demands that programs of population control be initiated now. For the immediate future, the food supply is critical.
3. Food supply is directly related to agricultural development and, in turn, agricultural development and overall economic development are critically interdependent in the hungry countries.
4. A strategy for attacking the world food problem will, of necessity, encompass the entire foreign economic assistance effort of the United States in concert with other developed countries, voluntary institutions, and international organizations.

In conducting its study, the PSAC panel members stated they had repeatedly asked themselves, Why is the race between food and population being lost? They listed seven contributing factors:

1. The overall problem of the world food supply is so large and so extremely complex that it is almost impossible for the casual or even the moderately concerned observer to comprehend its true dimensions or to grasp its intricate interrelationships with the many other aspects of economic growth and development.

2. Despite its true complexity, the problem, at first glance, seems deceptively straightforward and is, therefore, unusually susceptible to oversimplification. Because eating and even farming seem readily understandable to the average citizen in a developed country such as the United States, the temptation to act on the basis of superficial or incomplete information is almost irresistible. This leads to seizure and overemphasis upon panaceas and piecemeal "solutions" which are inapplicable, ineffectual, or inadequate. The cumulative delays engendered by false starts and stop-gap measures mask the requirement for broad and effective programs, tailored to the demands and dimensions of the overall problem.

3. The details of the task involved in increasing food production to meet world needs have never been charted with the clarity and exactness that the available information will permit. The problem has been treated dramatically but incompletely—usually to incite short-term action for humanitarian reasons. A wholehearted response to an incomplete proposal, however, lulls the participants into an unjustified feeling of security that the problem is coming under control.

4. Food shortage and rapid population growth are separate, but interrelated problems. The solutions, likewise, are separate, but related. The choice is not to solve one or the other; to solve both is an absolute necessity. The current tendency to think of food production and fertility control as alternative solutions to a common problem is dangerously misleading.

5. The twin problems of food and population imbalance have one feature in common that adds immeasurably to the difficulties of achieving control. Their eventual solution is crucially dependent upon success in convincing millions of citizens in the developing nations to take individual action. Fertility control cannot be achieved by declarations of government policy or by executive decree, although adoption of a policy and the provision of information, instruction, and materials are obviously needed and are helpful. Similarly, political declarations concerning agricultural productivity are ineffective unless individual farmers can be convinced to adopt the necessary improved practices. The provision of these personal incentives is a task that encompasses a vast array of social, economic, and political considerations which differ between countries and within countries. Indeed, the very fabric of traditional societies must be rewoven if the situation is to change permanently.

6. The eventual alleviation of world hunger will require many years. It is dependent on far-reaching social reforms and long-range programs of hard work which offer no promises of quick and dramatic results of the type so helpful in maintaining enthusiasm for a concerted, difficult undertaking. The results cannot be seen as a dedication of new buildings, as a successful launching into space, or as other spectacular, "newsworthy" events to punctuate the year-in and year-out toil.

7. The problem of food production is but one part, albeit a very important part, of the enormous problem of economic development in the poor nations. As the years have passed, the great expectations which ushered in our foreign assistance programs, fresh on the heels of the heady successes of the Marshall Plan, have not been realized. Domestic political constraints have so eroded the program and the agency responsible for it that there remains virtually no possibility of commitment to long-range, coordinated action, dedicated to the systematic solution of a series of interrelated problems, none of which can be solved in isolation from its fellows. The original emphasis upon technical assistance has been so diluted that it is almost correct to say that this form of aid, indispensable to the accomplishment of increases in food production, now receives little more than lip service. Despite chronic reiterations of the need to involve private industry in economic assistance, no significant progress in engaging this rich reservoir of resources and skills can be reported at this time.

The third point warrants reemphasis: "The details of the task involved in increasing food production to meet world needs have never been charted with the clarity and exactness that the available information will permit." The panel made a beginning at laying out a strategy, particularly for U.S. involvement. However, there is still an urgent need to go beyond descriptions of the problem to the identification and implementation of effective approaches.

In 1974 (just before the World Food Conference), the Committee on World Food, Health, and Population of the National Academy of Sciences, most of whose members had participated in the 1966–67 PSAC study, was asked to reexamine the world food situation. The committee found the problem still to be extremely serious, if not at a crisis stage. Moreover, it found the PSAC findings *still generally valid and still generally being ignored.*

THE INDICATIVE WORLD PLAN

At the First World Food Congress, convened in relation to the 1963 FAO Freedom from Hunger Campaign, a proposal was developed to survey the world food situation and to prepare a plan to increase food production to meet needs. Directed by Walter Pawley, this comprehensive effort resulted in three volumes totaling 714 pages. A first report was presented to the Fifteenth Session of the FAO Conference in 1969, and FAO's published version appeared in 1970 under the title *Provisional Indicative World Plan for Agricultural Development.*

The Indicative World Plan (IWP) was, in reality, as FAO stated, "an analysis of the major issues which are likely to be facing world agriculture in the 1970s and 1980s, together with some recommendations regarding the most important directions in which efforts will need to be made." It was not considered by FAO to be a "plan" for action in the usual sense. The IWP estimated that between 1962 and 1985 total agricultural production in the less-developed countries would have to grow by 3.7 percent per year, and food production by 3.9 percent per year, if overall development were not to be seriously slowed. Like the report of the PSAC panel, the IWP called for greatly increased efforts to improve cereal production plus attempts to diversify diets and to increase protein supplies, supported by greater efficiencies in production and marketing, more comprehensive economic policies, greater employment within, as well as outside, agriculture, and intensification of land use. For animal production, IWP emphasized swine and poultry, which have high reproductive rates.

The IWP not only improved understanding of the world food situation but led to the widespread conviction in the late 1960s that massive investment in improvement of conventional agriculture was urgently needed.

RECENT STUDIES

The green revolution, with its quick successes, held promise to many that the world food problem might at last be overcome. Lester Brown was illustrative of the general consensus when in 1970 he wrote: "the world has recently entered a new agricultural era. It is difficult to date precisely this new era since many of the contributing factors have been years in the making. But in terms of measurable phenomena such as the sudden sweeping advances in food production in several major developing countries, the old era ended in 1966 and the new began in 1967." Later in the same paper he asked: "Are the recent agricultural advances a temporary phenomenon, or a new trend? They appear to be the latter. The agricultural revolution seems to have gone too far now to be arrested. Too much is at stake, too much has been invested, the expectations of too many people have been aroused. The agricultural revolution in Asia should not, therefore, be viewed as an event but as the beginning of a process—the eventual modernization of Asia."

Although popular books were appearing which were skeptical of the depth and breadth of change, the late 1960s and early 1970s were generally a period of dearth in serious studies of the world food situation.[3]

This neglect changed dramatically, however, with the sharp decline in world food production in 1972. Since then, independent studies by agricultural economists at Iowa State University (*World Food Production, Demand, and Trade*), the Preparatory Committee of the World Food Conference (*Assessment: Present Food Situation and Dimensions and Causes of Hunger and Malnutrition in the World*), a multidisciplinary team at the University of California (*A Hungry World: The Challenge*

---

[3] The exceptions were excellent projections of supply and demand prospects carried out by FAO in 1967 and 1971 and by the Economic Research Service of the U.S. Department of Agriculture in 1967, 1970, and 1971.

to Agriculture), the U.S. Department of Agriculture (*The World Food Situation and Prospects to 1985*), D. Gale Johnson (*World Food Problems and Prospects*), the U.S. National Academy of Sciences (*World Food and Nutrition Study: The Potential Contributions of Research*), and the International Food Policy Research Institute (*Meeting Food Needs in the Developing World: The Location and Magnitude of the Task in the Next Decade*) have appeared. All confirm that, unless major efforts are mounted soon, the food-population-poverty crisis will become much worse.

The National Academy study, as reflected in its interim report, is noteworthy for its recognition of the problem of poverty—that is, income distribution—in addition to the problems of production and population emphasized in all the studies:

An immediate cause of most malnutrition is poverty: poor people cannot buy enough food. They cannot buy enough food because not enough food is produced at prices the poor can afford; and this interacts with other factors in a poverty environment to foster malnutrition. Increased food production would lower food prices, increase employment and income, and provide more and better quality food directly for the masses of people in subsistence agriculture. These benefits are most significant for the poorest populations and all of them, except for the price effect, depend on growing the additional food where the hungry people live, primarily in the developing countries. Moreover, these countries generally are unable to finance the import of more than a small percentage of their food needs on a sustained basis.

Better distribution of the food supplies available within each country and throughout the world could alleviate the most serious current instances of malnutrition. Better composition of diets would also help. These opportunities for reducing malnutrition should be pursued. Yet however successful such efforts might be, they cannot meet the demand for food generated by the rapidly rising world population and rising per capita incomes.

What to do: The battle of ideas

Agricultural development is a long, uphill struggle with few breakthroughs. Momentum lost at one place or time in the process is difficult to regain. Despite the apparent disarray of opinion in the popular media, a substantial consensus on several major issues has emerged among serious students in recent years. In this section we review several of the key issues on which some understanding has emerged.

FOOD AID

For many years food commodities have been made available to developing countries either on a grant (gift) or concessional-sale basis. Concessional sales are made at market prices but with long-term arrangements for repayment (loans) with low interest rates; sometimes the concessional sales are on such extended and soft terms that they could be considered grants.

Since 1960 the value of food aid has been relatively steady at from US$1,000 million to $1,300 million per year. Of the approximately $11,000 million in food aid provided during the decade ending in 1973, Canada accounted for 7 percent, Japan for about 3 percent, Germany and France for about 2 percent each, and the U.S. for the great bulk—80 percent. However, because the level of financial contributions has not been increasing and because prices of products have risen, especially in the 1970s, the actual volume of food has declined (Table 5.2).

The wisdom of large-scale food aid by the U.S. has been widely debated. There is broad support of food aid for any nation hit by natural disaster, for the innocent victims of civil or international conflict, and for programs that have other humanitarian aims or that clearly contribute to development of the recipient nation. U.S. food assistance, including the Food for Peace Program, has done much good. Many lives have been saved, as in South Asia in the mid-1960s and the Sahel in the 1970s. Foreign currencies generated by food aid have helped to pay the costs of American agencies or of agricultural research in those countries. Some development has been fostered abroad, and a number of humanitarian agencies have been supported. Disaster relief is not at issue. However, some aspects of food aid are controversial.

Table 5.2 Volume of food aid and concessional sales

Country	Shipments (thousand tons)					
	1960/61–1964/65 (avg.)	1965/66–1969/70 (avg.)	1970/71	1971/72	1972/73	1973/74
U.S.	15,634	12,806	9,425	9,533	6,989	3,475
Argentina	0	10	23	23	23	0
Australia	35	191	226	240	225	196
Canada	179	676	1,608	605	712	243
EEC	a	561	1,287	1,035	1,256	1,393
Finland	0	6	14	14	14	0
Japan	0	119	729	603	442	258
Sweden	0	22	54	35	35	0
Switzerland	0	15	36	37	32	0
U.S.S.R.	0	40	0	23	0	2,000
Others	0	43	379	577	88	25
Total	15,848	14,489	13,781	12,725	9,816	7,590

Source: United Nations, The World Food Problem.
a Less than 1,000 tons.

First, the U.S. food aid program has been closely associated with the existence of U.S. surpluses and, as such, has been seen by some as a form of domestic surplus disposal rather than as a true foreign-aid effort. This program has led to continued overproduction of commodities in relation to commercial demand abroad, and has probably contributed to continued low farm prices and the failure of U.S. farmers to switch to commodities for which market demand was greater.

Second, the large and burdensome surpluses that existed until 1968 encouraged the U.S. to maintain its policy of not assisting other nations directly with basic food-crop research or production programs.

Third, much of American food aid has gone to countries in which the U.S. has had obvious political interests. The intermingling of political and humanitarian activities has led to confusion about American objectives.

Fourth, *recurrent* supply of free food to agrarian nations has encouraged some governments to ignore their farmers. Food aid buys living time, an important objective, but if it delays serious food production campaigns in any food-deficit developing country, its humanitarian value is dissipated. Food aid can make the recipient dependent upon the donor, which can be uncomfortable, if not politically dangerous, for leaders of recipient countries. W. David Hopper has stated this argument forcefully:

Part of the blame can be placed on the developing countries themselves. Agricultural development is expensive and other, often more glamorous priorities of modernization shoulder aside its claim for scarce resources. Rural development is also a politically charged endeavor. City dwellers are more clamorous of attention, and their demands are more urgent and visible than those of a traditional peasantry. Keeping food cheap to appease urban consumers often leads to policies that destroy the economic incentive for modernizing farms. And the rich countries are always offering food on easily negotiated concessional terms. The food generosity of the industrial countries, whether in their own self-interest (disposing of food surpluses) or under the mantle of alleged distributive justice, has probably done more to sap the vitality of agricultural development in the developing world than any other single factor. Food aid not only has dulled the political will to develop agriculture but also, by augmenting domestic production with grain grown abroad, has kept local prices at levels that destroy incentives for indigenous farmers. In the last analysis making surplus food cheaply available to the developing countries in normal times has reinforced the already strong tendency of those countries to neglect local agriculture; it is easier on their national budgets to farm the fields of the U.S. and Canada.

Some U.S. farmers and farm leaders have looked upon concessional food aid shipments as developing "markets" for their products. Over the longer run, however, this may be a short-sighted view. To the extent that food aid delays agricultural development in the recipient country, it slows economic development and hampers the emergence of new cash markets, thus sacrificing longer-term American farm interests.

Food aid programs that are clearly humanitarian should be continued. There may also be times when low-income countries need commodities to stabilize domestic prices due to short-run circumstances. However, food aid programs which confuse humanitarian and political considerations and retard emergence of economically stronger trading partners are against the longer-term interest of both recipient and donor countries.

NONCONVENTIONAL FOODS

The idea of producing "nonconventional" foods to help feed the world was in vogue in the mid-1960s. Nonconventional foods use resources which otherwise might be wasted or go into low-value uses. Considerable effort has gone into a wide range of these foods. Algae culture has received much attention since the 1950s. "Cocktails" of plant foods, such as a mixture of peanut and chickpea flours, which combine complementary amino acids with added vitamins and minerals, have been used as food supplements in several countries. Fish protein concentrate, a tasteless, odorless mixture, has been used to reinforce deficient foods. Plant substances, such as cottonseed meal, can be treated for human consumption. Going further, chemical synthesis of food is possible.

One advantage of microorganisms as a source of protein is their ability to produce food fast from simple materials. A bullock weighing 500 kilograms, for example, may synthesize less than half a kilogram of protein a day, whereas it is claimed that the same weight of yeast can produce over 25,000 kilograms of protein a day. Development of single-cell protein (SCP) using petroleum or other substrates has moved from laboratory research through the pilot-plant stage to limited commercial production. While the results are sufficiently promising to keep researchers active in this area, problems still exist in finding organisms and techniques to produce SCP that will make it a sufficiently attractive and inexpensive food for the poor and undernourished people of the world.

Nonconventional foods must be provided as gifts or be purchased—and the mass of the hungry have little money. Moreover, conventional agriculture will continue to be the chief source of income for many of the poor. It is unreasonable to expect nonconventional foods to provide more than a small fraction of the food needs of the poor in the decades ahead.

IMPORTANCE OF AGRICULTURE TO NATIONAL DEVELOPMENT

Since developed countries generally are industrialized, some persons have reasoned that the best way for a poor agrarian country to leap into the 20th century is to emphasize industrial growth. This philosophy was publicized in the "big push" theories of the 1950s. It was actually embodied in India's Second Five-Year Development Plan, and it has influenced the planning efforts of numerous other countries.

The weakness of this argument is that financing for industrialization must ultimately come from some source other than the industrial sector, which in low-income countries is small. Agriculture accounts for half of the gross national product and three-quarters of employment in these countries. In the absence of rich reserves of natural resources or unusual trade opportunities, agriculture is the only realistic source for the financial resources to support economic development.

Agricultural growth can contribute to overall economic gains in six main ways:

First, agricultural profits may be deposited in financial institutions, which can then lend funds to the nonagricultural sectors as well as to the agricultural sector.

Second, if the growth in agricultural output exceeds the growth in demand and if food prices fall (or at least do not rise), pressure for increases in industrial wages and raw material prices will lessen and industrial input costs will be lowered. The resulting higher business profits could in turn lead to reinvestment and hence to faster manufacturing growth.

Third, if a continuous stream of new cost-reducing agricultural technology were available, it would lead to a continued high level of capital investments in order to lower costs below the falling product prices. These capital goods are produced by the nonagricultural sector. Although cultivators will consume some of their extra production, they will sell a large part for cash; their increased income can expand the market for nonagriculturally produced consumer goods. The greater demand for investment and consumption goods produced by the nonagricultural sector can lead to higher prices or fuller use (and probably lower unit costs) of nonagricultural profits for reinvestment and hence faster growth.

Fourth, higher agricultural incomes provide a source of taxes.

Fifth, as agricultural development proceeds, workers are both "pushed" out of the agricultural sector and "pulled" into other occupations, especially in rural trade centers, thereby serving as a source of labor for the expanding sectors.

Sixth, the agricultural sector contributes to overall economic growth by raising foreign-exchange earnings through increased agricultural exports, by reducing imports, or by attracting foreign loans, grants, or investments.

Therefore, the agricultural sector—because of sheer size, as well as its growth potential—must play a key role in the process of capital formation. Neglect of agriculture can severely curtail the chances for overall economic development. There is need to support agricultural development in such a way as to achieve a balance between agriculture and other sectors in promoting mutually reinforcing activities which characterize modern economic growth.

THE ROLE OF IMPROVED TECHNOLOGY

The postwar recovery of Europe led some authorities to believe that the technology of a developing country's own best farms, together with the technology available from economically advanced countries, could raise the developing country's production greatly. It was presumed that an educational and motivational program could close the gap between traditional and advanced farmers. Accordingly, in the early postwar years, policy focused on rural change through community development, extension education, land reform, and cooperatives, and through extensive techniques of production—mainly planting more land, building more irrigation canals, and, later, applying more fertilizer. This approach was consistent with the prevailing ideological framework of bringing about production increases without perpetuating or increasing income disparities among cultivators.

Frequently these policies did improve food production as countries snapped back from wartime conditions. It soon became clear, however, that there were limits to the new land that could be brought into cultivation and the amounts of fertilizer that could be applied profitably given existing crop varieties and farming practices. Production growth rates began to slow noticeably.

The problem was, and is, that farmers use resources efficiently. Once profitable new opportunities are fully exploited, farmers settle into a pattern of continuing the practices which have proved to be safe in the past; that is, they settle into a self-perpetuating equilibrium.

The only way to generate growth in such a situation is to create a disequilibrium—to introduce highly profitable new opportunities which will induce farmers to change their previous practices. The green revolution demonstrated that one way—often the best way—to force this change is to introduce improved technologies which promise economic returns of 25–100 percent. Several examples are described in Chapter 8.

PRECONDITIONS TO YIELD TAKEOFF?

In 1965 Lester Brown published a thought-provoking statistical study (*Increasing World Food Output*) associating several economic and social indicators with rates of increase of crop yields in 60 nations that grow 400,000 hectares or more of rice or maize or 800,000 hectares or more of wheat. Based on this analysis, he presented the concept of "necessary preconditions to yield-per-acre takeoff" by nations—an extension of the concept of income takeoff described at the time as "an integral part of development theory." Brown argued that a rapid increase in agricultural yields over a period of years probably could come about *only* if nations were *first* to (a) achieve a reasonably high level of literacy, (b) raise per capita incomes to approximately $200 or more, (c) increase shares of farm produce marketed relative to amounts consumed on the farm, thereby moving from a subsistence toward a commercial economy, (d) have reasonably well-developed nonagricultural sectors of the economy as a basis for providing the goods and services necessary to agricultural development, and (e) otherwise meet the minimum requirements for accelerating modernization and economic development. To these preconditions Brown added the requirement of favorable prices for farm products relative to the cost of inputs. Figures 5.2 and 5.3 show the associations underpinning his formulation of preconditions for rising yields.

While the statistical associations from his analysis are evident, it is not clear that cause can be inferred. The relation of yield increases to the preconditions of literacy and per capita income seems especially doubtful. It is more likely that improvement in literacy and per capita income, the accelerated development of a market economy, and the strengthening of nonagricultural sectors in many developing nations depend to a large extent upon raising agricultural yields and the incomes of great numbers of farm people, thereby leading to the increased national income required to finance costly programs.

Certain preconditions are necessary for increasing yields of basic food crops, but they differ in part from those presented by Brown. There

Fig. 5.2. Relationship between literacy levels and yield-raising capabilities of selected countries (data assembled in 1965)

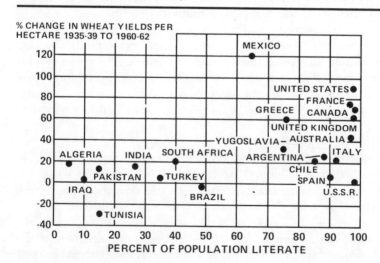

Source: Lester R. Brown, *Increasing World Food Output: Problems and Prospects.*

must be a commitment by the government. The program envisioned must be technically feasible and economically profitable for the farmer. Inputs must be available, and there must be reliable markets. Governments must make the necessary investments. While these preconditions are not as simple to achieve as they are to state, they are at least within reach of most nations.

NEW ATTITUDES TOWARD TECHNICAL ASSISTANCE

During the mid-1960s, a serious drought struck South Asia. The U.S. and other nations responded with emergency grain shipments to India and Pakistan on an unprecedented scale. The sudden drawdown in U.S. stocks, combined with a widening understanding of the seriousness and nature of the food problem in the developing countries, altered ideas about technical assistance. Until that time it had been the policy of the U.S. (and Canada as well) not to help nations directly to increase production of crops that might compete with its surpluses in the world market. In 1966 A. H. Moseman, then assistant administrator of the U.S. Agency for International Development, wrote:

The science and technology in foreign aid designed to increase food crop production has been rather limited. We have concentrated on the extension or transfer of our own crop varieties and our own production practices. We have not focused research attention on the increase of production of crops such as rice and wheat, which have been in surplus in the United States. This reflected

Fig. 5.3. Relationship between income levels and yield-raising capabilities of selected countries (data assembled in 1965)

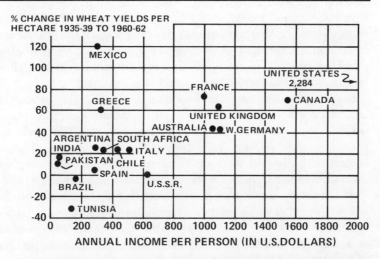

Source: Lester R. Brown, *Increasing World Food Output: Problems and Prospects.*

the attitude of the Congress, of the American public, and of American farm organizations—a handicap that is still to be overcome. I think this is one of the major jobs that we as scientists and as people who are concerned with world food supplies have a responsibility for, to develop that kind of constituency that recognizes the importance of filling the massive food deficits of the next two decades.

By 1969 the U.S. and Canada began to support direct efforts in developing countries to increase output of cereals and other basic food crops. This was a fundamental shift which has had far-reaching beneficial effects on the world effort to increase food output.

Now technical assistance is recognized as being a necessary component of international assistance. For instance, in 1977 the Steering Committee of the National Research Council Study on World Food and Nutrition recommended: "(a) expanded U.S. research efforts to improve food and nutrition policies, increase food availability, reduce poverty, and stabilize food supplies; (b) actions to help mobilize and organize research and development resources in the United States and throughout the world; and (c) a U.S. government mechanism to better interrelate actions that affect food and nutrition situations both at home and abroad."

Nevertheless, U.S. technical and financial assistance still is not immune to domestic political considerations. In 1976, for example, the U.S. attempted to discourage further palm oil production in developing countries because these imports were competing heavily with U.S. soybean oil production.

THE "SMALL FARMER" DILEMMA

By the early 1970s the improvement of conventional agriculture in the developing countries had been widely accepted as the primary means by which their food needs would be met. Moreover, it was becoming increasingly clear that agricultural development is an integral component of economic development. But agreement had not been reached on another fundamental question: Should agricultural production efforts center on the millions of farmers with small landholdings?

Small farmers whose livelihoods depend upon the production of the basic food crops have generally been neglected. Governments and international assistance agencies can give many reasons for overlooking farmers whose landholdings may be small, fragmented, and remote from centers of trade and services. Farmers in mountainous or otherwise inaccessible regions, people who practice shifting cultivation, and nomads, who seasonally move their herds long distances, are doubtless hard to reach. Nevertheless, in most developing countries there are large numbers of farmers with small holdings (Table 5.3), many of whom own land, or lease land, or work it as tenants, who remain outside the mainstream of agricultural development.

Table 5.3. Distribution of farm size in Indonesia, Bangladesh, and India

	Percentage		
Area (hectares)	Indonesia (1963)	Bangladesh (1960)	India (1961)
Less than 0.4	45	24	—
0.4–1	26	27	39[a]
1–2	18	26	23
2–3	5	12	13
3–5	3	7	15
5–10	2[b]	3	6
Over 10	—	—[c]	5

Source: Walter P. Falcon, "Green Revolution: Generations of Problems."
[a] Amount is for all holdings under 1 hectare.
[b] Amount is for over 10 hectares.
[c] Less than 0.5 percent.

One reason is that governments want fast, massive increases in output. When a nation with limited resources is faced with serious food deficits and must increase national food supplies rapidly, it will understandably attempt to produce important commodities in the most direct way possible. This often involves concentrating improved technology, inputs, credit, marketing, and technical services in areas that promise quick gains. Usually, those farmers who control relatively large landholdings are the most easily reached. This approach is especially appealing to nations with limited trained manpower.

Second, governments often rely on the "trickle down" mechanism. Many planners believe that if key farmers (usually meaning respected individuals with larger holdings) adopt new and better farming systems, then the smaller farmers in the community will follow their examples. This mechanism does work to a degree, but incompletely and slowly.

Third, governments often promote faulty technology. Recommended combinations of varieties and farming practices are supposedly more productive and profitable, but they are often incomplete or poorly adapted to farmers' conditions. Agriculturists by and large have not developed systems which are tailored to small farms and specific agro-climatic conditions.

Fourth, governments often blame the farmer when small farmers fail to adopt new technology. Those in charge of promoting new farming systems often say the farmer is too conservative, too unintelligent, too fearful of risk, or too apathetic to change. This conveniently relieves those who design or execute farm programs of responsibility for failure. However, the small farmers' reluctance to adopt new techniques is more likely a reflection of the fact that inputs or credit are not available when farmers need them and are unreasonably priced, that the market is unsure, or that farmers have not been shown how to use the new ideas in their locality. Little attention has been given to developing decentralized institutional structures (such as input delivery, credit, and marketing systems) for small farmers, who operate under different constraints than large farmers.

Fifth, governments often fail to appreciate indirect benefits. Far too often, particularly among economists, there has been a limited view of the costs and returns of programs involving small farmers. For example, other than increased food production, benefits include improved living standards for substantial numbers of people, the development of domestic markets for products of urban industry, the creation of demand for goods and services in rural trade centers, and a consequent generation of employment in rural trade centers, if not on the farms themselves. A sense of despair among villagers can be replaced with hope for a better future. Voluntary reduction in population growth rates is often related to economic progress. There may be a slowing of the flight to the cities. Maintenance of tranquility in the countryside may be facilitated. These benefits often are ignored by planners and assistance agency personnel because they cannot quantify their magnitude. Yet these are among the most important benefits of good programs.

Sixth, governments often fear farmer organization. Leaders in some countries oppose efforts to assist small farmers. The required organizational efforts, they believe, could enable the farmers to make continuing, bothersome demands upon government. Once rural people are organized, the greater pressures on government may be politically irreversible. Yet serious efforts to help small farmers will require farmers to organize for purchasing and marketing and to apply pressures on the institutions which must serve their needs.

Seventh, governments often doubt that small-farmer programs can succeed. Prior to 1965 there were many community development projects which aimed at raising the standard of living of the rural poor. Most projects did not greatly affect crop or animal productivity and farm incomes, because technologies for higher yields and more profitable farming systems were not available. However, this was not recognized at that time. The "failures" therefore provided support for the opponents of small-farmer programs, who called them welfare agriculture—too costly and not economical—said that there were better ways to increase production, and claimed that small farmers were unwilling to change.

Recently, several successful small-farmer programs have begun to receive recognition. Mexico has several programs for its small farmers. The Puebla Project is the best documented, but programs have been initiated in other areas of Mexico as well. Small-farmer production programs have also been launched in Colombia, Peru, Guatemala, and El Salvador. In the Philippines the International Rice Research Institute and government agencies have experimented with ways to increase the productivity and incomes of small farmers in by-passed rainfed rice areas. This effort led in part to the national "Masagana 99" program. In India the Indian Council of Agricultural Research has been making progress in extending benefits of advanced agriculture to its numerous small farmers and in promoting intensive multiple-cropping methods. The People's Republic of China has an extensive and highly effective program of increasing yields of small farmers. Taiwan and Japan are noted for their progress in increasing the productivity and profitability of small farm units.[4]

Critics of the green revolution have charged that it has widened the gap between the rich and the poor. This is a complex issue which cannot be adequately treated in a few paragraphs. However, several points are clear:

First, great numbers of producers, whether large or small, have increased their incomes; that is, the benefits have been widespread in an absolute sense.

Second, the change in incomes of poor farmers relative to wealthy farmers varies from location to location. The conclusion is that one cannot generalize.

Third, the effect on tenants and landless laborers is unclear. In some areas, leases have been revoked, while in others tenants have benefited as much as owners. In some areas, mechanization and labor disputes have led to replacement of labor, while in other areas wages and employment have risen on farms and in farm-related industries.

Fourth, nothing inherent in the biological components of new technologies biases them in favor of large farmers. The economies of size in farming are relatively limited. One area where biases do appear to enter the picture is water control. The new wheat and rice varieties have excelled where irrigation is good, and larger farmers have more money to spend on their own irrigation facilities and land shaping. However, more attention is now being given to producing new technologies for irrigated areas where water control is poor and for rainfed areas. While the absolute increases in yield in these areas may not be so startling as under more favorable conditions, the percentage increases and the contribution to production may be even greater because of the present low yields and the large areas involved. Much of the irrigated land is owned by small farmers. Another area of bias stems from the easier access larger farmers often have to credit, fertilizer, pesticides, technical information, new seeds, and markets.

[4] See Chapter 8 for more details on some of these cases.

Changes in rice farming in Asia

In *Changes in Rice Farming in Selected Areas of Asia*, the International Rice Research Institute and economists in several Asian countries have attempted to identify the major influences on the adoption of new practices in Asia. From studies in 26 villages they have concluded:

- The three factors mainly responsible for the differences among villages in rate of adoption are: availability of modern varieties suitable for a particular locale, differences in the rice-growing environment (including climate, soils, irrigation, and drainage), and price relationships between improved and local varieties.
- Nitrogen was the most significant variable explaining differences in yield.
- Explanations for differences in fertilizer use were, in order of importance, environment, quality of irrigation services, percentage of farmers using formal sources of credit, and the price ratio of nitrogen to rice.
- There was little relationship between use of modern varieties and the adoption of tractors or herbicides.
- Many farmers reported an increase in the use of family or hired labor following adoption of modern varieties.
- There was no consistent pattern in the relationship between farm size and yield of the modern varieties. In many situations smaller farms tended to have higher yields, presumably because of higher inputs of both labor and capital. Other factors, such as the distribution of farm sizes, the socioeconomic structure of villages, and the role of tenancy, interacted with farm size in different ways in different areas. For example, the high rate of tenancy in all surveyed villages in the Philippines tended to over-shadow the importance of farm size for adoption in that country. Generally the tendency for larger farms to adopt new technologies faster and in larger amounts was higher in South Asia than in Southeast Asia.
- A technology, some of whose elements require cash inputs, tends to exacerbate inequity in income distribution. Technological innovations alone cannot be expected to correct serious inequities to access to resources and benefits from them.

Fifth, the low-income consumer, whether he be a farmer, laborer, or city dweller, has benefited from increased agricultural production. He spends a large percentage of his income on food. Increased production has lowered prices and thereby increased his real income.

Multiple cropping, intercropping, relay planting, and other labor-intensive techniques involving "gardening" of crops, at which small farmers excel, offer possibilities of higher yields per day or per year than is possible with most Western-style "farming" or with large-scale, mechanized schemes. Nations that have little cultivable land per person, many small farms, underemployment, and precarious food supplies must concentrate on intensive techniques. They cannot afford large-scale, lower-yielding mechanized farming, except under special circumstances.[5] Furthermore, they must be sure that the small farmer gets a fair share of the gains from changes in agricultural production.

Agreement about small-farmer programs is still not widespread. Many developing countries are, however, now attacking small-farmer problems for the first time. While the debate continues, so do efforts to find ways to make small-farmer production programs successful, to learn the principles involved, and to identify appropriate techniques. More and more international agencies are giving small-farmer projects priority.

We believe that, due to the development of new agricultural technologies, small farmers can be helped and that all nations must do so soon if they wish to retain stable societies.

NUTRITION

It is sometimes charged that the spread of the new cereal varieties has harmed human nutrition in some regions. The reason for this assertion is that increases in area planted to the new cereal grains have sometimes occurred at the expense of food legumes, one of the primary sources of protein in the diets of cereal consumers.

Little reliable information is available to evaluate this issue, however. Virtually no controlled studies have involved these problems. Baseline health and nutrition data are rare in areas greatly affected by the new varieties. Moreover, it is difficult to identify the changes that have occurred, because of social and political influences operating at the same time.

Nutritionists have found that, generally, mixed diets which are adequate in calories are also adequate in protein. The new wheat varieties have 8–9 percent protein compared with 20 percent for the pulses, but the doubling of yields associated with the new wheat varieties produces more total calories and protein per hectare than could be obtained from growing pulses alone.[6] Furthermore, because the growth durations of the new cereal varieties are short, it is often possible to grow a second crop, which in turn yields even more protein, and more calories, per hectare. The new cereal varieties can also be grown in new areas during seasons when the land was previously unused. Therefore, it is not clear that protein availability has suffered because of the rapid spread of the new cereal varieties.

[5] For example: (1) sparsely populated regions that cannot attract enough labor, so mechanization must be used to exploit crop production potential; (2) regions of low potential crop productivity in which a family cannot farm a large enough area to be self-sufficient; and (3) situations in which, for reasons of distributional equity or economies of size, or because several years will be required to produce marketable crops, it is desirable to organize farmers into group efforts.
[6] The benefit to improved nutrition depends also on the amino acid balance of the protein among foods.

These advantages notwithstanding, diversification into more nutritious crops must remain an important objective, especially in localities that depend heavily on starchy foods.

AN INTERNATIONAL FOOD RESERVE

Few low-income countries have the surplus production or the financial resources needed to build up large holdover stocks of their own. Therefore, they have generally looked to food-exporting countries to assist them in crises.

Until the late 1960s the U.S. government was the major source of surplus foods. Recently, however, the U.S. reduced its stocks and no other nation has stepped forward to take its place. In large part, the developing world has been left to the mercy of the commercial market for supplies to supplement domestic production in poor years. For this reason, establishment of an international reserve system has been proposed.

The concept of an international reserve has been widely accepted in principle, but the specifics continue to be argued. There are disagreements over its size, who is to contribute and under what conditions, who is to be eligible for commodities, and where the stocks should be located. Each of these issues has economic as well as political implications. D. Gale Johnson estimates that a reserve of 30 million tons, which would be adequate to meet 95 percent of the shortfalls from the trend in world food grain production, would cost from about US$4,000 million to $5,000 million to acquire and from $400 million to $500 million in annual interest and storage costs. Reserves are quite expensive for the low-income countries or any entity to maintain. For an international reserve to function as well in periods of surplus as in periods of scarcity, participating nations would have to adjust their domestic trade and agricultural policies. For example, tremendous pressures could be placed on an international reserve if U.S. price-support policies resulted in large excesses in production, thus causing world prices to fall precipitously. Or the unwillingness of participating nations to lower trade barriers when world production is excessive would make the international reserve less effective.

In short, an international reserve could buffer the worldwide effects of unilateral actions by major exporters and importers in response to domestic problems. However, compromise and cooperation would be required. Resolution of the political questions, more than the economic ones, will probably determine whether or not an international reserve becomes a reality. Meanwhile, each nation must seek to provide its own buffer stocks —for its own protection. And those willing to do so should be helped.

Concluding comments

Much of the analysis of the food-poverty-population crisis and what to do about it is very recent. It is encouraging that so much has been learned so quickly.

In one respect the crisis might be called a problem of high population growth rates. Food production in the developing countries has expanded fast enough to increase per capita consumption in areas where population growth has been moderate. If population growth had been slower, however, more resources would have been available for investment, the engine of economic growth. *Decreasing birth rates in most areas where they are still high is a necessary component of the solution.*

The crisis is also a problem of inequitable income distribution. There is more than enough grain in the world—if consumed directly instead of being wasted or fed to livestock or put to other intermediate uses— to feed the world's population. Therefore, better distribution of income both among and within countries would theoretically be another solution.

Although there are signs of decreasing population growth rates in some developing countries, the phenomenon is not widespread and will not have a significant impact for some time. Furthermore, short of abrupt changes in political and economic systems, income redistribution within and among nations is very hard to bring about. The Chinese have developed one solution, but the price—regimentation—has been high. However, neither slower population growth nor more equitable income distribution is likely to occur independently of success in providing more food in the developing countries.

The developed countries are not capable of feeding the developing world indefinitely, nor is food aid in the long-term interests of developed or developing countries. Nonconventional foods are not the answer. Therefore, while efforts should be made to slow population growth and improve the distribution of income, the developing countries must act now to expand food production through conventional agriculture.

The potential of the world to feed itself—in terms of physical resources as well as understanding the nature of the problem and what to do about it—is stronger today than in any recent time in history. "Triage" and "lifeboat ethics" are cruel and false solutions to the world food situation.

References

INTRODUCTION

Borgstrom, Georg. *The Hungry Planet.* New York: Macmillan, 1965.
Brown, Lester R. *By Bread Alone.* New York: Praeger, 1974.
Brown, Lester R. "Population Growth, Food Needs, and Production Problems." In *World Production and Food Supplies, 1980.* Special Publication No. 6. Madison, Wis.: American Society of Agronomy, 1965.

Brown, Lester R. *Seeds of Change.* New York: Praeger, 1970.
Erlich, Paul R. *The Population Bomb.* New York: Ballantine, 1968.
Hardin, Garrett. *Exploring the New Ethics for Survival: The Voyage of the Spaceship Beagle.* New York: Viking Press, 1972.
Paddock, William, and Paddock, Elizabeth. *We Don't Know How: An Independent Audit of What They Call Success in Foreign Assistance.* Ames: Iowa State University Press, 1973.
Paddock, William, and Paddock, Paul. *Famine—1975!* Boston: Little, Brown, 1967.
Revelle, Roger. *Population and Resources.* Research Paper No. 5. Cambridge, Mass.: Harvard University, Center for Population Studies, July 1974.

THE NATURE AND SERIOUSNESS OF THE PROBLEM UNDERSTOOD

Abel, Martin E., and Rojko, Anthony S. *World Food Situation: Prospects for World Grain Production, Consumption, and Trade.* Foreign Agricultural Economic Report No. 35. Washington, D.C.: U.S. Department of Agriculture, 1967.
American Society of Agronomy. *World Population and Food Supplies, 1980.* Special Publication No. 6. Madison, Wis.: American Society of Agronomy, 1965.
Blakeslee, Leroy L.; Heady, Earl O.; and Farmingham, Charles F. *World Food Production, Demand, and Trade.* Ames: Iowa State University Press, 1973.
Brown, Harrison; Bonner, James; and Weir, John. *The Next 100 Years.* New York: Viking Press, 1957.
Brown, Lester R. *By Bread Alone.* New York: Praeger, 1974.
Brown, Lester R. *Increasing World Food Output: Problems and Prospects.* Foreign Agricultural Economic Report No. 25. Washington, D.C.: U.S. Department of Agriculture, 1965.
Brown, Lester R. *Man, Land, and Food.* Foreign Agricultural Economic Report No. 11. Washington, D.C.: U.S. Department of Agriculture, 1963.
Brown, Lester R. "Population Growth, Food Needs, and Production Problems." In *World Production and Food Supplies, 1980.* Special Publication No. 6. Madison, Wis.: American Society of Agronomy, 1965.
Brown, Lester R. *Seeds of Change.* New York: Praeger, 1970.
University of California. *A Hungry World: The Challenge to Agriculture.* Berkeley: University of California, Division of Agricultural Sciences, July 1974.
"Food and Agriculture" (entire issue). *Scientific American* 235 (September 1976): 31–205.
Food and Agriculture Organization. *Agricultural Commodity Projections, 1970–1980.* 2 vols. Rome: Food and Agriculture Organization, 1971.
Food and Agriculture Organization. *Agricultural Commodities—Projections for 1975 and 1985.* 2 vols. Rome: Food and Agriculture Organization, 1967.
Food and Agriculture Organization. *Provisional Indicative World Plan for Agricultural Development.* 2 vols. plus regional studies. Rome: Food and Agriculture Organization, 1970.
Food and Agriculture Organization. *Provisional Indicative World Plan for Agricultural Development: Summary and Main Conclusions.* Rome: Food and Agriculture Organization, 1969.
Hardin, Clifford M., ed. *Overcoming World Hunger.* Englewood Cliffs, N.J.: Prentice-Hall, 1969.
Harrar, J. George. *Strategy for the Conquest of Hunger.* New York: Rockefeller Foundation, 1963.
Harrar, J. George. *Strategy toward the Conquest of Hunger.* New York: Rockefeller Foundation, 1967.
International Food Policy Research Institute. *Meeting Food Needs in the Developing World: The Location and Magnitude of the Task in the Next Decade.* Research Report No. 1. Washington, D.C.: International Food Policy Research Institute, February 1976.
Jacobson, Dorothy H. "Our Mission Abroad—Opportunities to Aid Developing Countries." In *Symposium on Research in Agriculture, Feb. 23–25, 1966, Warrenton, Va.* Washington, D.C.: U.S. Department of Agriculture, 1966.

Johnson, D. Gale. *World Food Problems and Prospects.* Washington, D.C.: American Enterprise Institute for Public Policy Research, 1975.

Millikan, Max F., and Hapgood, David. *No Easy Harvest: The Dilemma of Agriculture in Underdeveloped Countries.* Boston: Little, Brown, 1967.

Moseman, Albert H., ed. *Agricultural Sciences for the Developing Countries.* Washington, D.C.: American Association for the Advancement of Science, 1964.

National Academy of Sciences. *Prospects of the World Food Supply.* Washington, D.C.: National Academy of Sciences, 1966.

National Academy of Sciences. Committee on World Food, Health, and Population. *Population and Food: Crucial Issues.* Washington, D.C.: National Academy of Sciences, 1975.

National Academy of Sciences. National Research Council. *World Food and Nutrition Study: Interim Report.* Washington, D.C.: National Academy of Sciences, 1975.

National Academy of Sciences. National Research Council. *World Food and Nutrition Study: The Potential Contributions of Research.* Washington, D.C.: National Academy of Sciences, 1977.

Paarlberg, Donald. "Food for More People and Better Nutrition." In *Overcoming World Hunger,* edited by Clifford M. Hardin. Englewood Cliffs, N.J.: Prentice-Hall, 1969.

Rockefeller Foundation. *Agricultural Development.* New York: Rockefeller Foundation, 1969.

Rockefeller Foundation. *Strategy for the Conquest of Hunger: Proceedings of a Symposium.* New York: Rockefeller Foundation, 1968.

Rojko, Anthony S., and Mackie, Arthur B. *World Demand Prospects for Agricultural Exports of Less Developed Countries in 1980.* Foreign Agricultural Economic Report No. 60. Washington, D.C.: U.S. Department of Agriculture, 1970.

Rojko, Anthony S.; Urban, F. S.; and Naive, James J. *World Demand Prospects for Grain in 1980 with Emphasis on Trade by the Less Developed Countries.* Foreign Agricultural Economic Report No. 75. Washington, D.C.: U.S. Department of Agriculture, 1971.

United Nations, Economic and Social Council, Preparatory Committee of the World Food Conference, 2nd Session. *Assessment: Present Food Situation and Dimensions and Causes of Hunger and Malnutrition in the World* (E/CONF. 65/PREP/6), May 8, 1974.

United Nations, World Food Conference. *The World Food Problem: Proposals for National and International Action. Item 9 of the Provisional Agenda* (E/CONF. 65/4), August 1974.

U.S. Department of Agriculture, Economic Research Service. *Changes in Agriculture in 26 Developing Nations, 1948–1963.* Foreign Agricultural Economic Report No. 27. Washington, D.C.: U.S. Department of Agriculture, 1965.

U.S. Department of Agriculture, Economic Research Service. *Economic Progress of Agriculture in Developing Nations.* Foreign Agricultural Economic Report No. 59. Washington, D.C.: U.S. Department of Agriculture, 1970.

U.S. Department of Agriculture, Economic Research Service. *The World Food Situation and Prospects to 1985.* Foreign Agricultural Economic Report No. 98. Washington, D.C.: U.S. Department of Agriculture, December 1974.

U.S. President's Science Advisory Committee. *The World Food Problem: Report of the Panel on the World Food Supply.* 3 vols. Washington, D.C.: U.S. Government Printing Office, May 1967.

WHAT TO DO: THE BATTLE OF IDEAS

Bachman, K. L. "Can We Produce Enough Food?" In *World Population and Food Supplies, 1980.* Special Publication No. 6. Madison, Wis.: American Society of Agronomy, 1965.

Brown, Lester R. *Increasing World Food Output: Problems and Prospects.* Foreign Agricultural Economic Report No. 25. Washington, D.C.: U.S. Department of Agriculture, 1965.

Brown, Lester R. "Population Growth, Food Needs, and Production Problems." In

World Population and Food Supplies, 1980. Special Publication No. 6. Madison, Wis.: American Society of Agronomy, 1965.

University of California. *A Hungry World: The Challenge to Agriculture.* Berkeley: University of California, Division of Agricultural Sciences, July 1974.

Falcon, Walter P. "Green Revolution: Generations of Problems." *American Journal of Agricultural Economics* 52 (1970): 698–712.

Hathaway, Dale E. "Grain Stocks and Economic Stability: A Policy Perspective." In *Analyses of Grain Reserves: A Proceedings,* compiled by David J. Eaton and W. Scott Steele. Washington, D.C.: U.S. Department of Agriculture, Economic Research Service, August 1976.

Hopper, W. David. "The Development of Agriculture in Developing Countries." *Scientific American* 235 (September 1976): 196–205.

International Rice Research Institute. *Changes in Rice Farming in Selected Areas of Asia.* Los Baños, Philippines: International Rice Research Institute, 1975.

Isenman, Paul J., and Singer, H. W. *Food Aid: Disincentive Effects and Their Policy Implications.* AID Discussion Paper No. 31. Washington, D.C.: Agency for International Development, Bureau for Program and Policy Coordination, October 1975.

Johnson, D. Gale. *World Food Problems and Prospects.* Washington, D.C.: American Enterprise Institute for Public Policy Research, 1975.

Johnston, Bruce F. "Agriculture and Structural Transformation in Developing Countries: A Survey of Research." *Journal of Economic Literature* 8 (1970): 369–404.

Johnston, Bruce F., and Mellor, John W. "The Role of Agriculture in Economic Development." *American Economic Review* 51 (1961): 566–93.

Josling, Timothy. *An International Grain Reserve Policy.* London and Washington, D.C.: British–North American Committee, 1973.

Kuznets, Simon. *Modern Economic Growth.* New Haven, Conn.: Yale University Press, 1966.

Levinson, James. *Morinda: An Economic Analysis of Malnutrition among Young Children in Rural India.* Cornell/MIT International Nutrition Policy Series. Cambridge, Mass.: Cornell University/Massachusetts Institute of Technology, 1974.

Moseman, Albert H. "Science and Technology in International Agriculture." In *Symposium on Research in Agriculture, Feb. 23–25, 1966, Warrenton, Va.* Washington, D.C.: U.S. Department of Agriculture, 1966.

National Academy of Sciences. National Research Council. *World Food and Nutrition Study: The Potential Contributions of Research.* Washington, D.C.: National Academy of Sciences, 1977.

Paarlberg, Donald. "Food for More People and Better Nutrition." In *Overcoming World Hunger,* edited by Clifford M. Hardin. Englewood Cliffs, N.J.: Prentice-Hall, 1969.

Rostow, W. W. *The Stages of Economic Growth.* Cambridge: Cambridge University Press, 1960.

Sanderson, Fred H. "Next Steps on Grain Reserves." *Food Policy* 2 (1977): 267–76.

Schultz, T. W. *Transforming Traditional Agriculture.* New Haven, Conn.: Yale University Press, 1964.

Srivastava, U. K.; Heady, E. O.; Rogers, K. D.; and Mayer, L. V. *Food Aid and International Economic Growth.* Ames: Iowa State University Press, 1975.

Streeter, Carroll P. *Reaching the World's Small Farmers.* Working Paper. New York: Rockefeller Foundation, February 1975.

Wharton, Clifton R., Jr. "The Green Revolution: Cornucopia or Pandora's Box?" *Foreign Affairs* 47 (1969): 464–76.

CHAPTER 6

The world assistance community mobilizes

Introduction

UNTIL THE MID-1940s, international agricultural assistance went mainly to colonies for the production of export crops.[1] The developed world had little money or appropriate technology to provide the developing world. Two world wars, between which a traumatic economic depression occurred, had forced industrialized countries to look after their own needs first. Moreover, the knowledge of food production possessed by the Western countries was applicable primarily to temperate climates.

After World War II, the situation changed. Some industrialized nations accepted responsibility for assisting developing nations, many of which were newly independent. Since then a growing complex of national and international agencies has provided financial, technical, research, and training help to expand food production and rural development in low-income nations. The first steps were taken in 1943, when the groundwork for the Food and Agriculture Organization of the United Nations (FAO) was laid. The first FAO conference was held in 1945, and permanent headquarters were established in Rome in 1951. In 1941 The Rockefeller Foundation sent a scientific mission to explore the feasibility of helping Mexico improve its food production, a study which marked the start of the foundation's program in international agriculture. In 1946 the World Bank was founded. In 1948 the Organization of American States, which provides major support for the Inter-American Institute of Agricultural Sciences, was established. In 1949, U.S. President Truman made his "Point Four" speech, and in 1950 the Act for International Development (setting up a predecessor of the U.S. Agency for International

[1] The U.S. Department of Agriculture carried on some foreign technical assistance beginning in 1872, but was given legal authority to do so only in 1938. Britain's Colonial Development Act, an important step in providing overseas assistance, was passed only in 1940, with an appropriation of £5.5 million.

Development) was signed. In the same year, the Ford Foundation started providing assistance in agriculture. With postwar economic recovery the European nations, Canada, and Australia (in time followed by Japan) built up bilateral assistance programs. The agreement for the Inter-American Development Bank was signed in 1959, the African Development Bank was established in 1964, the United Nations Development Programme was established in 1966, the Asian Development Bank opened for business in 1966, the International Development Research Centre of Canada was established in 1970, the Consultative Group for International Agricultural Research began in 1971, and other new institutions to provide assistance appear each year.

The purposes of this chapter are to describe this impressive international mobilization of resources in the areas of financial assistance, technical assistance, research, and training to help low-income countries and to indicate where weaknesses remain.

The financial network

External financial assistance for agriculture in low-income countries, excluding food aid, probably exceeded US$6,000 million in 1975.[2] Official development assistance in agriculture by bilateral agencies of the Development Assistance Committee (DAC) and by multilateral organizations,[3] the largest source of external financial assistance, was estimated at US$5,000 million in 1975, up from $2,600 million in 1973 and $4,200 million in 1974. Total official development assistance was about $16,000 million in 1973, $20,000 million in 1974, and $22,000 million in 1975. The share to agriculture in total development aid therefore rose from 16 percent to 23 percent during these 3 years.

A second source, members of the Organization of Petroleum Exporting

[2] Financial data in this section come primarily from the Consultative Group on Food Production and Investment in Developing Countries.

[3] The Development Assistance Committee (DAC) is a specialized committee of the Organisation for Economic Cooperation and Development (composed of industrialized countries of North America and Western Europe plus Australia, Japan and, for some purposes, Yugoslavia) which was set up "to secure an expansion of aggregate volume of resources made available to developing countries and to improve their effectiveness." The headquarters of the DAC is Paris.

According to Maurice Williams, "DAC countries adopted the term 'official development assistance' to apply to publicly-financed capital directed to the development programs of countries on concessional terms of at least a 25 percent grant element, compared to normal commercial loans. An outright grant, of course, has a grant element of 100 percent. The DAC objective was to establish the principle of providing capital to countries on terms appropriate to their financial situations. At the same time, the DAC sought, through adoption of the 'official development assistance' concept, to establish a basis for a broader sharing of the burden of the Common Aid Effort."

Countries, is estimated to have committed over $800 million for agricultural purposes in 1975, up from $300 million in 1974.[4]

A third source, centrally planned economies, is estimated to have contributed approximately $200 million in assistance to agriculture in 1975, half from East European countries and half from China. The U.S.S.R. is estimated to have contributed little.

Additionally, the total value of expenditures by private voluntary agencies of the DAC countries (excluding food aid) is estimated to have been over $1,000 million in 1973 and also in 1974, a large part of it being for agricultural and rural development.

MULTILATERAL AGENCIES

Multilateral agencies now account for almost two-thirds of the DAC's official development capital assistance to agriculture (Table 6.1). This has been the most rapidly growing source of capital assistance to agriculture.

The World Bank Group. With headquarters in Washington, D.C., the World Bank Group is the largest supplier of external funds for agriculture in developing countries.[5] It has three sources of loans. The International Bank for Reconstruction and Development (IBRD) makes long-term loans at conventional interest rates—mostly for large projects. The International Development Association (IDA) provides credits. These are loans for the same types of projects but on softer terms—longer repayment periods and nominal interest rates. Voluntary contributions have made it possible for the World Bank to establish an intermediate financing facility, more commonly known as the "Third Window," which permits loans on terms which are "half-way" between IBRD loans and IDA credits.

An affiliate of the World Bank Group, the International Finance Corporation, facilitates the investment of private capital in private enterprises of developing member countries.

Both the IBRD and IDA require that projects which they finance make a significant contribution to the economy of the borrowing country. Five basic steps in the granting of the loan—identification, preparation, appraisal, negotiation, and supervision—help to ensure that investments are financially sound from the viewpoint of both the World Bank and the developing country and that a reasonable certainty exists that the loan will be repaid. A World Bank loan normally is confined to foreign-

---

[4] The primary donors are Iran, Iraq, Kuwait, Libya, Qatar, Saudi Arabia, the United Arab Emirates, and Venezuela.
[5] Descriptions of the organization of the multilateral agencies borrow heavily from *International Organizations and Agricultural Development,* by Martin Kriesberg.

Table 6.1. Bilateral (Development Assistance Committee) and multilateral official development assistance commitments in agriculture, 1973-74 averages (million US$)

	Agriculture			All purposes	Agriculture (%)
	Capital	Technical	Total		
Bilateral					
Australia	16	18	34	362	10
Austria	7	1	8	43	18
Belgium	4	—	4	227	2
Canada	60	—	60	619	10
Denmark	5	3	8	116	8
Finland	—	1	1	27	3
France	37	63	100	1,748	6
Germany	127	114	241	1,560	16
Italy	—	—	—	90	—
Japan	80	12	92	1,354	7
Netherlands	15	12	27	321	8
New Zealand	4	2	6	39	16
Norway	22	3	25	91	28
Sweden	136	6	142	341	41
Switzerland	6	1	7	45	16
U.K.	54	20[a]	74	694	11
U.S.	325	66	391	3,016	13
Total	898	322	1,220	10,693	11
Multilateral					
EEC	66	2	68	499	14
European Investment Bank	—	—	—	90	—
World Bank	1,271[b]	—	1,271	4,434	29
Inter-American Dev. Bank	208[b]	—	208[b]	998	21
African Dev. Bank	22[b]	—	22	87	26
Asian Dev. Bank	104[b]	—	104	485	22
UNDP	—	90[c]	90	319	28
World Food Program	168	—	168	331	51
Total	1,839	92	1,931	7,243	27
Grand total	2,737	414	3,151	17,936	18

Source: Consultative Group on Food Production and Investment in Developing Countries, "Analysis of Resource Flows to Developing Countries in the Field of Agriculture—Progress Report."
[a] Estimate.
[b] Includes an element of technical assistance forming an integral part of project activities.
[c] Includes equipment and services provided for demonstration and training.

exchange costs of the project, but recently the bank has begun to help meet local currency costs. It is not now unusual for up to 25 percent of a loan to be for such costs.

The IBRD obtains funds for its operations from subscribed capital from member countries, by borrowing on world markets, and from interest on its loans. The IBRD established a sound credit rating during its early years of operation which has facilitated its ability to get favorable terms in international financial markets. The IDA is funded by subscriptions and contributions (grants) from member countries, transfers from the World Bank's net income, and income derived from IDA's own investments and lending operations.

The World Bank also sponsors consortia of donor countries to several large developing countries—including India, Indonesia, Nigeria, Pakistan, and Bangladesh—to coordinate external assistance to meet their development needs.

The World Bank's lending for agriculture and rural development has grown rapidly.[6] During the first 15 years of operation, lending for agriculture totaled almost $500 million, or 9 percent of the bank's total lending. For 1969 through 1973 the corresponding figures were $2,600 million and 20 percent. For 1974 through 1978, lending for agriculture and rural development was projected to increase to $4,400 million. In 1974 and 1975 alone almost $3,000 million in loans (29 percent of the bank's total lending) was approved for these purposes. Substantial sums are also lent for industrial and public works projects, such as fertilizer plants, roads, and rural electric systems, which greatly affect agricultural production and rural prosperity. Under this broader definition, total World Bank commitments for agriculture are estimated to have been $1,600 million in 1974 and $2,300 million in 1975, or 34 percent and 39 percent of total lending.[7]

The emphasis in the bank's agricultural loans also has changed markedly during this period. The bank's investment in irrigation projects has declined from 77 percent of total agricultural loans during the 1947–63 period to 32 percent in the 1969–73 period.[8] But, in the same periods, loans for agricultural credit have increased from 4 percent to 14 percent; for livestock development, from 1.5 percent to 20 percent; for agro-industries, from 1 percent to 9 percent; and for perennial crops, from zero to 11 percent. Its first loan for development of a national research system was given in 1970. During 1974–78, according to Robert McNamara, president of the World Bank, "programs which directly assist the small farmer to become more productive" are being emphasized.

[6] Rural development projects are those in which 50 percent or more of the primary benefits will accrue to the rural poor. Some loans for education and roads meet this definition.
[7] The contribution of IDA to the total remained static between 1973 and 1975; IDA's share of the bank's total financial assistance to agriculture has declined from 56 percent in 1973 to only 27 percent in 1975.
[8] Aggregate analyses such as these can be misleading. For example, the fall in percentage of funding for irrigation projects may not, in fact, lead to slower expansion of irrigated areas. Tube wells are much less expensive than dams and hydroelectric projects.

Inter-American Development Bank. The regional development banks have now established themselves as influential forces in agricultural and rural development assistance. The oldest is the Inter-American Development Bank (IDB); the Asian Development Bank and the African Development Bank are the others.

Membership in the IDB, headquartered in Washington, D.C., was initially restricted to nations of the region, but it is now open to others. In 1976 Belgium, Denmark, West Germany, Spain, Switzerland, the U.K., Yugoslavia, Israel, and Japan joined. Austria, France, the Netherlands, and Italy joined the bank in 1977.

Funds come primarily from member subscriptions, with the U.S. contributing a third of the total. Earnings on loans provide a second source of income. The IDB has borrowed extensively in private capital markets. The Fund for Special Operations, financed by member contributions proportionate to their use of IDB capital, permits the IDB to finance projects under concessional terms. Several trust funds enable the IDB to make loans for special purposes.

Agricultural projects (including fishing) have accounted for $2,400 million or almost one-fourth of IDB lending. Irrigation and agricultural credit each account for approximately 30 percent of total agricultural sector loans. Loans have also been made for integrated agricultural or rural development, land settlement and agrarian reform, livestock production, animal health, marketing and agro-industries, research and extension, fishing, and forestry. In addition, much of the almost $169 million in preinvestment loans has gone for projects in the agricultural sector. Moreover, IDB loans exceeding $780 million in sectors such as access and farm-to-market roads, rural water supply, farm electrification, agricultural education, and rural housing have fostered rural development.

Asian Development Bank. While situated in Manila and serving Asia, the Asian Development Bank has members outside the region. Funds are derived from capital stock subscriptions by its members (the U.S. and Japan being the largest contributors), special funds from contributions by countries, and bonds floated in world capital markets.

In 1976, agricultural projects accounted for just over $200 million, or over one-quarter of the bank's total lending. Loans for area and water resources development make up the largest part of the bank's agricultural activity, followed by industrial crops and agro-industries, fisheries and livestock, and agricultural credit. The bank gives special attention to projects which have regional significance. The first *Asian Agricultural Survey*, completed in 1968, provided a valuable inventory of resources and identified problems in the area. The most recent survey was made in 1976.

African Development Bank. Membership in the African Development Bank (located in Abidjan, Ivory Coast) is restricted to African nations, a condition which has limited the amount of capital it can marshal. It now has a soft window—the African Development Fund (target $300 million)—in which a number of non-African countries participate (Canada, Belgium, Denmark, Norway, Germany, Japan, the U.K., Italy, the Netherlands, Brazil, Finland, Saudi Arabia, Spain, Sweden, Switzerland, the U.S., and Yugoslavia). Through 1975, agriculture accounted for $36 million in loans (over 10 percent of the bank's total loans) and $59 million in credits (over 40 percent of its total credits).

The European Development Fund. The main instrument of multilateral financial and technical cooperation between the European Economic Community (EEC) and the 52 Associated Overseas States, countries, territories, and departments is the European Development Fund, headquartered in Brussels. The fund is administered by the Commission of the European Communities and supported by budgetary contributions from EEC member states.

The fund makes grants (which account for more than 80 percent of its total assistance) and loans, and gives special-terms aid for the payment of interest on ordinary loans granted by the European Investment Bank. The financing is primarily for investments or development activities, but also for technical assistance, research, and training. Rural development gets high priority; from 1970 to 1975 over 28 percent of disbursements went for this purpose, nearly all as grants.

International Fund for Agricultural Development. By 1977, members of the Organization of Petroleum Exporting Countries (OPEC) and other affluent countries had raised $1,000 million to establish the International Fund for Agricultural Development, an outgrowth of the World Food Conference of 1974. Temporary headquarters have been established in Rome. The fund will be a large new source of money for development efforts. Members of OPEC and low-income countries will have majority voting representation in the fund.

The World Food Program. Administered by a joint United Nations–FAO unit and directed by an intergovernmental committee of member nations of the United Nations and FAO, the World Food Program, headquartered in Rome, supplies food as partial payment in labor-intensive projects promoting social and economic development in recipient countries. It supports projects to build irrigation facilities and roads, to increase agricultural production, and to aid in resettlement. Emergency relief is provided in special circumstances. The World Food Program also helps promote price stabilization.

BILATERAL ASSISTANCE

Nation-to-nation assistance in recent years has increased in volume and in the proportion directed to agriculture. Several points stand out in an examination of bilateral assistance in agriculture.

- Total bilateral development aid (not limited to agriculture) as a percentage of gross national product is still relatively modest for most countries (Table 6.2).
- Political and economic interests affect which countries receive aid and what type of aid is given. Donor countries channel aid particularly to former colonies or to countries with similar philosophies.[9] And often the funds are "tied"—equipment and supplies must be procured in the donor country.
- A high proportion of bilateral assistance goes to low-income and medium-income countries (Table 6.3). There is considerable variation among donor countries. During 1975, Canada, Germany, the Netherlands, and the U.S. all explicitly stated they would give greater emphasis to the poorest countries.
- The poorest countries, especially the densely populated poor countries (most of which are in South Asia), receive relatively low levels of aid per capita.[10] There are several reasons for this situation. Some donor countries feel that, in a period of world grain shortages, priority should be given to countries where existing natural, infrastructural, and human resources permit the most rapid expansion of output at the lowest cost. The poorer countries have weaker overall planning. They have

[9] This orientation applies to OPEC as well as to DAC bilateral assistance. During 1973–75, Indonesia received the largest OPEC bilateral agricultural commitments, followed by Syria, Sudan, Egypt, Pakistan, and Malaysia—all Muslim countries (and accounting for two-thirds of total OPEC bilateral assistance during this period).

[10] Per capita aid does not necessarily fully reflect the efforts being made to assist a given country. For instance, while India's per capita aid figure is among the lowest of all developing countries, it has received a considerable share of total IDA resources.

Table 6.2. Official development assistance in 1975 relative to the gross national products of members of the Development Assistance Committee

Country	%	Country	%	Country	%
Sweden	0.82	Canada	0.58	Japan	0.24
Netherlands	0.75	Denmark	0.58	Switzerland	0.18
Norway	0.66	New Zealand	0.52	Finland	0.18
France	0.62	Germany	0.40	Austria	0.17
Australia	0.61	U.K.	0.37	Italy	0.11
Belgium	0.59	U.S.	0.26		

Source: Maurice J. Williams, *Development Cooperation: Efforts and Policies of the Members of the Development Assistance Committee.*

Table 6.3. Distribution of assistance in agriculture by per capita income class of recipient countries, 1973–74

	Assistance (%)		
Income class	DAC[a]	IBRD[b]	IDA[c]
Low (below $200/year)	48	8	75
Medium ($200–$375/year)	33	18	15
High (above $375/year)	14	55	1
OPEC members	5	12	9
Other	—	7	—
Total	100	100	100

Source: Consultative Group on Food Production and Investment in Developing Countries, "Analysis of Resource Flows to Developing Countries in the Field of Agriculture."
[a] DAC = bilateral assistance of the Development Assistance Committee countries.
[b] IBRD = International Bank for Reconstruction and Development.
[c] IDA = International Development Association.

lower repayment capabilities and must rely on aid given on highly concessional terms.

• Relative to the other low-income countries, very large and very small nations face special disadvantages in receiving aid. To avoid making seemingly disproportionate total aid commitments to populous countries, some donor countries apparently hold down the per capita aid. Small countries often have neither the talent to prepare attractive aid requests nor enough people to be politically important.

• National assistance agencies still appear to favor large projects, such as water development and fertilizer plants, rather than more dispersed programs, such as strengthening research and production capabilities. While some large-scale activities are important, production programs need support.

INTERNATIONAL TRADE

The financial resources transferred through international trade dwarf the amounts transferred through multilateral and bilateral assistance. In 1974 the total value of exports of the developing countries, excluding oil-exporting countries, was $94,000 million. About 80 percent of these exports were agricultural products, chiefly beverage crops, fibers, and forest products.

Three critical problems hamper the growth of exports from developing countries. First, high costs of domestic transportation, processing, and production make competition with products of the developed countries difficult.

Second, the markets of many developed countries are protected by high tariff barriers and rigid qualitative or quantitative restrictions. From

1953 to 1963, exports of manufactured goods by developing countries increased 13 percent a year and from 1965 through 1973 they rose by a spectacular 25 percent a year. Nevertheless, manufactured exports of developing countries are still less than 8 percent of total world exports of manufactured goods. This indicates not only dynamic expansion of the trade among industrialized countries but also the limited extent to which the developing countries are part of the industrial trading economy. There is considerable potential for future trade expansion. As D. Gale Johnson has observed:

It is unfortunate that there is so little understanding of the role of trade in increasing incomes and food supplies in the developing countries. The industrial countries have been willing to go to a considerable distance in removing barriers to trade in industrial products produced by other industrial countries, but they have been most reluctant to lower the barriers to their imports of agricultural products and labor-intensive manufactured products from the developing countries. It seems rather odd that it is accepted that there are gains from trade among industrial countries in industrial products yet little progress has been made in extending the same advantage to the developing countries where their products are competitive with either the industrial or agricultural products of the industrial countries.

. . . The additional foreign exchange earnings made possible by reduced trade barriers would permit the developing countries to obtain modern farm inputs at the lowest possible cost. There would be less need to engage in high-cost production of such inputs if the low-cost products of the developing countries had ready access to international markets.

The third problem is price instability, influenced in part by supply changes resulting from, for example, effects of weather and by demand changes resulting from, for example, changing business conditions in the developed countries. The exports of developing countries (excluding oil exporters) were worth 44 percent more in 1974 than in 1973, but the volume of exports was up only 4 percent. The difference was due to higher export prices. However, the prices of imports to these countries rose so much in 1974 that the aggregate purchasing power of the developing, non–oil producing countries' exports actually fell almost 2 percent.

THE DEVELOPING COUNTRIES

Most of the financing for development of low-income countries must come from their own resources. However, most developing countries are poor by North American or European standards (Table 6.4). For example, for most countries of Northern and Western Europe, the 1975 per capita gross national product (GNP) ranged from $3,000 to $8,000. Yet in Africa, Latin America, and Asia, 64 countries had per capita GNP levels of less than $500. In most countries, the incomes of rural people

Table 6.4   Number of countries at various levels of per capita gross national product, 1975

Per capita GNP (US$)	Africa	Latin America	Asia	North America, Europe, U.S.S.R., Oceania	Total
Less than 100	3	0	3	0	6
100–249	16	1	13	0	30
250–499	18	4	6	3	31
500–999	11	11	6	2	30
1,000–3,999	3	15	10	14	42
4,000 or over	1	0	4	17	22
Total	52	31	42	36	161

Source: International Bank for Reconstruction and Development, *World Bank Atlas.*

are well below national averages. Nations with such low income levels have difficulty mobilizing financial resources to invest in agricultural development, especially in the public sectors of research and infrastructure.

Complete and comparable data on domestic investments in agriculture by governments of developing countries, their private institutions, and farmers are difficult to assemble. FAO data on the share of agriculture in national development plans indicate that most governments are allocating 15–25 percent of expenditures (representing intended target figures) to the agricultural sector. Generally the relative contribution to agriculture is larger in the public sector than in the private sector. In several countries the share devoted to agriculture in current development plans is higher than in previous ones. In the Philippines, for example, public-sector investment in agriculture rose from 17 percent in the 1971–74 plan to 20 percent in the 1974–77 plan; in Venezuela the share of agriculture in total plan outlay increased from 8 percent in 1970–74 to 14 percent in 1974–79.

The technical assistance network

Technical assistance has increased in volume almost as fast as financial assistance. Recently the multilateral development banks have begun to include funds for technical assistance in their loans. However, technical assistance in agriculture is still supplied primarily by UNDP/FAO, the bilateral-assistance programs (Table 6.1), voluntary nonprofit agencies, and private companies.

FAO

The Food and Agriculture Organization of the United Nations is the largest source of technical agricultural assistance for developing countries. By the end of 1977, 144 nations had joined FAO. Each member government has a single vote in the Conference, the supreme governing body.

FAO funding comes from the contributions of its member countries, the United Nations Development Programme, the Freedom from Hunger Campaign, and the United Nations Children's Fund. In addition, some FAO programs are financed from trust arrangements with recipient countries, some by the international and regional banks under special agreement, some under special programs sponsored by developed countries, and some with funds from private sources.

FAO has a wide range of activities. It and the U.S. Department of Agriculture are the major bodies collecting and reporting data on world agriculture. FAO carries out a world census of agriculture every 10 years. It is part of a worldwide food aid program. It has joined with the World Bank in a cooperative program to identify and appraise investment projects. In 1976 it created the Technical Cooperation Program to permit it to become more directly and quickly involved in development efforts, particularly program development.

FAO's program of providing technical assistance has grown steadily. Its staff is recruited internationally, with substantial representation from the developing countries. At present it has programs in land and water resources, rural institutions, food policy and nutrition, plant production and protection, animal production and health, development planning, fisheries, and forestry. As of January 1975, FAO was assisting 1,700 field projects in 126 countries and territories.

THE UNITED NATIONS DEVELOPMENT PROGRAMME

In 1966 the United Nations Expanded Program of Technical Assistance, established in 1949, merged with the Special Fund, established in 1959, to form the United Nations Development Programme (UNDP), the financial hub for technical assistance activities in the U.N. system. The financial resources of UNDP come principally from voluntary contributions pledged by member governments. In 1976, $101 million, or 28 percent of the UNDP budget, was spent for technical agricultural assistance in 140 countries and territories.

Although it follows policies established by a governing council composed of representatives of developing and developed countries, the key element in its operation is the field representative, who helps the host government with development planning and U.N. assistance and who coordinates the UNDP-financed programs under his jurisdiction. In 1976, field representatives were stationed in 108 developing countries. FAO staff members have been assigned to many of these representatives as agricultural advisors.

REGIONAL AGENCIES

In Latin America the Organization of American States aids the development of agriculture in member states by technical assistance and training activities directly and through its agricultural arm, the Inter-American Institute for Agricultural Sciences.

In Asia, the Southeast Asian Regional Center for Graduate Study and Research in Agriculture (SEARCA), located at the University of the Philippines, operates under the auspices of the Southeast Asian Ministers of Education Organization. It sponsors research in water resource management, food technology, information science, extension, agribusiness, and development economics. SEARCA maintains a practical orientation in its work and focuses on regional problems.

BILATERAL ASSISTANCE

Most large donor countries provide technical support along with their capital assistance programs. In fact, the program of the U.S. Agency for International Development (USAID), which now consists predominantly of financial assistance, began as a technical assistance program under "Point Four." Experience soon demonstrated that technical assistance by itself produced limited results, and therefore capital assistance was added. In 1973–74 three nations—Germany, the U.S., and France—accounted for 75 percent of the bilateral technical assistance in agriculture given throughout the world (Table 6.1).

As with bilateral financial assistance, bilateral technical assistance is often directed toward developing countries that have political or historic ties with the donor country. French technical aid, for example, goes largely to Francophile Africa; British aid is concentrated in its former colonies; and Swedish aid favors developing nations that have socialist forms of government or that have projects with strong egalitarian objectives.

The donor agencies have difficulty maintaining effective, professionally qualified technical staffs to implement their programs. Agricultural scientists can lose touch with current practices in rapidly changing fields when they are stationed away from the mainstream of professional ideas. Furthermore, the constantly changing aims of bilateral aid programs, both geographically and in subject matter, make professional continuity difficult to maintain. The French and British have been more successful in maintaining long-term career staffs than the U.S., but donor countries are increasingly using universities and private firms as reservoirs of technical personnel for overseas programs. For example, USAID, which at one time employed a large technical staff, now relies heavily on U.S. universities, private firms, and the U.S. Department of Agriculture for overseas technical personnel.

NONPROFIT ORGANIZATIONS

Several private foundations have played innovative roles in technical agricultural assistance to developing countries. They are able to recruit and maintain qualified staff, provide career opportunities in international agriculture, provide program flexibility to respond to the needs of the developing countries, and stay with programs long enough to achieve measurable results. The Rockefeller Foundation's assistance in Mexico, Colombia, and India has been a prime example. The Ford Foundation has carried out productive assistance programs in a number of countries. Between 1943 and 1975 these two foundations spent over $300 million on international agricultural development. Their most significant joint achievement was perhaps starting the international agricultural research institutes, which are now financed by members of the Consultative Group on International Agricultural Research. The International Development Research Centre of Canada, established in 1970, is a newer addition to this set of organizations which encourages innovation or support programs for long periods (or at least until other, larger sources of funding are obtained). The Swedish Agency for Research Coordination with Developing Countries was established in 1975 to improve the scientific and technological infrastructure in developing countries in order to lessen their dependence on developed countries and increase their capacity to establish economic and social justice.

The foundations must operate on their own funds; that is, they generally do not accept funds from outside sources for specified purposes. Therefore, their contribution to direct technical assistance focuses on innovation rather than long-term financial support of programs.

Many voluntary agencies are engaged in food production and agricultural assistance internationally. The Technical Assistance Information Clearing House of the American Council of Voluntary Agencies for Foreign Service, Inc., lists over 150 nonprofit organizations in this field in the U.S. alone. These range from Catholic Relief Services, which has a $226-million program embracing almost 50 countries and geographical entities, and CARE, Inc., which operates a $170-million program in 23 countries, to some 50 small organizations operating in single countries. Nonprofit organizations exist in some other donor countries—for example, OXFAM, Voluntary Service Overseas, and War on Want in the U.K.

The activities of these agencies range from distributing surplus foods to programs to increase food production.

PROFIT-MAKING ORGANIZATIONS

Profit-making assistance organizations represent another large source of technical assistance. They range from multinational corporations, which carry on farming operations in low-income countries in cooperation with governments, to private firms such as IRI Research Institute, Inc., Arthur D. Little, Inc., and the Stanford Research Institute in the U.S., Tate and Lyle in the U.K., and Euroconsult in the Netherlands, which supply technical assistance on a contractual basis.

The research network

In the past, many agricultural programs have been ineffective because improved agricultural production systems, with locally adapted biological components, were lacking. The biological components, such as high-yielding varieties or animal strains or techniques of disease and insect control, must be associated with new production practices. Agricultural progress therefore requires competent, problem-oriented scientific and technical studies. This work is often expensive and time-consuming. The recent emergence of an international agricultural research network gives some reason for confidence that improved biological materials and production practices will continue to be developed in the future. The network has three interlocking components: national research and production systems, the international agricultural research institutes, and research in developed countries.

NATIONAL RESEARCH AND PRODUCTION SYSTEMS

Agricultural technologies having biological components must be tailored for a variety of crops and a range of unique conditions of different seasons of many regions. Scientists who are developing technologies must take account of locally prevalent strains of insects and diseases, characteristics of soils, prevailing rainfall patterns, and consumer preferences. At the minimum, each nation or group of nations needs the research capacity to identify, through farm-level experimentation, more highly productive crop and animal production systems (see Chapter 12). Countries that are scientifically well staffed may, in addition, be able to carry out strategic or supporting research. Progress is most rapid when the research is closely related to the production goals of the country.

Research in most developing countries suffers from a common handicap. National investment in agricultural research is by any measure

Table 6.5. Public expenditures on agricultural research by region in selected years

Region	Expenditures (million US$)				Research expenditures as % of value of agricultural production, 1965
	1951	1958	1965	1970	
North America	225	333	448	478	1.01
Northern Europe	60	104	217	258	0.93
Southern Europe	8	15	27	32	0.38
Oceania, South Africa & Rhodesia	25	45	100	176	1.61
Eastern Europe & U.S.S.R.	65	150	265	300	0.64
Latin America	8	11	24	42	0.17
Mideast & North Africa	19	26	38	47	0.55
South & Southeast Asia	10	16	42	54	0.24
East Asia	24	36	91	113	0.79
Sub-Saharan Africa	10	20	39	69	0.45
Developed countries	405	679	1,126	1,324	0.87
Less-developed countries	49	77	163	236	0.26
World total	454	756	1,289	1,560	

Source: James K. Boyce and Robert E. Evenson, *National and International Agricultural Research and Extension Programs*.

(percentage of GNP, per capita expenditure, or percentage of value of agricultural production) pitifully low (Table 6.5).[11] Furthermore, a much smaller proportion of research is done by the private sector in low-income countries than in high-income countries (Table 6.6).

Many national agricultural institutions in developing countries are unable to cope with their agricultural problems without external assistance.

[11] In contrast, the low-income countries spend a higher percentage of the value of agricultural production for agricultural extension than do high-income countries; in 1974, for example, countries with per capita incomes below $150 spent 1.82 percent, compared with the 0.60 percent spent by countries with per capita incomes above $1,750.

Table 6.6. Estimated share of private research activities in current total agricultural research spending

Country	%	Country	%
U.S.	35	Oceania	10
Canada	30	Mexico, Brazil & Argentina	5
Northern Europe	20	Israel & Japan	4
Central & Western Europe	12	Other African & Asian countries	3
Southern Europe	8	Eastern Europe & U.S.S.R.	2

Source: James K. Boyce and Robert E. Evenson, *National and International Agricultural Research and Extension Programs*.

Typically, developing countries—especially the smaller ones—lack trained manpower; they also lack strong, problem-solving, development-oriented research institutions and sound policies to foster the development of agricultural technology. The commitment to implement such policies also is frequently wanting.

This situation is changing. In several countries agricultural production has been accelerated through national research efforts. Among the most notable are the experiences of Mexico in the 1950s and 1960s and of India in the late 1960s (see Chapter 8).

Public expenditures on agricultural research between 1951 and 1970 (Table 6.5) increased faster in the developing countries (a quadrupling) than in the developed countries (a tripling). International donors are providing more support for national research systems. The World Bank gave its first loan to support a national agricultural research program to Spain in 1970. Subsequently it has made large loans to Malaysia, Indonesia, and Brazil for this purpose. Some bilateral-aid agencies also are adopting this pattern.

THE INTERNATIONAL AGRICULTURAL RESEARCH INSTITUTES

The international institute system began with the International Rice Research Institute, established in the Philippines in 1960. By 1969 The Rockefeller Foundation and the Ford Foundation, together with host governments, had sponsored the creation of three other international agricultural institutes. Since the formation of the Consultative Group on International Agricultural Research (CGIAR), a multilateral forum of donors, in 1971, five more institutes have been launched. Several other international institutions cooperate closely with the CGIAR-sponsored centers. This research system, although still quite new, now covers most of the major food crops and animals, and extends to most areas of the developing world (Table 6.7). The budgets of the international institutes totaled about $85 million in 1977 (compared with $6 million in 1968).

The basic purpose of the international agricultural institutes is to help nations develop their capabilities to increase agricultural production. Toward this end, institute staff members work cooperatively with those of national institutions on the more difficult problems of regional or international importance, train staff members for national institutions, and facilitate international cooperation on matters of importance. Experimental strains and practices developed at the institutes are tested at many locations in the world along with materials developed in cooperating national programs. This permits selection of varieties best suited for specific environments. The international institutes make germ plasm freely available to cooperating countries, provide scientists to work cooperatively in national programs, hold meetings to review programs and exchange

Table 6.7. The international agricultural research institute network

Center	Program
International Rice Research Institute	Rice, multiple cropping
International Maize and Wheat Improvement Center	Wheat, maize, barley, triticale
International Institute of Tropical Agriculture	Maize, rice, cowpeas, soybeans, lima beans, cassava, yams, sweet potatoes, and farming systems
International Center of Tropical Agriculture	Beans, cassava, beef and forages, maize, rice, and swine
International Potato Center	Potatoes
International Crops Research Institute for the Semi-Arid Tropics	Sorghum, millets, peanuts, chickpeas, pigeon peas
International Laboratory for Research on Animal Diseases	Blood diseases of cattle
International Livestock Centre for Africa	Cattle production
International Center for Agricultural Research in Dry Areas	Wheat, barley, lentils, broad beans, oilseeds, cotton, and sheep farming

Source: Ralph W. Cummings, Jr., *Food Crops in the Low Income Countries: The State of Present*

information, and train national scientists. Similar work is being carried out in animal production.

Individually, most of the characteristics of the international agricultural research institutes are not new. Commodity-oriented research institutes have been in existence for over half a century. The Experiment Station of the Hawaiian Sugar Planters' Association and the Pineapple Research Institute, both in Hawaii, are examples. The Central Rice Research Institute has been a center of rice work in India for several decades.

The French government provides technical assistance primarily through two institutions: The Office de la Recherche Scientifique et Technique d'Outre-Mer (ORSTOM) and the Groupement d'Études et de Recherches pour le Développement de l'Agronomie Tropicale (GERDAT). ORSTOM handles disciplinary research oriented toward development (17 disciplines are represented in ORSTOM) as well as interdisciplinary research through integrated research teams. GERDAT is composed of eight crop-oriented institutes and one center for tropical agricultural engineering, which can work in developing countries on the basis of agreements signed for specific research action related to agricultural development (Table 6.8); each of the institutes is placed under the authority of a general director, with GERDAT maintaining an overall unity of action.

The British government supports important centers of agricultural development concerned with the tropics and subtropics, including the Tropical Products Institute, the Centre for Overseas Pest Research, and the Tropical Stored Products Centre.

Year founded	Headquarters	Agro-climatic area served
1960	Philippines	Rainfed and irrigated areas—subtropical/tropical
1966	Mexico	Rainfed and irrigated areas—temperate/tropical
1968	Nigeria	Rainfed and irrigated areas—lowland tropics
1969	Colombia	Rainfed and irrigated tropics—1,000 meters to sea level
1972	Peru	Rainfed and irrigated areas—temperate-to-tropical
1972	India	Semi-arid tropics
1974	Kenya	Mainly semi-arid tropics
1974	Ethiopia	Humid-to-dry tropics
1976	Lebanon, Syria, Iran	Mediterranean

and Expected Agricultural Research and Technology.

The "invention" of the International Rice Research Institute in 1960 drew on the accumulated experience of many such institutions and individuals. What makes the international institutes—and their support by the CGIAR—unique is that each combines the following eight attributes in single institutions:

First, each institute is governed by an autonomous, self-perpetuating board of trustees, the majority being distinguished citizens of the nations served.[12] This independence enables the institute to focus on problems of first importance.

Second, because the institutes are independent and are staffed by the best talent available, regardless of nationality, and because the doors of the institutes are open to people of any interested nation, they are increasingly accepted by nations of diverse ideologies as apolitical institutions.

Third, institutes generally are mission oriented. A well-organized, well-run, hard-working institute is not the ultimate objective; improved productivity on each nation's farms is.

Fourth, an institute can initiate a program to assist cooperating nations quickly. It can provide support (including interim leadership, if needed) if it receives a request from a nation, if it has funds for the undertaking, and if it obtains the approval of its trustees.

[12] For example, the 14-member board of trustees at the International Rice Research Institute in 1977 included three members from the Philippines and one each from Bangladesh, Indonesia, India, El Salvador, Egypt, Burma, and Thailand.

Table 6.8.   Institutes with international research responsibilities sponsored by
the French government

GERDAT—Groupement d'Etudes et de Recherches pour le Développement de l'Agronomie Tropicale—is composed of eight commodity institutes and an agricultural engineering institute:

- Centre Technique Forestier Tropical (CTFT) [Technical Center for Tropical Forestry]
- Institut d'Elévage et de Médecine Vétérinaire des Pays Tropicaux (IEMVT) [The Livestock Breeding and Veterinary Institute of the Tropics]
- Institut Francais des Recherches Fruitières Outre-Mer (IFAC) [French Institute for Overseas Fruit Research]
- Institut Francais du Café, du Cacao et des Autres Plantes Stimulantes (IFCC) [French Institute for Coffee, Cacao, and Other Stimulant Plants]
- Institut de Recherches Agronomiques Tropicales et des Cultures Vivrières (IRAT) [Institute for Agronomic Research on Tropical Food Crops]
- Institut de Recherches sur le Caoutchouc en Afrique (IRCA) [Research Institute for Rubber in Africa]
- Institut de Recherches du Coton et des Textiles Exotiques (IRCT) [Research Institute for Cotton and Exotic Textile Crops]
- Institut de Recherches pour les Huiles et Oléagineux (IRHO) [Research Institute for Oils and Oilseeds]
- Centre d'Etudes et d'Expérimentation du Machinisme Agricole Tropical (CEEMAT) [Center for Tropical Agricultural Mechanization Research]

Source: National Academy of Sciences, *World Food and Nutrition Study.*

Fifth, the institutes have unusual flexibility in responding to the program requests of nations. They can tailor their programs to specific needs. Some solutions will emerge from work done in an institute's own laboratories or in its experimental fields. Other solutions will be obtained by national organizations. Still others will result from cooperative work between the institute and organizations of the nations with which it is associated. The institute may receive grants from any source. It can cooperate with nations on a scientist-to-scientist basis as well as an institution-to-institution basis, and in fact institutes usually insist on doing so. The point is that the interdisciplinary staff of an institute has the freedom to do what is necessary to organize a concerted international effort—an international, comprehensive campaign, if necessary—to find solutions to critical problems.

Sixth, institutes can tailor training to specific needs. Previously there was almost exclusive reliance on the scientific training of personnel in the industrialized nations. Such education and training could not be closely related to the needs of the individuals and their institutions, since agricultural problems of the temperate regions differ from those in the tropics. Moreover, institutions in the two regions are dealing with the agricultural development process at different stages of evolution.

Seventh, the institutes permit knowledge to become institutionalized. The core staff of each international institute is made up of career people,

Conservation of germ plasm

For many years scientists have been worried that with the spread of high-yielding varieties over the world's agricultural lands or for other reasons, valuable indigenous varieties and wild relatives might be displaced and hence unavailable for future crop improvement. World germ plasm banks for maize and rice are reasonably complete and in safe storage. But for most crops, collections are incomplete, poorly maintained in scattered locations, and even threatened with loss.

In 1974, an international organization was formed which has the expertise and the funds with which to arrange systematic collections of important germ plasm; to evaluate, describe, and maintain it; and to make it available to scientists anywhere. The International Board for Plant Genetic Resources, established under the aegis of the CGIAR, consists of 15 specialists representing all parts of the world. In 1976 the board received $1.2 million from a consortium of nine governments and the United Nations Environment Programme.

Initial priorities for attention to crops and regions have been established and published. The board's first symposium, on wheat, was held in the U.S.S.R. and a second, on groundnuts, was held in the U.S. International advisory committees for each major crop have been established.

individuals who will likely remain on the job, provided their performance is effective. And as the institute and its cooperators advance their knowledge and improve the materials with which they work, such knowledge and materials tend to be preserved by the international institute and a few strong national organizations. Information and materials are not lost as individuals switch positions or retire. Because of the long periods of service, scientists at the institutes become acquainted with advanced work being done anywhere in their specialties. Consequently, when national organizations turn to the institutes, they know they will probably receive reliable and up-to-date information or materials of a quality high by world standards.

Eighth, the institutes can maintain continuity of work, even though the contributions of most donors are made on a year-to-year basis. Because each institute has a broad base of financial support, each donor is assured that it is contributing to an effort of a magnitude and type which it would find difficult to support on its own. This factor undoubtedly accounts for the support of institutes by a growing number of national and international assistance agencies. Together they can create and sustain an organization which individually they could not.

The international institutes constitute one of the more successful modern-day examples of international cooperation. They hasten development of new technologies. While they have this critically important role, they are not a substitute for strong national programs in the achievement of the end result of agricultural research—accelerating the pace of agricultural and rural progress.

RESEARCH PROGRAMS IN DEVELOPED COUNTRIES

Laboratories and research centers in the developed countries play an important role in carrying out basic or supporting research (Chapter 12) which is outside the commodity or production-systems orientation of organizations in developing countries or international institutes or which currently does not justify priority use of the scarce scientific resources in the developing countries.

For example, the high-yielding varieties of wheat and rice were developed in the low-income countries by restructuring plant types, introducing genes for disease resistance, and incorporating fertilizer responsiveness, early maturity, daylength insensitivity, and other desirable traits (see Chapter 7). Much of this work was based on earlier scientific work in more affluent countries, notably Japan and the U.S.

The concept of breeding plants to specification (sometimes called biological engineering) leads logically to the idea of crossing unrelated species to achieve superior plants not found in nature. Triticale, a hybrid of wheat and rye, represents one such man-made species that has been successful. Breeders and geneticists are now attempting to cross wheat with barley, wheat with oats, barley with rye, and maize with sorghum, to name a few.

Symbiotic and nonsymbiotic fixation of atmospheric nitrogen by soil bacteria has been an object of scientific research for years, but a marked rise in interest occurred when sharply higher prices of petroleum raised the price of nitrogen fertilizer significantly. Nitrogen-fixing soil bacteria live both independently and in association with certain plants, chiefly (but not exclusively) the legumes. Scientists are searching for ways to extend biological nitrogen fixation to the grasses.

Major attention is being directed toward reducing losses in the field caused by pests and diseases. Researchers are continuing to develop pesticides that attack target insects and do not harm other species or remain long in the environment. Progress is also being made in insect control through the use of pheromones (insect communication media, chiefly sex attractants). Juvenile hormones, antijuvenile hormones, and hormone mimics have been used experimentally to disrupt insect development at early stages of their life cycles, either killing or sterilizing them. However, the tool that holds the greatest promise for the low-income farmer who cannot buy agricultural chemicals is the development of crop varieties having built-in resistance. Plant pathologists and geneticists are currently aiming at so-called horizontal, or generalized disease resistance—that is, to incorporate into a single variety genes for resistance to a number of pests and pathogens, as contrasted with single-gene resistance to one plant enemy. Plant pathologists and entomologists are not counting on any one of these approaches to do the job alone; their aim is to achieve integrated strategies based on a combination of methods which can be used in comprehensive plant protection programs.

The foregoing examples of "frontier" research (wide crosses and nitrogen fixation) do not begin to exhaust the list of the many promising opportunities which exist. Not all of the advances have come, or will come, from industrialized nations. However, the developed countries can afford to put a larger proportion of their research into these efforts.

Support for agricultural research at all levels—national research and production systems in the low-income countries, the international agricultural research institutes, and laboratories and research centers in the developed countries—and mechanisms to improve cooperation and reduce duplication in the research network deserve to be strengthened.

The training network

Because agriculture has been a profession of low prestige, most high-level government officials in the developing countries are military officers, lawyers, businessmen, doctors, engineers, economists, or religious leaders, and thus their knowledge of agriculture is slight. Young people who went abroad for training in the 1950s or earlier were financed by their families, and they unsurprisingly chose high-prestige fields. Individuals from less affluent backgrounds in many instances received military training abroad, at the expense of either their own government or that of an international power which hoped to influence the armed services of the trainees' home country. Former colonies commonly find that the departure of expatriates has left them with too few qualified people. As a result, biological scientists and economists are needed who can plan sound programs and describe the proposed programs in nontechnical language to national leaders, who can direct programs to achieve high productivity of the basic food commodities, and who can train young people in managing crops and animals for high yields.

Several mechanisms are evolving to improve the quality of training of agriculturalists in the low-income countries (see Chapter 14). Some colleges of agriculture are reorienting their programs to be more responsive to local needs. New colleges and schools of agriculture are being formed. Regional postgraduate programs are being developed. Each of the international agricultural research centers has a variety of training programs, lasting from a couple of weeks to several months. The Economic Development Institute of the World Bank, the International Agricultural Center in the Netherlands, and the Agricultural Extension and Rural Development Centre in the U.K. operate nondegree training programs in agriculture. The well-established system of postgraduate universities in the developed countries provides yet another component of this growing and maturing list of institutions engaged in training agriculturalists.

Too few persons are receiving advanced foreign and in-country training in agriculture, however. In a recent study, H. M. Phillips indicates that more than 7,000 students and trainees in agriculture were assisted under official bilateral education aid in 1973, apparently a fifth less than in the previous year. Phillips advances several possible explanations. For example, the decrease may have reflected concentration on large urban centers in developing countries, a trend which may now be reversed by the rekindled interest in food production. Or people who work on rural development activities, which have received more recent emphasis, may not be identified as being trained in agriculture. Phillips also concludes that, "roughly speaking, more than twice as much effort (in terms both of numbers of educational aid personnel and students and trainees aided) was expended on the developing countries with higher per capita incomes than upon the lowest income group," even though the lowest income group "had over twice their population."

New forms of cooperation

The 1970s have been marked by the encouraging emergence of new forms of international cooperation.

Perhaps the most effective example is the Consultative Group on International Agricultural Research (CGIAR), which provides financing for the international agricultural research institutes. The CGIAR includes international agencies, bilateral donors, and several private foundations (Table 6.9). It brings together financiers and agriculturalists, officers of governments and foundations, economists, biologists, and international lawyers. Its Technical Advisory Committee, composed of 13 highly regarded agriculturalists from both low-income and developed countries, determines which investments are of highest priority and monitors the relevance and quality of work of the institutions supported.

The World Food Conference (held in 1974) resulted in the formation of new intergovernmental bodies in the food field and a strengthening of several previously established ones (Fig. 6.1):[13]

[13] The staff of the U.S. Senate Select Committee on Nutrition and Human Needs has identified a total of 89 international governmental organizations which, to a greater or lesser degree, have an interest in or responsibility for food, agricultural, and nutrition issues, policies, or programs.

- The World Food Council is the primary instrument for coordinating the recommendations of the World Food Conference. It was established by the United Nations General Assembly in December 1974. Its headquarters are in Rome. The council's 36 member countries represent a careful balance of food exporters, food importers, food-deficit countries, rich countries, poor countries, large countries, and small countries. All world regions are represented, as is a wide spectrum of political and economic systems. The council's first meeting, in 1975, provided an occasion for reassessing the current world food situation as well as for confirming the council's mandate to monitor and encourage action on all phases of the World Food Conference's resolutions and to make recommendations to other U.N. bodies. The council determined that its future activities should include identification of problem areas, gaps in activities, and time lags in performance and reporting on and encouragement of progress made toward an integrated and coordinated approach to the world food problem.
- The Consultative Group on Food Production and Investment in Developing Countries, located in Washington, D.C., was established in February 1975, under the joint auspices of the World Bank, FAO, and UNDP, to promote investment in the food production sectors of developing countries, to coordinate the activities of donors, and to increase the efficiency of investments made in agriculture. It did not have funds of its own to distribute. By the end of 1976 it had held

Fig. 6.1. Major intergovernmental bodies in the food field

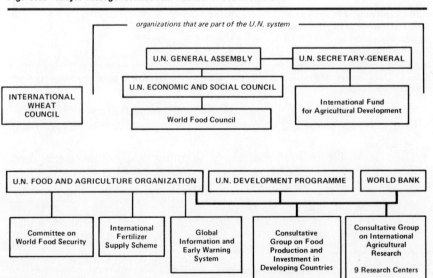

Source: Martin M. McLaughlin, *World Food Insecurity: Has Anything Happened Since Rome?*

Table 6.9. Contributors to nine international agricultural centers, 1978

	International Center for Tropical Agriculture (CIAT)	International Maize and Wheat Improvement Center (CIMMYT)	International Potato Center (CIP)	International Crops Research Institute for the Semi-Arid Tropics (ICRISAT)
Arab Fund				
Asian Development Bank				
Australia	x	x	x	x
Belgium	x		x	x
Canada	x	x	x	x
Denmark		x	x	
European Economic Community				x
Ford Foundation	x	x		
France				
Germany	x	x	x	x
Inter-American Development Bank	x	x	x	
International Development Research Centre			x	x
Iran		x		
Italy				
Japan	x	x		x
Kellogg Foundation	x			
Netherlands	x		x	x
New Zealand				
Nigeria				
Norway	x			x
Rockefeller Foundation	x	x		
Sweden			x	x
Switzerland	x	x	x	x
United Kingdom	x	x	x	x
U.N. Development Programme		x		x
U.N. Environment Programme				x
United States	x	x	x	x
World Bank	x	x	x	

Source: Consultative Group on International Agricultural Research, tentative estimated 1978 financial allocations.

three meetings with a wide participation of donors, developing countries, U.N. agencies, and representatives of business. It was discontinued in 1978.

• The Global Information and Early Warning System was established under FAO in 1974—with the notable nonparticipation of the U.S.S.R. and China. It monitors world food supply and demand and provides warning of approaching shortages.

• The International Fertilizer Supply Scheme was established under FAO in July 1974 and is now operating in 30 countries. By June 1975 it had made 73,000 tons of fertilizer available to importing countries designated "most seriously affected" by FAO.

• The Committee on World Food Security was established by FAO in

International Institute of Tropical Agriculture (IITA)	International Rice Research Institute (IRRI)	International Livestock Centre for Africa (ILCA)	International Laboratory for Research on Animal Diseases (ILRAD)	International Center for Agricultural Research in Dry Areas (ICARDA)
				X
	X			
X	X	X	X	X
X	X	X	X	X
X	X		X	X
	X	X		
	X			
X	X			X
		X		X
X	X	X	X	X
	X			X
X	X	X		X
				X
X	X			
X		X	X	X
	X			
X		X		
X		X	X	X
	X		X	
	X	X		X
		X	X	
X	X	X	X	X
	X		X	
X	X			X
X	X	X	X	X
X		X	X	X

November 1975 as a successor to the FAO Ad Hoc Working Party on World Food Security to bring about the creation of a world food reserve.

• The Industry Cooperative Program and the Bankers' Cooperative Program were organized by FAO to make private-sector institutions more aware of the opportunities in the developing world.

Although not yet part of the intergovernmental system, three other new organizations promise to make significant contributions to agricultural development in the future. Each employs an internationally recruited staff, has an international board of directors, and already has or expects to have multiple sources of funding.

- The International Fertilizer Development Center, located in Muscle Shoals, Alabama, was established in 1974 to improve fertilizers and fertilizer know-how in developing countries. Its research emphasizes development of more efficient fertilizers, processing and manufacturing, use of indigenous raw materials, marketing, and fertilizer-soil-plant problems. Technical assistance is available to those concerned with supplying fertilizers to the developing countries. Training is provided in aspects of fertilizer production, supply, and use. The center also collects and exchanges information on fertilizer technology and use.
- The International Food Policy Research Institute, established in Washington, D.C., in 1975, brings a politically independent viewpoint to food policy analysis. It focuses on four areas of research: trends in food production, consumption, and trade; food production policies; food consumption and distribution policies; and international trade policies.
- The International Agricultural Development Service was established in 1975 as a private, professional, nonprofit organization to provide technical assistance to developing countries. Initially it drew on the experience and talent of The Rockefeller Foundation and other organizations, while being able to accept grants or contract funds from outside sources for specific types of assistance to developing countries.

These new forms of cooperation increase the ability of the low-income countries to raise money and secure technical expertise. They help the assistance agencies to be better informed regarding needs, and they help the developing countries to be better informed regarding sources and conditions of assistance. Moreover, they build stability into assistance, so that if one donor institution has temporary difficulty in providing funds or technical assistance, its role can be smoothly assumed by others.

Concluding comments

Since World War II, and especially during the last decade, the world has mobilized an impressive array of financial and technical assistance mechanisms in support of the developing countries' efforts to alleviate hunger and associated poverty. Led by the World Bank, assistance agencies have reoriented their lending for agricultural and rural development, placing more emphasis on basic food crops and small farmers. More effective forms of international cooperation are being identified and implemented. Some developing nations are now exhibiting the will to give agricultural and rural development high priority in their development plans. While the severity of food-poverty-population problems has increased, so have the world's capabilities to deal with it.

But, laudable as past efforts have been, they are not enough. Weaknesses remain. The developed countries' financial assistance is inadequate in relation to the needs of the recipients and to the abilities of the affluent to pay. Just as the poorest individuals within countries are neglected in national development efforts, so do the poor, small nations tend to be neglected by the international assistance community. The industrial countries tend to overlook the large potential resource transfers which can result from encouraging imports from the developing countries. Too often government policies within the developing countries themselves, aimed at generating revenues or holding down food prices in urban areas, inhibit their own agricultural development. Assistance agencies tend to think more in terms of discrete, often unrelated, projects rather than in terms of coordinated contributions to comprehensive national development efforts. The developed countries have too few agriculturalists experienced in planning and implementing the accelerated agricultural efforts now required in the low-income countries. Too few programs are available to train public-sector personnel in the management of forced-paced agricultural production programs. Only limited literature exists which can help policymakers, many of whom are not specialists in either agriculture or economics, understand the basis for organizing national research and production programs or the world system from which nations can draw assistance.

Greater efforts are needed to promote practices which have proved effective in the past and promise to be so in the future. New directions are needed in many problem areas.[14]

References

THE FINANCIAL NETWORK

Asian Development Bank. *Asian Agricultural Survey, 1968.* Manila: Asian Development Bank, 1968.

Asian Development Bank. *Asian Agricultural Survey, 1977.* Manila: Asian Development Bank, 1977.

Consultative Group on Food Production and Investment in Developing Countries. "Analysis of Resource Flows to Developing Countries in the Field of Agriculture—Progress Report, November 25, 1975." Mimeographed.

Donaldson, G. F., and Bates, D. J. "Changes in Emphasis in World Bank Lending for Agriculture." *Span* 17 (1974): 98–100.

European Communities Commission. *The European Development Fund: From the Introduction of the Project to its Completion.* Rev. ed. Luxembourg: Office for Official Publications of the European Communities, 1973.

Hopper, W. David. "The Development of Agriculture in Developing Countries." *Scientific American* 235 (September 1976): 196–205.

International Bank for Reconstruction and Development. *World Bank Atlas: Population, Per Capita Product, and Growth Rates.* Washington, D.C.: World Bank, 1975.

[14] Implications for international assistance will be treated in Chapter 15.

Isenman, Paul. "Biases in Aid Allocations against Poorer and Larger Countries." *World Development* 4 (1976): 631–41.

Johnson, D. Gale. "Food for the Future: A Perspective." *Population and Development Review* 2 (1976): 1–20.

Kreisberg, Martin. *International Organizations and Agricultural Development.* Foreign Agricultural Economic Report No. 131. Washington, D.C.: U.S. Department of Agriculture, May 1977.

McNamara, Robert S. *Address to the Board of Governors, Nairobi, Kenya, September 24, 1973.* Washington, D.C.: International Bank for Reconstruction and Development, n.d.

"Some Policy Initiatives in Development Cooperation." *OECD Observer* No. 79 (1976): 4–5.

United Nations, Department of Economic and Social Affairs. *World Economic Survey, 1974: Part Two. Current Economic Development* (E/568/Rev. 1/ST/ESA/26), 1975.

Valdes, Alberto, and Huddleston, Barbara. *Potential of Agricultural Exports to Finance Increased Food Imports in Selected Developing Countries.* Occasional Paper 2. Washington, D.C.: International Food Policy Research Institute, August 1977.

Williams, Maurice J. *Development Cooperation: Efforts and Policies of the Members of the Development Assistance Committee—1976 Review.* Paris: Organisation for Economic Cooperation and Development, 1976.

THE TECHNICAL ASSISTANCE NETWORK

American Council of Voluntary Agencies for Foreign Service. Technical Assistance Information Clearing House. *A Listing of U.S. Non-Profit Organizations in Food Production and Agricultural Assistance Abroad.* New York: Technical Assistance Information Clearing House, December 1974.

Cummings, Ralph W., Jr., and Weinstein, Linda. *Agricultural Assistance Sources.* New York: International Agricultural Development Service, 1978.

Osoyo, Roberto. "Mexico: From Food Deficits to Sufficiency." In *Strategy for the Conquest of Hunger.* New York: Rockefeller Foundation, 1968.

Streeter, Carroll P. *Agricultural Change: The Men and the Methods. Columbia.* New York: Rockefeller Foundation, 1972.

Streeter, Carroll P. *A Partnership to Improve Food Production in India.* New York: Rockefeller Foundation, 1969.

THE RESEARCH NETWORK

Boyce, James K., and Evenson, Robert E. *National and International Agricultural Research and Extension Programs.* New York: Agricultural Development Council, 1975.

Consultative Group on International Agricultural Research. *International Research in Agriculture.* New York: Consultative Group on International Agricultural Research, 1974.

Cummings, Ralph W., Jr. *Food Crops in the Low Income Countries: The State of Present and Expected Agricultural Research and Technology.* Working Paper. New York: Rockefeller Foundation, May 1975.

Dalrymple, Dana G. *Measuring the Green Revolution: Impact of Research on Wheat and Rice Production.* Foreign Agricultural Economic Report No. 106. Washington, D.C.: U.S. Department of Agriculture, July 1975.

Hardy, R. W. F., and Havelka, U. D. "Nitrogen Fixation: A Key to World Food?" *Science* 188 (1975): 633–43.

Hulse, Joseph H., and Spurgeon, David. "Triticale." *Scientific American* 231 (August 1974): 72–80.

International Board for Plant Genetic Resources. *Annual Report, 1975.* Rome: Food and Agriculture Organization, International Board for Plant Genetic Resources Secretariat, 1976.

International Board for Plant Genetic Resources. *Priorities among Crops and Regions.* Rome: Food and Agriculture Organization, International Board for Plant Genetic Resources Secretariat, 1976.
National Academy of Sciences. *World Food and Nutrition Study: The Potential Contributions of Research.* Washington, D.C.: National Academy of Sciences, 1977.
Wittwer, Sylvan H. "Maximum Production Capacity of Food Crops." *BioScience* 24 (1974): 216–24.
Wortman, Sterling. "Extending the Green Revolution." *World Development* 1 (December 1973): 45–51.
Wortman, Sterling. "International Agricultural Research Institutes: Their Unique Capabilities." In *Rice, Science, and Man: Papers Presented at the Tenth Anniversary Celebration of the International Rice Research Institute, April 20 and 21, 1972.* Los Baños, Philippines: International Rice Research Institute, 1972.

THE TRAINING NETWORK
Phillips, H. M. *Higher Education: Cooperation with Developing Countries. An Analysis of the Sources and Amounts of Funding for Educational Assistance, and of the Distribution of Those Monies—Geographically and by Level of Education.* Working Paper. New York: Rockefeller Foundation, February 1976.

NEW FORMS OF COOPERATION
Consultative Group on International Agricultural Research. *International Research in Agriculture.* New York: Consultative Group on International Agricultural Research, 1974.
International Agricultural Development Service. *First Report, 1976.* New York: International Agricultural Development Service, [1977].
McLaughlin, Martin M. *World Food Insecurity: Has Anything Happened Since Rome?* Communiqué on Development Issues No. 27. Washington, D.C.: Overseas Development Council, 1975.
"New Donors Support Agricultural Centers." *RF Illustrated* 2 (March 1976): 1, 8.
U.S. Senate. *The United States, FAO, and World Food Politics: U.S. Relations with an International Food Organization. A Staff Report.* Prepared for the Select Committee on Nutrition and Human Needs, U.S. Senate. Washington, D.C.: U.S. Government Printing Office, June 1976.

CHAPTER 7

New focus on food crops and animals

Introduction

HUMANS DERIVE food directly from many crops and animals and indirectly from plants such as pasture grasses. The food crops and animals grown by the greatest number of farmers and contributing most to the world food supply are listed in Tables 7.1 and 7.2.

During recent decades, science has increasingly modified farming. That is, intensive agriculture is now based on the application of scientific principles to growing and marketing these crops and animals. The purposes of this chapter are to show the depth of research required to increase production of food in the tropics and subtropics, to suggest how recent such research efforts are, to describe the types of research that are under way, and to indicate some potential breakthroughs.

The decades of neglect

In low-income countries most food crops and animal species are produced by subsistence farmers who often live in remote areas. These farmers use traditional practices to eke out meager harvests on impoverished soils.

Cash crops, such as bananas, cotton, pineapples, rubber, tea, and sugarcane, have for decades received substantial attention from companies engaged in international trade as well as from governments which depended on them for foreign exchange. There were clear incentives to increase output and to seek better yields through research, fertilization, irrigation, and disease and pest control. Wherever management was skillful, relatively high yields were obtained.

But the basic food crops and animal species were neglected until re-

Table 7.1. Major food crops in developing market economies by region, 1973–75 averages

Food crop	Area harvested (million ha)					
	Africa	Latin America	Near East	Far East	Total for developing economies	World total
Cereal						
Rice	3.7	6.6	1.2	83.0	94.4	137.4
Wheat	6.1	8.9	20.8	25.3	61.1	224.1
Maize	11.7	25.6	1.9	14.7	54.0	149.1
Sorghum	10.7	4.4	3.8	17.1	36.0	43.3
Millets	14.4	0.2	1.6	20.8	37.0	70.4
Barley	4.1	1.3	6.2	3.8	15.4	89.1
Oats	0.1	0.6	0.3	—	1.0	31.5
Rye	—	0.5	0.6	—	1.1	16.0
Food legumes						
Soybeans	0.2	5.6	—	1.3	7.2	45.3
Dry beans	2.9	6.6	0.2	9.2	18.9	24.9
Groundnuts	5.5	1.0	0.9	8.5	15.8	19.1
Dry peas	0.4	0.1	—	0.8	1.4	10.6
Broad beans	0.5	0.3	0.2	—	1.0	5.4
Chickpeas	0.6	0.3	0.3	8.6	9.7	10.0
Pigeon peas	0.1	—	—	2.6	2.8	2.8
Cowpeas	4.8	—	—	—	4.9	4.9
Root and tuber crops						
Potatoes	0.3	1.0	0.3	0.8	2.5	21.9
Sweet potatoes	0.9	0.4	—	1.0	2.4	14.7
Cassava	5.7	2.6	0.2	2.6	11.2	11.3
Yams	1.9	—	—	—	2.1	2.1
Other crops						
Bananas	0.7	1.2	—	0.8	2.8	2.9
Sugarcane	0.5	5.8	0.1	4.4	10.8	12.2

Source: FAO, *Production Yearbook 1975.*

cently, for several reasons. First, food production could be expanded in most countries by increasing the area planted or grazed. Intensive production was less economical. Critical population pressure on limited land area is a phenomenon of recent decades.

Second, until the early 1960s, in many developing countries the cost of fertilizers was high relative to the value of basic food crops, and means of fertilizer distribution were not well established. In the mid-1960s, however, costs declined with improvements in manufacturing and delivery processes, and it became feasible to use fertilizers on food crops together with chemical control of diseases and pests and often with irrigation. With the introduction of fertilizer-responsive, high-yielding varieties, fertilizer use on food crops is now spreading through the developing world.

Table 7.2. Livestock in developing market economies by region, 1973–75 averages

	Number (millions)				
Livestock	Africa	Latin America	Near East	Far East	Total for developing economies	World total
Cattle	119.4	252.5	43.4	255.1	671	1,175
Buffalo	—	0.2	3.7	93.5	97	130
Sheep	98.1	123.7	138.1	64.8	425	1,029
Goats	102.0	41.0	60.3	107.0	310	399
Swine	6.4	68.7	0.3	38.8	116	665
Chickens	390.7	676.2	191.8	574.7	1,836	5,925

Source: FAO, *Production Yearbook 1975.*

Third, research on most basic food crops and livestock (and the pastures on which cattle are produced) has been the responsibility of the public sector—as it has been in the developed countries. But the technical services of the developing countries have commonly been weak, so their impact on production of food crops and animal species has been slight.

Fourth, until the late 1960s it was the unspoken policy of the U.S. and Canada to avoid helping other nations directly with crops which might compete in world trade with North American surpluses. The Communist Bloc still has not become substantially engaged in assisting others technically with food production.

Finally, a major reason for the scientific neglect of food crops and animals in the developing countries has been the widely held belief that the technology of the temperate-climate countries could simply be transferred to the developing countries—that what was needed was more investment in agriculture or changes in policies. Much technology is transferable, but the biological components—the varieties, disease and pest control measures, and related practices—generally are not.[1]

---

[1] Beginning in 1943, scientists of Mexico and The Rockefeller Foundation cooperated in the improvement of Mexico's basic food crops, with initial emphasis on maize and wheat (Chapter 8). From that cooperative program in Mexico, high-yielding varieties of wheat were sent to India and Pakistan in the early 1960s. These semidwarf types were found to be directly usable in some areas and added substantially to output in the ensuing years. This could be interpreted as an example of direct transferability, even of biological components—an exception to the rule. However, Indian scientists had to tailor agronomic practices for these wheats to their own conditions. And after the initial wave, they had to breed varieties which were resistant to local disease strains and more acceptable to consumers. Now all wheat varieties grown in India have been developed by Indian scientists.

The current status of agricultural technology

In part as a result of the decades of neglect, crop and animal productivity and farm income on most farms in developing countries are extremely low. For example, FAO assembles maize yield figures for 141 countries. The highest yield reported (1973–75 average) was 7,300 kg/ha in New Zealand. The U.S. average was 5,200 kg/ha. Nine other countries exceeded 5,000 kg/ha. Yet in 114 countries, most of which produce maize for human food rather than animal feed, average yields were less than 3,000 kg/ha. Moreover, 80 of these countries reported average yields of under 1,500 kg/ha. Yields of most other food crops are equally dismal, as are production data for livestock.

These statistics indicate a low level of agricultural productivity in the developing world. They also reveal the potential for increasing production. *This production gap represents a tremendous food reserve on which governments must now attempt to call* (Table 7.3).

Inadequate agricultural technology, particularly the biological components, has been a barrier to increased agricultural productivity in the developing regions. When crop varieties will not respond to intensive management by yielding more, or when animal production is inhibited by deficiencies of minerals in pastures or the prevalence of uncontrolled diseases, there often is little that can be done to stimulate output by

Table 7.3. Average and record yields, 1975

Food	Average yield		World record yield
	Developing countries	U.S.	
Maize (kg/ha)	1,325	5,398	21,216
Wheat (kg/ha)	1,295	2,085	14,526
Soybeans (kg/ha)	1,544	1,883	7,398
Sorghum (kg/ha)	867	3,295	21,521
Oats (kg/ha)	1,199	1,722	10,617
Barley (kg/ha)	1,154	2,367	11,405
Potatoes (kg/ha)	9,129	26,632	94,153
Milk (kg/cow)	624	4,725	22,500
Eggs (per hen)	—	230	365
Cassava (kg/ha)	9,113	—	60,000
Rice (kg/ha/crop/112 days)	—	2,500	14,400
Sugarcane (kg/ha/year)	—	50,000	150,000
Sugarbeets (kg/ha/year)	—	50,000	120,000

Source: Adapted from Marylin Chou, David P. Harmon, Jr., Herman Kahn, and Sylvan Wittwer, *World Food Prospects and Agricultural Potential.*

Table 7.4. Estimated status of international food crop research efforts

Crop	Asia Southeast	Asia South	Asia East	Near East/North Africa
Rice				
Irrigated/controlled	S	S	S	S
Irrigated/casual	I	I	I	—
Rainfed (water-bunded)	W	W	I	—
Upland (no bunds)	W	W	—	—
Deepwater	W	W	—	—
Wheat				
Irrigated	—	S	—	S
Rainfed spring	—	I	—	I
Rainfed winter	—	—	I	W
Durum	—	I	—	W
Maize				
Irrigated	—	S	—	W
Rainfed/low altitude	W	W	W	W
Rainfed/intermediate/high altitude	W	W	—	—
Sorghum				
Rainfed/humid	W	W	W	W
Rainfed/semi-arid	W	W	W	W
Millets				
Pennisetum	W	W	—	W
Eleusine	—	W	—	—
Food legumes				
Dry beans	W	W	W	W
Cowpeas	W	W	W	—
Chickpeas	W	W	W	W
Pigeon peas	—	W	—	—
Dry broad beans	—	—	?	W
Leguminous oilseeds				
Peanuts	W	W	?	—
Soybeans	W	W	I	—
Starchy crops				
Cassava	W	W	W	—
Yams, sweet potatoes	W	W	I	I
White potatoes	—	W	W	I

Source: Ralph W. Cummings, Jr., *Food Crops in the Low Income Countries: The State of Present and Expected Agricultural Research and Technology.*

manipulation of prices, provision of credit, or organization of programs by extension services. Where technology is adequate, production may be able to keep pace with demand. This has prompted growing support for the three-component interlocking international agricultural research system (described in Chapter 6), which involves national research and production programs of developing countries, international agricultural institutes, and research organizations and laboratories in developed countries.

Africa				Latin America		
Savanna	Sahel	Forest	Highlands	Tropical	Temperate	Andean
I	—	I	W	S	S	—
—	—	W	W	I	I	—
—	—	W	—	W	—	—
—	—	W	W	W	—	—
—	—	W	—	W	—	—
W	—	W	—	—	S	I
—	—	W	I	—	I	I
—	—	—	—	—	I	W
W	—	—	—	—	I	W
—	—	—	—	I	I	—
W	W	W	W	W	I	—
W	W	I	W	W	I	I
W	—	W	W	W	I	—
W	—	W	W	W	I	—
W	W	W	W	—	—	—
—	—	—	W	—	—	—
—	—	—	W	W	W	W
W	W	W	—	W	—	—
W	—	—	—	—	—	W
W	—	—	—	W	—	—
—	—	—	—	W	—	W
I	—	I	W	W	I	—
W	—	W	W	W	I	—
—	—	W	W	W	W	W
W	?	W	W	W	W	—
—	—	—	W	—	W	I

Note: S = strong; I = intermediate; W = weak; ? = insufficient information to guess; — = crop of little economic importance in area.

But how adequate is existing and expected agricultural technology, region by region, crop by crop, animal by animal? Ratings made by international agricultural specialists in the mid-1970s are given in Table 7.4. For simplicity, 11 regions and 16 food crops were chosen, some with subdivisions. These choices undoubtedly do injustice to the wide range of agro-climatic and cultural conditions throughout the world, but they give a manageable set of situations to evaluate.

Where research efforts were classified as "strong," as for irrigated rice in Asia, Near East–North Africa, and Latin America, it was considered that major problems were receiving attention by competent scientists in international centers or national programs and that nations of these regions had places to turn to for help with technical problems and for training their personnel. An "intermediate" rating indicated that considerable progress had been made in generating and applying technology and in developing international training programs. A rating of "weak" indicated that either international research and training activities were absent or were so new that needs of nations were only beginning to be satisfied.

In the following sections the activities of centers of international research and training are reviewed and the status of technology as applied to major food commodities is discussed. To emphasize the complexity of the research required, special attention is given to two major cereals—rice and wheat—and to two major root crops—cassava and potatoes. Briefer descriptions are given of other important commodities.

Rice

There are a number of types and cultures of rice (*Oryza sativa*), each of which requires a somewhat different research approach. An understanding of the fundamental differences reveals some of the problems which have limited the spread of high-yield technology.

"JAPONICA" AND "INDICA" TYPES

The predominant type of rice grown in Japan, northern China, and Korea has been the "japonica," which is characterized by short, relatively sticky grain and by lack of seed dormancy. In the tropics the generally preferred type of rice is the "indica," which is characterized by long, relatively dry grain and several weeks of seed dormancy, which prevents sprouting of seed in the panicle in the field during the often rainy harvest periods.

IRRIGATED, RAINFED, UPLAND, AND DEEPWATER CULTURES

Like most crops, rice generally yields best under irrigation. If water is not a limiting factor in production, maximum performance is obtained with optimum combinations of variety, fertilizer use, and insect control. In the tropics up to three crops per year can be obtained with varieties that mature in 3–4 months.

Nonirrigated rice production is of two general types. First, throughout much of Asia, rice lands are bunded to trap rainwater and keep the soil submerged all or part of the growing season. For such rainfed rice, planting dates vary according to the onset of heavy rains, so research on this type of culture is complicated. Second, upland rice—rice grown in conventional fields without bunds—can be found in Africa, Asia, and Latin America. Uncertainty about the amount and distribution of water makes the use of fertilizers or pesticides risky and affects planting dates. Weed control is particularly difficult in upland rice.

Deepwater rice culture occurs in the flood plains of Thailand, Bangladesh, and India, where water may range from 0.5 to 6.0 meters in depth during the growing season (Fig. 7.1). In such areas rice varieties have evolved with stems that can elongate several centimeters per day as the water rises, thereby keeping some leaves above the water's surface.

Scientists at the International Rice Research Institute have estimated the area in South and Southeast Asia devoted to each type of rice culture

Fig. 7.1.   The world's rice land classified by water regimes and predominant rice types

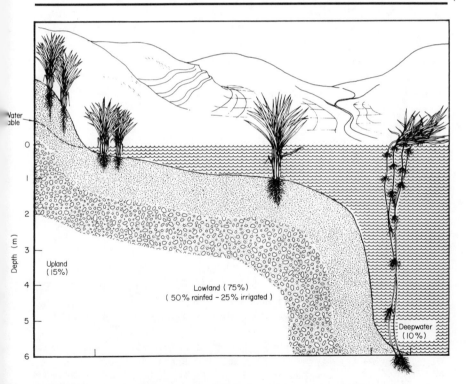

Source: J. C. O'Toole and T. T. Chang. *Drought and Rice Improvement in Perspective.*

and the contribution of each to total production in the early 1970s as follows:

Culture	Crop area (%)	Production (%)
Irrigated	33	48
Rainfed	47	40
Upland	10	5
Deepwater	10	7

In Africa perhaps 80 percent of the rice is grown under upland conditions. In Latin America a substantial proportion of rice is upland, especially in Brazil.

ESTABLISHMENT OF THE INTERNATIONAL RICE RESEARCH INSTITUTE

In the early postwar period several efforts were made to improve rice productivity in the tropics. For example, India established its Central Rice Research Institute in 1946. An effective national research program was developed in Taiwan. FAO supported efforts to cross indica and japonica rice types. However, field problems received little attention from the scientists who had the best training and ability. The potential for higher yields under tropical conditions was severely limited.

The experience of the joint Mexican/Rockefeller Foundation effort with wheat demonstrated the results that might be expected from a directed, multidisciplinary assault aimed at raising crop yields (Chapter 8). In 1959 the Ford and Rockefeller foundations decided to establish an international research institute for rice. Robert F. Chandler, Jr., was dispatched to Manila to conclude arrangements with the government of the Philippines. The International Rice Research Institute (IRRI) was incorporated in early 1960 and Chandler was designated its first director. Bids for construction of its facilities, to occupy an 80-hectare tract adjacent to the University of the Philippines College of Agriculture, were received in January 1961. One year later, the US$7 million research center was completed and occupied by its international staff.

Some of the world's finest young scientists were recruited.[2] They were men with a mission and in a hurry. Their goal was to find ways to increase rice yields and to train scientists for national programs in Asia. The problems were many. When in late 1962 it was agreed that on the basis of the first year's work a 3-day staff conference should be held to

[2] Included were P. R. Jennings (U.S.) and T. T. Chang (Taiwan) in plant breeding and genetics, S. H. Ou (Taiwan) in plant pathology, Mano Pathak (India) in entomology, F. N. Ponnamperuma (Ceylon) in soil chemistry, James Moomaw (U.S.) and S. K. de Datta (India) in agronomy, Akira Tanaka (Japan) and Benito Vergara (Philippines) in physiology, Takashi Akazawa (Japan) and Bienvenido Juliano (Philippines) in chemistry, and Vernon Ruttan (U.S.) in economics.

Why new types of tropical rice were needed

When closely planted and treated with nitrogen fertilizer in early tests at IRRI, the available tropical indica rice varieties grew excessively tall (sometimes to 2 meters) and leafy, and fell over (lodged) long before harvest, often reducing yields. There appeared to be no way to raise yields of existing tropical indicas substantially through good management.

The Japanese varieties had multiple defects when grown in the tropics. Their sensitivity to daylength and temperature often caused them to flower entirely too soon or too late, depending on the time of sowing. They had the short, sticky grain, which is not popular in tropical countries. They lacked seed dormancy, and their seed sprouted in the panicle when harvest periods were rainy. They lacked resistance to the diseases and insect pests prevalent in the tropics. While meeting the needs of Japan, they were of little use in the tropics.

U.S. varieties produced too few tillers for a system involving transplanting.

Materials from Taiwan fared better. In fact, some of the earliest high-performing varieties at IRRI were Tainan-8 and Chianung 242, both of which were unfortunately of the japonica type. One dwarf indica, Taichung (Native) 1, gave exceptionally high yields, but was highly susceptible to some diseases. These materials allowed the IRRI staff to proceed immediately with work on disease and insect control and on agronomic and physiological studies while the plant breeders attempted to create new, high-yielding varieties for the tropics. The varieties from Taiwan were planted on sizeable areas in India in the mid-1960s.

create an institute research strategy, the staff preferred to devote a weekend to it—starting at 7:00 o'clock on a Friday night—rather than lose 3 days of work in the fields and laboratories. They worked as a multidisciplinary team. They were selected in part because of their belief in the team system. With only one person per discipline, there was no opportunity for departmentalization.

Varietal development. IRRI's scientists systematically set out to develop the required varieties. Prior research in Japan suggested to them that short, stiff-strawed rice varieties were needed for the tropics—varieties which would respond to high levels of fertilizer application by producing more grain rather than more foliage. It was decided that the varieties should have narrow, erect leaves to allow maximum light penetration into the canopy. Other characteristics sought included long, relatively slender grains; dormancy to prevent sprouting of the grain in the panicle during a rainy harvest season; insensitivity to daylength, which would permit varieties to mature in a fixed period, regardless of the date of planting; earlier maturity; and resistance to blast and other diseases.

As a first move, the plant breeders brought together a collection of 10,000 of the world's varieties and strains. Not a single one met all the requirements specified by the plant breeders.

IRRI's scientists therefore embarked on a major rice breeding program. Fortunately, among the varieties from Taiwan, they found some which carried a recessive gene for dwarfness. Through an intensive breeding program, they developed a series of short, stiff-strawed varieties into which the desired characteristics were gradually incorporated.

IR8 was the first of several varieties released by IRRI and cooperating national programs. This variety and its many successors of similar plant type responded to high rates of fertilizer application by producing more grain rather than excess straw (Fig. 7.2). Because varieties such as IR8 are insensitive to daylength, they are widely adapted; excellent yields have been reported from many areas throughout the world. The initial varieties represented what might be called the first phase of the research program—a focus on higher yields. A second phase, represented by IR20

Fig. 7.2.   Response of four rice varieties to nitrogen, 1966 dry season, the Philippines

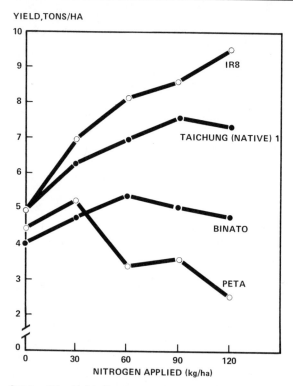

Source: "Ten Metric Tons per Hectare—High Dry Season Yields," *IRRI Reporter.*

High-yielding varieties and high rates of fertilizer

Some observers suggest that high yields and high-yielding rice varieties *require* use of higher levels of fertilizer. Others say that if high-yielding varieties are grown without use of fertilizers, they will yield less than the indigenous varieties they replace. Experience with high-yielding varieties which efficiently convert light, nutrients, and water to harvestable product generally supports the following observations:

- The high-yielding varieties usually perform as well at low levels of fertility as the indigenous varieties (Fig. 7.2).
- When conditions of low light intensity or unfavorable temperatures prevail (as with heavy cloud cover during the wet season), the response of high-yielding varieties to increased levels of nitrogen fertilizer may not be great.
- When conditions are favorable for high productivity, nitrogen-responsive varieties such as IR8 may yield up to 10,000 kg/ha in 130–140 days, whereas traditional varieties such as Peta seldom yield in excess of 6,000 kg/ha, even under the most favorable circumstances. The new varieties do not *require* more fertilizer; they simply use it much more efficiently for grain production.
- The high-yielding varieties themselves are not responsible for high yields; rather, they make it possible for other practices such as close spacing, high levels of fertilizer application, and weed and insect control to be used effectively and profitably.

and IR22, focused on grain quality—an attempt to produce longer, slender grains which would bring higher prices in the market. The current phase, one which IRRI and the cooperating national programs are now deeply into, is to incorporate broad-based disease and insect resistance into plants for more stable high yields while giving continuing attention to yield and grain quality.

More than 30,000 strains are now maintained in the IRRI germ plasm collection. They are systematically screened to identify characteristics that can be used in breeding for resistance to diseases, resistance to insects, high protein levels, tolerance to drought, tolerance to toxic soils, tolerance to deep water, and tolerance to cold. This supply of germ plasm is available as a basic research resource to scientists anywhere.

Fertilizer response. Figure 7.2 shows that with no fertilizer (that is, with only the soil's residual fertility) the better traditional and high-yielding varieties differ little in performance. Had IRRI's scientists chosen to work only at the lower levels of fertility, IR8 and Taichung (Native) 1 would not have demonstrated their unique ability to turn nutrients into grain.

Diseases. Blast, caused by *Pyricularia oryzae*, is one of the most important diseases of rice. There are many strains (physiological races) of the organism, to which individual lines or varieties of rice differ in reaction. To complicate the matter, the high levels of nitrogen fertilization needed for high yields predispose rice to attack by the organism.

Pathologists at IRRI cooperated with other Asian scientists in determining the distribution and the virulence of the many races of *Pyricularia* which exist in the tropics. With the plant breeders they identified the resistance of new experimental varieties to the prevalent races. In a massive field program using high levels of nitrogen fertilizer, they then tested thousands of new experimental rice varieties against the prevalent races. As a result, some blast resistance has now been incorporated into newer varieties.

At the time IRRI was formed, the importance of viral diseases was not recognized in the tropics, and no provision was made for a virologist on the staff. But shortly thereafter yields were drastically reduced at IRRI by a then-unknown disease which, because of its pattern of attack, appeared to be a virus.

With the assistance of experts from Japan, it was found that in fact four viral diseases were involved. Efforts were then initiated to control each virus disease through varietal resistance to the virus or the insect, through chemical control of the insect vector, or both.

Insects. Although some insects can drastically reduce rice yield, in the early 1960s chemical control had not been widely adopted. With low yields, insects could reduce output by only a few hundred kilograms per hectare. This was a substantial loss if considered as a percentage of the grain harvest, but saving a few hundred kilograms of rice would not pay for the insecticides and their application. On the other hand, at potential yields of 5,000 kg/ha or more, insects, if uncontrolled, could reduce yields by 2,000 kg/ha. Thus, under intensive production conditions, use of insecticides can pay handsomely.

Control of the stem borer, one of the major insects causing direct damage, is complicated by the life history of the insect. The moths lay eggs on the leaves and, within a few hours after hatching, the larvae descend from the leaves and bore into the stem. There is only a short period in the life of each larva when it can be reached by contact insecticides. The hatching process is continuous, and it is difficult to protect a crop with a few insecticide applications because they are washed off during frequent rains. Scientists have therefore developed safe techniques for the tropics involving application of systemic insecticides to the irrigation water, where they are absorbed by the plant; some now give acceptable control at reasonable cost.

The experiments at IRRI have demonstrated the need to involve highly competent economic entomologists in tropical agricultural research teams.

Weeds. Flood waters eliminate some weeds and retard growth of others in irrigated rice. Still, supplementary control is needed. Weeds as well as rice respond to fertilizer, and, once established, compete with the crop—experiments with flooded rice at IRRI indicate additional yields of 500–1,500 kg/ha as a result of weeding alone.

Whether to weed by hand or with chemicals—that is, with herbicides—is a matter of economics. IRRI research shows that two hand weedings give significantly higher yields than the preemergence application of granules of 2,4-D, the most popular herbicide in the Philippines. But the 2,4-D treatment costs less than even one hand weeding, and at least two hand weedings are necessary to adequately remove weeds. The more selective herbicides, such as butaclor or benthiocarb, cost three or more times as much as 2,4-D and, under most conditions, are more expensive than hand weeding.[3] Weed control does not need to be all chemical or wholly performed by hand. Good land preparation, multiple cropping, and straight-row planting, with subsequent use of the rotary weeder, all aid in weed control.

Weeding under upland conditions is much more difficult. Some weed species that flourish under upland conditions, such as nut sedge (*Cyperus rotundus*), are difficult to control with chemicals. In early stages of growth (and it is essential to weed early), it is difficult to distinguish some of the grasses from rice. Hand weeding is slow (often being finished too late to be of benefit) and expensive. Effective weed control can increase yields of rice by as much as 2,000–3,000 kg/ha under upland conditions, thereby entirely changing the outlook for the crop.

IRRI is devoting considerable attention to improving weed control under upland conditions. The utility of herbicides in Asia will depend upon their effectiveness, their cost relative to the value of hand labor as judged by the farmer who must put in the time, and safety. The higher the potential yield, the higher the wage, and the greater the safety, the more likely it is that weed control will be achieved through herbicides. Therefore, several methods—hand, mechanical implements, biological aids, and chemicals—are being tested, separately and in combination. Integrated weed management systems, involving rotations of crops, also are being tested. Such systems are possible and practical for small farm-

---

[3] Ironically, water management and control of weeds has now made the perennial sedge *Scirpus maritimus* one of the most serious weed problems in lowland rice fields in Asia. When the farmer applies herbicides that control annual weeds, he creates conditions that are ideal for *Scirpus* and other perennial weeds to move into. Once established, they grow rapidly.

ers, but they will require rice varieties—probably of intermediate height, high tillering capacity, large total leaf area, and able to establish stands rapidly—that can compete with weeds.

Upland rice. The varieties for upland areas must be exceptionally tolerant to moisture stress. Research attention has been focused on this problem only recently.

Breeding lines previously selected from crosses between upland and semidwarf lines are being mass-screened at IRRI. The most promising selections are then tested in farmers' fields to permit observation of the differences in response to and recovery from dry periods. Screening is also being carried out in greenhouses and in the laboratory under controlled moisture conditions. The characteristics of drought-tolerant varieties are being recorded. Agronomic practices are receiving increasing attention.

Upland rice is also becoming a high priority of several national programs with which IRRI is cooperating.

Cooperative testing. The International Rice Testing Program links IRRI with national programs. Its principal objectives are to interchange superior germ plasm among rice scientists, to allow scientists to have their materials evaluated under diverse conditions, to identify varieties that are broadly resistant to diseases, insects, and other stresses, and to evaluate the genetic variation in pathogens and insects. Table 7.5 lists some of the international cooperative trials now under way.

Several other international networks of cooperative research have been

Table 7.5. International cooperative trials coordinated by IRRI, 1975

Trial	Year started	No. of countries cooperating
Upland Rice Observational Nursery	1975	9
Upland Rice Yield Nursery	1974	5
Rice Salinity Tolerance Observational Nursery	1975	3
Rice Cold Tolerance Nursery	1975	12
Rice Observation Nursery	1974	11
Rice Yield Nursery—Early (120 days or less)	1973	8
Rice Yield Nursery—Medium (more than 120 days)	1973	6
Rice Blast Nursery (originated by FAO)	1961	13
Rice Sheath Blight Nursery	1973	9
Rice Tungro Nursery	1975	5
Rice Brown Planthopper Nursery	1975	5
Rice Gall Midge Nursery	1973	4

Source: International Rice Research Institute.

established to identify problems slowing adoption of improved varieties and technology (International Agro-Economic Network); to identify superior intensive farming schemes involving rice and other crops, especially for the small farmer (International Cropping Systems Network); and to concentrate on design and manufacture of machinery appropriate for land preparation, seeding, threshing, and drying on small rice farms (Farm Machinery Development Network).

NATIONAL RESEARCH PROGRAMS

Several national rice programs in Asia are now turning out rice varieties and technologies which are contributing significantly to production. Among the stronger research programs are those of the Philippines, which cooperates closely with IRRI; India, which has developed varietal resistance to gall midge and to tungro virus and which has an active deepwater program from which varieties have already been released; Bangladesh, which has a research institute to work on rice (Chapter 12); South Korea, which has developed new cold tolerant varieties; Thailand, which has become a center of research in deepwater rice; and Indonesia, Malaysia, and Sri Lanka.

AFRICA

Several organizations conduct rice research in Africa. The International Institute of Tropical Agriculture, located in Nigeria, operates a rice program in cooperation with IRRI. It is carrying out basic studies under upland conditions, a major need for that continent. In addition, 14 tropical countries are working together in the West Africa Rice Development Association.

LATIN AMERICA

The International Center of Tropical Agriculture (CIAT), located in Colombia, is conducting research on rice in Latin America in cooperation with IRRI and national programs. Several varieties have been named and released by CIAT and its cooperative national partner, the Instituto Colombiano Agropecuario (Chapter 8). Investigations are carried out in agronomy, pathology (particularly attempting to incorporate generalized blast resistance into the varieties grown on large areas under upland conditions), entomology, weed control, agricultural engineering, and economics.

Wheat

While often referred to as a single crop, "wheat" embraces a complex of species and types. Common or bread wheat (*Triticum aestivum*) is the most important. Because of its gluten content, it is suitable for leavened breads. There are gradations in texture from hard, higher-protein classes, which are highly water absorbent, to softer, lower-protein classes (pastries, French-type breads).

Most of the wheat in the developing world is spring wheat, which grows where the weather is generally mild. Wheat requires cool weather only through the tillering stage. Much of the spring wheat crop is irrigated, especially in India, Pakistan, and Mexico.

Winter wheat production predominates in regions where winters are too cold for most other crops but not cold enough to kill wheat. It is planted in the autumn, lies under a blanket of snow in the winter, and is harvested early the following summer.

Second in importance is the hard-grained durum wheat (*Triticum durum*), used for such products as spaghetti, macaroni, and "arab bread." Durum wheats are grown primarily in Mediterranean nations and in Argentina and Chile.

The other cultivated species are of lesser importance and receive little scientific attention.

SPRING WHEAT

Scientific work on wheat has a long history in developed nations. And some low-income countries such as India maintained wheat improvement programs before the 1960s (although increases in production potential were limited).

In Japan intensified agricultural research began in the 1920s (Chapter 8). Mounting food needs put pressure on the small land area available. Since Japan was one of the first countries to use high levels of nitrogen fertilizer, its scientists were confronted by the severe lodging of crops under intensive management. Out of their work came the first semidwarf varieties, the now famous "Norin" varieties. Following World War II, these short, stiff-strawed, lodging-resistant types were introduced into breeding programs in the Pacific Northwest of the U.S. Concurrently, an expanded wheat program, developed in the Ministry of Agriculture of Mexico with assistance from scientists of The Rockefeller Foundation, particularly Dr. Norman Borlaug and his co-workers, also exploited the potential superiority of the short-strawed characteristics of the Norin wheats.

In 1966, the International Maize and Wheat Improvement Center CIMMYT was organized in Mexico, borrowing from the experiences of IRRI, which in turn had benefited from earlier work in Mexico. CIMMYT has now assumed major international responsibility for wheat research, working in cooperation with the International Center for Agricultural Research in Dry Areas in the Mideast.

The yield plateau. Over the years, steady progress was made in Mexico · in shortening the straw and increasing the yielding ability of the spring bread wheats. However, a new problem has emerged: an apparent yield plateau of about 8,000 kg/ha (Fig. 7.3). Breaking that yield barrier is a challenge to wheat scientists. Still, the yield potential of the varieties which have been released to date is well beyond what is being achieved in farmers' fields; there is a large, unexploited capacity for yield increases at the farm level through improved cultural practices where permitted by economic considerations.

Minimizing disease damage. The plant breeders' battles with rusts and other diseases are perennial ones. The standard approach has been to identify genes in the crop for resistance to known races of the micro-organisms in each region, and to attempt to incorporate them into varieties having other desired characteristics. This is a slow, expensive, and often frustrating process. Several new techniques are being developed.

One is the use of "slow-rusting" gene complexes, which apparently remain effective far longer than do single, major genes for resistance, despite changes in the rusts. For example, the variety Yaqui-50 has been relatively unaffected by changes in rusts for decades. By rating plants for

Fig. 7.3. Pushing back the yield barrier: Average yield of Mexican wheat varieties at Ciudad Obregon, Mexico, under optimum management and in the absence of disease

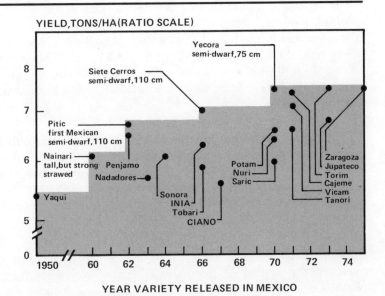

Source: International Maize and Wheat Improvement Center, *CIMMYT Review 1976.*

resistance three times per growing season, pathologists believe they can identify the slow-rusting lines.

Another technique is the "multiline variety" being developed by CIMMYT and collaborating national programs using cross 8156 (otherwise known as Siete Cerros) as the basic germ plasm. This popular variety, which in 1973 was grown on 13 million hectares worldwide, is still among the highest-yielding entries in international spring wheat trials. CIMMYT is testing over 200 strains of the 8156 multiline in different localities so that, based on their performance in each region, composites of the best lines can be made, multiplied locally, and released to farmers. Although genetically different in their resistance to rust, the lines appear to be similar. As certain lines become susceptible, they are replaced by others with resistance. In irrigated trials in Mexico in 1974–75, seven 8156 multiline composites yielded from 7,300 to 9,400 kg/ha, equal to or better than the conventional Siete Cerros and other commercial varieties.

A third technique is the early warning system being developed by CIMMYT plant pathologists in cooperation with national agencies in North Africa, the Mideast, and South Asia. It should soon be able to give plant breeders 2 or 3 years' notice of the buildup of new races in the region, together with reports on the susceptibility of commercial and experimental varieties.

Wheat for the humid tropics. Spurred by the recent cereal shortages and higher prices, scientists have been challenged by the possibility of growing wheat in the humid tropics. In 1974, CIMMYT began screening wheat lines on the humid Gulf Coast of Mexico. Siete Cerros grows reasonably well there in the absence of disease, but is severely damaged by bacterial diseases. Some sources of resistance have been identified, but many problems remain.

Tolerance to aluminum toxicity. Large areas of tropical soils have concentrations of aluminum which are toxic to most wheat varieties. Some relatively low-yielding, tall Brazilian varieties are tolerant. Since 1974, Brazilian and CIMMYT scientists have been cooperating in efforts to combine this tolerance with the desirable qualities of the Mexican varieties.

International cooperative field trials. For spring wheat, CIMMYT coordinates a system of international trials involving advanced germ plasm. Cooperating scientists in any country are encouraged to select, name, and release any materials that perform well for them, as well as to submit their own lines to international evaluation. Any nation may participate in this testing program, which consists of nine trials and nurseries. In 1976, seed for 655 such bread wheat tests were distributed by CIMMYT to cooperators in 95 countries: 21 in Latin America, 21 in Africa, 11 in the Mideast, 15 in Asia and Oceania, 25 in Europe and the U.S.S.R., and 2 in North America.

WINTER WHEAT

The most comprehensive winter wheat research programs are carried out in the U.S., U.S.S.R., Eastern Europe, and Turkey.

In 1968 the International Winter Wheat Performance Nursery was organized by the Nebraska Agricultural Experiment Station and the U.S. Department of Agriculture, with the cooperation of FAO and CIMMYT. Each year, the seed of 30 important varieties is shipped to cooperating institutions which conduct uniform field experiments, sending data back to Nebraska for summary. In 1973 a fifth such nursery was conducted at 52 locations in 31 countries, and in 1976 a detailed report of the results was published. Six of the varieties were from the U.S., 10 were from Western Europe, 8 were from Eastern Europe, 3 were from Latin America, and 1 each were from Japan, Turkey, and the U.S.S.R. Such cooperative work, spanning continents and ideologies, permits comparison of progress, the exchange of germ plasm, and an understanding of the range of adaptation of these biological materials.

In the late 1960s, Turkey undertook to strengthen its national wheat program with the cooperation of several foreign organizations (Chapter 8). Introduced varieties and new practices were having a substantial impact on spring wheat production in the coastal areas. Turkish leaders concluded that winter wheat production, concentrated in the Anatolian Plateau, could be increased substantially if a coordinated national campaign were launched. Major gains in yield in winter wheat areas would for the most part depend not on new varieties (good ones existed), but on methods of retaining soil moisture and controlling weeds in fallowed land. Oregon State University, CIMMYT, and the Rockefeller Foundation have assisted this program.

SPRING × WINTER WHEAT CROSSES

In 1968 a program was begun by CIMMYT, with support from the Rockefeller Foundation and in cooperation with Oregon State University, to cross spring and winter wheats to combine the more favorable characteristics of each group. Winter wheats have greater resistance to certain diseases, such as Septoria, and generally greater tolerance to low temperatures and drought than spring wheats. Spring wheats, however, are superior in response to nitrogen application, have better rust resistance, and have certain desirable bread-making qualities.

This program was expanded considerably in 1972, when it was found that by staggering sowing dates in the Valley of Toluca (2,600 meters above sea level) in Mexico, both types, winter wheat and spring wheat, would flower simultaneously, making large-scale crossing possible. By 1975, seeds of segregating populations of these crosses were being sent to cooperators at 100 locations, and the resulting experimental varieties were entered in worldwide yield trials for the first time in 1977.

DURUM WHEAT

Many of the problems of bread wheats in developing regions are shared by the durums, among them susceptibility to rusts and Septoria and narrow range of adaptation. But there were other weaknesses in the crop when CIMMYT expanded its work on durums in 1968.

First, virtually all varieties in the world durum collection were tall and had weak stems. Applications of nitrogen fertilizers induced severe lodging. Crosses of the tall durums with semidwarf bread wheats resulted in plants of low fertility— that is, many florets contained no grain. This troublesome linkage now has largely been overcome, and in the mid-1970s semidwarf durums with good yields were being named and released by Mexico.

Second, the durums were largely of the spring type, with relatively little tolerance to low temperatures. Winter durums are needed in some areas at high elevations. Breeders are now using selected winter wheat varieties and materials from the spring-winter wheat crossing program as parents in crossing programs.

Third, entirely vitreous (or hard) grain is desired in durums for manufacture of macaroni and spaghetti. But in developing countries, where durums are used for making such products as *couscous* or *chapatis*, macaroni quality is not required. Nevertheless, attention is being given to eliminating the poor grain characteristics found in the earlier dwarf durums.

Even though the durum breeding program was not officially initiated at CIMMYT until 1968, progress has been rapid. Better durum varieties now equal the better bread wheats in yield and have similar wide adaptation. By 1975, seven different types of international durum nurseries were being distributed to 47 nations—an indication of the growing interest in durums in the developing countries.

Barley

The opportunities for developing countries to exploit barley (*Hordeum vulgare*) are great, if only because the crop has been so neglected. Research on barley has been substantial in North America and Europe—

but not on barley as a human food. Barley produced in the industrial countries is primarily used in beer-making or as feed for cattle.

In 1972 CIMMYT began a barley research program. Wheat and barley production areas usually are contiguous, barely being grown at the drier margins of areas suitable for wheat. Research objectives for wheat and barley are generally similar—dwarf plants, stiff straw, short growth duration, disease resistance, and high and dependable yields. International testing techniques are similar, and in most countries wheat and barley research is handled by a single technical group.

Since 1972 considerable progress has been achieved in shortening the plant height of most strains selected for use in the breeding program, with a resulting substantial increase in potential productivity. Through CIMMYT's multiple-location research and testing system, wide adaptation (insensitivity to climatic variation) of the barleys is replacing the narrow geographic range characteristic of most local varieties.

Efforts are being made to develop new food barleys that have a reasonably high protein level, rather than the low protein level characteristic of malting varieties. Moreover, using the "hiproly" gene discovered in Sweden, attempts are under way to improve the nutritional quality of the protein through adjustment of amino acid balance.

Most barley varieties used for malting or feed have hulls which must be separated from the grain by pounding or soaking. A high proportion of the experimental lines at CIMMYT are already hull-less but have shortcomings in size and plumpness of grain.

An international search is under way for resistance to two of the more serious diseases, scald (*Rhynchosporium secalis*) and powdery mildew (*Erisyphye graminis*). Breeders in several countries are cooperating in this work; the experimental materials are being tested in many areas of the world.

Scientists at CIMMYT are projecting that the first barley varieties emanating from this worldwide cooperative effort will be ready for release by governments in 1980. Most will combine short, stiff-straw, naked (hull-less) kernels; moderate to good resistance to several diseases; wide adaptation; good protein levels and quality; and substantially increased yield potential. A range of maturities will be available.

Maize

Maize (*Zea mays*) is one of the world's most diverse crop species. Originating thousands of years ago in the tropics of Middle America in all probability, it spread far to the north and south in the Americas. Types evolved which were adapted to the highlands (at 3,000 meters or more, where 9–12 months may be required for maturity of the crop), to the humid tropical coasts, and to a wide assortment of intermediate conditions. Ear and grain type and texture vary tremendously, comprising the small-eared popcorns, the "sweet corns," the tropical flints of Asia and Africa, the Corn Belt dents of the U.S., the extremely tall, leafy tropical dents, and the soft, floury maizes of the Andean highlands, to name only a few. And, in addition, great variation occurs in seed color and length of growing period.

THE CIMMYT PROGRAM

During the first half of this century a remarkable scientific base was laid, mostly in the U.S., for the improvement of maize worldwide. But the crop received only scattered attention in the low-income regions of the world.

Shortly after initiation in 1943 of the cooperative agricultural program involving the Mexican Ministry of Agriculture and The Rockefeller Foundation, a series of surveys of the world's diverse germ plasm was begun. Over 300 names of races were discovered and named, of which authorities considered at least 100 to be authentic and distinct races. Perhaps no other crop with which scientists and governments must deal encompasses such a variety of grain types, texture, and color. CIMMYT is now providing international leadership for work in the tropics and subtropics.

New sources of germ plasm. During the past 30 years a collection of some 12,000 maize varieties or strains has been accumulated at CIMMYT through the cooperative action of scientists throughout the world. It is held in cold storage for use by scientists anywhere; each accession has been described, and data are stored in a computer for easy retrieval. To give national program personnel access to better genetic materials, CIMMYT scientists have now formed several dozen "pools" of germ plasm which consist of mixtures of better varieties for specific purposes. There are pools for the lowland tropics (early, medium, and late maturing versions of white and yellow, flint and dent types), for the tropical highlands, and for temperate climate areas. With the support of the United Nations Development Programme, most are also being converted to high-quality protein types through the incorporation of "opaque-2" genes.

Through a system of worldwide cooperative testing of breeding materials managed by CIMMYT, scientists in national programs each year may obtain progenies, experimental varieties, and elite experimental varieties for trial and further refinement in their own localities and for possible release to their own farmers. In addition, national program personnel have access to pools, to advanced populations developed for specific climates, and to international experimental variety trials. This system has been developed, for the most part, since 1970. In 1975, maize trials from CIMMYT were grown by collaborators in 19 countries in Latin America and the Caribbean; 9 in tropical Africa; 5 in the Mediterranean and Mideast; and 8 in Asia.

Recent advances. Several basic changes are being made in the maize plant by scientists at CIMMYT and cooperating countries which, individually and collectively, should significantly improve maize yields and quality in those countries that make use of them:

- *Wide adaptation.* Traditional maize varieties are narrowly adapted to agro-climatic niches as a result of sensitivity to daylength and temperature as well as long-term farmer selection for adaptation to local rainfall and temperature patterns, soil, and disease complexes. Since 1968, CIMMYT has been seeking wide adaptation of maize germ plasm. Mixtures of maize varieties have been grown and tested each year at selected locations worldwide. By 1976 several mixtures were producing seed in all climates. Only a start has been made, but true wide adaptation, if achieved, could greatly simplify the task of creating high-yielding maize varieties which would perform well in many ecological niches.
- *Reduced plant height.* Many tropical maize varieties are excessively tall and leafy and therefore lodge badly when grown densely and with high levels of nitrogen fertilizer. Through breeding, CIMMYT has reduced the height of varieties by 1.0–1.5 meters, bringing them down to about 2 meters. With shorter varieties, plant population and fertilizer levels can be increased, raising average yields by about 2,000 kg/ha.
- *Earlier maturity.* In many parts of the world, extremely early maturing maize varieties are needed for intensive multiple cropping systems. CIMMYT has achieved earliness in some of its advanced populations; however, additional increments must be sought in each nation concerned.
- *Improved plant architecture.* Tropical maize materials generally produce about as much dry matter per day as do the very high yielding types of the U.S. Corn Belt, but many tropical types are much less efficient in converting nutrients, water, and light energy to grain. Three characteristics which are believed to contribute to this inefficiency—excessive height, excess foliage above the ear, and large tassels—are being altered.
- *Enhanced protein quality.* Most maize grain contains 9–11 percent protein, but that protein is deficient in two amino acids, lysine and tryptophan. CIMMYT is converting many populations to "high-lysine" types that have a better amino acid balance, while simultaneously selecting for high yield, normal grain appearance, and resistance to

diseases and insects. Several promising experimental varieties are now in international field tests.

• *Crop resistance to diseases and insect pests.* International collaborative work is now under way on both breeding and pesticide treatments for the wide range of disease and insect problems which affect maize.

THE IITA, CIAT, AND ASIAN PROGRAMS

At the International Institute of Tropical Agriculture (IITA) in Nigeria, a scientific team is at work on problems of maize production in sub-Saharan Africa. High-yielding composites are under continuous development. Beginning in 1974, emphasis was placed on evaluation of materials under a wide range of plant stress and field management levels to achieve wider adaptation and stability of yield. Varieties and hybrids are now available from African national programs and IITA that are superior to those being used by farmers in various localities. Tillage practices, nutrient requirements, planting densities, insecticides, time of planting, weed control, use of maize in cropping systems, and development of genetic resistance also are receiving attention.

At CIAT (the International Center of Tropical Agriculture) in Colombia, a maize improvement program has been developed in cooperation with CIMMYT to serve the needs of South America, particularly the Andean region.

CIMMYT has also assigned two maize specialists to the International Crops Research Institute for the Semi-Arid Tropics in India to serve the Asian region.

ACTIVITIES OF COMMERCIAL COMPANIES

Several seed companies with international interests have been active in developing hybrids and in the production and sale of seed to farmers in the tropics and subtropics. A number of companies have been formed in the developing countries, on occasion as joint ventures with international companies, to develop hybrids and produce seed. Some, such as the Kenya Seed Company (Chapter 8), have been credited with major roles in the success of local production campaigns.

Sorghum

Sorghum, like maize, is a highly variable species. There are 16 identified races of sorghum, 14 of which apparently originated in northeast Africa, and all of which are now subsumed under the single species *Sorghum bicolor*. Among them are the grain sorghums, which differ greatly in type of head and in size, color, and texture of grain and include milo, kafir, hegari, feterita, guinea corn, the beer sorghums of East Africa, shallu, and kaoliang. There are also "sorgos," used principally for fodder, hay, silage, or syrup production; and the grass sorghums, including sudangrass, broomcorn, and several special-purpose types.

Sorghum is generally grown in areas where climatic risk is high. It is more tolerant than maize to drought (it can become dormant during periods of moisture stress), excess moisture, heat, and soil or water alkalinity.

INTERNATIONAL RESEARCH

The research problems with sorghum are formidable. Most of the farmers who grow sorghum have very low incomes, so the technology must be labor intensive. Since pesticides are costly and often difficult to obtain, genetic resistance to birds, insects, and diseases is a high priority. Development of short varieties which are relatively insensitive to daylength (maturing within a set period of time following planting) is necessary to allow sorghum to fit into various cropping patterns. In dry areas, varieties must be able to withstand drought and still yield adequately. In moist areas, varieties are needed which will withstand mold and produce high yields under cloudy, humid conditions. Incorporation of genes for high protein and lysine levels would improve the diets of low-income consumers, but production practices lag behind known technology in almost every region.

The International Crops Research Institute for the Semi-Arid Tropics (ICRISAT) in India has since 1974 served as a world center for research on sorghum. It has built a 17,000-item world collection on which to base breeding work. Cooperating centers are being developed in Senegal, Upper Volta, Nigeria, and Ethiopia. Cooperating centers may also be established in South America.

COOL-SEASON SORGHUM

Since 1958, plant breeders at CIMMYT in Mexico have operated a small program aimed at developing sorghums that would produce grain in the cool highlands of the country. In the early 1970s three varieties from East Africa were found that set seed at CIMMYT's headquarters— at an altitude of 2,200 meters. Since that time 150 lines have been obtained from Ethiopian highlands, most of which are cold tolerant. The sensitivity of the lines to daylength must be eliminated to make such varieties or their derivatives useful in other latitudes. Moreover, most African varieties are tall and tend to lodge, and their grains are opaque— all undesirable characteristics, but all of which scientists believe can be overcome.

In 1975 nearly 3,000 sorghum crosses were made at CIMMYT to combine cold tolerance with other characteristics needed in high-altitude sorghum. In the same year, sets of 380 cold-tolerant lines were sent to collaborators at 29 locations throughout the world for testing. Replicated yield trials of the best varieties were begun in 1976. The program is now being operated in cooperation with ICRISAT.

The millets

For years "the millets" has been used as a general term for a large category of crops. Among the millets are at least 14 species, representing 10 different genera, and for each there are distinct problems and potentials. The millets are among the few crops adapted to the sandy soils of the Sahel region, the Rajasthan Desert, and the extreme western Punjab. Their yield potential seems to be lower than that of sorghum, but their ability to withstand harsh conditions gives some of them an important place adjoining sorghum-producing zones.

ICRISAT is doing research on millets at Hyderabad, India, and expects to cooperate with research organizations in Africa, where work on millets has been under way on a modest scale for some years. ICRISAT is rapidly assembling a broad base of genetic germ plasm. Breeding approaches which can generate hybrid or open-pollinated products (varieties or synthetics) are being pursued in ICRISAT's pearl millet (*Pennisetum typhoides*) breeding program. Experimental varieties were tested for the first time in 1976. A cytoplasmic male-sterile line from the U.S. has been used for hybrid seed production, but it is susceptible to downy mildew and ergot, both of which are major problems.

The food legumes

The food legumes are a diverse group botanically.[4] About 20 species of food legumes are used in appreciable quantities in the human diet in various parts of the world. In spite of this diversity, the problems facing farmers in increasing production are quite similar. Plant diseases and insect pests cause significant damage. Although many of the diseases are seed-borne, most small farmers save seed from previous harvests. Since

[4] "Food legumes" have been defined by L. M. Roberts as "those species of the plant family Leguminosae (pea or bean family) that are consumed directly by human beings, most commonly as mature, dry seeds, but occasionally as immature, green seeds or as green pods with the immature seeds enclosed. It does not include species that provide leaf or stem tissue that is used as cooked or uncooked greens. Food legumes utilized as dry seed are often referred to as pulses or grain legumes." Soybeans and groundnuts are included within this grouping.

these crops are grown primarily for home consumption, application of pesticides or chemical fertilizers is not economical. Farmers in many areas do not inoculate to stimulate the natural nitrogen-fixing abilities of the legumes. Legumes are often grown in association with other crops; yet agronomic practices for these intercropped conditions have received little attention from scientists. Within each species, tremendous variation exists in the size, shape, color, texture, and taste of the grain. These differences lead to narrow and strongly held consumer preferences.

After long neglect, some food legumes are receiving attention from researchers in the developing regions of the world. The ones being given primary attention are dry beans, cowpeas, chickpeas, pigeon peas, soybeans, and groundnuts (peanuts).

DRY BEANS

Probably more research is under way on dry beans (*Phaseolus vulgaris*) than on any other food legume except soybeans. About 20 countries have been identified as carrying out research, but much of this is on narrow, local problems, and only a beginning has been made in developing a broad research effort.

In 1972 the International Center of Tropical Agriculture (CIAT) in Colombia began a major program on beans for Latin America and the Caribbean. For bush beans, CIAT expects short-term advances through the introduction of improved agronomic practices to minimize yield variability. Varietal selection is envisioned as a major contributor to higher yields in the intermediate term. Genetically improved varieties are just beginning to be released. Since consumer preferences and production conditions differ widely, strong national programs will be essential to provide finished varieties and associated practices suitable to many areas. The potential of climbing beans, for example, for intensive production by small farmers has not been thoroughly studied, so improvements cannot be expected for several years.

A network of bean improvement programs is being built in Latin America which may eventually involve national institutions in the developing countries, international and regional institutes, and institutions in the developed countries throughout the world. For several years the Inter-American Institute of Agricultural Sciences (IICA) has assigned a coordinator and provided technical support for the Central American Regional Project for Production and Improvement of Beans and Other Food Legumes as part of the Central American Cooperative Food Crop Improvement Program. It has also recently published a comprehensive bibliography on beans. The Center for Research and Training in Tropical Agriculture (CATIE) in Costa Rica and the Brazilian Corporation for Agricultural Research (EMBRAPA) have funds and the capability to train bean workers. The Institute of Nutrition for Central America and Panama (INCAP) is making valuable contributions to these efforts, especially through its research on the nutritional aspects of food legumes and consumer preferences. Links with several research institutions in the industrialized countries have been developed.

COWPEAS

In the early 1970s the International Institute of Tropical Agriculture (IITA) at Ibadan, Nigeria, became a world center for research on cowpeas (*Vigna unguiculata*). Its cowpea germ plasm collection contains over 7,000 accessions. These are being grown in several seasons and environments, and their characteristics are being recorded and entered on computer cards.

IITA has started an extensive crossing program. Elite genetic stocks with excellent disease resistance, pest tolerance, and wide adaptation have been developed.

Testing has begun for host-plant resistance to insect pests such as thrips and leafhoppers to complement control with insecticides. Other pests receiving attention are the hemipterous bug, the red-banded blister beetle, and pod borers. Work has also started on important diseases such as Cercospora leaf spot, rust, anthracnose, bacterial pustule, cowpea mosaic virus, and the root-knot nematode. A cowpea mosaic virus nursery is being sent to cooperators in six countries.

Agronomic work also is under way. Planting-density trials reveal that the optimum number of plants per hectare depends upon plant type and season. Some varieties give top yields at 40,000 plants per hectare; others require up to 100,000 for best performance. Studies have shown that indigenous cowpea *Rhizobium* strains are more efficient than imported strains. The overall performance of cowpea varieties has been found to differ significantly in the absence of inoculation.

International cooperative yield trials have been initiated in several African and Asian countries. Yields have ranged from 1,000 to 1,600 kg/ha for the better varieties.

CHICKPEAS AND PIGEON PEAS

Among the international agricultural centers, ICRISAT has the major responsibility for chickpeas (*Cicer arietinum*). Its program began in the mid-1970s. Because of their cultivation in the Mideast, the Mediterranean area, and Ethiopia, chickpeas and the other grain legumes adapted to that region are also part of the research program of the newly founded International Center for Agricultural Research on Dry Areas, located in Lebanon, Syria, and Iran.

ICRISAT is also responsible for pigeon peas (*Cajanus cajan*). An

All-India coordinated research program has carried out much previous work and has assembled more than 5,000 entries in its collection. IITA is concerned with the development of pigeon peas for the humid tropics.

SOYBEANS

Until recently, little research was conducted on soybeans (*Glycine max*) for tropical and subtropical regions. The unimproved types widely grown in these areas are viney, susceptible to many diseases and insect pests, subject to seed shattering at maturity, and produce low yields. The sensitivity of soybeans to daylength determines to a considerable degree the area of adaptation and time of maturity of each variety. Soybean varieties adapted to U.S. conditions flower soon after emergence and require careful management to produce satisfactory yields when planted in tropical and subtropical regions.

To serve broader needs related to soybean production and consumption, the International Soybean Program (INTSOY) was established in the early 1970s in the U.S. as a cooperative program between the University of Illinois and the University of Puerto Rico. INTSOY provides a vehicle by which the vast amount of research on soybeans in the U.S. (the major producer) and elsewhere can be applied more directly to conditions of the developing world. During 1975, coordinated variety trials were conducted at 256 locations in 90 countries. Joint IITA–INTSOY soybean variety trials are being conducted in 33 tropical African countries.

The Florida Agricultural Experiment Station and the U.S. Department of Agriculture have developed the "Jupiter" variety (a cross of one of the best U.S. types with a type introduced from the Philippines), which has shown good adaptability and productivity in several tropical regions.

The Asian Vegetable Research and Development Center (AVRDC) in Taiwan is attempting to develop lines that are tolerant to humid tropical climates; have greater resistance to diseases, especially rust, and insect pests; and are insensitive to daylength. AVRDC has found that under Taiwanese conditions the soybean responds positively to nitrogen applications; it is now investigating the reasons. A top yield of more than 5,000 kg/ha has been obtained.

GROUNDNUTS

Yields of groundnuts (*Arachis hypogaea*), also known as peanuts, are usually low. The short-season varieties required in many areas of production have genetic limitations. The agronomic technology developed in the temperate climates is not applicable to the tropics and subtropics. Disease and pest attacks are widespread. Finally, researchers in the developing regions have been slow in deriving profitable agronomic and plant protection practices which can be recommended to farmers with confidence.

The genetic variation in cultivated groundnuts is surprisingly narrow. There are no more than 30 distinct clusters of varieties. However, since the groundnut is largely self-fertilized and every plant is the potential parent of a pure line, there is scope for further selection.

ICRISAT is establishing a world collection and register of varieties and wild stocks. Evaluation of the collections was begun in 1975, and full-scale work in plant breeding and genetics, production studies, and plant protection got under way in 1976. Breeders are attempting to produce widely adapted varieties as well as stocks with superior characteristics which can be used in national programs to produce local varieties. At first these ICRISAT stocks will be based largely on selections; later, stocks derived from crosses between *Arachis hypogaea* and wild species will be employed. Disease and insect resistance are the major objectives of the breeding program. Chemical control measures also will be tested.

Agronomic work will largely be left to the national programs, but ICRISAT is investigating water relations and the activity of *Rhizobium*, by which the nitrogen-fixing ability of groundnuts can be maximized. Work is planned in postharvest technology and economics.

The root and tuber crops

Roots and tubers—primarily white potatoes, cassava, sweet potatoes, and yams—are major components of the diets in regions where they are grown.

THE POTATO

Partly to reduce the probability of severe losses from plant diseases and partly because of the temperature requirements for best growth, production of potatoes in the tropics is normally confined to high elevations where temperatures are relatively low and to seasons when rainfall is not excessive.

Research in the developing regions was expanded in 1971, when the International Potato Center (CIP) was established in Peru. Research is carried out in three ecological zones: the subtropical desert at La Molina (240 meters above sea level), the temperate highlands or "sierra" of Huancayo (at 3,300 meters), and the tropical rain forest at San Ramon (800 meters). CIP is developing a decentralized international research program through contracts for cooperative work with institutions in Denmark, Mexico, the Netherlands, Peru, Sweden, and the U.S. Cooperative work also extends to national programs in a number of countries in Africa, Asia, the Mideast, and Latin America. To facilitate such cooperation CIP has established regional programs in major potato-growing areas.

There are 2,000 species of *Solanum*. One hundred fifty are tuber-producing types, of which only two subspecies of *S. tuberosum* have been developed as major sources of human food. Thousands of collections of the cultivated potato and its relatives have been assembled by CIP and are being field tested, described, and maintained for study, for use as parent stocks for plant breeding programs, and for international exchange. Maturity periods range from 75 to 150 days; skin color ranges from white to red to blue; and tuber size, shape, and texture are highly variable.

Expeditions are being organized to make CIP's world collection more broadly representative of the world's diverse germ plasm. Working collections are kept by a number of research organizations in countries where the potato is important. Study and use of this immense reservoir of germ plasm is a central component of the expanding world research on potatoes.

Potatoes can be produced vegetatively, using tubers or portions of tubers as "seed," or through sexual reproduction, which results in segregation into diverse genetic types. But the potato is subject to infection by several viral diseases. This creates a special problem for the world's potato research workers, since vegetative material cannot be exchanged readily among countries for fear of spreading dangerous viruses. Work currently under way to develop techniques for producing virus-free clones may soon allow safe international exchange of genetic materials.[5]

As with most crops in tropical or subtropical areas, the potato is subject to attack by numerous diseases and insect pests. Late blight, a highly destructive disease, is prevalent in most areas where the potato is grown. The causal organism, transmitted through the air or via infected tubers, is highly variable genetically. Chemical control is possible, but costly. Development of "field-resistant" varieties is promising. Brown rot, which has been a major deterrent to production of the potato at low elevations in the tropics and subtropics, is receiving attention.

Attention is also being given to chemical control of other diseases and the insect vectors of the viral diseases. Varietal resistance will be required, and some progress has been reported from Nigeria and Peru.

Both CIP and the Asian Vegetable Research and Development Center are at work on the problems which must be solved if the potato is to be grown successfully in the humid tropics.

---

[5] CIP is also developing techniques for the sexual reproduction of potatoes, since true seed could be exchanged more readily.

CASSAVA

Cassava (*Manihot esculenta*) is generally grown on tropical soils of low fertility. It can exist in areas where there is little rainfall. Moreover, its starchy roots can be left in the ground, sometimes for months, until needed.

Scattered work on cassava has been undertaken in recent decades in a number of countries. Not until CIAT and IITA were established in 1967, however, was a world effort undertaken to attack the abysmally low yield of cassava.

The CIAT program. Cassava is one of CIAT's major interests—nine scientists are at work on the crop at CIAT headquarters in Colombia. A germ plasm bank consisting of 2,300 collections has been established.

CIAT's intensive breeding program produces about 20,000 crosses a year. Better selections are multiplied vegetatively and are tested at CIAT and three additional locations. In Colombia, farm yields of from 3,000 to 12,000 kg/ha are common. It has been demonstrated that with the use of disease-free seed stocks, weed control, optimal plant populations, and good husbandry, the yields of these local varieties (clones) can be increased to about 18,000 kg/ha. Moreover, with improved varieties, yields have increased to an average of 30,000 kg/ha. CIAT soon expects to have varieties which will regularly produce 50,000 kg/ha at CIAT (1,000 meters above sea level) or 30,000 kg/ha on the tropical coast.

The search for higher-yielding types is intensifying. Physiological studies suggest that high yield will be associated with a short plant, small stem, and the ability to retain a large leaf area until harvest. Efforts are being made to develop "sweet" types, which contain minimal amounts of poisonous hydrocyanic acid. Work on fertilizer response has been initiated. Certain varieties show some acid-soil tolerance. Several potentially useful herbicides and weed control systems have been identified.

Good resistance to the devastating bacterial blight disease has been identified in only a few experimental lines, but it has been learned that such resistance is transmitted to the progeny of crosses—an important finding. Many items in the world collection are resistant to thrips, and some may be resistant to spider mites.

Production trials are conducted at nine sites in Colombia, and regional testing programs have been established in cooperation with institutions in 16 countries. In 1977, CIAT established cooperative research projects in Latin America and Asia.

The IITA program. A major biological constraint to cassava production in Africa is disease, especially cassava mosaic disease (CMD), which exists in Africa and India and can reduce yields by 50 percent; cassava bacterial blight (CBB); and anthracnose. Insects such as green mite and mealy bug, recently identified in Zaire and the Congo, are very serious pests in Africa. The objectives for cassava improvement at IITA are: (1) high rates of dry matter production per unit of land and time in both monoculture and mixed cropping systems; (2) resistance to and cultural control of important diseases and insects; (3) better consumer acceptance, nutritional value, and processing characteristics; (4) better plant canopy and root characteristics; and (5) adaptation to a wide range of environments.

A large germ plasm collection in seed form has been assembled from Africa, Latin America, and Asia. It has been evaluated for resistance to diseases and for agronomic traits. Extensive crosses have been made, and every year about 100,000 seedlings are raised and screened for disease resistance and root characteristics. Several thousand seedlings are selected annually in 5 locations in Nigeria and 24 locations in Zaire. These selections are used for cloning and for further evaluation for resistance to diseases and lodging, for root and plant characteristics, and for high-yield potential.

Progress has been made in producing cassava clones which are resistant to diseases (especially CMD and CBB), give higher yields, have improved root characteristics, and are resistant to lodging.

Through selection for several generations, hydrocyanic acid content has been lowered and many "low" clones have been selected.

SWEET POTATOES

Sweet potatoes (*Ipomoea batatas*) are eaten in large quantities in parts of Africa and the Far East.

In the 1970s, IITA has instituted a systematic search for better varieties. Strains from the IITA breeding program have yielded about 33,000 kg/ha and have exhibited field resistance to both viral infection and weevil damage plus good storability. The yield of IITA varieties in Cameroon and Liberia topped that of local and introduced varieties.

Working with a world collection of over 200 varieties, breeders at the Asian Vegetable Research and Development Center in Taiwan are aiming for high yield, acceptable quality, high amounts of protein and beta-carotene, early maturity, and resistance to the leafhopper-transmitted "witches broom" and the sweet potato weevil. In yield trials, some varieties have produced 30,000–60,000 kg/ha.

YAMS

Yams belong to the genus *Dioscorea*, which consists of some 600 species, most of which are found in the tropics and subtropics. The important edible species, which produce tubers, are water yam (*D. alata*) from Asia, yellow yam (*D. cayensis*) from West Africa, white yam (*D. rotundata*) from West Africa, and cush-cush yam (*D. trifida*) from Central America. In the early 1970s, IITA began work with the white, yellow, and water yams, with primary emphasis on white yams.

Techniques for seed germination and artificial hybridization of white yam have been developed at IITA. Breeding clones are being evaluated for disease resistance, tuber shape, yield potential, storage, and quality characteristics. A number of promising clones have been identified.

Means have been developed to produce white-yam seed tubers from rooted cuttings, thereby speeding the increase of desirable clones free of nematodes and tuber-borne diseases. A white-yam virus has been characterized and a method of mechanically transmitting the virus has been developed, so large numbers of breeding stocks can be screened for resistance.

IITA is also attempting population improvement. Good breeding populations would allow scientists to produce white yam from uniform true seed rather than from the vegetative sets which are traditionally used. This would reduce the cost of planting stocks and permit production of white yams with fewer problems from soil-borne diseases and diseases normally transmitted through vegetatively propagated sets. This would also facilitate the distribution of stocks to national programs with less risk of spreading diseases.

Neglected crops

Many important crops receive little attention from scientists. Vegetable crops are mankind's richest source of vitamins and minerals. They are a readily available solution to problems of malnutrition which cannot be entirely met by increasing the availability of calories from cereals or root crops. They also provide one possibility for raising farmers' income on small parcels of land. Little research on vegetables has been carried out in developing regions, although the Asian Vegetable Research and Development Center has focused on Chinese cabbage, mungbean, soybean, sweet potato, tomato, and the white potato for the tropics.

Other major neglected crops are plantain, or cooking banana; several species of oilseed field crops, such as sesame, sunflowers, safflower, and castor bean; nearly all tropical fruits not managed as estate crops; and pasture and forage crops.

Major animal species

All forms of livestock are found throughout the world, with two exceptions: the buffalo is concentrated in Asia, and swine are raised primarily in Latin America and non-Muslim Asia (Table 7.2). Production systems in the low-income countries vary considerably, but most involve minimal competition with humans for food.

In Asia, livestock is usually raised in subsistence systems requiring few external inputs. Animals add to the food, fiber, and shelter of the farm family, provide a means of savings, and serve as a way to acquire other goods through sale or barter. Animals may contribute draft power, manure, and food, but seldom consume materials eaten by the human population. Their feed may consist of weeds pulled from croplands, grass growing on roadsides and unused land, crop residue, or cereal by-products such as rice bran. Grain or other concentrated feeds are given only to milk-producing animals or hard-working draft animals. Waste materials, sometimes cooked or fermented, are often fed to swine. Occasionally pig-producing units are located near small ponds or lakes stocked with fish and become part of a highly integrated, intensive farming system. Only recently have modern pig-producing units been established near urban areas. Commercial egg and chicken production for urban markets is well established, however; flocks are large and mixed feeds are used. Backyard poultry, kept by small farmers, is still the major production system in villages.

Latin America has large areas of grassland, much of which is of little use other than for grazing. Consequently, production systems based primarily on pasture are used for most beef cattle, dairy cattle, and sheep. Pig production utilizes agricultural by-products, with the animals often being allowed to run loose on small farms. However, most poultry for urban consumption is now raised under intensive production systems, generally near cities.

In Africa, most ruminants are raised on open grazing lands. As in Latin America, swine are largely fed waste agricultural products. Because of the high cost of imported grains and feed rations most poultry is raised in small flocks by many farm families utilizing agricultural by-products. However, commercial poultry production is being widely adopted.

In the developing regions, research on the major animal species has in recent decades been as weak and as fragmented as that involving the basic food crops. International agricultural research institutes involved with farm animals are now beginning to correct this situation.

RUMINANTS

Inadequate nutrition and poor health are the principal biological constraints to production of cattle, water buffalo, sheep, and goats throughout the developing world. In tropical regions there is intense sunlight, a long, warm growing season, and often adequate moisture, all of which are important for production of the forage needed by ruminants. However, in many areas a combination of low soil fertility and long seasonal dry periods greatly restricts year-round production of quality forage.

Management and pasture improvement. Since ruminant animals can utilize the forages and grasses on land which is unsuitable for cropping, beef production is an attractive investment for countries that have extensive rangelands. Latin America and Africa have vast areas that could be developed. Information is accumulating on ways to correct most nutrient deficiencies of pastures, to extend the grazing season, and to preserve forage. However, since fertilizer is rarely economical on grazing lands, the more fertile soils must be exploited first.

CIAT works on husbandry practices and improvement of forage legumes for pasture and rangeland in the lowland tropics. Research in Colombia indicates that modern technology could raise carrying capacity and calving rates so that annual offtake could triple. CIAT research on cattle and rangeland should be applicable to Brazil and Venezuela, which also have poor soils and alternating extremes of dry and rainy seasons.

The International Livestock Center for Africa (ILCA), located in Ethiopia, is developing more efficient animal husbandry systems for sub-Saharan Africa. In drier areas where animals have overgrazed the grasslands, there are often long periods when no grass regrows, so livestock lose weight and many starve. Moreover, standing forage becomes progressively lower in protein, minerals, and vitamins during the dry season, resulting in severe adverse effects on pregnancies, birth of young, and lactation. Corrective actions include reducing livestock pressure on lands through controlled grazing, planned marketing of portions of herds, and providing supplemental feeds. On controlled rangelands low-value annual grasses can be replaced with higher-yielding perennial grasses and legumes to lengthen the grazing season and increase the nutritive value of the forage. The control necessary to carry out this operation is difficult to achieve under present policies. Use of harvested feeds (grain, hay, silage) to support livestock in seasons when plant growth does not occur (in winter) has long been traditional in temperate zones, but the need was not recognized in the tropics until recently. Improved animal husbandry is in its infancy in most regions. There is little segregation of breeding herds, young stock, and market animals, although the requirements for each differ.

Nutrition. The benefits of supplementary feeding are under extensive investigation. If the digestibility of the rations for most ruminants were raised by less than 10 percent, the output of livestock products could be doubled given present livestock numbers. Nearly all of the additional energy consumed would be used for productive purposes, the needs for maintenance having already been satisfied. Limited feed-lot operations, depending largely on agro-industrial wastes, may be feasible. In some areas, stall operations on small farms—using high-energy crop residues and harvested forages—may be feasible.

Disease. Animal disease control is an aspect of livestock production that governments recognize and usually seek assistance to improve. However, failure to recognize that adequate feed supplies and good husbandry are necessary supplements to effective disease control programs has reduced their benefits. A large assortment of serious diseases and parasitic infections plague livestock. Effective control measures are known for rinderpest, anthrax, blackleg, pasteurellosis, brucellosis, and rift valley fever. Control measures are still urgently needed for trypanosomiasis, contagious bovine pleuropneumonia, east coast fever, streptothricosis, lumpy skin disease, and piroplasmosis.

In approximately one-third of the African continent south of the Sahara, trypanosomiasis makes livestock raising either hazardous or impossible. Trypanosomes are carried by the tsetse fly (*Glossina morsitans*), which infests the area. It has been estimated that this region could support about 125 million head of cattle if the disease could be eliminated. East coast fever, caused by a protozoan parasite, *Theileria parva*, occurs in about one-quarter of the same area; the vector is chiefly a tick, *Rhipicephalus appendiculatus*. A severe epidemic can wipe out entire herds. Control of these two diseases is the initial goal of the International Laboratory for Research on Animal Diseases (ILRAD), located in Kenya. Immunological research may lead to the development of vaccines which, in combination with other techniques, will radically increase the livestock production potential of African countries.

Research is also in progress at CIAT on some tropical animal diseases (particularly the hemoparasitic diseases) and on factors affecting the reproductive performance of cattle.

Breeding. Substantial upgrading of indigenous herds can be accomplished by selection of superior dams and sires and by controlled breeding to propagate superior stock. An important factor is the fate of improved breeding stock placed in the hands of a herdsman who may not provide adequate feed supplies, good husbandry, and animal disease control—all prerequisites for successful animal improvement programs. The indigenous stock has the great advantage of being well adapted. If importations appear necessary, stock should probably be sought in other tropical regions rather than in temperate zones.

The laws of genetics are fully applicable to livestock improvement.

However, the livestock geneticist will require large populations of animals and many animal generations in order to select desired traits and to fix these for a high degree of heritability. Such projects require competent geneticists and continuity of financial support over many years.

Marketing. The most casual survey of practices and facilities for the marketing of meat animals in Africa and other developing areas reveals opportunities for enormous improvement. ILCA is focusing on such improvement.

Goats. Arid or semi-arid tropical and subtropical areas have about 70 percent of the world's 383 million goats. As ruminant animals, they can consume forages, so they need not compete with man. From the research standpoint they remain almost totally neglected.

SWINE

The worst problem facing the swine industry in developing regions is nutrition. Animal health has been considered of secondary importance.

Technology for swine is apparently largely transferable from the temperate regions to the tropics; therefore the major needs are improved local feed sources and more efficient production systems and processing and marketing systems tailored to local conditions. Research is under way in many areas to find inexpensive local feed ingredients for the swine industry.

POULTRY

Technology for poultry, as with swine, is largely transferable from the temperate zone to the tropics, so the major needs are improved feeds, production systems, and processing and marketing systems. Inadequate nutrition is the principal constraint. Research in many areas is aimed at finding inexpensive feed ingredients from local sources. Health also is a problem; diseases such as Newcastle can wipe out whole flocks in a few days. Vaccines are available, but they are often too expensive or are utilized too late, either because of distances to be traveled, lack of trained persons to administer them, or failure to identify the disease in its early stage.

Summary

In developing regions crop yields are only a fraction of their potential. New areas can still be brought into cultivation, and much currently cultivated area can be cropped more intensively. However, substantial investment will be required to develop new lands; build irrigation systems; manufacture fertilizers, pesticides, and machines; generate technology; and train people. Governments must have the commitment and will to pursue aggressive agricultural development policies, one of which should be to support research on a much larger scale than in the past.

A three-component international agricultural research system is expected to speed the generation of needed technology for low-income countries. This research system, although still only emerging, now covers many of the major food crops and animals and extends to most geographical areas of the developing world.

The next "breakthroughs" can be expected to involve durum wheats, tropical maize, and barley as human food. The new high-yielding dwarf varieties of durum wheat and barley are being tested. Tropical maize varieties are being shortened, and their yield potentials raised. Improvements in the other major food crops are on the way, but several years of work are still required to achieve significant contributions to yield increases. The initial stages of defining programs, collecting germ plasm, building physical facilities, and recruiting staff take time. Efforts to date appear to have been sound and, if adequately supported in the future, should provide payoffs of considerable magnitude.

Improvement of livestock production in the tropics is a relatively new item on the research agenda. The international assistance community is taking on major responsibilities in this area with the establishment of the research institute network, and through support of the regional and national programs with which these centers collaborate. Advances in livestock technology for the tropics can be one of the chief determinants of change in these nations.

References

INTRODUCTION
Food and Agriculture Organization. *Production Yearbook 1975.* Vol. 29. Rome: Food and Agriculture Organization, 1975.

THE CURRENT STATUS OF AGRICULTURAL TECHNOLOGY
Chou, Marylin; Harmon, David P., Jr.; Kahn, Herman; and Wittwer, Sylvan. *World Food Prospects and Agricultural Potential.* New York: Praeger, 1977.
Cummings, Ralph W., Jr. *Food Crops in the Low Income Countries: The State of Present and Expected Agricultural Research and Technology.* Working Paper. New York: Rockefeller Foundation, May 1975.
Food and Agriculture Organization. *Production Yearbook 1975.* Vol. 29. Rome: Food and Agriculture Organization, 1975.
Litzenberger, Samuel C., ed. *Guide for Field Crops in the Tropics and Subtropics.* Washington, D.C.: U.S. Agency for International Development, 1977.
Nelson, Michael. *The Development of Tropical Lands: Policy Issues in Latin America.* Baltimore and London: Johns Hopkins University Press for Resources for the Future, 1972.
Sanchez, P. A., and Buol, S. W. "Soils of the Tropics and the World Food Crisis." *Science* 188 (1975): 598–603.

RICE

Barker, R.; Kauffman, H. K.; and Herdt, R. W. "Production Constraints and Priorities for Research." Agricultural Economics Paper No. 75–8. Mimeographed. Los Baños, Philippines: International Rice Research Institute.
Chandler, Robert F., Jr. "Rice in the Tropics: A Guide for Policy Makers and Administrators." Unpublished manuscript, International Agricultural Development Service, New York, N.Y.
International Rice Research Institute. Major Research in Upland Rice. Los Baños, Philippines: International Rice Research Institute, 1977.
International Rice Research Institute. Research Highlights for 1974. Los Baños, Philippines: International Rice Research Institute, 1975.
Jennings, Peter R. "The Amplification of Agricultural Production." Scientific American 235 (September 1976): 180–94.
O'Toole, J. C., and Chang, T. T. Drought and Rice Improvement in Perspective. IRRI Research Paper Series No. 14. Manila, Philippines: International Rice Research Institute, 1978.
"Ten Metric Tons per Hectare—High Dry Season Yields." IRRI Reporter 2 (July 1966).

WHEAT

Breth, Steven A. "Durum Wheat: New Age for an Old Crop." CIMMYT Today 2 (1975): 1–16.
Breth, Steven A. "Multilines: Safety in Numbers." CIMMYT Today 4 (1976): 1–8.
Breth, Steven A. "The Return of Medic." CIMMYT Today 3 (1975): 1–16.
Breth, Steven A. "Turkey's Wheat Research and Training Project." CIMMYT Today 6 (1977): 1–16.
International Maize and Wheat Improvement Center. CIMMYT Review 1976. El Batan, Mexico: International Maize and Wheat Improvement Center, 1977.
International Maize and Wheat Improvement Center. CIMMYT Review 1977. El Batan, Mexico: International Maize and Wheat Improvement Center, 1977.

BARLEY

International Maize and Wheat Improvement Center. CIMMYT Review 1976. El Batan, Mexico: International Maize and Wheat Improvement Center, 1977.

MAIZE

Centro Internacional de Agricultura Tropical. Annual Report: 1976. Cali, Colombia: Centro Internacional de Agricultura Tropical, 1977.
Harpstead, Dale D. "High-Lysine Corn." Scientific American 225 (August 1971): 34–42.
Hayes, H. K. A Professor's Story of Hybrid Corn. Minneapolis, Minn.: Burgess, 1963.
International Institute of Tropical Agriculture. 1975 Annual Report. Ibadan, Nigeria: International Institute of Tropical Agriculture, 1976.
International Maize and Wheat Improvement Center. CIMMYT Review 1976. El Batan, Mexico: International Maize and Wheat Improvement Center, 1977.
International Maize and Wheat Improvement Center. CIMMYT Review 1977. El Batan, Mexico: International Maize and Wheat Improvement Center, 1977.
International Maize and Wheat Improvement Center. High Quality Protein Maize. New York: Wiley, 1975.
Mangelsdorf, P. C. Corn: Its Origin, Evolution, and Improvement. Cambridge, Mass.: Belknap Press, 1974.

SORGHUM

Doggett, H. Sorghum. London: Longmans, 1970.
International Maize and Wheat Improvement Center. CIMMYT Review 1976. El Batan, Mexico: International Maize and Wheat Improvement Center, 1976.
Quinby, J. R. Sorghum Improvement and the Genetics of Growth. College Station: Texas A & M University Press, 1974.

Rao, N. G. P., and House, L. R. *Sorghum in the Seventies.* New Delhi and Bombay: Oxford University Press, 1972.
Wall, J. S., and Ross, W. M. *Sorghum Production and Utilization.* Westport, Conn.: Avi, 1970.

THE MILLETS
Rachie, K. O. *The Millets: Importance, Utilization, and Outlook.* Hyderabad, India: International Crops Research Institute for the Semi-Arid Tropics, 1975.

THE FOOD LEGUMES
Centro Internacional de Agricultura Tropical. *Potentials of Field Beans and Other Food Legumes in Latin America.* Cali, Colombia: Centro Internacional de Agricultura Tropical, 1973.
Hulse, J. H.; Rachie, K. O.; and Billingsley, L. W. *Nutritional Standards and Methods for Evaluation for Food Legume Breeders.* Ottawa: International Development Research Centre, 1977.
International Institute of Tropical Agriculture. *1975 Annual Report.* Ibadan, Nigeria: International Institute of Tropical Agriculture, 1976.
Roberts, L. M. "The Food Legumes: Recommendations for Expansion and Acceleration of Research." Mimeographed. New York: Rockefeller Foundation, 1970.

THE ROOT AND TUBER CROPS
Centro Internacional de la Papa. *Annual Report, 1973.* Lima, Peru: Centro Internacional de la Papa, 1974.
Centro Internacional de la Papa. *Annual Report, 1974.* Lima, Peru: Centro Internacional de la Papa, 1975.
Kay, D. E. *Root Crops.* Crop and Product Digest No. 2. London: Tropical Products Institute, 1973.
Nestel, Barry, and Cock, James. *Cassava: The Development of an International Research Network.* Ottawa: International Development Research Centre, 1976.

NEGLECTED CROPS
Mortensen, Ernest, and Bullard, Ervin T. *Handbook of Tropical and Subtropical Horticulture.* Washington, D.C.: U.S. Agency for International Development, 1970.

MAJOR ANIMAL SPECIES
Blaxter, K. L. "Increasing Output of Animal Production: Technical Measures for Increasing Productivity." In *Man, Food, and Nutrition,* edited by M. Rechcigl, Jr. Cleveland: CR Press, 1973.
Centro Internacional de Agricultura Tropical. *Annual Report: 1976.* Cali, Colombia: Centro Internacional de Agricultura Tropical, 1977.
Cunha, T. J. "Role of Ruminant Production in Increasing Animal Foods in Latin America." Paper presented at the International Conference on Nutrition and Agricultural and Economic Development, December 6, 1974, Guatemala City, Guatemala. Mimeographed.
Davendra, C. "Goats: Their Productivity and Potential." *Span* 17 (1974): 130–32.
McDowell, R. D. "Inventory and Capacity for Expanding Protein Available from Animal Sources." Paper presented at a Symposium on Protein and the World Food Situation, June 5–7, 1974, North Carolina State University, Raleigh, N.C. Mimeographed.
Rockefeller Foundation. *The Role of Animals in the World Food Situation.* Working Paper. New York: Rockefeller Foundation, December 1975.

CHAPTER 8

Toward forced-pace campaigns

Introduction

A NUMBER OF COUNTRIES have had success in markedly accelerating agricultural production. Their experiences can be divided into three categories: comprehensive national efforts, national commodity programs, and defined-area projects. In the first category would be the efforts such as those in Taiwan, Mexico, India, and China; in the second, programs in Kenya (maize), Turkey (wheat), Colombia (rice), and the Philippines (rice); and in the third, projects in the Comilla district of Bangladesh and in the state of Puebla in Mexico.

This chapter reviews these representative experiences in order to identify the motivations for the campaigns, the difficulties faced, the actions taken, and the lessons learned. Before turning to the efforts of developing countries, however, it may be useful to consider the experiences of the U.S. and Japan.

Early success stories

Under quite different circumstances, the U.S. and Japan used agriculture to accelerate their overall economic development. Although these models are not directly applicable to developing countries today, useful lessons do emerge.[1]

THE U.S.: 1880 TO THE PRESENT

Between 1880 and 1960, agricultural output in the U.S. increased at 1.5 percent annually (Table 8.1), a rate which is well below that needed

---

[1] This section relies heavily on *Agricultural Development: An International Perspective*, by Hayami and Ruttan.

(and even well below that being achieved) in many developing countries today but which was adequate both to produce large surpluses for export and to contribute significantly to overall capital formation in the U.S. Today, less than 5 percent of the population feeds the remainder of the country at an extraordinary material standard of living and produces enough in addition to provide major world exports of food and fiber.

The period 1900–1940 marked a transition in U.S. agriculture. Before 1900, new land and labor plus some mechanization were primary causes of increased production. The growth rate then slowed markedly. But since the mid-1930s rising productivity—that is, increase in yields—has been the major component of higher output; both land area cultivated and number of agricultural workers have decreased.

During the transition, four developments contributed greatly to growth. First, there was a deliberate effort to impart technological knowledge and skills to large numbers of rural Americans (see Chapter 14). The responsiveness of the American farmer to profitable new opportunities and the aggressiveness with which private industrial and service companies met his production and marketing requirements were primary driving forces in this process.

Second, the invention of hybrid maize greatly increased the yield potential of the nation's largest crop.[2] The hybrids gave much higher returns to use of chemical fertilizers and pesticides, and fertilizer consumption began to increase markedly. Moreover, this breakthrough triggered increased research efforts with other crops.

Third, induced by the higher demand, technical changes in fertilizer production and marketing lowered the real price of fertilizer relative to the price of agricultural products and of land. At first, higher fertilizer use may only have offset declining yields brought on by depletion of soil fertility, especially in the South, where cotton and tobacco had been grown extensively, and in the Midwest, where the virgin lands had been farmed for many years. However, from 1930 on, yields per hectare increased steadily.

Fourth, the availability of inexpensive fuel permitted tractors to substitute for horses, sharply reducing the demand for fodder and grain to feed farm animals. Much land was freed for commercial crop production and tractors enabled a farmer to manage larger areas of land. Widespread use of tractors was the most dramatic of the mechanical innovations which have characterized the history of U.S. agricultural growth.

Government actions promoted the technological basis for modernized intensive agriculture:

[2] Maize accounts for three-fifths of the total energy production from the basic food and feed crops in the U.S.

Table 8.1. Changes in output, input, productivity, and factor proportions in U.S. and Japanese agriculture, 1880–1960, selected years

	Index: 1880 = 100					Annual compound rate of change				
	1880	1900	1920	1940	1960	1880–1900	1900–1920	1920–1940	1940–1960	1880–1960
United States										
Output (net of seeds and feed)	100	155	180	232	340	2.2	0.8	1.3	1.9	1.5
Total inputs	100	138	172	181	190	1.6	1.1	0.3	0.2	0.8
Total productivity (output/total inputs)	100	112	105	128	179	0.6	−0.3	1.0	1.7	0.7
Number of male workers	100	124	128	107	50	1.1	0.2	−0.9	−3.9	−0.9
Output per male worker	100	125	141	217	680	1.1	0.6	2.2	5.8	2.4
Agricultural land area	100	157	180	203	215	2.3	0.7	0.6	0.3	1.0
Arable land area	100	170	249	246	238	2.7	1.9	−0.1	−0.2	1.1
Output per hectare of agricultural land	100	99	100	114	158	−0.1	0.1	0.7	1.6	0.5
Output per hectare of arable land	100	91	72	94	143	−0.5	−1.1	1.4	2.1	0.4
Agricultural land area per male worker	100	127	141	190	430	1.2	0.5	1.5	4.2	1.9
Arable land area per male worker	100	137	195	230	476	1.6	1.7	0.8	3.7	2.0
Japan										
Output (net of seeds and feed)	100	149	232	264	358	2.1	2.2	0.7	1.5	1.9
Total inputs	100	105	119	127	156	0.2	0.6	0.3	1.0	0.6
Total productivity	100	142	195	208	229	1.9	1.6	0.4	0.5	1.0
Number of male workers	100	98	97	81	79	−0.1	0	−0.9	−0.1	−0.3
Output per male worker	100	152	239	326	453	2.2	2.2	1.6	1.6	1.9
Arable land area (= agricultural land area)	100	110	126	129	128	0.5	0.7	0.1	0	0.3
Output per hectare of arable land	100	135	184	205	280	1.6	1.5	0.6	1.5	1.3
Arable land area per male worker	100	112	130	159	162	0.6	0.7	1.0	0.1	0.9

Source: Yujiro Hayami and Vernon W. Ruttan, *Agricultural Development: An International Perspective.*

- In 1862, acts were passed which established the U.S. Department of Agriculture (USDA) and the land-grant college system of state universities of technical and agricultural education. (The first state agricultural experiment station was established in 1875 in Connecticut.) In 1890 federal financial support was extended to the Negro land-grant institutions in the southern states.
- The Hatch Act in 1887 provided federal funding, to supplement state sources, for land-grant college agricultural experiment stations.
- The Smith-Lever Act of 1914 provided the firm institutional basis for a cooperative federal-state extension service. By the early 1920s a nationwide agricultural research and extension system had effectively been established.
- Long-term credit for land purchase (through the federal land banks) and short-term credit on reasonable terms from a variety of sources permitted U.S. farmers to build their capital resources quickly.

Government policy encouraged the industrial sector to introduce a stream of new mechanical equipment and other production inputs. Farmers invested in improved implements which, after proving to be technically feasible and economically profitable, were manufactured on a large scale. Public research expanded knowledge of the use and production of chemical fertilizers which was then extended by the private fertilizer industry. After the public sector had provided the early research leadership, the private sector took over the roles of providing commercial seeds, animal feeds, and pesticides. The patent system provided incentives to manufacturers by protecting them from competition until development costs could be recovered and reasonable profits could be realized. Today the private sector plays an important role in research, accounting for over one-third of agricultural research expenditures in the U.S.

Contributing to the success of all of these agricultural activities were public investments in roads, rural electrification, communication systems, and other services necessary for an advancing agriculture.

U.S. public agricultural policy has increasingly focused on easing the adjustment of the agricultural sector to the changing economy. The objectives have been to enable farmers to approach economic equality with other segments of the economy and to ensure that consumers get a reliable supply of farm products for a relatively small proportion of their income. The Agricultural Adjustment Act of 1933 was the first of a series of legislative actions which provided for agricultural price supports, reductions in cropped land, and market development. Schemes such as the Soil Conservation and Domestic Allocation Act of 1936 have encouraged the use of soil-conserving practices. More recently the government has spent substantial amounts of money on programs for disposing of surplus crops while developing foreign markets (in the 1960s) and for supplementing the diets of the domestic poor (in the 1970s).

Hybrid maize in the U.S. One aspect of U.S. agricultural development deserves special mention—the introduction and adoption of hybrid maize. Hybrid maize was first distributed in the U.S. in the early 1930s. It then spread rapidly throughout the Corn Belt and elsewhere. There were marked geographic differences in this development.

Figure 8.1 demonstrates the influence this revolution has had on the representative states of Iowa and Kentucky. In 1932, yields of maize averaged 2,500 kg/ha in Iowa. Just 10 years later, hybrids covered virtually the entire area planted to maize in that state. During this period, even in the absence of widespread heavy fertilizer applications, average yields climbed to 3,500 kg/ha. The use of chemical fertilizers began to increase after World War II and the true potential of the hybrids began to be expressed. By 1972 the statewide average yield for maize in Iowa was over 6,000 kg/ha.

The pattern in Kentucky, a southern state, was similar, although characterized by a lower initial average yield level (1,500 kg/ha), later introduction of hybrids (1936), a slower rate of adoption (in 10 years 65 percent of the area was covered by hybrids), but an earlier increase in the use of chemical fertilizers. Over the 35-year period to 1972, average yields in Kentucky almost quadrupled.

Hybrid maize was not immediately available everywhere. The state agricultural experiment stations or local companies had to create suitable hybrids for each area. Some state experiment stations started earlier than others, thereby making the more productive hybrids available to the farmers in their regions earlier than elsewhere. A USDA-sponsored cooperative maize improvement program was instrumental in speeding the development of inbred lines and hybrids.

The rate at which the farmers accepted the new hybrids depended on the magnitude of profit to be realized from the changeover. This in turn depended upon the absolute superiority of the hybrids in yield per hectare and on the average area per farm planted to maize.

The extension service influenced the pattern of adoption by seeing that the less progressive farmers, often the farmers with smaller landholdings and less education, knew about the new varieties and the associated agronomic practices and therefore eventually joined the adoption process. However, most of the responsibility for success—especially so over the years—must be attributed to the many private seed companies which invested heavily in the development of ever better hybrids, distributed seed of highest quality, and aggressively promoted good production practices.

Side effects of the U.S. system. Farmers with larger landholdings took the lead in adopting new maize varieties. Historically, they have bene-fited from accessibility to markets and from economies of size, particularly as applied to management, but also as reflected in their ability to get discounts on inputs and better deals on marketed products. National and state agricultural policies have benefited the larger, more commercialized farmers. The credit system has been more responsive to their needs.

Fig. 8.1. Percentage of area planted to maize hybrids, nitrogen use on all crops, and maize yields, Iowa and Kentucky, U.S., 1932–69

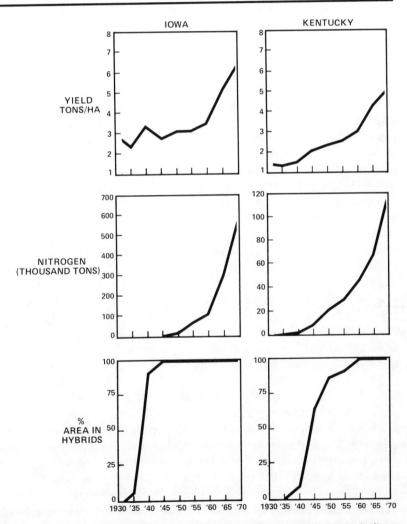

Source: Statistical Reporting Service, U.S. Department of Agriculture.

Finally, U.S. agricultural development has been characterized by progressive mechanization, and the producers with larger farms have had substantial advantages both in financing these capital investments and in farming areas large enough to make the investments pay off quickly.

During recent decades there has been a rapid emigration of rural people to urban areas. Some poorer, smaller farmers—especially black farmers in the South—lost their holdings because of crop failures, low prices, and inability to meet mortgage payments. Many more left because the economic opportunities offered by farming small holdings were less promising than opportunities they thought existed in the city. Often their land was then consolidated into larger farms. Between 1930 and 1967 the farm population declined from 30.5 million to 10.7 million and the average farm size increased from 61 to 157 hectares. The U.S. rural problem was "solved," in part, by creating an urban problem.

JAPAN: 1880 TO THE PRESENT

Between 1880 and 1960 in Japan, agricultural output increased at the rate of 1.9 percent a year. This seemingly modest rate of increase was adequate to provide a substantial contribution to overall Japanese economic growth. Production growth based on yield increases began earlier in Japan than in the U.S., but Japan, too, had to undergo a transition midway to provide the basis for sustained progress (Table 8.1).

When Admiral Perry arrived in 1854, Japan was opened to Western influence, and the existing feudal rule was undermined. A major effort was then made to catch up with the West.

The first attempt to increase agricultural production was to import Western agricultural technology in the form of both machinery and education. Soon, however, it became apparent that this approach was unsuccessful. The Western methods of extensive cultivation were inappropriate for a land-short nation. Japan therefore began a determined effort to develop a modern agricultural technology based on its own needs.

Rapid growth in the late 1800s and early 1900s was based on exploiting a backlog of indigenous technological potential. Farmers were given the freedom to use land and grow crops as they chose. Such decisions had previously been dictated by feudal lords. The Land Tax Revision of 1873–81 changed the basis of agricultural taxation from a levy on production to a cash tax on the value of the land, giving farmers more incentive to increase production and become involved in the market economy. Agricultural discussion societies and seed-exchange societies were encouraged among the farmers. The Ministry of Agriculture and Commerce was founded in 1881. The National Agricultural Experiment Station began to intensify rice-breeding efforts to exploit the potential of farmer-produced varieties. Responding to demand from farmers, fertilizer traders and manufacturers brought in organic fertilizers. Manufacture of superphosphate of lime on a commercial scale became the major source of supply by the 1910s. Agricultural banks were encouraged to provide long-term credit to farmers at low interest rates. Substantial investments were made by the government in improving transportation and developing irrigation. A compulsory education system was established.

Significant changes in research began around 1900. A decentralized research system was organized. The number of prefectural agricultural research stations was increased and these gradually accepted responsibility for conducting applied research tests and demonstrations. Agricultural associations, organized in a pyramid fashion from village associations upward, began to take on extension activities. Relieved of these duties, the National Experiment Station then directed its resources toward more strategic research.

In 1904 the National Agricultural Experiment Station began to develop new varieties by cross-breeding. In 1905, improvement of varieties by pure-line selection began, systematically following practices used previously by veteran farmers; this process resulted in faster payoff and was the major research focus for the next 20 years, until commercial varieties from cross-breeding were ready. At the end of the 19th century, Japan's national average rice yield was a little less than 2,000 kg/ha. With the introduction of improved varieties in the early 1900s, Japanese rice yields began to rise.

Agricultural growth stagnated during the interwar period (1920–40). The production "slack" was largely exploited. Attractive nonfarm investments began to siphon off much of the available capital. New sources of growth had not yet appeared. The Rice Riot in 1918, caused by high rice prices, emphasized the difficulty which Japanese agriculture was facing. The Japanese authorities combatted the high prices by increasing rice imports. However, they also increased their efforts to reexamine and improve their production practices.

Faced with rising pressures for food, an "Assigned Experiment System" was instituted in 1926. National experiment stations were given the responsibility for crossing and selecting promising strains during the first several generations. Eight major regional stations made further plant selections for adaptation to regional ecological conditions. Selected varieties were then sent to prefectural stations to be tested for acceptability in various localities.

Use of chemical fertilizers on the new varieties produced by cross-breeding began to have an effect by the time of World War II, and national average yields rose to about 3,000 kg/ha.

Following World War II, several changes were made. Far-reaching land reform was carried out. The major contribution of this change was not so much to increase capital formation and productivity as to raise standards of living and consumption in the rural areas. Agricultural

> "There are 47 prefectures in Japan, and each prefecture has its own research and experiment stations for agriculture, forestry, and fisheries. The number of stations in 1973 was 411 with about 18,000 personnel, 7,000 of which were researchers and about 11,000 were technical and clerical employees. Such a large number of research and experiment stations is attributable to the fact that many . . . specialize in specific fields such as agriculture, horticulture, animal husbandry, dairy farming, chicken raising, sericulture, tea, forestry and fisheries."
>
> Azio Suzuki
> "Agricultural Research Situation in Japan"

cooperatives were reorganized to give farmers a more effective voice to counter the power of large private businesses. In 1950 the experiment-station system was modified again. Reflecting increased technical capacity, local experiment stations began to conduct independent cross-breeding programs to design varieties more specifically for local conditions. The extension service was reorganized under prefectural governments and was closely tied to the research stations; this made it more responsive to local needs, permitting more effective use of results from the revamped research system.

Industry redirected its wartime efforts. It quickly began to supply fertilizers and other complementary inputs. Substantial areas were improved with flood control and irrigation facilities. Industry produced large numbers of mini-tractors—small-scale machines (less than 10 horsepower) suited for the small Japanese plots. Industry was also able to absorb the people released from agriculture by mechanization.

The agricultural production effort was further stimulated by high government support prices (occasionally as much as four times the world rice price level), which were implemented in response to farmer pressures.

As use of improved dwarf varieties, intensively managed, was combined with high rates of fertilizer application and disease and insect control in response to high prices, yields climbed still higher—to 5,600 kg/ha by 1970. Productivity rose faster than consumer demand, causing large surpluses which have been reduced only recently by disposal programs and the recent world food shortage.

IMPLICATIONS OF U.S. AND JAPANESE EXPERIENCES

Neither the U.S. nor Japan developed under conditions in which pressures were nearly as intense as those facing low-income countries today. Still, at least four implications can be drawn from their experiences which are instructive for developing countries.

First, research tailored to the requirements of each area of each state or province played a key role in each country's modern growth. The central government took the initiative in establishing the agricultural research system. Research responsibilities were deliberately allocated among national, regional, and local agencies, each being assigned the tasks it was best equipped to perform. Pressures were exerted by farmers —through farmers' associations in Japan and by allocation of state funds in the U.S.—to guide research toward solution of problems of importance to them. In both countries there were relatively long gestation periods before research results began to pay off in increased farm production.

Second, the government generally encouraged private action or, sometimes, moved the private sector in seemingly more socially productive directions. The reinforcing interaction of the public and private sectors— close and effective cooperation among public agencies, farmers, scientists, and agricultural supply firms to increase agricultural productivity—stands out clearly in both countries.

Third, researchers developed production practices and machines geared to the farm sizes typical of each country. The large number of small farms in Japan resulted in technology different in important aspects from that developed for the large U.S. farms.

Fourth, sustained growth over long periods was perhaps even more important than the rates obtained (which were relatively modest) in explaining the large contribution of agriculture to overall economic growth.

Comprehensive national efforts

A serious challenge facing developing countries today is to accelerate agricultural output generally. Several developing countries have recently done so. In the following case studies, we sought answers to such questions as:

- What special circumstances led to the initiation of efforts? Was it a planned approach, a crash program, or what?
- To what extent were government organizations involved? How, and at what stages? What were the associated problems and issues, as well as the advantages and disadvantages?
- In productivity programs were realistic goals specified? When? By whom? Through what process were revisions made over time?
- Was equitable distribution of landownership established? What influence did size of holding have on adoption?
- Were the technical feasibility and economic profitability of the technology established in advance? How? By whom?
- How was the program or campaign organized? Were local rural people effectively involved?

- How did the program or project incorporate components such as development of technology; communication of technology; institutional participation and support in providing improved services for credit, input distribution, commodity marketing, and economic policy; and necessary infrastructure?
- At what stages did evaluation take place? How? With what results? What were the consequences of evaluation?
- How were people trained for the program, and did the program provide for the training of others?
- What were the accomplishments of the program or project in terms of increased production, higher incomes, and distribution of benefits?

In some cases, we were successful in finding answers to these questions in published studies. In many others, less so. There appears to be an urgent need for studies which systematically analyze the key points of success and failure of representative national efforts and from which principles applicable to other situations can be derived.

TAIWAN

Between 1950 and 1965, agricultural output in Taiwan increased at an annual rate of 4.5 percent, contributing significantly to the 7.6 percent yearly growth of national income. Agricultural productivity (yields) rose 2.5 percent per year, accounting for more than half of the total agricultural growth. Intensification of production through multiple cropping of previously single-cropped land was a second major growth force. This performance was achieved in an agricultural system in which farm families average 6.5 persons, or about 1 hectare of cultivated land each, and in which farms have increasingly been mechanized with small-scale equipment.

The foundation for modern agricultural growth in Taiwan was laid during the Japanese colonial period, 1895–1945. During this time, irrigation projects and transportation facilities were constructed, rural electrification was extended, chemical fertilizer and dwarf rice were introduced, disease and pest control measures were implemented, agricultural research and education programs were initiated, and local farmers' organizations were supported as a means of providing technical information, inputs, and marketing assistance to farmers. As a result, even before World War II, production was increasing faster than population, and large amounts of agricultural products were available for export.

The disruptions of war, independence from Japan, and separation from Mainland China caused setbacks in production. The 1939 level of output was not re-achieved until 1951. Large migrations from the mainland, combined with high birth rates and rapidly declining death rates (the result of improved health and sanitation), caused population growth to increase to over 3.5 percent yearly. The potential for expanding the area under cultivation or increasing the irrigated area had largely been exploited. Generous foreign aid was available from the U.S. and other countries, but it was obvious that domestic production rates had to be raised even higher than those achieved during the successful prewar period if the country was to prosper.

The production campaign that was organized to meet this challenge had three key elements. First, far-reaching land reform was carried out in three stages: in 1949, rent reductions and other improvements were initiated; in 1952, public land was sold on a large scale to tenants; and in 1953, a land-to-the-tiller program began in which 60 percent of the privately owned tenanted land was purchased by the government and resold to the tenants. The proportion of farmers owning their own land rose from 36 percent to 60 percent by 1957. This reform contributed to political stability and, perhaps more important for production, shifted the leadership of rural organizations to the farmers who tilled the land.

Second, in 1953, farmers' associations and cooperatives were reorganized. Marketing, credit, and agricultural extension were closely linked. At the base were small agricultural units made up of several farmers who were collectively represented in township farmers' associations. Above them were provincial associations.

Third, assured local markets for farm products and readily available local supplies of inputs, which reduced price uncertainty and risk, were probably as important as favorable input-output price ratios (which were not exceptionally attractive) in providing economic incentives to expand farm production. Fertilizer use in Taiwan is high (237 kg/ha in 1966), even though prices paid by farmers for fertilizer have been higher there than in most countries. Small-scale machinery tailored to the size of Taiwan's farms has been designed, manufactured, and widely used (Table 8.2). Institutional credit, which increased from 12 percent of the total credit supplied by all sources in 1949 to 65 percent by 1965, was made available through a number of agricultural credit institutions and government agencies.

The extension system has been tied in closely with research, credit, and farmer organizations. It has organized numerous demonstrations of new technologies in farmers' fields. A continuing flow of new technology has been made available by an agricultural research system, organized with centralized institutes and district improvement stations on a basis similar to the U.S. system of state branch experiment stations. The lag between identification of improved, profitable farming methods and their application on farmers' fields has been short.

Acceleration of agricultural and rural development was the primary concern of a semi-autonomous central development agency known as the Joint Commission on Rural Reconstruction (JCRR). Established through

Table 8.2. Major agricultural machines in Taiwan

Machine	Number of units			
	1960	1965	1970	1975
Power tiller	3,700	12,200	28,300	48,600
Tractor	—	400	500	1,500
Rice transplanter	—	—	300	2,800
Power sprayer	300	4,500	17,800	45,400[a]
Water pump	8,400	32,100	52,800	119,900[a]
Rice thresher	177,300	205,800	186,400	135,200[a]
Power thresher (with cleaning device)	—	—	—	2,800
Grain dryer (bin- and circulation-type)	—	150	200	1,700
Rice combine	—	—	20	2,100

Source: T. H. Shen, *Taiwan's Family Farm during Transitional Economic Growth.*
[a] Data for 1974.

joint U.S. and Chinese funding in 1948, JCRR has been involved in all phases of agricultural development. It has had direct ties with the Ministry of Economic Affairs, which in turn has been responsible for planning and supervising agricultural programs and for coordinating the programs, operations, and budgets of agricultural agencies. JCRR supports activities or programs which meet four criteria: (a) rural people have expressed needs for the services and activities; (b) the distribution of program benefits is fair; (c) the sponsoring agency is qualified to use the assistance and carry on the activities or programs after JCRR support is withdrawn; and (d) the feasibility of the project is demonstrated before it is expanded broadly. JCRR has thus played both catalytic and direct roles in the development process.

Taiwan's experience, like that of Japan, demonstrates that production in a nation of small, privately owned family farms can be efficient and can grow rapidly. By 1968 the value of crop production per hectare was about six times higher than that of the U.S. The essential ingredients were effective land reform, an adequate infrastructure (especially irrigation and transportation), a continuing source of new technology adapted to farm conditions and communicated to the farmer, integrated associations to ensure a responsive institutional structure serving agricultural needs, an intelligent, strong government involvement, the imagination and drive of the JCRR group, and good farmers responding to profitable opportunities.

MEXICO

In the early 1940s, Mexico's food production was stagnant and population was growing rapidly. It was an extremely poor nation. Yields were low

—about 800 kg/ha for wheat and 650 kg/ha for maize. However, in spite of a population growth rate exceeding 3 percent, Mexico was transformed from a country importing 163,000 tons of maize and 432,000 tons of wheat in 1944 to one exporting 497,000 tons of maize in 1965 and 276,000 tons of wheat annually from 1962 to 1965.

Mexico's own actions have contributed to her progress. Land reform, beginning in 1915, put substantial amounts of land, much of it in small parcels, into the hands of owner-operators. Agricultural education was strengthened. The number of institutions of higher learning devoted to agriculture increased from three to twelve. In 1958 a graduate school was created in conjunction with the National School of Agriculture at Chapingo. It now offers training through the Ph.D. level. An extensive program was implemented to improve rural infrastructure. Between 1940 and 1967, irrigated area increased by approximately 2 million hectares. The administration of irrigation was strengthened. Numerous new roads were built and old roads upgraded. Between 1940 and 1967 the land suitable for agriculture more than doubled and pasture land increased by over 20 million hectares. Agricultural credit was extended to the rural areas, with special efforts (although with varying success) being made to reach small farmers.[3] Public and private industries stepped up production and distribution of a wide variety of agricultural chemicals and mechanical equipment.

However, probably the most important factor contributing to Mexican agricultural performance was establishment of a strong research program. In 1943, at Mexico's request, the Rockefeller Foundation sent three well-known scientists—Richard Bradfield, P. C. Mangelsdorf, and E. C. Stakman—to analyze Mexican agricultural potential. They concluded that agricultural progress could be made if technological problems could be solved and people trained. To that end, the Office of Special Studies was established in the Ministry of Agriculture with Rockefeller Foundation assistance. Work was initiated on maize, wheat, beans, and potatoes. In later years, research attention spread to other basic food crops and animal species. Instructive lessons can be learned from examination of the wheat and maize programs.

The wheat program. The structure and the essential components of a successful national commodity production program can be illustrated by the cooperative wheat program initiated in Mexico in 1944. By 1969, yields had climbed nearly fourfold. Mexico has become a center for assistance to other nations, providing high-yielding wheat varieties, serving as a major source of quality wheat seed, training young scientists, and lending its own specialists to lead programs elsewhere.

[3] See the discussion of the Puebla Project later in this chapter.

At least eight important components of this successful program can be identified. First, ambitious objectives were established. In 1944 the program was designed to eliminate Mexico's wheat deficit, which it did by 1954, in spite of the growing population. Every effort was made to raise production in the shortest possible period of time.

Second, there was continuous emphasis on research. New varieties were resistant to rust and had short, stiff straw to permit profitable use of high levels of nitrogen fertilizers. Building in insensitivity to daylength extended the range of adaptation of wheat in Mexico and elsewhere. Soil management, weed control, and irrigation techniques were developed. By growing two and sometimes three generations, or crops, per year, the research program made fast progress. Although Mexico had to produce its own wheat varieties starting from a low base of technology, it did so; and by 1954, 70 percent of Mexico's wheat land was planted with new varieties developed, tested, and increased in Mexico.

Third, in-service training (internships) was emphasized. Some 700 nationals were locally trained to a point of proficiency in crop and animal production, many in the wheat program.[4]

Fourth, outstanding and dedicated young men—graduates of Mexico's agricultural colleges, most of whom had received additional field experience—were sent abroad for advanced studies. Mexico developed the competent leadership needed to assume the direction of its own wheat improvement and other work.

Fifth, leadership was continuous. The wheat program was initiated by J. G. Harrar and Jose Rodriguez Vallejo, with the counsel of E. C. Stakman. Shortly thereafter, Norman Borlaug assumed responsibility for the project. Borlaug stayed with the program during the next 16 years, until Mexico's own scientists were prepared to assume leadership.[5] A number of the Mexican scientists who joined the project in its early years are now leaders in the national research program.

[4] Graduates of Mexico's colleges of agriculture were given one or more years of local experience working as members of the staff of the various projects. They learned about the crops, how to improve them, and how to farm them, or obtained similar experience with animals. A fraction of these individuals stayed in research, but over the years many others accepted positions in extension, in teaching, in seed production, with agricultural banks, or with industrial firms. Through this process a large number of exceptionally well-trained technicians were infused into Mexican agriculture, laying the basis for what today is an effective governmental staff. These individuals helped to do the jobs of research, seed production, and extension as they learned. That kept costs minimal. (See also Chapter 14.)

[5] In 1961 the cooperative Mexico–Rockefeller Foundation program was phased out. To consolidate programs, the National Institute of Agricultural Research (INIA) was organized. INIA now has 17 departments, 7 major research centers, and 22 experiment stations. Since 1966 a high degree of coordination and interchange of experimental data has been maintained between INIA and the International Center for Maize and Wheat Improvement (CIMMYT). The director of INIA is both a trustee and a member of the Executive Committee of CIMMYT.

Sixth, as trained people became available, the research program was systematically broadened to all important wheat-growing regions and seed production was intensified through private growers and government farms.

Seventh, research and extension were combined. As the researchers solved the problems limiting production, they demonstrated repeatedly —at field days, on private farms, to national leaders and to farm groups— how higher yields could be obtained. Instead of separating research and extension, there was one program that began on the research station and ended with use of the varieties and practices by the farmers.

Eighth, government and private services and policies encouraged wheat production. Price supports were provided, farm credit became more widely available, and supplies of farm machinery, fertilizers, and agricultural chemicals increased. Without the interest and support of leaders of the Mexican government, this record of unusual achievement could not have occurred.

The maize program. Between 1943 and 1968, national average maize yields in Mexico doubled. This was a substantial rise, but considerably less than the increase in wheat yields. The factors responsible have been well summarized by Delbert Myren in "The Rockefeller Foundation Program in Corn and Wheat in Mexico," and include the following:

Locational differences. Maize was grown on 6.8 million hectares, mostly rainfed, scattered over the country; wheat was grown on only 850,000 hectares, almost all irrigated, concentrated in the northwest.

Market orientation. Maize was grown on two-thirds of the farms of Mexico by 2 million farmers with average landholdings of about 3 hectares. Wheat was grown by fewer than 50,000 farmers with an average of 17 hectares each. Maize was grown primarily for home consumption; wheat was grown for sale.

Technical differences. Two yield-limiting factors for wheat, stem rust and excessive plant height, could be quickly and effectively overcome by plant breeders, thereby offering a dramatic yield increase through new varieties at practically no cost to the farmer. In contrast, because of variations in soil and climatic conditions, and because of consumer preferences, many types of maize were required, ranging from tropical white dents and both yellow and white tropical flints for the coasts, to a wide assortment for intermediate areas and the highlands. In some localities, long-growing maize types were needed for those farmers who could plant early with irrigation, intermediate maturity strains were required for years in which rains began on normal dates, and very early varieties were necessary for some areas in years when planting was delayed by late rains. At one time, when wheat breeding work was concentrated in only two locations, maize breeding programs were under way at 10 widespread locations. And at each location several distinct maize varieties and types had to be sought. Finally, as fertilizer use was increased, plant population usually had to be increased as well in order to get high maize yields. For wheat, on the other hand, the heavy labor investment in overplanting and hand thinning was not needed because of the wheat plant's natural tillering ability.

Seed production and distribution. Since the wheat plant is self-pollinated, seed can be multiplied rapidly and repeatedly by farmers from their own fields without change in the variety, if done with care. With hybrid maize, which was emphasized early in the program, the farmer had to purchase new seed for each planting for best results. Open-pollinated maize varieties can of course be increased rapidly, but seed producers must be careful to isolate seed fields to prevent mixture with other types since maize pollen is wind-borne. Hybrids needed for each of the many different ecological niches of Mexico must be produced anew each year, requiring enormous seed multiplication and distribution networks of the types that only specialized commercial companies have successfully developed and managed.

Information and extension. Since wheat growers were concentrated in a few well-defined areas, an important part of the communications work was undertaken by the research scientists themselves; no large-scale extension effort was needed. The maize research workers also participated in promotional activities, but the problems of communicating with numerous, small, widely scattered maize farmers were great.

The element of risk. A basic limitation in maize production is the uncertainty of both the amount and the distribution of rainfall. Even in areas of more adequate rainfall in Mexico, the relatively slow rate of adoption of improved practices seems related to the uncertainty and risks involved, as well as to lack of information about new practices for many localities.

Given the complexity of maize improvement in a country with the ecological variability of Mexico, the doubling of national average yields represents a substantial accomplishment.

Epilogue. The experience of Mexico provides models for crop-oriented production programs which deserve the study of agronomists and national leaders elsewhere. However, in spite of the rapid progress which has been made, it has not been enough. A combination of the steadily increasing population, high rates of per capita income growth, and incentives to produce nonfood crops has conspired to move Mexico back into a food-deficit position. (In 1975 the rate of Mexican agricultural growth exceeded the rate of population increase, estimated at 3.5 percent annually, for the first time in 10 years.) An important lesson of the Mexican experience is that increased food production only buys time to introduce programs to limit population growth. Even agricultural progress as spectacular as Mexico's can be neutralized by increases in human numbers.

INDIA

Following independence in 1947, India embarked on a series of 5-year plans emphasizing agricultural development. Land reform was carried out. An extensive system of rural roads and irrigation channels was constructed. The Community Development Program and the Intensive Agricultural Districts Program began to bring services to rural people. An effective agricultural research system was organized. Foodgrain production expanded from 51 million tons in 1950/51 to 89 million tons in 1964/65.

However, in the view of Minister for Food and Agriculture C. Subramaniam, India "stretched traditional agriculture almost to the very limit during the first three plans." Cereal production stagnated around 80 million tons from 1960/61 to 1963/64 and rose higher in 1964/65 only because of exceptionally good rains. The scope for planting more land and expanding the use of chemical fertilizers by large numbers of new cultivators, the two main factors accounting for previous growth, was limited. Major technological changes were required.

The new strategy. Fortunately, semidwarf Mexican wheat varieties had been introduced experimentally in India in 1962/63 as part of trials of exotic wheats. On the basis of these tests, Indian scientists, in consultation with Norman Borlaug, concluded that India's growing conditions were similar enough to those of Mexico to make direct transfer of the dwarf wheats a good gamble. Bulk samples of four commercial varieties were shipped to India. Production trials and seed multiplication followed.

A similar pattern of research and testing was being carried out with rice varieties from the International Rice Research Institute and from Taiwan. Varietal development research within India also had been accelerated in the late 1950s. By 1966, high-yielding varieties of the five major cereals had undergone at least limited testing under Indian conditions. The stage was set for their widespread introduction.

A crisis in food production occurred when India suffered two consecutive droughts of unprecedented severity. In 1965/66, foodgrain production dropped 8 million tons below the average of the first 5 years of the 1960s and in 1966/67 it was 5 million tons lower than average.

The "New Strategy of Agricultural Development," India's response to the crisis, marked a bold departure from previous policies. The New Strategy proposed combining high-yielding varieties, a "package" of complementary inputs in selected irrigated or reliable-rainfall areas, and incentive prices. Availability of high-yielding varieties was the critical new element. The decision to initially concentrate inputs—fertilizers and pesticides—in areas of high productivity represented a fundamental policy change. This was an expedient to obtain quick production gains among the more progressive farmers, to be followed by widespread adoption as a result of the initial successes. Investment in agricultural supply industries was encouraged. Programs in research, extension, and rural credit were reorganized and strengthened.[6] It was proposed to have 13 million hectares under the high-yielding varieties (primarily of wheat and rice) by 1970/71—a clear and ambitious goal.

The drought of 1966/67 kept the results of the first year of the program modest. However, in the second year, the New Strategy set off widespread enthusiasm and exceeded expectations. Foodgrain production in 1967/68 rose to over 97 million tons, almost 10 percent above the previous record output. By 1974/75, high-yielding varieties were sown on 62 percent of the total wheat area and on 30 percent of the total rice area. This rapid spread of new technology surpassed even the speed of adoption of hybrid maize in the U.S. Midwest. In 1975/76, total foodgrain production was estimated at 118 million tons.

Characteristics of adoption. The main reason for the rapid spread of the new varieties was the higher net income expected from their adoption. Production costs per ton were comparable to those for older varieties, but the new varieties produced 50 percent higher yields, on the average, with the application of modern inputs.

The large cash requirements for purchased inputs and the risk implicit in the adoption of new practices made it inevitable that those who had savings or easy access to loans should be among the earliest adopters. Farmers with large holdings—5 hectares or more—most easily satisfied these requirements.[7] Supplementary water was very important, and owners of private tube wells had significant management advantages over users of public irrigation. Tractors were needed for land shaping to make best use of available water and for timely operations for multiple cropping. Generally, the larger farmers also devoted larger proportions of their total wheat planting to the new varieties. As a result, per hectare returns tended to be higher on large farms than on small farms.

However, the gains were not confined to larger farmers. Small farmers rapidly adopted the new varieties, although sometimes a year or two after the larger farmers. Tenancy and illiteracy were not insurmountable

[6] The Indian research system is described in Chapter 12.
[7] According to the 1961 census, 90 percent of the holdings in India were smaller than 5 hectares and 96 percent were smaller than 10 hectares.

barriers to adoption. Returns were high enough to compensate for the sometimes onerous terms on which tenancy was contracted. In traditional societies like India, farm demonstration plots and talks with neighbors, relatives, and opinion leaders are much more important than the written word in spreading new agronomic practices. The new technologies required more labor per hectare for cultivation and harvesting. Additional demands on agricultural supply industries were created to provide machines and implements for cultivation, harvesting, and threshing. Larger volumes were marketed. Wages were pushed up in the nearby towns as well as on the farms, thereby helping the landless laborers. The Small Farmers Development Program and other institutional reforms have been initiated to ensure that gains from new technologies are shared even more equitably in the future.

The future. India has established a basis for accelerated agricultural growth. The increased use of modern inputs has signaled the beginning of a structural change: a significant part of the country's productive resources are now being purchased from outside the agricultural sector. This has made the farm and nonfarm sectors more interdependent, a characteristic which is critical to the agricultural development process. The use of modern inputs also signals a change in the technology of production resulting in lower per unit costs of production and higher per unit profits for farmers who are able to purchase and efficiently use such inputs. The key elements have been introduction of new technology adapted to local conditions, reorientation and coordination of public and private organizations serving agriculture, and incentive prices to farmers (for wheat). Continuing efforts are being made to ensure that higher production is sustained and that the gains are extended to an ever-increasing range of commodities, regions, and people.

THE PEOPLE'S REPUBLIC OF CHINA

The recent agricultural and rural development of China, given its population of over 900 million, its limited amount of cultivated land area per person, and its low per capita income, is one of the remarkable achievements of this century.

From 1956 to 1971, Chinese grain production increased from almost 190 million tons to 250 million tons, an annual rate of about 1.9 percent, about equal to population growth. Rural income roughly doubled between the early 1950s and the late 1960s. Average food availability is higher than in most other Asian countries. And distribution of income has become markedly more equitable.

In 1974, 10 U.S. agricultural scientists spent 1 month in China visiting 20 agricultural research centers or colleges of agriculture, and seven communes, including the component production brigades and production teams. The team traveled 5,000 kilometers, much of it by train and by car. The team was impressed by several factors. Crops generally looked good wherever the team traveled—largely as a result of expansion and extension of traditional practices. Moreover, within localities production seemed *uniformly* good. There seemed to be within local areas no "exceptional" or "poor" farms.

Although the government is authoritarian, there seemed to be a substantial amount of local initiative and local participation in management decisions. Farm people seemed to have hope for more prosperous times, for improvements in their personal standards of living. It appeared that China was making every possible effort to reduce its rate of population growth. Malnutrition seemed nonexistent.

There was pervasive emphasis on year-round productivity by all individuals, on achieving maximum yields per year from each hectare, on stabilizing agricultural yields at high levels through massive irrigation and drainage works, on extensive use of both organic and inorganic fertilizers, and on reforestation to control erosion.

Chinese agriculture and rural development seemed to involve an unusual degree of financial accounting; there was much discussion of gross and net income at various levels of organization, of bank deposits of members of communes, of reinvestment of commune income in enterprises of the commune, and of levels of taxation.

There was a remarkable amount of light industry in the rural areas to provide employment for rural people, especially in off-seasons, and to generate income to finance social services and reinvest in elaboration of local enterprises.

Because crops were generally good—rice yields of 5,000 or 6,000 kg/ha were routinely observed—the team searched for the basic reasons, the incentives, for the generally good farming. Clearly, China had given high priority to agricultural development, but how and why had it succeeded?

Organization of agriculture. The organizational system for agricultural production was created over a long period (1949–62) of experiment and change. The starting point was radical land reform in 1949, when land and political power were taken from the rural elite and peasants were mobilized politically and psychologically to shape their lives and environments.[8] The key unit in rural China today is the commune, which in turn is made up of production brigades and, within brigades, of production teams.

---

[8] While all land is basically under collective ownership, up to 7 percent of the cultivated area is set aside for allocation to the families within the production teams as private garden plots. Some activity in private handicrafts also is encouraged.

The production team comprises 15–30 households whose lands have been pooled and are operated as a single unit. The production team is governed by a revolutionary committee (board of directors).

The production brigade comprises 8–15 production teams and represents a natural grouping of hamlets with contiguous landholdings. The brigade may cultivate 80–120 hectares in an irrigated area. The brigade is generally responsible for providing services such as the primary school and the health clinic. It may own farm equipment, including small hand tractors, small pumps, and other implements, which it contracts to the production teams. Brigades are encouraged to develop diverse enterprises by which they generate income for schools, health clinics, and other services. Brigade management consists of a revolutionary committee made up of representatives of production teams, the army, the Party, and others.

The commune, consisting of 10–20 brigades and up to 50,000 members, is essentially a self-contained, operational community with substantial autonomy and business orientation. It is responsible for overall maintenance of the lands, for operation of the irrigation and drainage systems, and for road maintenance, enterprises, and other community services such as hospitals and secondary schools. Each commune strives for self-sufficiency in basic food crops. This lessens allocation problems for the central government and eases the burden on the nation's transportation system, particularly the railways, in moving the nation's massive food supplies. Each commune has a marketing enterprise which sells farm products and buys and distributes the inputs required by its members. Heavy equipment is owned and operated by commune enterprises. Plant protection is largely a commune (or brigade) responsibility, particularly when use of spraying or dusting equipment is required. Diverse businesses are operated by the commune to generate income. The commune is, like other units, governed by a revolutionary committee or board of directors.

Production plans are established by negotiation among the various levels each year. The central authorities work out a national plan for production of various crops and also for sale of crops to the state. Quotas are then progressively negotiated for each province, county, commune, brigade, and, finally, production team. In turn, each production team specifies the inputs and services that it needs to meet the quota. When supplies are adequate, the production team is free to purchase what it wants. When supplies are scarce, an allocation mechanism which works upward through planning departments facilitates decisions. Day-to-day production decisions are left solely to the production teams.

The system provides incentives both to improve productivity and to reduce the rate of population growth. First, there is the obvious incentive to raise total output of the production team. The income of individuals or households can rise only with increase in productivity or value of output and with individual efforts. For example, an individual's income for a given year depends upon the profit of the team (total value of the team's output for the year minus the costs involved and reserves set aside and minus the tax paid to the state). The individual receives a share of the profit, according to work points earned. Because the amount of cultivated land per person is limited, the above consideration explains the uniform quality of the farming within the area of a single production team; quality of farming is raised to the maximum permitted by local skill and experience. Very intensive care can be given to the crops by members of the production team. In a sense there is no farming in China —even the grain crops are "gardened."

At the same time, there is a strong incentive to hold the number of members in the production team down, for individual income depends directly on the numbers in the local unit. The problem of population growth is an immediate one for each individual rather than a general problem for some distant unit of government to solve. Together with aggressive promotion of techniques to reduce births, this results in a system which appears to be effective in limiting population growth.

Technical support to communes. An important feature of China's drive for higher productivity has been the direct support of communes by agricultural research institutes and colleges of agriculture and the direct support of commune industrial enterprises by research and educational institutions in other fields.

Institutes and colleges are required to cooperate directly with communes in work on farm-level technology. Certain brigades establish experiment stations of several hectares for research or technological work by teams of scientists, local farm managers, and peasants—the so-called 3-in-1 approach. In 1974, a third of an institute's scientists and technicians reportedly were in residence at brigades, working as members of local research and development teams. Another third of the staff members of any institute or college were doing general extension work with brigades and communes that did not have "experimental places." The decentralization of the academies' research and technological activity undoubtedly accelerated farm-level improvements in productivity. This means, however, that only a third of the scientists and technicians were at central experiment stations working on in-depth research.[9] Most fundamental work had been shelved, at least for the time being.

A major objective of technical support has been to stabilize yields at

[9] In 1977, exchanges of visits of scientific teams were initiated between China and both IRRI and CIMMYT.

high levels. China has built irrigation and drainage systems and massive dikes in some coastal and river delta areas to reduce the effects of "nature's adversity." Scientists have developed and promoted short-duration crop varieties which are exposed to the vagaries of weather for shorter periods than the traditional ones and which, if calamity occurs, can be replanted between the rows of the damaged crop. Practices for relay planting, intercropping, and catch cropping have received considerable attention. Mechanized methods are used to prepare land rapidly for succeeding crops in China's intensive agricultural system, to apply crop management or protection techniques which could not be done by hand, and to gradually release labor for other enterprises of the communes or brigades. These techniques make possible a substantially higher rate of production per hectare per year than could be achieved under monoculture.

Strengths and weaknesses. The Chinese system of organization permits rapid transfer of technology, facilitates the allocation of resources (partly on noneconomic grounds), and enforces a high degree of savings and a commensurate high level of investment.

This system also has problems. Difficulties in the organization of technical and administrative services stem largely from the desire to discourage formation of elite groups. The agricultural research system therefore appears stronger in the application of existing technology than in the generation of new technology. There have reportedly been difficulties in keeping tractor fleets fully operational. The system is so delicately balanced that disruptions can quickly become serious if not checked in time, leading to rigidities and inflexibilities which can slow progress.

China has clearly embarked on a campaign to increase agricultural output, to increase per capita income of rural people through intensified agriculture, massive public works, and decentralized industry, and to reduce population growth rates. Any system contains a series of compromises, and no one system can be judged best in every respect. The Chinese system succeeds in applying existing technology with widely distributed benefits within its farming community.

National commodity programs

Several nations have had success in increasing production of food crops through national commodity programs. Instructive lessons can be learned from the experiences of Kenya with maize, Turkey with wheat, and Colombia and the Philippines with rice.

KENYA: MAIZE

In 1955 Kenya began a maize improvement program that has been so successful that today over half of all maize planted is hybrid and the introduction of hybrid maize has been used to stimulate better management generally.[10] The price of maize has remained reasonable while demand from a population growing at more than 3 percent a year has been satisfied, livestock feeding is increasing, a maize products factory has been set up, and maize can now be exported at a profit. The development of hybrid maize in Kenya was in no way a "forced-pace" campaign. It is, rather, an example of development without formal planning and shows what a dedicated local effort can achieve with a minimum of outside assistance.

Kenya already had several of the requisites for increasing production when the maize improvement program began. The road system throughout most of the country was adequate. Fertilizers, seeds, and other inputs were distributed throughout the country on time and at reasonable cost by private traders.[11] The price of maize was fixed annually before planting and supported at a constant level over the year through purchases at a network of buying points. Local African shopkeepers extended this network to the small-scale farming area by the time the maize research package become available.

Availability of suitable technology was the key missing component for success. The Maize Improvement Section of the Ministry of Agriculture aimed for a complete package of recommendations to maximize farmers' yields and profits. The first step was to breed a higher-yielding variety responsive to good conditions, but with a yield under poor growing conditions at least equal to that of local maize. Farmers were free to choose hybrids or improved open-pollinated varieties. This research strategy provided continuous long-term yield improvement: the yield superiority of hybrids over local varieties progressed from an average of 30 percent in 1961 to 60 percent by the mid-1970s.

The next step was to identify the factors that affected yield most and

[10] In the high-altitude and good rainfall areas of western Kenya, 90 percent of the farmers, both small and large, are using hybrids.

[11] The Kenya Seed Company played a key role in the maize improvement program from the beginning. Its hybrid seed was certified to international standards, its seed price was lower than that of hybrids in other countries, and it developed a large number of registered sellers (now over 5,000). The company realized its main market was with small farmers and became very active in extension. It participated frequently, though irregularly, in exchanges of ideas with the Maize Improvement Section of the Ministry of Agriculture in planning and implementing the program.

Originally the company was entirely private, being formed by a group of European farmers when research first produced improved strains of indigenous pasture grasses and legumes. Now there are few European settlers left; most of the seed producers are African. Government has a controlling interest, and continuity of management has ensured improvement of standards.

Table 8.3. Results from 11 district crop management trials in western Kenya, 1966 and 1967[a]

Factors	Treatment	Yields (kg/ha)	Yield (kg/ha)	Returns ($/ha)	Cost ($/ha)	Net profit ($/ha)
			Differences between treatments			
Timely planting	Start of rains	5,800	2,400	96	3	93
	4 weeks later	3,400				
Plant density	39,000/ha	5,100	1,000	40	3	37
	20,000/ha	4,100				
Seed	Hybrid	5,400	1,600	64	4	60
	Local	3,800				
Weeding	3 times	5,200	1,200	48	7	41
	Once, late	4,000				
Phosphorus at planting	56 kg/ha	4,700	100	4	11	−7
	0 kg/ha	4,600				
Nitrogen top dressing	78 kg/ha	4,900	600	24	25	−1
	0 kg/ha	4,300				

Source: Personal communication from M. N. Harrison of work conducted by A. Y. A llan.
[a] Trials of six factors each at two levels, with a total of 64 treatment combinations .

to study their interactions to arrive at a recommended package. Table 8.3, which presents only the main treatment effects, shows that the factors which cost little more (time of planting, seed, weeding) tended to give the greatest returns. The use of fertilizer by itself, on the average, resulted in financial loss. Figure 8.2 shows the large positive interaction among

Fig. 8.2. The Kenya maize demonstration diamond: Data on four treatment combinations showing positive interactions

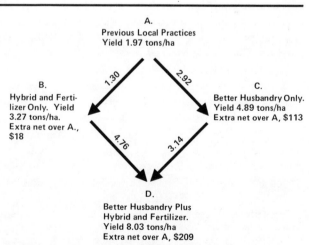

A.
Previous Local Practices
Yield 1.97 tons/ha

B.
Hybrid and Ferti-
lizer Only. Yield
3.27 tons/ha.
Extra net over A.,
$18

C.
Better Husbandry Only.
Yield 4.89 tons/ha
Extra net over A, $113

D.
Better Husbandry Plus
Hybrid and Fertilizer.
Yield 8.03 tons/ha
Extra net over A, $209

Source: Personal communication from M. N. Harrison; based on trials reported in Table 8.3 on work conducted by A. Y. Allan.

factors. Hybrid plus fertilizer increased yields by 1,300 kg/ha with poor management (late planting, poor stand, and poor weeding), but by 4,760 kg/ha more with good management. Similarly, good management increased yields by 2,920 kg/ha without hybrids and fertilizer, but by 3,140 kg/ha more with them. When these four treatments were combined in demonstrations on farmers' fields, the lesson was clear: hybrids and fertilizers by themselves are no substitute for good farming. They give worthwhile profit only when combined. If the full recommendations were followed, farmers could quadruple yield and get a good profit.

Strong cooperation was formed between research and extension staff by seminars, demonstration plots, and district tours. At annual seminars led by provincial extension officers, researchers presented their latest trial results and the extension staff decided on the package of recommendations. Demonstration plots were explained. At least one research officer each year visited each district to meet with the extension staff, to monitor progress, and to identify weak links. Weaknesses found were then reviewed at the next seminar. The Kenya Seed Company and other companies took part in these seminars and policy coordination activities. This kept conflicting advice from reaching the farmer and combined the considerable strengths of commercial enterprise with government programs.

With these combined efforts, the farmers showed little resistance to change. The large expatriate farmers initially insisted on hybrids. A few subsistence farmers, seeing and appreciating the advantages, also demanded the hybrids for themselves. They traveled long distances to buy the seed because there were no distribution points in their localities. Their fields provided the best demonstration plots. Thereafter the problem was to expand seed supplies fast enough. From 1965 through 1967 the Kenya Seed Company almost doubled seed production each year and still was unable to meet demand. Large-scale farmers planted over 80 percent of their maize land to hybrids within 6 years from first introduction. The time required for 80 percent of peasant subsistence farme s to adopt hybrids varied from 8 to 11 years.

Extension policy was to use hybrids as a lever to stimulate better management generally. Before hybrids were introduced subsistence farmers used no fertilizer on maize. Ten years after the introduction of hybrids, fertilizer use reached 50 percent of the recommended rate in western Kenya. Small farm size, low educational level, low income from cash crops, long distance from source of inputs, and limited work experience on large commercial farms slowed the adoption of some aspects of the recommended hybrid-maize package, although not greatly.

Continuity of leadership was important to the success of Kenya's effort. Michael Harrison, maize breeder, and Alistair Allan, maize agronomist, each spent about 15 years in the program. Festus Ogada, after 3 years as a maize breeder, took over from Harrison as senior maize research officer, while Harrison stayed on for 2 years as regional coordinator for the International Maize and Wheat Improvement Center (CIMMYT), a total transition period of 5 years. Ogada is still director of the National Agricultural Research Station, Kitale, where the maize work is headquartered. Wim Verburght, managing director, later joined by Ted Hazelden, commercial director, have been with the Kenya Seed Company throughout the development of hybrid production. Hazelden was previously an assistant maize breeder with Harrison and his transfer typified the close cooperation between the Maize Research Section and the Kenya Seed Company.

Effective use was made of foreign technical assistance to supplement local resources. In 1955 Kenya recruited Harrison, its first full-time maize research worker, and British government assistance soon afterward extended this effort. Later The Rockefeller Foundation gave a grant to add an agronomist, and the U.S. government supported a project that studied maize breeding methods. Both grants were designed to enable Kenya to work in a cooperative regional program for eastern Africa. CIMMYT assisted the regional program for a short period. The British government added four agronomists when The Rockefeller Foundation grant ended.

Kenya's Maize Research Section currently operates four main research stations in different ecological zones, but is still a comparatively small program with no specialists other than breeders and agronomists, all Kenyan nationals. Outside assistance ended in 1977. From the beginning of the maize improvement program, the largest single source of funds was a research grant from Kenya's Maize and Produce Marketing Board. This grant financed farmer membership on the Cereals Research Advisory Committee and so ensured that farmers participated in preparing budgets and making policy.

Several lessons can be learned from Kenya. A profitable technology package, giving significantly higher yield levels than traditional farming, was the basic requirement. Kenya was fortunate in having people and organizations that could be mobilized, adapted, and coordinated to provide the services needed to make the new technology available to farmers. A land of extreme contrast between types of farmers, Kenya has shown that small subsistence farmers, given the opportunity, will adopt appropriate new technology almost as rapidly as large commercial farmers.

TURKEY: WHEAT

Wheat is the principal food of the 40 million people of Turkey. Annual consumption of 200 kilograms per person is among the highest in the world. This cereal accounts for approximately half the calories and protein in the diet of the average Turkish consumer. In 1972, 8.2 million hectares were sown in wheat, and an almost equal area was kept in fallow to accumulate moisture for the following year's crop. The total area utilized for wheat therefore totaled approximately 15 million hectares, 60 percent of Turkey's tillable land. In 1961, Turkey produced slightly less than 7 million tons of wheat. By 1970, production had risen to only about 10 million tons. By 1977, output had jumped to 17 million tons. Average yields had climbed more than 60 percent to 1,800 kg/ha (Fig. 8.3).

The coastal regions, where spring wheat is grown, contain 15–20 percent of the total wheat area and account for 25–30 percent of total wheat production. In 1967, based on previous testing, 22,000 tons of spring wheat seed were imported from Mexico. Some 60,000 farmers with 170,000 hectares took part in the 1967 campaign. Most of these farmers had to be instructed quickly in the new practices, including use of grain drills for shallow, precision planting. An extension effort involved 250 agents aided by U.S. specialists. Initial recommendations for planting dates and fertilizer use were based on experience in similar environments elsewhere. Information was also gathered from thousands of demonstration plots throughout the country. In subsequent years, as Turkish research organizations began to focus on the new problems, more precise recommendations for the local conditions were developed. Government-managed production farms provided seeds at stable prices. Some government credit was made available to support input purchases. A government program guaranteed minimum support prices.

Fig. 8.3. Wheat production and yields in Turkey, 1962–76 (3-year moving averages)

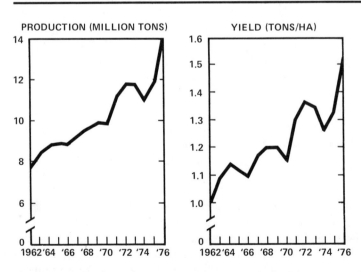

Source: Bill C. Wright, "A Brief Review of the Turkish Wheat Research and Training Project."

By 1971/72, the high-yielding varieties were estimated to be sown on 900,000 hectares, about two-thirds of the wheat area in the coastal regions. Yield potentials of the varieties in use by 1976 were 5,000–6,000 kg/ha; of this, farmers were realizing 40–60 percent, leaving considerable room for improvement in yields.

An extensive research effort is now being devoted to increasing the production of winter wheat on the Anatolian Plateau and the highlands to the east, which account for 60 percent of total wheat area. Rainfall is low and variable. Major changes are being introduced in the system of fallow to conserve moisture and control weeds. These changes will require substitute feeds for the large numbers of sheep which graze the weeds and stubble during the fallow period. Once government programs begin actively to promote these systems, production gains in the winter wheat areas of Turkey can be expected to be as impressive as those experienced in the coastal, spring wheat areas.

COLOMBIA: RICE

In 1967 the Inter-American Rice Improvement Project was initiated by the International Center of Tropical Agriculture (CIAT) in close cooperation with the Instituto Colombiano Agropecuario (ICA). Peter Jennings, who had previously headed the rice-breeding program at the International Rice Research Institute (IRRI), worked closely with Manuel Rosero and his colleagues at ICA during the next 8 years. The best varieties from IRRI were released in 1968. In 1971 the first of several varieties produced in Colombia was made available to farmers.

Adoption of the new varieties and related technology for use on irrigated lands was extremely rapid, in part because of the superiority of the new technology and in part because of the cooperation of the National Rice Growers' Federation, which provided extension services, sold inputs, offered training courses, and collaborated in field testing. National average rice yields in Colombia rose from 1,800 kg/ha in 1965 to 4,400 kg/ha in 1975, when virtually all irrigated areas were planted with high-yielding varieties (Fig. 8.4). The average yield for the irrigated sector rose to 5,400 kg/ha, one of the highest in the world. Between 1969 and 1975, total rice production more than doubled.

The scientists responsible for the development of the new rice technology for Colombia now feel that an opportunity exists to produce rice by means of a modified Asian technology on perhaps 60 million hectares of poorly drained coastal lands in Latin America. They further believe that this could be accomplished at a much lower cost and in a shorter time than would be needed to build large irrigation facilities. The technology would include construction of drainage canals, leveling of lands and construction of bunds by tractor, the sowing by hand of pregerminated seed of high-yielding varieties, hand application of fertilizers, use of small-scale threshing, and the training of technicians and farmers. Family farm units of from 2 to 3 hectares would be appropriate, if grouped to allow use of one tractor and implements per 100 hectares. Low-lift pumps could supply supplementary irrigation from rivers and streams.

THE PHILIPPINES: RICE

Like other Asian countries, the Philippines was hard hit by a poor rice crop in 1973. Its rice shortage was about 700,000 tons, of which it was expected that less than 30 percent could be imported before the tradi-

Fig. 8.4. Percentage of irrigated area planted to modern dwarf rice varieties and total rice production in Colombia, 1968–74

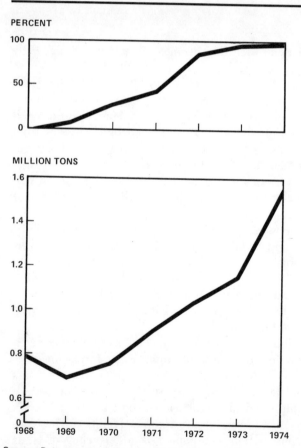

Source: Data on area under new varieties supplied by Peter R. Jennings; production data from U.S. Department of Agriculture

tional lean months. In this time of emergency, the Philippines launched the "Masagana 99" rice production program.[12] J. D. Drilon has identified major elements of the campaign:

- A package of improved production practices had been developed for rainfed lowland farms by the International Rice Research Institute and the Department of Agriculture and Natural Resources of the Philippines over the previous 2 years.[13] Four hundred research trials in two provinces provided information about planting methods (broadcast or transplanted), time of planting, optimum nitrogen application, best varieties to use, best types of herbicides and insecticides, and best combined management levels. During the following year, a pilot program with almost 100 farmers was set up to test the new technology on a whole-farm basis.
- The government and private dealers, who handled the distribution, promoted the adoption of seed of recommended varieties.
- Fertilizers were distributed to participating farmers on a priority basis at a subsidized price. Efforts were coordinated by the Fertilizer Industry Authority. During 1973, fertilizer consumption nationwide increased almost 90 percent above that of the previous year.
- A campaign to control pests and diseases was organized and the needed pesticides were made available through private suppliers, coordinated by the Pesticide Institute of the Philippines, a private organization. During 1973, pesticide consumption was twice the previous year's level.
- The task of credit distribution was divided among three institutions: the Philippine National Bank, the Rural Banking System, and the Agricultural Credit Administration. The Agricultural Loan Fund guaranteed 85 percent of all losses sustained by lending institutions, reducing the need for collateral. A new rediscounting procedure enabled lending institutions to recycle loan funds at a faster rate to achieve greater volume. Farmer-borrowers were formed into small groups; each group member guaranteed his fellow members. In the first year of the program almost 650,000 farmers were reached by credit, with an average loan repayment of 91 percent; over 300,000 other farmers participated in the program without obtaining credit from banks.
- Irrigation improvement and pump distribution programs were intensified to make double cropping possible and to provide adequate water during the growing season.
- Over 2,000 technicians were trained; a special loan fund provided

[12] *Masagana* means "abundance," and 99 was the target yield of the program—99 cavans (44 kilograms each) of paddy rice per hectare.
[13] Forty-seven percent of Philippine rice land is under rainfed lowland conditions and 28 percent is farmed under upland conditions.

motorcycles to enable the technicians to get into the countryside to work directly with farmers.

- An informational and education drive was organized through the use of radio and other media. Half-hour programs were beamed to farmers each morning. Newspapers gave coverage. Posters were printed and distributed. A commercial advertising company assisted in designing the media campaign.
- The price support, procurement, and storage program was strengthened.
- Target areas of high production potential were identified to focus program inputs.
- A management system, operating at each level from the national government down to the farmer, was instituted to plan, implement, and monitor the progress and problems of the program. A central government council, headed by the secretary of agriculture and composed of representatives of the Department of Agriculture and National Resources, the financial institutions (both public and private), the research institutions, and the planning agency, reviewed policy decisions and coordinated activities. A working group handled operational matters at the national level, advised by a technical committee and an information committee. Regional coordinators, provincial action teams, municipal action teams, and production group leaders helped to ensure that directives reached the farmer and that, in turn, information on local problems moved back through the system to allow corrective changes.

Several problems arose during early stages of the program. Subsidized fertilizers, intended for rice production, were diverted to more profitable export crops; then farmers were squeezed when the government raised fertilizer prices in response to higher production and import costs at the time when rice prices were falling. Several seasons were required before a sufficient number of technicians could be trained to respond to the needs of the farmers in the program. Credit repayments fell significantly after the first couple of seasons.

These problems notwithstanding, the results of the program during the first 3 years were gratifying. Rice production in 1974 rose about 25 percent over the previous year (admittedly a year of depressed production), another 1 percent in 1975 (despite 22 typhoons sweeping over parts of the largest rice-producing regions in the latter half of 1974), and an estimated 10 percent more in 1976. Perhaps as important as the production increase were some of the indirect benefits. Philippine land reform, by taking land from some larger farmers who had also served as money lenders, had reduced the sources of credit for many small farmers. The Masagana 99 program substituted institutional credit for private credit.

It brought government to many farmers in a positive way for the first time.

Masagana 99 was a forced-pace campaign to quickly move research results to the farmers. Improved technology was accompanied by simultaneous efforts to supply material inputs, credit, information, and markets. The delivery system involved the activities of a wide-ranging group of organizations. A modern management system was designed to direct the campaign.

Defined-area projects

A third approach to agricultural development involves increasing output and incomes in a specific area.[14]

COMILLA

Between 1963/64 and 1969/70, average yields of rice doubled in the Comilla Project of East Pakistan (now Bangladesh). The incomes of cooperators more than doubled. Small and large farmers benefited.

The Pakistan Academy for Rural Development at Comilla was one of two institutions set up by the government in 1959 to study and teach ways to promote rural development. It was allocated one thana (the administrative unit below the district, consisting of 250 square kilometers) to serve as a laboratory in which it could experiment with cooperatives and rural development. Akhtar Hameed Khan became the founder-director.

The Comilla Project emphasized four interdependent activities to teach farmers to be effective in managing their own resources and public resources to attain objectives they chose. First, the Thana Training and Development Center was organized to mobilize the people through their elected leaders to coordinate government affairs and ensure responsiveness to the people. A local government council was created. Public and private services, such as credit and extension, were headquartered at the center, facilitating coordination among the economic development departments and institutions of central and local government.

The second activity was the Rural Works Program, which was organized to construct roads, drainage channels, and embankments and thereby provide employment to landless laborers during the idle dry months. Protection from flooding and better access to markets were priority needs

---

[14] Morss et al. give a comprehensive review of 36 small-farmer projects in Latin America and Africa, most of them in defined areas, in *Strategies for Small Farmer Development*. Michael Nelson has provided an excellent review of land settlement projects in tropical Latin America in *The Development of Tropical Lands*.

of the area. This program was financed in large part by U.S. funds. By fulfilling popular expectations and by promoting popular participation, it gave vitality to the self-governing bodies and laid the foundation for rural progress.

The third activity, the Thana Irrigation Program, was organized to carry the road and flood control works one step further—to provide water during dry periods through more effective use of water in rivers and canals and through the drilling of tube wells.

Fourth, cooperatives were organized to safeguard the farmers from moneylenders and to enable them to modernize their farming methods. The cooperatives gave the small farmers solidarity. It taught them how to acquire capital through thrift. Collective action was essential for irrigation management. Each cooperative selected a "model" farmer from its members who spent 1 day a week at the Thana Training and Development Center learning better production techniques to teach his neighbors.

These activities significantly improved the standard of living of members of cooperatives. But the program has had problems. First, massive and seemingly unremovable subsidies, such as concessional interest rates, were at the heart of the program and over time became a drain on the economy. Second, the wealthy began to capture the cooperatives and use the credit funds for their own good. The center has continued to flourish for training and exchange of ideas, but its coordinating function has weakened considerably. The rural works program died. However, the irrigation program is going well. Government, responding to the traditional power structure of the area, has continued to give attention to production increase, although perhaps at the cost of equity and the widespread involvement of farm people.

Nevertheless, Comilla stands out as one of the first and more innovative of the world's rural development projects. It demonstrates that much can be done, in large part through encouragement of local initiative, to improve production by many people, even those with few resources.[15] Charismatic leadership, a factor difficult to replicate, was instrumental in its success. But Comilla also warns that successful rural development requires sustained support and vigilance if the powerful economic forces, such as large landholders, are to be prevented from capturing programs for their own benefit.

PUEBLA

Between 1968 and 1972 the average yield of maize increased by 30 percent on unirrigated land in the valley of Puebla in Mexico. Between

[15] For a thorough review of the positive influence of local organization on rural development in Asia, see *Local Organization for Rural Development*, by Uphoff and Esman.

1967 and 1970, net income from crop production by farm families in the area (adjusted for inflation) increased by 45 percent. These results have drawn attention to the Puebla Project.

In the late 1960s, scientists were concerned that maize varieties and agronomic practices developed on research stations in Mexico were not reaching small farmers. The question was why not? The Puebla Project was established in 1967 to achieve two primary objectives: (1) To determine if efficient techniques for promoting a rapid increase in maize production could be developed; and (2) if so, to train leaders for maize promotion programs and to assist them in initiating and operating programs.[16]

The project area chosen was in the valley of Puebla, about a 2-hour drive from Mexico City. In this area approximately 43,000 families farmed about 116,000 hectares of unirrigated cropland (about 2.5 hectares per family), three-quarters of which was in maize. Average maize yields were only 1,300 kg/ha and were static. Area roads were adequate. Government agencies for credit, fertilizer supply, crop insurance, and price supports had offices nearby, but were not serving most small farmers. Land reform had been carried out previously.

The project was conceived as an experiment.[17] It tested a planned approach, based initially on what was known, with built-in mechanisms for learning and subsequent adjustments. The team consisted of a coordinator, four specialists in agronomic research, an evaluator, and five technical assistance agents. Twenty-five local farmers were selected and trained to assist the professional staff. Several Mexican institutions were involved as collaborators, and the International Maize and Wheat Improvement Center (CIMMYT) and the Graduate School at the National Agrarian University at Chapingo provided overall control and coordination.

The project began with an assessment of the problems, resources, and activities of people in the project area and a series of field trials in 26 locations. Rainfall at each site was recorded. Visits were made regularly to determine the condition of the experiments. The results of the trials were striking. Local varieties, with all their defects, clearly were as good as available hybrids. With this information in hand, the field research for 1968 was narrowed to provide more detailed information on fertilizer rates, plant populations, dates of planting, time of application of fertil-

---

[16] In addition, the project staff members added an internal challenge to themselves: to double the yield of maize within a 5-year period. This was not a formal objective of the project, although of course its achievement would have been welcomed.

[17] Several people played key roles in this project. Perhaps the most prominent were Leobardo Jimenez-Sanchez, Heliodoro Diaz-Cisneros, Mauro Gomez-Aguilar, Antonio Turrent-Fernandez, Edwin J. Wellhausen, Reggie J. Laird, Delbert T. Myren, and Hector Porras-Howard.

izers, depth of the second cultivation, fertilization of maize in orchards, residual effects of fertilizers, and so forth.

Only through this field research phase could two critical questions be answered: Could appropriate combinations of available technology increase yields substantially? If yields could be raised with combinations of available technology, would it be profitable for the farmer? If the answer to either question was "no," there was obviously no basis for a campaign to involve farmers. If answers to both were positive, then efforts to work with farmers were justified.

The project staff recognized that identification of superior technology for local environmental conditions was only a first step. The staff tried to develop a mechanism for reaching as many of the farmers as possible to increase yields and incomes—that is, to provide *technical assistance* to the farmers.

In repeated visits to the villages, the staff studied the organization of the communities, the power structure, and the informal systems of communication. Information about the project was given to families at meetings held in the villages. Several things were accomplished in this process: the farmers felt involved; problems most important to the community were noted; community leaders were identified; and the key role of credit as a motivating force was recognized.

By 1969, several major organizational changes had been made. The project area was divided into four (and eventually into five) agro-climatic zones. A technical assistance agent was assigned to each zone. Each agent had one or two nonprofessional assistants—locally trained farmers—who worked with other farmers. The number of participants had risen to over 2,500 so the official credit banks joined one fertilizer distributor in offering credit. And because the number of farmers had become large, the participating farmers were organized into groups.

Agricultural service institutions to supply production inputs, to provide credit, and to ensure a reliable market for outputs already existed, but they were not serving small farmers. They resisted becoming directly involved in the project. Favorable program experience and pressure from the farmer groups eventually persuaded them to participate.

An evaluation unit was established within the project. The process of evaluation, exercised through informal as well as formal methods, helped uncover problems and provide a basis for program changes to improve those conditions.

A training component was also built into the project on the premises that expansion to other areas would require substantial numbers of specially trained individuals, that professional competence is a key ingredient for transferring experiences from one project to another, and that a pilot

"While formal participation in the program has remained constant (varying from 8,300 to 8,500), yearly evaluations have shown a growing number of campesinos adopting the new technology. In 1976, it was estimated that close to 80 percent of the campesinos in the area were using it. This has meant considerable increase in corn yields. The record was established in 1976, the last growing season for which we have data. A good rainy season, combined with wide use of the new technology, brought in an average of 3,400 kilograms per hectare, compared to the average of 1,300 for 1967. While part of the good results in 1976 were due to favorable weather, much was also due to correct use of the new technology.

The Puebla strategy now has become a national strategy . . . [for] the President of Mexico asked the Minister of Agriculture to promote the strategy at the national level. The President approved a budget to operate Plan Puebla and to build a training center to prepare technical workers. More than 250 such workers have been trained since the first course was offered in 1974. They are the technical personnel for 36 regional programs now under way."

Heliodoro Diaz-Cisneros
"Grass-Roots Research That Really Paid Off"

program is the best arena for teaching the principles and practices required to make a project succeed.

By 1975, almost 9,000 farmers (20 percent of the total number of farmers in the Puebla area), who cultivated 35 percent of the maize land, were obtaining credit from official sources, one means of identifying participation. Many others not in organized groups also benefited.[18]

By 1973 the project could no longer be operated as an experiment. The activity was taken over by government agencies. Subsequently, many of the principles and practices of the Puebla Project were used in other countries in the hemisphere and the approach had by 1976 been utilized in other states in Mexico as well as in Colombia and Peru.

The Puebla Project was initiated as an experiment in 1967—a time when the feasibility and desirability of work with small farmers was highly controversial in professional circles. It had limited, but important,

[18] Winkelman, in *The Adoption of New Maize Technology in Plan Puebla*, notes the difficulties of evaluating a project of this nature: "If the progress is to be evaluated in terms of farmer response to precise recommendations and if the precise recommendations don't exactly fit all the farmers, then adoption rates will be low and the evaluation will be unfavorable. This would be the conclusion from a stringent evaluation of data from the 1975 yield survey which shows adoption, defined in terms of the recommendations, on less than 10 percent of the plots. Measured in terms of general recommendations, however, program progress would be more favorably viewed. And this view would seem to accord better with what has occurred—a sharp reduction in the proportion of farmers applying low levels of fertilizer and a sharp increase in the proportion applying high levels."

goals. The project followed a planned approach based initially on what was already known, but with built-in mechanisms for learning and subsequent readjustment. A methodology for promoting a substantial increase in maize production was developed. Intensive field research identified new practices which were not radically different from what farmers had been doing; the new recommendations utilized the same varieties, higher rates of fertilization, denser plant populations, and better management of crops. The project leaders and farmers, organized in groups, promoted the new technologies and induced the relevant service institutions to become more responsive to farmers' needs.

Summary

These brief descriptions of selected experiences, covering a wide range of agro-climatic conditions, cultural systems, and forms of political organization, demonstrate that the means to accelerate agricultural production are well within the reach of most nations. Most nations *can* increase their agricultural production and raise the standards of living in their rural areas if they *will*.

References

EARLY SUCCESS STORIES

Bishop, C. E. *The People Left Behind: A Report by the President's National Advisory Commission on Rural Poverty.* Washington, D.C.: U.S. Government Printing Office, 1967.

Bishop, C. E. *Rural Poverty in the United States: A Report by the President's National Advisory Commission on Rural Poverty.* Washington, D.C.: U.S. Government Printing Office, 1968.

Crabb, Richard A. *The Hybrid-Corn Makers.* New Brunswick, N.J.: Rutgers University Press, 1948.

Griliches, Zvi. "Hybrid Corn: An Exploration in the Economics of Technological Change." *Econometrica* 25 (1957): 501–22.

Griliches, Zvi. "Hybrid Corn and the Economics of Innovation." *Science* 132 (1960): 275–80.

Hayami, Yujiro; Akino, Masakatsu; Shintani, Musahiko; and Yamada, Saburo. *A Century of Agricultural Growth in Japan: Its Relevance to Asian Development.* Minneapolis: University of Minnesota Press, 1975.

Hayami, Yujiro, and Ruttan, Vernon W. *Agricultural Development: An International Perspective.* Baltimore: Johns Hopkins University Press, 1971.

Hayes, H. K. *A Professor's Story of Hybrid Corn.* Minneapolis, Minn.: Burgess, 1963.

Heady, Earl O. "The Agriculture of the U.S." *Scientific American* 235 (September 1976): 106–27.

Heady, Earl O., ed. *Benefits and Burdens of Rural Development.* Ames: Iowa State University Press, 1970.

Rasmussen, Wayne D.; Baker, Gladys L.; and Ward, James S. *A Short History of Agricultural Adjustment, 1933–75.* Agricultural Information Bulletin No. 391.

Washington, D.C.: U.S. Department of Agriculture, Economic Research Service, March 1976.

Suzuki, Akio. "Agricultural Research Situation in Japan." In *Institutionalizing Research Management in Asia.* College, Laguna, Philippines: Southeast Asian Regional Center for Graduate Study and Research in Agriculture, 1974.

COMPREHENSIVE NATIONAL EFFORTS

Abbott, John C. "Food and Agricultural Marketing in China." *Food Policy* 2 (1977): 318–30.

Borlaug, N. E. "Wheat, Rust, and People." *Phytopathology* 55 (1965): 1088–98.

Christensen, Raymond P. *Taiwan's Agricultural Development: Its Relevance for Developing Countries Today.* Foreign Agricultural Economic Report No. 29. Washington, D.C.: U.S. Department of Agriculture, 1968.

Cummings, Ralph W., Jr., and Ray, S. K. "1968–69 Foodgrain Production: Relative Contribution of Weather and New Technology." *Economic and Political Weekly* 4 (September 27, 1969): A163–A174.

Dalrymple, Dana G. *Development and Spread of High Yielding Varieties of Wheat and Rice in the Less Developed Nations.* Foreign Agricultural Economic Report No. 95, fifth ed. Washington, D.C.: U.S. Department of Agriculture, August 1976.

Mellor, John W. "The Agriculture of India." *Scientific American* 235 (September 1976): 154–63.

Myren, Delbert T. "The Rockefeller Foundation Program in Corn and Wheat in Mexico." In *Subsistence Agriculture and Economic Development,* edited by Clifton R. Wharton, Jr. Chicago: Aldine, 1969.

Osoyo, Roberto. "Mexico: From Food Deficits to Sufficiency." In *Strategy for the Conquest of Hunger: Proceedings of a Symposium.* New York: Rockefeller Foundation, 1968.

Sen, Sudhir. *Reaping the Green Revolution: Food and Jobs for All.* Maryknoll, N.Y.: Orbis Books, 1975.

Sen, Sudhir. *A Richer Harvest: New Horizons for Developing Countries.* Maryknoll, N.Y.: Orbis Books, 1975.

Shen, T. H. *Taiwan's Family Farm during Transitional Economic Growth.* International Agriculture Mimeograph 40. Ithaca, N.Y.: Cornell University, 1976.

Shen, T. H., ed. *Agriculture's Place in the Strategy of Development: The Taiwan Experience.* Taipei: Joint Commission on Rural Reconstruction, 1974.

Sprague, G. F. "Agriculture in China." *Science* 188 (1975): 549–55.

Stakman, E. C.; Bradfield, R.; and Mangelsdorf, P. C. *Campaigns against Hunger.* Cambridge, Mass.: Belknap Press, 1967.

Stavis, Benedict. *Making Green Revolution: The Politics of Agricultural Development in China.* Rural Development Monograph No. 1. Ithaca, N.Y.: Cornell University, Rural Development Committee, 1974.

Streeter, Carroll P. *Reaching the Developing World's Small Farmers.* New York: Rockefeller Foundation, 1973.

Subramaniam, C. "India's Program for Agricultural Progress." In *Strategy for the Conquest of Hunger: Proceedings of a Symposium.* New York: Rockefeller Foundation, 1968.

Vyas, V. S. *India's High Yielding Varieties Programme in Wheat, 1966–67 to 1971–72.* El Batan, Mexico: Centro Internacional de Mejoramiento de Maiz y Trigo, 1975.

Wellhausen, Edwin J. "The Agriculture of Mexico." *Scientific American* 235 (September 1976): 128–50.

Wortman, Sterling. "Agriculture in China." *Scientific American* 232 (June 1975): 13–21.

NATIONAL COMMODITY PROGRAMS

Breth, Steven A., "Turkey's Wheat Research and Training Project." *CIMMYT Today* 6 (1977): 1–16.

Demir, Nazmi. *The Adoption of New Bread Wheat Technology in Selected Regions of Turkey.* El Batan, Mexico: Centro Internacional de Mejoramiento de Maiz y Trigo, 1976.

Drilon, J. D., Jr. "Masagana 99: An Integrated Production Drive in the Philippines." Paper prepared for a Seminar on Accelerating Agricultural Development and Rural Prosperity, September 5–18, 1976, University of Reading, England. Mimeographed.

Eberhart, S. A., and Sprague, G. F. "A Major Cereals Project to Improve Maize, Sorghum, and Millet Production in Africa." *Agronomy Journal* 65 (1973): 365–73.

Gerhart, John. *The Diffusion of Hybrid Maize in Western Kenya.* El Batan, Mexico: Centro Internacional de Mejoramiento de Maiz y Trigo, 1975.

Harrison, M. N. "Maize Improvement in East Africa." In *Crop Improvement in East Africa*, edited by C. L. A. Leakey. Commonwealth Bureau of Plant Breeding and Genetics Technical Communication No. 19. Farnham Royal, England: Commonwealth Agricultural Bureaux, 1970.

Jennings, Peter R. "The Amplification of Agricultural Production." *Scientific American* 235 (September 1976): 180–94.

Jennings, Peter R. *Plant Breeding Contributions to Food Production in Developing Countries.* Paper presented at the Centennial Meeting of the American Chemical Society, New York, N.Y., April 4–9, 1976. Mimeographed. (Abstract available from the American Chemical Society, Washington, D.C.)

Mann, Charles K. "The Impact of Technology on Wheat Production in Turkey." *Gelisme Dergisi* (Middle East Technical University Studies in Development) 14 (Winter 1977): 30–47.

Sprague, G. F. "Factors Affecting the Adoption of Hybrid Maize in the United States and Kenya." In *Change in Agriculture*, edited by A. H. Bunting. London: Duckworth, 1970.

Wright, Bill C. "A Brief Review of the Turkish Wheat Research and Training Project." Mimeographed. Wheat Research and Training Project, Ankara, 1971.

DEFINED-AREA PROJECTS

Blair, Harry W. *The Elusiveness of Equity: Institutional Approaches to Rural Development in Bangladesh.* Special Series on Rural Local Government No. 1. Ithaca, N.Y.: Cornell University, Rural Development Committee, 1974.

Centro Internacional de Mejoramiento de Maiz y Trigo. *The Puebla Project: Seven Years of Experience: 1967–1973.* El Batan, Mexico: Centro Internacional de Mejoramiento de Maiz y Trigo, 1975.

Diaz-Cisneros, Heliodoro. "Grass-Roots Research That Really Paid Off." *Christian Science Monitor*, January 12, 1978, p. B-10.

Khan, Akhtar Hameed. *Reflections on the Comilla Rural Development Projects.* OLC Paper No. 3. Washington, D.C.: American Council on Education, Overseas Liaison Committee, March 1974.

Morss, Elliot R.; Hatch, John K.; Mickelwait, Donald R.; and Sweet, Charles F. *Strategies for Small Farmer Development.* 2 vols. Boulder, Colo.: Westview Press, 1976.

Nelson, Michael. *The Development of Tropical Lands: Policy Issues in Latin America.* Baltimore: Johns Hopkins University Press for Resources for the Future, 1973.

Uphoff, Norman T., and Esman, Milton J. *Local Organization for Rural Development: Analysis of Asian Experience.* Special Series on Rural Local Government No. 19. Ithaca, N.Y.: Cornell University, Rural Development Committee, 1974.

Winkelmann, Donald. *The Adoption of New Maize Technology in Plan Puebla, Mexico.* El Batan, Mexico: Centro Internacional de Mejoramiento de Maiz y Trigo, 1976.

The basis
for hope

OVER THE PAST decade, world agriculture has increasingly preoccupied international diplomatic, financial, and scientific circles. A new era is emerging. Knowledge, financial resources, and management capabilities are being mobilized nationally and internationally to achieve break-throughs in crop and animal productivity. This trend is fueled by a heightened concern with the world food situation—and with the extreme poverty associated with hunger—and by the realization that concerted action could change the situation.

A worldwide assault on hunger and poverty today, if wisely organized and pursued, could reduce suffering and lead to a new sense of hope for the hundreds of millions whose future now is bleak, as well as create a new sense of satisfaction among the many who wish to help.

Successful policymaking is the art of the possible. Establishing a basis for hope, an optimism for success tempered by caution, is a prerequisite to any program for change. Recapitulating the main points made in the preceding chapters, the basis for hope that agricultural production can be increased and that standards of living can soon be improved signifi-cantly for the world's poor rests on several recent developments:

The area of unused and underused land in the low-income countries that can be safely cultivated or otherwise used more productively is larger than previously thought. Less than half of the world's potentially arable land is currently being cropped. There are large amounts of under-utilized land—89 percent of potentially arable land in Latin America and 78 percent in Africa. The possibilities for constructing irrigation and drainage systems, and of improving the efficiency of existing ones, are great in some regions, although the cost may be high. Multiple cropping can be expanded. The maximum potential gross cropped area of the earth may be as much as five times the area now cultivated. (Chapter 4.)

Chemical fertilizers are now being produced in sufficient volumes to allow their use on vast areas of food crops, even in the developing coun-

tries. The world's chemical fertilizer production following World War II was about 7.5 million tons; production tripled by 1955, doubled again by 1965, and now exceeds 90 million tons per year. Fertilizers were once so costly and available in such limited quantities that they could be used only on luxury crops, but now they are increasingly profitable on food crops. This shift has accelerated as scientists have developed varieties— with associated production systems—which use nutrients, water, and solar energy more efficiently. Low-income countries currently use little fertilizer—Africa averages one-seventeenth as much per hectare as the U.S., and Asia and Latin America average one-third as much as the U.S.— indicating immense scope for growth. (Chapter 4.)

New biological technologies for the tropics and subtropics are being developed. Inadequate technology is a major reason why much potentially arable land is not cultivated and why currently cultivated land produces such low yields. A decade ago many assumed that technology could be transferred wholesale from temperate regions to the tropics. Much agricultural technology is transferable, but generally speaking it must be modified to meet local conditions; this is particularly true for the biological components. New crop and animal production systems that are higher yielding and more profitable must be devised for thousands of combinations of soil, climate, and plant-pest complexes, as well as consumer preferences. New production systems must be devised for every crop for every season of every region of every nation and must be adopted by hundreds of millions of farmers, many of whom are uneducated and live in remote areas. The myth of general transferability of agricultural technology has been set aside.

Over the past decade a scientific and technological base on which countries can draw to bring agricultural advances to their own farms has begun to be established. A network of international agricultural research and training centers is helping low-income regions deal with long-neglected crop and animal species; international research began in rice in the early 1960s, in maize and wheat in the late 1960s, and in other food crops in the 1970s. Moreover, some low-income countries are embarking on large-scale development of their national agricultural science capabilities. And the research carried out in the developed countries is being more effectively linked to the needs of the low-income countries. (Chapters 6 and 7.)

The seriousness and complexity of the food-poverty-population problem is becoming understood. Before World War II, Asia, Africa, and Latin America were all net exporters of grain. Since then, those regions have been importing increasingly large quantities. Today only the U.S., Canada, Australia, Argentina, and Thailand consistently export food.

Long-range studies of world food supplies date back only to 1963, when

Lester Brown wrote *Man, Land, and Food.* It was not until 1967 that a comprehensive analysis of the situation was undertaken. That study, a three-volume work entitled *The World Food Problem*, remains generally valid. Since that report, other reports with similar conclusions, including FAO's *Indicative World Plan* and the findings of the World Food Conference of 1974, have been published. Considering how recently widespread concern has developed, it is reassuring that the food problem is receiving serious attention at the highest political levels. (Chapters 2, 3, 4, and 5.)

It is now recognized that increased productivity in developed countries will not by itself solve the world food-poverty-population problem. Since all nations cannot be self-sufficient every year, the few areas of surplus production will continue to sell food to nations that need to supplement domestic production or to maintain stable consumer prices. For humanitarian reasons, food stocks must be available to meet emergencies anywhere. However, the few exporting countries are not able to feed the rest of the world, and the food-deficit countries do not have the financial resources to import large quantities of food indefinitely.

The shrinking surplus of grains in the 1960s and 1970s and the accompanying price increases convinced some importing nations that they must develop their own agricultural areas. Any confidence that governments may previously have had in the international availability of low-cost or free food supplies was severely jolted. If these crises forced governments to address the problems of their rural people, the disappearance of the surpluses may well have been a fortuitous event. While there is growing recognition that the higher-income countries must, in the interest of all, help the developing countries improve their agriculture and achieve greater rural prosperity, the primary responsibility rests with the government of each developing country. (Chapters 2 and 5.)

More leaders of developing countries now understand that improvement of agriculture is fundamental to economic development. A decade ago many development authorities advocated industrialization to provide employment for the masses and to thrust poor agrarian countries into the 20th century. However, most citizens of low-income countries produce basic food crops for a living. Increasing production of basic food crops in the developing countries will both make more food available and expand purchasing power, which will allow the hungry to afford more food. And greater demand for goods and services in the countryside will quicken economic activity in rural trade centers. (Chapters 2, 5, and 6.)

In numerous areas, poor farmers have demonstrated that they will change to a more productive farming system if they are convinced it is profitable. A decade ago conventional wisdom held that uneducated farmers who have tiny landholdings are too conservative and too ignorant to shift to high-yielding, more complex systems. That myth has been set aside. Scientists or administrators who once blamed failures of production programs on apathetic farmers now must look to the weaknesses of their own programs. (Chapters 3, 5, and 8.)

Governments and assistance agencies are placing increasing emphasis on helping small farmers grow basic food crops. Increasing the production and profitability of small farms gets at both sides of the hunger equation: increased food production and increased purchasing power among the poor. (Chapters 1 and 10.)

Several poor countries with widely divergent ideologies have demonstrated that rapid agricultural progress is possible. Among the reasonably successful programs are comprehensive national efforts in Taiwan, Mexico, India, and the People's Republic of China; national commodity programs in Kenya (maize), Turkey (wheat), Colombia (rice), and the Philippines (rice); and defined-area projects in the Comilla district of Bangladesh (then called East Pakistan) and in the Puebla district of Mexico. Farmers will increase their agricultural production if they can; governments can increase national agricultural production if they will. (Chapter 8.)

International assistance agencies have increased their lending for agricultural and rural development. The volume of financial assistance in agriculture from developed to low-income countries probably reached US$5,000 million in 1974 and exceeded $6,000 million in 1975. (Chapter 6.)

New, more effective forms of international cooperation are working. Examples of the new forms are the Consultative Group on International Agricultural Research and several initiatives resulting directly or indirectly from the World Food Conference of 1974. (Chapters 6 and 7.)

A strategy for action is emerging. This strategy will be explored in the remaining portion of this book.

Despite these hopeful signs, high population growth rates must still be brought down quickly. If population growth in low-income nations continues indefinitely at over 2 percent per year, no thinkable solution to the world food problem is possible. But in a number of countries population growth rates seem to be coming down. Those who seek to increase food production around the world, thereby increasing opportunities for effective employment and improvements in income, are buying time for nations to lower population growth rates. The time provided must be effectively used by those working on the population portion of the equation.

The strategy

CHAPTER 10

The basic strategy

Introduction

THE WORLD is entering a third era of agricultural development which is characterized by governments' heightened awareness of the urgent need to accelerate agricultural and rural development in their own countries. This upsurge has many roots:

- an understanding that higher incomes among large numbers of rural people are fundamental for general economic advance, for enhancing rural standards of living, and for enlarging domestic markets for products of urban industry;
- a desire, insofar as possible, to be self-sufficient in food supplies and to be insulated from international uncertainties;
- a wish to spend less foreign exchange on farm products that could be produced within the country, thereby increasing employment of the rural people;
- a fear that neglect of rural populations will lead to unrest and violence; and
- a realization that agricultural progress can be rapid.

The acceleration of agricultural development can only be the responsibility of the government of each country, large or small, rich or poor. Only the government of each sovereign nation can set the policies, organize or strengthen the institutions, and reach its own rural people in ways that conform to the objectives of the society.

Some government leaders are now asking what to do and how to do it quickly and at acceptable costs.

There is, of course, no blueprint for rapid agricultural development which is applicable to all countries or regions within countries. But for virtually every region, commodity, or problem, certain actions can be

Development goals

According to the *Asian Agricultural Survey 1976* of the Asian Development Bank, some consensus is emerging among governments regarding development goals for agriculture. Typical objectives include:

- stepping up food production to meet the continually growing demands of an increasing population, to reduce reliance on overseas suppliers, and to provide reserves to cushion the effects of crop failure in bad seasons;
- increasing nonfood agricultural production to meet the raw-material needs of expanding industries and to provide foreign exchange for the economy through exports to markets abroad;
- increasing the opportunities for productive employment in agriculture and raising the income of the agriculturally supported population;
- diversifying agricultural activity in order to provide greater insulation for both farmers and the economy in general from large disturbances in international markets, and in order to take full advantage of changing patterns of demand, domestic and foreign;
- giving more producers better access to basic resources such as land and water, and eliminating inequitable relationships in agricultural factor and product markets; and
- adopting a more comprehensive approach to the development of the rural economy, with emphasis on improving the quality of life in rural areas.

initiated at once. Several alternatives are now reasonably well understood. Once alternatives are identified, national authorities can weigh their relative merits and choose on the basis of the political, social, and economic criteria peculiar to their country.

This chapter presents an overview of the strategy by which nations can accelerate increases in agricultural production and rural incomes. More detailed explanations follow in succeeding chapters.

The priorities

Development goals, as stated in official plans, are often numerous and diverse. The highest priorities in the agricultural sector should be placed on increasing farm income through increased productivity and on achieving widespread participation of rural people.

INCREASED PRODUCTIVITY AND INCOME

Rural development is receiving much attention today. A World Bank Sector Policy Paper defines rural development as a "strategy designed to improve the economic and social life of a specific group of people—the rural poor." Its objectives "encompass improved productivity, increased employment and thus higher incomes for larger groups, as well as minimum acceptable levels of food, shelter, education and health."

Our focus is on rapid means of raising agricultural output and achieving widespread increases in farm income, a central requirement of rural development. Evidence indicates that the first concern of most rural dwellers is higher income, for purchasing power provides access to other benefits. *Each agricultural development effort should have income generation through increased productivity as a primary objective.* This goal can be associated with provision of other important elements of rural development—improved water supply, health care, education, and housing, topics which we leave to others with competence in those areas. But increased productivity and income are the prime components. Any attempt to reach this objective must be made in a setting which has a potential for change.

Four requisites. Farmers, regardless of size of landholding, generally will increase their productivity provided four requisites are met:[1]

- *An improved farming system.* A combination of materials and practices that is clearly more productive and profitable, with an acceptably low level of risk, than the one he currently uses must be available to the farmer.
- *Instruction of farmers.* The farmer must be shown, on his own farm or nearby, how to put the practices into use, and he should understand why they are better.
- *Supply of inputs.* The inputs required, and, if necessary, credit to finance their purchase, must be available to the farmer when and where he needs them, and at reasonable cost.
- *Availability of markets.* The farmer must have access to a nearby market that can absorb increased supplies without excessive price drops.

[1] A. T. Mosher, in *Getting Agriculture Moving*, identifies five "essential elements for agricultural development": markets for products, constantly changing technology, local availability of supplies and equipment, production incentives for farmers, and transportation. The differences between our four requisites and his five "essential elements" are minor. We believe there are two major contributors to constantly changing technology. First, the continuing development of more highly productive systems tailored to each locality and, second, instruction of farmers in their use. We have subsumed under assured markets not only the physical existence of markets but the elements of an incentive price at the farm level and of transportation. To his essential elements, Mosher correctly adds five "accelerators": education for development, production credit, group action by farmers, improving and expanding agricultural land, and national planning.

"Our situation today is that we have had almost thirty years of experience testing and implementing a variety of projects, programs, and strategies. We have conducted extensive research under a variety of socio-economic and agronomic conditions in most regions and nations of the developing world. Much has been learned; much remains to be learned. On the whole this cumulative experience has brought us to the stage where, while we may disagree on minor details, by and large we have significantly large areas of consensus among the various disciplines and professions about the key factors and strategies to impact the complex process called 'agricultural development.' "

Clifton R. Wharton, Jr.
"The Role of the Professional
in Feeding Mankind"

If all of these conditions are met simultaneously in any locality, it is likely that a high proportion of farmers will, in time, change. If the combination is incomplete in any respect, farmers will hesitate to abandon their traditional ways.

Let's look at the four requisites.[2] The first requisite is *improved farming systems.* Improvements in technology or production systems which promise significantly higher yields and incomes than previous practices are essential to initiate change. The potential benefits must be clearly visible to the farmers. One frequent weakness of agricultural programs has been the assumption that farmers will respond to technologies that give small yield increases, say, 10 percent. Usually such minor improvements are not apparent to the eye, and are even difficult to demonstrate. What will command the farmer's attention, at least in early program stages, are changes which will give visibly higher yields and income—at least 20–30 percent higher.

Developing improved farming systems for farmers' use, systematically and quickly, is a complex operation. If a farmer is to use a new cropping system, he must know for each crop, among other things, which variety to use; the best rate, date, and depth of planting; the right amounts of nitrogen, phosphorus, or other nutrients, and when to apply them; how and when to apply supplemental water if the crop is irrigated; the appropriate pesticides, and the manner, times, and conditions under which they should be employed; and the means of preparing the soil and of controlling weeds. If major errors are made in *any* factor, yield may be substantially reduced. The farmer must determine how to fit a crop into his total farm system, including sequences of crops to use and often how to mesh cropping systems and animal production.

[2] The requisites are discussed in detail in Chapters 12 and 13.

The farmer must know, in addition, which combination of all the production factors and crops will give him maximum net income, for that is the farmer's measure of success.

In developing improved farming systems the proper combinations of production practices and economic decisions must generally be determined at each locality through on-farm experimentation. The level of skill required to carry out these on-farm experiments is often greatly underestimated by scientists, administrators, and planners.

The second requisite is *instruction of farmers*. While information about new developments may be all that managers of large farms require, small farmers need more. As new practices are introduced, local technicians must be able to teach farmers, in the farmers' own fields, how to employ the new systems to best advantage.

To know what combinations to employ in a locality usually requires that experiments be conducted there. Since the number of competent scientists is limited, at least in the smaller countries, they cannot work in many sites simultaneously. But they can work through technicians, who are trained in installation of field tests by the scientists. Such training usually can best be done by allowing field technicians to work at least a full agricultural season at an experiment station as a member of the staff—as an intern.

Additionally, the field technician must be able to diagnose and prescribe remedial action for production problems, much as does a general practitioner in medicine. Since field technicians will encounter many problems they cannot handle, they must be able to turn to the country's scientists for help. Field technicians and agricultural scientists therefore must be well acquainted and must communicate freely. Both must be mobile.

The third requisite is *supply of inputs*. For their year-to-year operations, subsistence farmers normally use only their seed, their land, their household labor, and their animals, if they have any. To shift to a high-yield system, farmers must invariably purchase inputs. Farmers usually have limited mobility. Unless outlets in a nearby village sell the required seeds, fertilizers, pesticides, or other materials, the inputs remain inaccessible. The farmer should be able to buy all the inputs he needs at a single location, in the small amounts he needs, and on credit if he needs it. Prices of inputs must be reasonable to allow their profitable use.

The fourth requisite is *availability of markets*. Most agricultural commodities are bulky; some are highly perishable. Consequently there must be purchasing points near each farm to which the farmers can bring products and receive a fair price. Moreover, a farmer must know before investing in inputs (before planting, in the case of crops) that he will be able to sell at an incentive price at harvest; that is, that he can expect a profit. For basic food commodities produced by large numbers of small farmers, this normally requires that a guaranteed price be announced early each season. And governments must be prepared to honor such commitments at harvest. Failure to do so will cause farmers to lose faith in government programs.

Roads, transport, markets, processing facilities, and communications must be adequate to allow new technology and inputs to reach farmers and to allow farmers to sell their products easily. Appropriate location and quality of these facilities, by increasing farmers' access to technology and reducing their buying and selling costs, can profoundly influence the pace and pattern of development.

Yield and production "equations." One way of thinking about the many interrelationships in agricultural production is to use the concept of an equation. In such an equation for crop yield—that is, a *yield equation*—one can assume that a combination of production factors and conditions in a given farm situation will result in a given yield. If all factors are optimum—variety, fertilizer types and rates, soil condition, water, spacing, climate, disease and insect control, and weed control—yield will be maximum. But if any factor is less than optimum, yield will be reduced proportionally. If *any* factor in the equation has a value of zero, even if all others are optimum, the resulting yield will be low or nil. For example, with the proper variety properly planted on good land at optimum fertilizer rates, but with no moisture for growth, yield is zero. If all else is perfect, but nitrogen fertilizer is absent, yield is low. With all else optimum, but poor weed control, yield is low or nil. This is elementary and widely understood by farmers and agricultural scientists. It dramatizes the interaction of production factors; they are not simply additive. The "package of practices" should be complete.

The concept can be carried further. The farmer's primary interest is usually net income rather than yield. He will wish to identify the combination of components that gives maximum economic return on his investment. Suppose high-performance technology has been identified by scientists and proves to be useful in on-farm tests. Still, the lack of any of a long list of factors—seed or fertilizer supply, credit, vaccines, a market—can prevent the farmer's use of that technology. Adequacy of the technological package becomes but one of a still larger series of factors in the *production equation,* and the inadequacy of any of them reduces net income.

Availability of all materials and services—on time and at prices which permit profits—is crucial. Addition of a single component alone is sufficient only when merely that component is lacking or when that component (often the technology) has a catalytic effect, causing other missing factors quickly to be supplied.

"Even small holdings, which previously conformed to pessimistic portraits of low incomes and low motivation to invest, have now become profitable. This has led to a great resurgence of investment in exploitation of ground-water resources in various parts of the country. Even the cropping pattern is changing, making land reproduce itself, as it were. Where only one crop was raised before, the new short-term varieties have made it feasible to raise two. With this development will emerge a new land-use pattern. Other related changes have created a pressing demand for mechanical aids in various parts of India today. With double cropping, the farmer needs aids to shorten the period of land preparation between one crop and the next. He needs mechanical threshers, seed dryers, power tillers, etc. A valuable by-product of the strategy may well be the growth of a new type of rural industrial base to serve these needs."

> C. Subramaniam
> "India's Program for Agricultural Progress"

Synchronization of public and private services to satisfy all requisites simultaneously, locality by locality, is fundamental.

REACHING SMALL FARMERS

Most low-income, densely populated agrarian countries must lift productivity and profitability on large numbers of small farms. There is no other way to raise *both* agricultural output (to provide the volume of products needed) and the incomes of the bulk of the rural people (to allow them greater access to food and other necessities). Large-scale mechanized farming—whether by corporations, on the estates of individuals, or on state farms—may increase production, but it usually will not expand employment and raise incomes of large numbers of rural people. It should usually be avoided in densely populated countries.

The rationale of the small-farmer approach merits repetition. Family ownership of farms provides incentives to increase productivity through more intensive agricultural systems and to reinvest in farm improvements. Increasing productivity and real incomes of large numbers of farm families creates demand for goods and services. Economic activity in rural trade centers is stimulated, creating employment. The domestic market for products of urban-based industry is expanded. The sense of helplessness of rural people is replaced by a sense of hope. In summary, economic development of rural areas creates a multiplier effect, contributing to general economic progress and perhaps stemming the flow of people to urban areas.

There are other reasons for deliberately designing programs to involve and benefit small farmers. First, they grow large proportions of the basic food commodities. Second, systems designed to meet the requirements of

Who receives help?

As the International Center of Tropical Agriculture (CIAT) was being established in Colombia in 1967, President Carlos Lleras Restrepo indicated his own concern about the welfare of large numbers of farmers on the hillsides. As he noted, they vote. He went on to ask on what basis decisions are made to provide technical assistance and other services to farmers. Should the amount of attention a farmer receives depend on the number of hectares he has? Or should each citizen receive equal attention because he is a citizen?

small farmers will generally serve *all* farmers—large or small—in any region; biological components of technology tend to be, for the most part, scale neutral, and the more progressive entrepreneurs will find ways to take advantage of any advance introduced. Contrarily, failure to design programs to benefit small farmers will cause many to be by-passed. Few programs have been developed for small farmers, and it is time we learned how to design and organize them. Third, in most countries small farmers are increasingly important politically.

The distribution of wealth, whether it be in the form of land or livestock, is practically synonymous with control of labor, wealth, social prestige, and political power. These factors determine who will participate in development and how the benefits will be divided. If the distribution of rural wealth is grossly inequitable, development programs, despite success in increasing production and absolute living standards, are likely to have little effect on raising the relative living standards of the poor.

A range of types of organization, from small, privately owned family farms to group farming, including corporate contracts with agricultural producers, are suitable as the basis for a reasonably equitable rural system. Means of achieving a system of family farms or group farms are discussed in Chapter 11.

The strategy

Authorities in developing countries are confronted with proposal after proposal for stimulating agricultural and rural development. These come from bureaucrats, scientists, economists, businessmen, farm leaders, and representatives of assistance agencies. Governments are asked to provide research and extension services, colleges and schools of agriculture, fertilizer plants, roads, irrigation, credit banks, forestry projects, and community development schemes. Many of the activities are useful. But each requires money, plus the time of institutions and individuals.

Government officials must weigh alternative uses for scarce funds and trained manpower. They must consider the desires of conflicting political pressure groups. They must understand the intricacies of agricultural and rural development. And they must be prepared to defend their plans against nonagricultural and nonrural forces competing for the same resources. It is not surprising, then, that decisions are often delayed, not infrequently by calling for another time-consuming study.

In addition, forces are at work which encourage piecemeal approaches instead of comprehensive programs. Many nations find themselves with a multitude of unrelated agricultural development projects which, while locally helpful and meritorious, often fail to raise national production and standards of living as rapidly as expected. One reason is that authority for action in agriculture, transportation, education, finance, health, and commerce is spread among numerous ministries and subministries. Moreover, some sources of external assistance seemingly prefer to finance projects that have narrowly defined goals, carefully calculated cost-benefit ratios which establish that the project is "justifiable," and, often, rigorous timetables for accomplishing specific aspects of each proposal.

The best way to intensify agricultural productivity rapidly will differ among countries, among regions within countries, and even among localities within regions. However, there are three well-proven and complementary approaches to accelerated agricultural development available to governments:

- commodity-oriented production programs designed to achieve established goals for domestic consumption or export;
- defined-region campaigns to increase productivity and incomes of as many people as possible, using whatever combinations of commodities, techniques, and services are feasible; and
- synchronized and reoriented government services to speed progress.

For greatest success, the strategy should combine all three approaches. The relative emphasis on each approach, and the ways in which each is implemented, will be dictated by the goals established.

COMMODITY PRODUCTION PROGRAMS

The agricultural economy of every nation is based on a wide array of crop and animal species. For each commodity there are one or more unique systems by which the commodity is produced, harvested, purchased, processed, stored, transported, and marketed locally or internationally.

There are many examples of successful commodity programs in the developing countries. Most have involved cash crops—estate, plantation, export, or industrial crops, as they are variously called. Vigorous programs for such crops as coffee, tea, cacao, cotton, sugarcane, bananas, jute, and rubber exist throughout the developing regions. The most successful efforts have clear goals, with arrangements for production, processing, marketing, research, and training of personnel synchronized by a governing body comprising representatives of diverse groups interested in the commodity. The principles that have made estate-crop systems successful can be extended to basic food crops and animal species (Chapter 8).

Properly organized and adapted to local conditions, national commodity programs can raise productivity and incomes rapidly and widely. The concept is simple, execution need not be difficult, and results can be dramatic if governments are willing to invest needed resources, establish clear goals for output and farmer participation, and insist on interagency cooperation.

The approach. For each commodity a central group with technical expertise must be organized to establish goals and devise strategies for accelerating output, to determine how input supply, marketing, and technical services should be improved, to identify target regions for early attention, to establish relations with scientific and other institutions in other countries from which information and materials for trial can be requested, and to ensure smooth operations involving all relevant institutions and individuals.

Choosing commodities for early emphasis and establishing long-term as well as short-term goals for each commodity is of high priority. The need to overcome national commodity deficits or to supply anticipated export markets, the opportunity to improve productivity and incomes of large numbers of farms, and likely technical and operational difficulties should be considered. Governments with few trained personnel and inexperience with such systems should initially concentrate on one or two commodities.

By comparing the farmers' yields for a particular commodity with yields being obtained in other countries that have similar ecological conditions, the magnitude of possible gains can be roughly estimated. These estimates are more likely to be reliable if they are based on the judgments of authorities who have participated in campaigns with the commodity under similar conditions.

Technical and operational feasibility can be established at most within a few seasons by installing experiments on farms to determine what crop or animal yields can be obtained with existing technology or with improved technologies. Such experiments should be designed, monitored, and evaluated by competent agricultural specialists. By calculating the costs of inputs, the product prices, and the risk associated with year-to-year climatic variations, the profitability of new practices also can be estimated—from the same on-farm experiments.

Scientists must then determine (and develop if necessary) the combinations of technologies which will succeed in various target regions.

Usually the scientists will operate from experiment stations, but they must be concerned with farm-level experimentation as well.

Both experiment stations and farms should be used to train technicians in field experimental techniques and production practices. Without such skills and knowledge, farm-level technicians will have neither the competence nor the confidence to work effectively and enthusiastically with farmers.

As new higher-yielding crop varieties or crop or animal production practices are developed, tested, and demonstrated, farmers will begin to adopt them, but only where all other basic requirements, such as roads, markets, and input supplies, are satisfied.

Planning commodity programs. The key to planning a successful commodity approach is a reasonably clear understanding of the likely future demand for each commodity, of the potentials of the country for meeting that demand, of the problems likely to be encountered in exploiting the potentials, and of the costs involved. For high-priority commodities, the understanding should be reached quickly.

One means of bringing such information together within a few months is to commission a series of papers on important aspects of the commodity for presentation at a national workshop. This procedure has two advantages. First, it spreads the workload among the agencies and individuals in the country who are best capable of summarizing information on each topic, and, second, it brings diverse personnel together to consider how the system might be improved. Each participant will then better understand the total system and the importance of the activity of his agency in that system. A situation paper could then be prepared from information assembled from the separate studies, after evaluation at the workshop.

A second, perhaps even quicker, approach is to assemble a task force consisting of the most knowledgeable people in the agencies and private sector of the country. The task force would review the commodity system thoroughly in a series of meetings and then itself prepare the situation paper.

Attempts to achieve precision through lengthy studies should be avoided. Immediately available data can be bolstered by judgments of qualified people. The goals and procedures of each commodity program will have to be adjusted periodically as new evidence and experience are developed. The situation papers should be written in language that political leaders can readily understand.

As background for the situation reports, projects of anticipated market demand for 5, 10, 15, and 20 years in the future should be prepared for all significant commodities. The data will reveal the urgency, if any, of stimulating production to meet needs, indicate the value of each com-

Situation reports, by commodity

Description and analysis of a commodity system should, if possible, include the following, each related to the same long-term periods:

- *Projections of market demand.* List imports and exports, with monetary values and data on past trends; make projections for 10–20 years.
- *Current area of production, by season and region.* For ruminant animals add data on numbers of animal units to information on pastures and feed supply. For nonruminants, numbers and major feed sources should be included.
- *Nature and size of farm enterprises producing the commodity, by region.* Determine which types of farmers produce what proportions of the commodity for home consumption and for sale.
- *Prospects for expanding output.* By planting or grazing larger areas, or otherwise increasing numbers of animals using existing levels of technology, where and by how much can an increase be expected to occur without a concerted effort to intensify production?
- *Marketing arrangements.* Describe how farmers sell products and what proportions are sold to what kinds of buyers. The purpose is to understand major features of the marketing systems, whether available purchasing points serve all farmers adequately, and what weaknesses in marketing exist. Consider requirements for products of specific quality or grades.
- *Nature and adequacy of input and credit supply systems.* Are the right amounts of the correct inputs reaching all farmers when and where they need them, and at reasonable cost? If small farmers need the inputs or credit, are they served adequately?
- *Pricing systems.* What prices are being offered to farmers (support prices?), and what prices are farmers actually receiving at the farm gate? Will current prices to farmers permit a reasonable profit, or are prices kept at unprofitable levels to satisfy urban consumers, to generate

modity to the country, and expose the financial implications of raising, or failing to raise, productivity. The relative importance of commodities can therefore be established to provide a framework for considering priorities.

Most countries should be able to produce this information within a few months. Planning units should be a first source of data. Colleges of agriculture or universities should participate actively. As a last resort, external help can be sought to work with local groups in preparing projections.

Flexibility of design. Commodity systems are so diverse that in each country an array of approaches to strengthen them can be expected. For basic food crops produced over wide areas by many small farmers, a

revenues for government, or for other reasons? What modifications, if any, would be required to permit farmers to intensify production?

- *Processing.* In what ways is the commodity processed and where? Are processing plants situated near producers or in ports to serve importers? What potentials exist for expanding or diversifying processing?
- *Transport and storage systems.* How is the commodity moved from farm to market town to retail outlets? Are there weaknesses in the system?
- *Current yields obtained by farmers, by region and by season.* Determine the highest yields under varying soil and climatic conditions, national average yields, and where yields are low and static. Compare yields in other countries under similar climatic and soil conditions. The objective is to determine the magnitude and nature of yield gaps—the difference between what yields are and what they could be.
- *Major technological and economic problems limiting productivity.* What are the potentials for expanding markets, the availability of existing remedies, and the major problems which require local research for solution? Compare needs with the existing research effort and determine any additional high-priority research which could be justified financially. Does current research match needs?
- *Availability of adequately trained personnel in various components of the system.* Identify weaknesses to be overcome by in-service or other types of training. Who are the national authorities on each aspect? Should more authorities be developed?
- *Opportunities for greater cooperation among such organizations as planning bodies, cabinet ministries, banks, private industry, and farmer organizations.* Which elements of government and the private sector have what major interests in the success of the system?
- *Connections with external centers of advanced technological work on the commodity.* Are there links which should be fostered?
- *External technical assistance received.* What, if any, should be sought?
- *Actions which should be taken immediately.* Based on projected market requirements and an understanding of the system, what strategy or alternative strategies can be suggested?

nationwide, publicly financed effort will usually be needed. Agencies of government, including research and extension services, credit agencies, colleges and schools of agriculture, input suppliers, and purchasing agencies, will have to work together and be supported openly by political leaders.

For export crops the approach may be narrower. Production is generally concentrated in a few localities. Work on the crop is often financed with a levy. Often only a few business-oriented groups are involved with the commodity, including those responsible for exports. Research and training are usually centered at institutes under a management group or board or council that is concerned with the success of the entire system.

For each commodity one or more suitable courses of action can be quickly identified by appropriate authorities. These should be found and implemented.

Implementation. Although the size and nature of national programs can vary considerably, six techniques or components can be considered:[3]

- National focus on each commodity system can be fostered by periodic, preferably annual, national or regional workshops at which goals are reviewed, progress assessed, problems discussed, and cooperative action for the next period determined. All major agencies, industry groups, and producer organizations should be asked to participate. Information on key aspects of the concerted effort should be presented by planning agencies, research and extension services, input suppliers, marketing agencies, processors, and producer groups. Political leaders should be asked to participate to underscore the importance of cooperation of all concerned, to promote enthusiasm, and to indicate political support at the highest levels.
- The technological basis for production efforts must be established and upgraded systematically for each crop season (for example, dry or wet, summer or winter) and for each region, through continuing regional and on-farm trials. This will require that research and extension organizations cooperate closely in developing recommendations for crop, or animal, or mixed-farming systems that are more highly productive and more profitable.
- Identifying leaders for commodity programs, improving their expertise, and ensuring that new leaders are being developed is a major responsibility of the national entity responsible for commodity programs.

  Candidates to direct commodity programs should be well grounded in the technology required to raise productivity, should have the proven ability to lead, and should be dedicated to making the commodity system work to the advantage of producers and the nation. Such individuals should be capable of taking advantage of contacts with other national and international centers that work on the commodity.

[3] In 1968, in a paper published in *Strategy for the Conquest of Hunger*, Norman Borlaug, who directed the successful wheat program in Mexico and who has cooperated with many other governments in launching high-payoff wheat campaigns, emphasized eight factors as important to success: (1) crop-oriented programs, starting initially with those important to the economy and nutrition of the country; (2) adaptive research; (3) training of young people, including practical experience, with opportunities to "learn how to grow a crop, to learn something about all of the factors that are involved in crop production, including the dignity of human sweat"; (4) assembly of the package of improved practices; (5) commitment at the top levels of government to back agricultural programs aggressively; (6) continuity of programs for periods of at least five years; (7) sound fiscal policy and incentive prices; (8) appropriate systems to make inputs available.

New commodities

New commodities call for a highly exploratory approach. In the 1950s, authorities of the Joint Commission on Rural Reconstruction in the Republic of China decided that mushroom production might provide additional income to small rice farmers. They therefore supported research on the production of mushrooms using waste materials, particularly rice straw, available on small farms. At the same time, laboratories developed superior spawn, work was supported on ways to collect and to process the crop (as canned products), and efforts were made to develop export markets. Creating this system required continuing professional guidance by a central body, flexible funding to enable diverse organizations and individuals to participate easily, authority to take quick action on many small but related matters, and willingness to look ahead and sustain courses of action for long periods.

Like experts in any other high-technology field, such commodity experts are of extraordinary value to their countries. Efforts must be made to develop and retain such individuals in their specializations. They should be encouraged with financial and administrative support and should be able to keep in touch with advances elsewhere by visiting other programs and attending important international meetings.

Additionally, a means of identifying and preparing future leaders must be developed so that vacancies can be filled with competent individuals.

• Cooperation among organizations and individuals should be a central feature of commodity programs. Field stations, production centers, colleges or schools of agriculture, and farms should participate in nationwide field trials and demonstrations. Producer groups can help arrange farmer participation in tests and demonstrations, promote interest, and identify logistical problems. Faculty members of educational institutions can undertake part-time research or promotion if funds to supplement their salaries, to pay assistants, and to cover other expenses are available. Personnel of private industries, religious groups, and other private organizations may be included in training sessions, so that they can contribute more effectively to the campaign. Media should be used to get timely information to rural people and to keep the public informed of activities.

Other opportunities for cooperation will usually be found by asking who could help and in what ways, especially if modest funds can be made available to finance marginal costs of participation.

• Continuity of cooperative efforts can be provided through a permanent task force for each commodity comprising representatives of the major organizations involved in operational work. These will include the research and extension services, credit agencies, commodity purchasing agencies, processors, and input suppliers. Task forces should meet frequently to deal with details of planning and implementation.

- For each commodity, concentrating initially in one or a few defined regions may be desirable, especially in countries that lack experience with concerted interagency work, that are short of trained field workers, or that have few basic services countrywide.

Administration and control. The rapid strengthening of commodity systems, including arrangements for cooperative action by all relevant parties, will require some national mechanism for guiding and promoting the work. The governing body should:

- include high-level representatives of ministries or agencies concerned with agriculture, finance, planning, and commerce, plus selected representatives of the private sector, including industry. The entity should be permanent and should be set up to avoid frequent turnover of members. The members should have the power to involve their agencies and implement programs. Groups that are merely advisory seldom function well.
- receive funds from government or other sources for flexible support of activities involving interagency cooperation or activities otherwise not covered by budgets of participating agencies.
- receive progress reports and plans from commodity program leaders and approve major goals, strategies, work plans, personnel, and budgets for activities it sponsors.

The assumption is that the governing body would promote and support voluntary but concerted action among organizations and interest groups. Each organization should receive full recognition for its own activities and should join with others in common cause simply because that will contribute to the greater success of all.

Getting under way. The impetus for arousing the interest of national leaders in development-oriented commodity production systems can come from many sources. Frequently a proposal will come from individuals in a research organization who realize that technology for a commodity either is available or could quickly be generated to allow major advances in productivity.

Sometimes local scientists or administrators find it difficult to get the attention of their own political authorities for worthwhile proposals, but outsiders—even if no more competent—can. The leverage of outside authorities, who can be invited to review local prospects and report to national authorities, should be considered. Personnel of international organizations or private foundations can help legitimize the views of local staff and otherwise help bring opportunities to the attention of national authorities, sometimes offering to finance part of the efforts.

In short, the initiation of the commodity approach can be stimulated by government leaders, by scientists, by businessmen, by assistance agencies, or by others working alone or in coalitions of various sorts.

Local vested interests—often scientists or extension organizations—may deter initiation of commodity programs. That problem can be circumvented by starting with a commodity for which there are few vested interests and on which exploratory activity can be undertaken with least opposition.

Most programs should start small to avoid outrunning the supply of adequately trained people. To prepare enough people with specific expertise to permit expansion, on-the-job training will be essential.

Weaknesses. The commodity approach has weaknesses. While the technology may flow quickly to farms in regions where it is well adapted, there may be farmers, localities, or entire regions that do not benefit. New technology usually will not meet the requirements of all local farming systems. Some farmers may not have access to markets. Prices of produce or costs of inputs may not permit profits for all farmers. Some farmers may not be aware of new systems and how to use them. Any of a myriad of reasons can keep farmers from changing. Usually, those involved in national or regional promotion of a particular commodity will not be able to identify and overcome the constraints in every locality. That requires a different methodology, which we term the defined-region or defined-area approach.

DEFINED-AREA CAMPAIGNS

The second major approach to rapid agricultural development is through concerted efforts to raise the productivity and incomes of farm families in designated regions of a country—and to do so rapidly and at low cost. This approach will be most successful if there are strong commodity research programs to provide improved components for local farming systems and if the local efforts are supported by groups with expertise on special problems—input supply, credit, marketing, transport, and communications, to name a few. Therefore, defined-area campaigns should be viewed as integral components of national development and not as isolated projects.

"Defined-area" means a region with an identifiable boundary represented by a political unit or subunit, or by an irrigation command area, a watershed, valley or hill area, or river basin. Intensity and scope of effort may vary, but we are primarily concerned with planned, concerted, forced-pace, and sustained efforts—campaigns—to increase agricultural productivity and incomes of farm families as rapidly as possible, so they can improve their diets and lives.

Experience with defined-area development. Defined-area efforts are not new, and there is abundant evidence on which governments can draw in tailoring such programs to the requirements of their own countries. In Japan, for example, there were strong decentralized efforts in each prefecture. In the U.S., the agricultural development of each state has been the responsibility of state agricultural research and extension systems, with work carried out in close cooperation with industrial and farmer groups. Taiwan used the defined-area approach extensively. India has had experience with intensive agricultural district programs.

The Puebla Project in Mexico and the Comilla Project in East Pakistan were described in Chapter 8. In Nepal, there are the Gandaki Project supported by Germany, an Integrated Hill Development Project assisted by Switzerland, and hill development programs financed in part by the United Kingdom. Under the auspices of the World Bank, Uma Lele has described and analyzed 17 projects in Cameroon, Ethiopia, Kenya, Malawi, Mali, Nigeria, and Tanzania; some were concerned with regional rural development, while others focused on commodities (mostly export crops) or on functions (agricultural research, extension, feeder roads, agricultural credit). Morss, Hatch, Mickelwait, and Sweet have evaluated 22 rural development projects in 5 countries in Africa and 14 projects in 6 countries of Latin America. Michael Nelson has analyzed 24 tropical highway and colonization ventures in Latin America. There have been many diverse approaches in Asia, the Mideast, and elsewhere, including the industrialized countries. The system of communes in the People's Republic of China involves integrated development in defined areas, with agriculture as a leading component.

The approach. Agricultural development, if managed properly, is usually the most direct way to bring a higher standard of living to rural people in most low-income countries. Furthermore, once the credibility of government authorities is established by increasing productivity and incomes through agriculture, it is much easier to introduce programs, such as education or public health, in which local participation is important. And, as incomes rise, local people will be better able to contribute to their own advance.

Adequately organized campaigns to promote agricultural development in defined areas

- permit the authorities to better understand the aspirations, resources, sources of livelihood, and often complex agricultural and social systems of rural people;
- enable scientists to test technologies under farm conditions and to tailor complete systems to local requirements;
- permit personnel of government service agencies and private businesses to work out policies and procedures that are politically and administratively feasible and to learn how to synchronize them;
- allow progress toward goals, or lack of it, to be measured, and responsibility for action and for success or failure to be assigned;
- minimize the impact of errors—mistakes made in early experimental programs, once recognized, need not be repeated elsewhere;
- provide locations to train people for programs in other areas.

Criteria in selecting areas. Possible locations for initial defined-area campaigns are numerous in any country. Making a choice involves economic, political, and technical considerations. From the economic standpoint, the need to increase output of particular commodities (or to learn how) suggests concentrating on areas that produce significant volumes of those commodities. Or areas may be chosen where transport and marketing systems are more highly developed and where the likelihood of rapid advances in productivity and incomes is greatest. From the political viewpoint, areas may be chosen because of large concentrations of poor people, or because of political leaders' interest in promoting change in their constituencies, or because they have unrest or potential unrest. All are valid considerations.

In estimating the probable success of each venture, there are additional factors to weigh:

- The area served by each program should be substantial so that the undertaking is economically and politically significant.
- The area should be located within a single administrative or political unit so that support of local, regional, and national political leaders can be obtained, and so that it fits the geographic responsibilities of existing agencies.
- The soil, climate, and accessibility of the area should permit progress (but if an initial pilot program is being considered, these factors must not be so favorable that success, if achieved, would be considered irrelevant to the problem of other areas of the nation).

- The technology required to increase yields of target commodities must be available or possible to develop quickly.
- Land tenure should be reasonably equitable. Or opportunities should exist to change the land distribution and to work directly with small farmers.
- In rainfed agricultural areas, the availability of rainfall and temperature records will be helpful.

In most countries, because of shortages of resources and of properly trained personnel, it is sensible to start in one or a few defined areas and then expand as feasibility studies suggest major new opportunities and as availability of trained personnel permits. In countries with diverse ecological conditions and basically different agricultural systems, if resources permit, one defined-area program should be started in each major ecological zone as promptly as possible. The objective should be twofold: to learn how to raise productivity and incomes in each ecological zone and to train people for expansion. Where strong state or provincial governments exist it may also be wise to establish a defined-area program under each, provided enough capable personnel are available.

Planning defined-area programs. Situation papers on any region should be prepared before any major campaign with farmers is launched. Many features of commodity program situation papers (discussed earlier in this chapter) will apply as well to proposed defined-area programs. But attention must be paid to all commodities, to all agricultural or nonagricultural sources of employment and income, and to characteristics of the population and the political and economic structure of the region.

Benchmark data will be needed on the physical, human, and economic resource bases of the area. Information from censuses, previous studies in the area, and studies in similar geographical areas can be evaluated to determine:

- agro-climatic conditions—soil types, topography, rainfall amount and distribution, temperatures, and incidence of hail, drought, frost, or other factors affecting risks;
- major economic components, including alternative employment opportunities or other nonagricultural endeavors nearby;
- the nature of farming systems;
- available agricultural technology;
- access to markets;
- structure of the political system; and
- how farmers are organized.

Where gaps are identified, statistical surveys can be made and observations of informed persons sought. This information will reveal conditions under which the project must be implemented and will provide a baseline against which changes can be measured.

Experiments with a few crops or animal species believed most promising should be initiated in farmers' fields to determine whether yields and output can be raised, in what ways, under what conditions, and how quickly. For annual crops with experiments in numerous locations, this should usually take no more than 2 years.

Concurrently, estimates of profitability of the components of the technologies, individually and in combination, at several levels of management and at a range of possible price levels, are necessary. These estimates also should be completed within the first 2 years of study, using data from the agricultural experiments (see the "maize diamond" technique used in Kenya, Chapter 8). Special consideration should be given to risks in introducing new practices, particularly with respect to year-to-year variability of weather or other factors which might penalize the farmer who innovates.

Only after the technical feasibility and potential economic profitability have been established through field tests under actual farm conditions has a basis been laid for a campaign in any area.

Implementation. For each area, prospects for success can be enhanced in a number of ways.

Narrowing the focus. Within each designated area, work should be limited initially to a few commodities or activities which could raise productivity and incomes dramatically and quickly. Goals should be clearly defined, with targets for farmer participation and commodity yields and output.

Team approach. A team of dedicated, well-trained, and skilled individuals (see Chapter 12) must be given the specific mandate of working with local farmers and organizations to achieve the goals of the program.

The project staff normally will have fundamental educational preparation but limited specialized training or previous experience. They should receive help from specialists in designing, implementing, analyzing, and interpreting surveys and experiments; preparing detailed plans of operation; and resolving social and technical problems that arise during the campaign. It is useful for the program staff to meet often with scientists experienced with commodities and in fields such as agronomy, plant protection, animal science, veterinary medicine, economics, sociology, and communication.

Joint undertakings. Development of the region should be a joint undertaking of all relevant entities. This will most likely occur if the team members are provided by the organizations concerned in an agreed-upon manner, or better yet if the team is responsible to a governing board comprising representatives of relevant agencies, of political entities, of business interests, and of local farmers.

Zones of action. In programs involving large areas, the area should be divided into zones and one or more technicians should be given primary responsibility for work in each. Criteria for establishing zones may include, in addition to climate and soil, such factors as social and political organization of the population, degree of mobility of the technicians, and financial resources available.

Simultaneous satisfaction of requisites. In each locality, institutions must work jointly to provide complete and more profitable crop and animal production recommendations, to instruct farmers in their use, to supply inputs and credits on time, and to arrange marketing, storage, and transport. Cooperation at the local level usually succeeds only if agencies cooperate at all levels.

Building on available technology and experience. Priorities for experimentation should be based on an understanding of the technologies and practices already being used in the area and why farmers use them. Existing technologies should be analyzed. Modifications that might substantially increase output and net income should be tested. Technologies in successful use elsewhere should then be introduced in the region, with appropriate modifications. Research should move outward from controlled experiments to farmers' fields. Eventual recommendations, involving use of costly inputs, should take into consideration the risks of climatic variation and fluctuations faced by farmers (see Chapter 12 for details).

Establishing centers of development activity. Establishment of a production center (described in Chapter 12) will be helpful. At the production center, specialists can test a wide range of commodities and techniques of promise for the region, even though the initial campaign is limited to a few lines of work of greatest potential for raising farm productivity and incomes. The production center should be a site for training the area development teams and the headquarters of agencies providing supporting services locally.

Use of all channels of communication. Getting information to farmers, agricultural leaders, agricultural institutions, businesses, and government officials will be an important component of the regional campaign. Likewise, developing means of learning *from* these people will greatly strengthen the program.

Rural people frequently will have had adverse contacts with outside parties. Many promises may have been unfulfilled and previous assistance

Succeed jointly or fail separately

In discussions in 1975 with technical personnel of several departments of a Latin American government regarding the urgent need to increase production of wheat in its highland areas, it was learned that the research agency felt it had the technology needed to at least double average yields, that fertilizer was available at subsidized prices, that the price for grain was at world market levels, and that use of a high-yielding system should be quite profitable—yet production was stagnant. Among the constraints were inadequacy of seed supplies of recommended varieties, inability of farmers to transport tons of fertilizers long distances to their farms or tons of grain to distant receiving points, and an extreme shortage of field personnel skilled in installing on-farm experiments and demonstration plots or otherwise working with farmers to increase production. The agencies at least had the capability to mount a campaign with the crop in one province, which could then serve as a pilot area and permit the training of more field personnel. The problem was that each agency—research, extension, fertilizer supply, marketing—was pursuing its own separate interests in isolation from the others. This isolation of agencies prevented any one of them from mounting a successful program—all were doomed to fail.

In such a case agencies have only two alternatives: *succeed jointly or fail separately.*

efforts may have resulted in frustration. Villagers may be suspicious of outsiders and lack trust in government and organizations associated with it.

Credibility must be established quickly. Technical assistance agents should have an adequate knowledge of technology and farming systems and have confidence in the practices they are recommending. Face-to-face communication will help establish rapport with the farmers. Team members should, if possible, be of local origin and fluent in the language of the area. Continuity of senior technical personnel in the early period will help establish trust.

Local people, especially community leaders, should be involved in the campaign from the beginning. Cooperating farmers can facilitate contact between technical assistance agents and other farmers at little cost, and farmer-to-farmer communication is an effective way to spread information. Farmers usually trust certain other farmers more than program technicians, at least in the early years of a program. Cooperating farmers should receive special training, and new information should be made available to them on a continuing basis. If such links are established, they will significantly reduce the size of the project staff required.

Other community figures can be helpful. Midwives may be effective in communicating with rural women. Religious leaders may serve as effective communicators of information to their followers. Certain individuals who hold socially powerful positions should also be brought into the campaign, if only as advisors, so they will not feel left out and block the program.

To reach larger groups of rural people, radio and pamphlets, village meetings, interchange between farmer groups, and field demonstrations by farmers at harvest should be used.

Input supply, credit, markets, and prices. Two rules apply fairly widely for improving the delivery of inputs, the availability of credit, and the stability of market prices. First, if possible, work should be done within the existing governmental or private system, reinforcing and supporting it, rather than by creating new institutions. For example, project personnel should establish cooperatives for credit or fertilizer distribution only if existing agencies cannot. Second, even if economic power is equitably distributed (and more so if it is not), special efforts must be made at the outset to meet the needs of small farmers and other rural poor. A focus on small farmers will benefit all farmers, including the larger farmers whose political support for the program will be important. Any other approach will fail to reach the smaller farmers.

Strengthening local institutions. Since development is a never-ending procedure, a basic policy should be to help local people and institutions learn to handle their own problems rather than expect most services from government.

Groups. Associations of rural people can be powerful forces for long-term change. Farmers banded together can be more effective in dealing with agencies than the same number acting separately. Three conditions will determine the effectiveness of groups: (1) They must be formed to achieve objectives about which the members feel strongly, usually to increase income. (2) Organizing must be carried out intelligently. If a major purpose is to arrange for credit and marketing, the success of groups will depend on the existence of new and more profitable production systems and the availability of inputs and stable and accessible markets. Credit services should be available to all. (3) The natural leaders among the small farmers and other rural people of the area must emerge in leadership roles. Groups often fail to achieve their purposes if they are captured by those already served well by existing institutions.

Improvements in infrastructure. Underlying the economic system of any area are the roads, markets, and communication system (mails, telephone, telegraph, radio) which facilitate the exchange of information and movements of production inputs, agricultural commodities, consumer goods, and people between farms and other locations. Rural electrification is a powerful stimulant of rural progress. Even though the project team may not be responsible for planning or building these facilities, it can seek improvements in these services by encouraging local initiative.

Training. Each defined-area program should be operated in large part by young people in training who work under a relatively few senior specialists. This is the key to both continuation and expansion of such activities. Basic skills in agronomic or animal experimentation, communication, and evaluation should be stressed. Each trainee should work in a project for at least a year, preferably two, becoming increasingly responsible for important components of the work. For some individuals, this practical phase might be followed by advanced specialized training at a university. The goal is to produce a stream of skilled individuals to help others to help themselves using the campaign approach.

Financial support. An adequate budget should be provided in a manner which makes it relatively easy to administer. Flexibility in use of funds should permit specialists to be brought to the area when needed and supplies to be obtained when required. Delays can be disastrous in agriculture. Costs should, however, be kept at levels which would allow the approach to be duplicated in other areas.

Long-term flexible efforts. Development of any region will be a continuous and long-term process. All efforts should be organized to permit continuity of work and innovation toward long-term goals. Flexibility of action—basing plans for each year on the progress of the previous year— is advisable. It should also be recognized that activity must continue for a long time, often 10 years or more.

Annual reviews. As in commodity programs, annual workshops are desirable for defined-region programs. Reviews, lasting several days, allow all cooperators, public and private, to examine the past year's progress and to establish plans for the ensuing year.

Political support. Political leaders should be encouraged to become involved on a continuing basis. Support may weaken when political leaders fail to grasp the magnitude of the importance of the program and become disillusioned when short-term accomplishments do not measure up to expectations, when the achievements of the later years do not keep pace with those (often more easily reached) during the early years, or when there is a change in political leadership.

Weaknesses. Defined-area projects have several built-in weaknesses. The staff usually must be small, in keeping with the limited area and numbers of people to be served. Most of the technical people cannot be specialized. The danger is that their work will be superficial, and superficiality has caused numerous rural development projects to fail. This weakness can be overcome in two ways: by limiting the initial number of commodities or problems to those which the staff can handle adequately and by arranging for close support of defined-area programs by commodity specialists and others, and by relevant government agencies.

Too often, defined-area projects are isolated from the mainstream of government agency activities. The isolation may be intentional—to avoid the stifling effects of bureaucracies. In fact, in some countries, organization outside government is the only practical way to start. Even programs undertaken within government structures or in initial close cooperation with particular public agencies can become isolated. The attention such projects receive may be resented by agencies not directly involved. Projects may not get close support if the regular agencies reserve their best personnel and first call on funds and services for other purposes. Such isolation must be avoided. Instead, close cooperation among all concerned parties should be fostered to accelerate progress in agricultural or rural development.

Area development projects are often small and isolated. Some small projects may have value for educational or research purposes. However, the principles already established appear to justify making the defined-area development approach an integral part of national development efforts, with the full weight of government financial and political support behind it.

REORIENTATION AND SYNCHRONIZATION OF SERVICES

Many national organizations and agencies were not designed to support forced-pace action; rather, they were organized for a slower rate of progress—satisfactory, perhaps, for times past.

The third component of a nation's strategy for accelerated development is reorientation of agencies of governments and colleges and schools of agriculture to enable them to support national development goals directly, synchronizing services at all levels, particularly within farm districts, and, if necessary, reorganizing agencies and services. Mosher deals effectively and at length with many of these subjects in *Creating a Progressive Rural Structure* and *To Create a Modern Agriculture*. In 1977, he reiterated a five-point strategy for improving agencies and procedures.[4]

First, strengthen the delivery of all services required by farmers so that they are available at points easily reached even by small farmers.

Second, arrange the mix and intensity of public agricultural activities "from place to place in such a way as to meet most urgent current needs in each part of the country."

---

[4] Mosher described this strategy in "Reorganizing Regular Agencies and Procedures."

Synchronization: Horizontal and vertical

Use of the term "synchronization" is intended to cover simultaneous provision in each locality of all materials, services, and conditions (including incentive prices) necessary for farmers to adopt more highly productive farming systems or practices. Embraced are collaboration of various units of government at each level (horizontal) and integration of the activities of local and district units involved in a particular program with those of regional and national units of the same component (vertical).

Our concept of vertical synchronization goes still further: for commodity programs, it includes concurrent and systematic efforts under an appropriate governing body to direct research and extension activities to most important problems; to gear production to demand for products; and to improve transport, storage, processing, and domestic or international marketing in such ways as to speed the development process.

Third, reorganize all public agricultural agencies to make them development oriented. Mosher notes that governments have agencies to support farming, but

the ways in which they are now organized, and the responsibilities each has, were not set up with rapid development in mind. Instead the existing pattern has been heavily influenced by one or more of three considerations: political considerations (to make room for or to squeeze out a particular Minister); colonial antecedents when special export crops dominated governmental interest and the possibility of rapid improvement with respect to domestic crops was not yet realized; and borrowing from the organization of agencies in developed countries where rapid current development is not the dominant concern.

Fourth, install an appropriate pattern of agricultural planning to provide for (a) both long- and short-range national requirements on a continuously revised basis; (b) the varying needs of regions that have "immediate growth potential," "future growth potential," and "low growth potential" (see Chapter 12); (c) involving all relevant agencies and technical personnel in the planning process, particularly personnel who must implement plans.

Fifth, modernize operating procedures and patterns of administration in all public agencies to attract and retain competent staff, to expedite purchase and delivery of materials and services, to streamline transactions between ministries, and to permit greater delegation of authority. "There is no one pattern of administration and operating procedures that is best. Different activities have different requirements. And different total administrative patterns do and should prevail in countries having significantly different prevailing cultures. But achieving effective patterns of administration and operating procedures is *essential* if rapid growth is to be achieved."

Intensifying agriculture generally requires that several ministries of government as well as private businesses be involved. Failure to synchronize activities at all levels, from cabinet to the individual rural community, will delay, reduce, or prevent progress. Wherever agricultural progress has been rapid, coordination has been achieved by some means. Governments of any political orientation can find ways to do so, if they have the political will.

Chapters 12 through 14 suggest means of organizing crucial research and extension services, colleges and schools of agriculture, and input and marketing organizations to allow them to contribute more substantially to the acceleration of progress.

Operational principles

All three approaches—commodity-oriented production programs, defined-region development campaigns, and synchronized supporting services—can be harmed by inappropriate and short-sighted goals, vested interests contending for limited resources in ways inimical to the national good, fragmentation of effort, and shortages of trained personnel. Such difficulties can be minimized by adopting several operational principles.

LONG-TERM GOALS

Long-term objectives (up to 20 years or more) for agricultural and rural development should be established, commodity by commodity, region by region, as a guide to shorter-term actions as often enunciated in national development plans. The goals will reveal the magnitude of gains required and the speed of action necessary. These in turn will affect the choice of strategies commodity by commodity, region by region, problem by problem. They will suggest how public agencies, private industry, and farmers and farm groups should be involved. They will shed light on the size, nature, and sequence of investments required by government or assistance agencies. In short, governments must establish the long-term targets to allow design of efforts toward which all agencies can work, innovating as they go along.

John Kenneth Galbraith, in an article in *Foreign Affairs*, referred to the disappointing progress of some national economic development programs for which external assistance had been provided. He stated rather bluntly:

There will be improvement only when we begin seriously to ask what is needed—when targets are established and attention becomes focused on what

THE BASIC STRATEGY 261

"In every developing country I have visited, agricultural policy is a strange schizophrenic creature that serves many masters. The goal of cheap food for urban consumption is incompatible with the goal of incentives for production. The goal of an efficient grain processing industry is incompatible with the goal of preserving and protecting wasteful small-scale mills. The desire to save foreign exchange and hold currency to overvalued exchange rates is likely to be incompatible with the need to increase the supply and lower the farm price of modern inputs. The insulation of inefficient public- or private-sector enterprises from competition is incompatible with the oft-proclaimed aim of providing farmers with quality inputs and maximum incentives to move to higher levels of production. Policies to discourage the development of mechanized agriculture because of its assumed impact upon rural labor-force employment are incompatible with the need for careful timing and precision in farm operations for multiple cropping in areas where growing conditions and the availability of water would permit the harvest of two or three crops per year. And so on; the list is long and depressing, for it frequently leads to the conclusion that, protestations to the contrary, many countries have accepted increased food production as a political objective so hedged by reservations and so conditioned by objectives of higher priority that it is lost as a focus for action. Under such circumstances there can be no strategy for eliminating hunger. Some nations can afford the luxury of mixed goals and of uncertain, unproductive policies. For others, the production of food must be accepted as the priority objective, and the strategy for its attainment must be drawn in accordance with Beauffre's dictum that it make the most effective contribution to achieving the objective."

W. David Hopper
"Investments in Agriculture:
The Essentials for Payoff"

is required to reach them. Then it will be impossible (or anyhow difficult) to avoid thinking about the missing elements, and once targets are established, we shall have measures of success—or failure. Then conspicuous failure will have to be explained and responsibiltiy for a wrong decision assigned.

Goals must be quantitative as well as qualitative, to be most useful in preparing plans and in measuring progress. Goals may be expressed as numbers of hectares or numbers of farmers to be benefited in specified ways. Or targets may be the amounts by which crop tonnage or animal production is to increase and gains in national average yield are to be achieved, in specified periods of time.

Long-term goals will at best be estimates, and should be stated in rounded terms or as orders of magnitude. These quantitative projections should be accompanied by statements of the assumptions on which they are based. For example, if a government has a goal of self-sufficiency in certain basic foods, it will be helpful to estimate requirements (consumer demand) for each commodity at, for example, points 5, 10, 15, and 20 years in the future. To do so, assumptions must be made regarding rate of population increase, changes in purchasing power of consumers, and the possibility of consumer shifts to purchase of other commodities should relative prices among them change.

Targets are normally revised from time to time based on experience. And, since development is a continuous and long-term process, all efforts should be organized to permit continuity of work and of innovation toward long-term goals. Flexibility of action, allowing plans for each year to be based on the progress and problems of the previous year, is advisable.

SPEEDY FEASIBILITY STUDIES

Program decisions can be only as good as the information on which they are based. The best information systems have been developed in response to specific program needs. Ways to rapidly determine the technical and economic feasibility of increasing farm productivity must be employed. If scientists and economists work together designing, locating, and interpreting surveys and field experiments for each commodity and each region and locality, they will be able to quickly assess the gains that are technically possible and the yield levels that are economically advantageous.

INVOLVING LOCAL PEOPLE

Local people, especially small farmers and community leaders, should be involved in the campaigns from the beginning. They can contribute to agricultural development efforts in several critical ways.

First, farmers' explanations of their farming systems can be enlightening to those attempting to identify and promote improvements. Preferences for certain characteristics of crops (flavor, cooking quality, storage properties) may be strongly held and soundly based. Customs are likely to affect the availability of labor and draft power. Such factors must be understood by those promoting improvements in commodity or defined-area programs so that technologies can be oriented accordingly.

Second, most farmers can readily understand why new practices are more productive and profitable, if they are. Experiments carried out in farmers' fields can show farmers the effects of variations in plant population, dates of planting, levels of fertilizer use, or degree of weed control. Similarly, the effects of vaccination, feed supplements, pasture management, or sanitation can be revealed through on-farm experiments with animals.

Third, farmers often trust other farmers more than outsiders. In seeking to reach all farmers, technicians can enlist the help of respected local

Goals versus activities

Goals or targets should not be confused with "activities." When the International Rice Research Institute was established in 1960, its stated "objectives" were to study the rice plant in all its aspects, to train personnel for national programs, to establish an information center and a world rice germ-plasm bank, and to facilitate cooperation on rice problems. Actually these were the proposed *activities* of IRRI. Its *goal*, according to its founders, was to raise rice yields in Asia. It is the ends, not the means, which are goals.

Hidden or unstated goals can be troublesome. Investments are now being made in research or extension services and in credit and input supply systems, with emergence of strengthened institutions or improved services as the stated goals. Some government authorities probably assume that the result of such investments will be increased output and improved incomes in rural areas. If so, these real goals should be plainly stated, along with strong indications of how institutions will be held accountable. If *real goals* are stated as plans are being made, programs are much more likely to work in the right direction.

farmers (not necessarily the more "progressive" or affluent) in conducting farm-level experiments and in explaining results to neighbors. The participation of numbers of local farmers may allow a handful of qualified technical people to influence many farm families.

In some societies, cooperating farmers may be able to do still more— organizing groups or assisting with input supply, credit arrangements, and marketing. Governments are justified in considering ways to make full use of the capabilities of farmers while increasing the qualifications, rather than the numbers, of technicians.

COMMITMENT BY GOVERNMENTS

Crucial to any nation's agricultural progress is the willingness of the government to make difficult decisions, establish policies, reorient institutions, and provide the necessary human and financial resources. Such a commitment can be expected only if understandable evidence is presented to political leaders, who are often lawyers, medical doctors, engineers, businessmen, military officers, or other nonagriculturists. They are entitled to know what needs to be done to promote agricultural and economic advance, how urgent it is, how it could be accomplished, what the costs would be, and the probable penalties for inaction. This brings us full-circle to the need for goals which clearly identify each nation's problems and for plans of action which promise to realize each country's potential for progress—all presented in language which political leaders can understand.

FINANCIAL SUPPORT

If progress is to be rapid, adequate budgets for work must enable programs to be relatively easy to administer, make the work of staff professionally and personally rewarding, permit specialists to be brought to the program when needed, allow supplies to be obtained on time, and enable staff to have required mobility. Financing should be sustained long enough to allow goals to be reached and at realistic levels so that replication of the approach with other commodities or in other areas would be justified.

REGION-BY-REGION ATTACK

In most countries, shortages of resources and of properly trained personnel limit initial efforts to one or a few commodities and one or a few defined areas. Expansion can occur when feasibility studies suggest major new opportunities and when availability of personnel permits.

Since farmers will shift to higher-yielding systems only when all requirements for marketing, input supply, technology, and farmer instruction are met, it is clear that progress can occur more quickly in some areas than in others. Roads connecting farms to markets are basic, but are time-consuming and costly to provide. For nations in a hurry, agricultural campaigns should be concentrated in areas favored with adequate transport and other resources.

In more remote areas, research should be undertaken on new farming systems in preparation for the time when the areas will have better transportation. In these areas a clear demonstration by scientists of how productivity can be increased, and by how much, will encourage investment in transportation, marketing, and input supply. Technical and economic studies of the potentials of more remote regions deserve high priority—second only to support of campaigns in more favored areas.

SYNCHRONIZATION OF EFFORTS

To accelerate agricultural progress, governments must ensure that the actions of all relevant public and private agencies are effectively coordinated. Establishing long-term goals and clarifying responsibilities for each component will be helpful. To improve coordination, some governments are establishing interministerial councils; others are considering semi-autonomous development commissions with relevant ministers and key members of industry participating.

Stimulation of agriculture can be vested in a permanent and separately funded commission which works with government agencies and the private sector to achieve rapid progress. The Joint Commission on Rural Reconstruction in Taiwan—a small board of scientists and administrators—is an example worthy of study (Chapter 8). JCRR financed studies, prepared plans for ministeries (which implemented them if they agreed), and supported a wide array of exploratory work which led to imaginative and rapid development of agriculture. No power was taken away from ministries; rather, as a permanent development organization with a highly capable, interdisciplinary professional staff and great flexibility of action, JCRR still works in a catalytic way in direct support of political units and private industry, helping to make their activities successful.

Another means of synchronization would involve establishing a national development agency which would implement programs requiring concerted action at all levels by various ministries. The agency could be directly responsible to a council of ministers and would receive funds for cooperative work directly from the central treasury, while individual ministries would continue to finance and implement activities which are clearly their responsibilities.

TRAINING

Regardless of the approach to development, insufficient qualified personnel is usually a barrier to expansion. And failure to appreciate the complexities of farm-level development work often results in inadequate training of technical people. Nations must plan how they will train enough personnel. Means of accelerating training, in large part through dual-purpose activities, are discussed in Chapter 14.

NONAGRICULTURAL SECTORS

Finally, agricultural planning and implementation must not be carried out in isolation from the other sectors of the economy. In the economic world, "everything depends on everything else," and the process of economic development is really based on establishing a series of growing and reinforcing relationships within and among sectors. Agriculture in particular has responsibilities for the process of capital formation for itself as well as for the other sectors. Agricultural planning must be carried out as an integral part of the overall economic development effort.

Considerations in planning

Countries faced with diverse and massive needs and a shortage of human and financial resources, yet desirous of rapid agricultural progress, must plan carefully, but imaginatively.

In his paper "Reorganizing Regular Agencies and Procedures" Arthur Mosher notes:

Agricultural planning is a complicated task and few countries do it well. In some cases it is little more than a statement of general objectives and an allocation of funds with little or no specification of how the objectives are to be achieved. In others, it consists primarily of developing budgets for individual public agricultural agencies. But the allocation of funds should be only one, and it is not the most important aspect of effective planning. Effective planning needs to embrace, in considerable detail, *what* is to be done in or for each farming district, *who* is to do it, and *how* it is to be done within a particular time period, with adjustment of *how much* of each is to be done being conditioned by available resources of finance and technical manpower.

Albert Waterston put it another way:

The current artificial separation between the formulation and implementation of plans accounts for the failure of planners, concentrating as they do on aggregative planning, to recognize soon enough that the weakness in most developing countries is not the lack of an elegantly integrated comprehensive plan based on economic potentialities but the lack of well-planned individual projects that can really be carried out. . . .

Only a few of the less developed countries are fully aware of the need for selecting soundly conceived projects with potentially high yields defining their scope with clarity, estimating their national currency and foreign exchange requirements with a sufficient degree of accuracy, and laying down realistic schedules for their execution; even fewer have the administrative capacity and political will to cope with these needs and especially to carry out projects in accordance with carefully developed programs of action.

. . . It seems clear, therefore, that improvements in project preparation and budgetary controls, where needed, are at least as urgent as the preparation of aggregative plans.

Much emphasis in recent years has been placed on strengthening national planning groups, which are usually heavily staffed with economists. Simultaneously, a substantial body of literature on the development process, including agricultural development, has evolved; most of the comprehensive books or papers on agricultural development also have been written by economists or, occasionally, by political scientists, if only because few others (except journalists) are writing on the subject. Biological scientists have been remarkably silent, as evidenced by their scant writings on strategies for development. There has been little joint work among specialists in the biological sciences, industry, and economics. It should not be surprising, then, that some concepts or attitudes which rest primarily on economic considerations deserve to be reexamined in relation to their influence on the speed and direction of agricultural development.

POLICY CONTROL OF AGRICULTURAL GROWTH

When technology is a factor limiting yield increases, no change in policy, no exhortation from government, no rise in prices, not even the use of force, can get those yields up. Until short, stiff-strawed rice varieties tailored to specific tropical conditions were produced, it was impossible to raise rice yields much in the tropics. The same was true for wheat in the low latitudes. Numerous examples exist for other crops, animal species, and regions.

ESTIMATES OF POTENTIALS AND PROBLEMS

Evaluation of the technological barriers to increased yields usually requires the judgments of biological scientists. Moreover, the scientists should normally be specialists in production of the particular crop or animal species in regions like those under study in order to determine production potentials, problems likely to be encountered, and the speed with which advances could be made. The assessment demands judgment based on field observations and experiments, in addition to surveys and interpretation of data. Economists may contribute significantly to such an evaluation, but few have the technical training or experience to make such judgments on their own. On the other hand, few biological scientists have been trained to think comprehensively about agricultural development or the planning of it. A new generation of leaders with strength in both biological science and economics, and with a development orientation, could contribute importantly to the rapid increases in agricultural output which so many nations need.

COMPARATIVE ECONOMIC ADVANTAGE

The costs of producing different commodities in a particular country or area, or of a particular commodity in different areas, are important considerations in planning agricultural development. The rule of comparative advantage has taught that if each area specializes in producing commodities which are most profitable and trades for others that it needs, all areas will be economically better off.

The rule of comparative advantage has validity on strictly economic grounds and often should be observed, especially with export crops. However, in the case of basic food commodities, political and social considerations also have great, often overriding, weight in a nation's strategy because of problems of employment, poverty, and internal security.

In some cases the rule of comparative advantage is easy to apply. For example, since ability to sell profitably in international markets is so important, the production of export crops is usually concentrated in a relatively few countries and even in regions within countries where conditions are most favorable. However, the rule is more difficult to apply to food crops. Due to domestic political pressures, Japan has paid its farmers three to four times more than world market prices. Other countries have supported domestic grain prices at well above world market levels to minimize imports, thereby making themselves less reliant on other countries for so basic a commodity as food. The People's Republic of China has promoted self-sufficiency in basic food production in all regions in order to spread risk, minimize transport of foodstuffs (perhaps in part to lessen the burden on an over-taxed rail system), and promote employment and prosperity as widely as possible. Planning decisions based only on perceived comparative economic advantage in production of basic foods are likely to be unrealistic.

RETURNS TO INVESTMENT

A common method of deciding among alternative investment opportunities is to calculate the expected net returns to each and then select the most attractive for implementation. While this exercise can be a valuable planning tool, errors arise from misunderstanding the factors that affect the profitability of the activity, and from the inability to state in quantitative terms the benefits to be derived. Two examples will illustrate these difficulties.

In preparing the rationale for major irrigation schemes, the estimates of crop yields possible with irrigation are often based on levels of productivity which should be obtained from use of high-yielding varieties, disease and pest control, proper application of fertilizers, reasonably priced fertilizers, incentive prices for products, application of irrigation water in correct amounts and at the right time, effective extension services, and, finally, adoption of practices by the farmers. While the factors which might contribute to high yields can easily be listed, it is often difficult to ascertain whether that high-yielding system can be developed quickly. Many estimates of returns to investment in irrigation schemes are therefore seriously overstated. Often designs of major irrigation works are approved, funds provided, and construction of dams and major canals completed on assumptions that major gains will occur in productivity and profitability of irrigated farming systems. Yet, frequently, no provision is made for land leveling, construction of the system of canals to deliver water to individual farms as needed, or for development or testing of high-yielding cropping systems which could be employed. Only the relatively straightforward engineering aspects of the project receive serious attention. That such incomplete projects are approved and initiated is a credit neither to the country nor to the funding agency.

In contrast, estimates of returns to crop production schemes in which large numbers of small farmers adopt high-yielding, more profitable farming systems probably are often *understated* by wide margins because only a few of the benefits can be given in quantitative terms. One can measure the costs of such programs reasonably well, yet, on the returns side, only the value of the product added can be measured. It is difficult to place a value on the effects of successful experience with one crop (use of fertilizers, weed control, shifts in dates of planting) on farmers' innovation with other crops; the effects of transfers of knowledge from farmers in a program to those not in it; the effects of employment on the farm or in nearby trade centers; the effects of increased purchasing power on diets, health, or other factors involved in standards of living; or the effects of happier rural people and tranquility in the countryside.

Summary

Farmers will change surprisingly quickly to higher-yielding crop or animal production systems if the requisites for their participation are satisfied in their entirety. This requires that the public and private agencies work in concert to synchronize their activities from establishment of basic services (roads, communication systems) to design of agricultural systems on-farm.

Nations in a hurry to develop agriculture are advised to use a strategy embracing a combination of commodity production programs, defined-area campaigns, and reorientation and synchronization of services of institutions.

If nations are to advance agriculture with minimum errors, planning and policy must be based on actual knowledge of systems and of what is required to make them function. Expertise in economics and biological science are but two of several important components.

References

THE PRIORITIES

Asian Development Bank. *Asian Agricultural Survey 1976*. Manila: Asian Development Bank, 1977.

de Janvry, Alain. "The Political Economy of Rural Development in Latin America: An Interpretation." *American Journal of Agricultural Economics* 57 (1975): 490–99.

International Bank for Reconstruction and Development. *Rural Development*. Sector Policy Paper. Washington, D.C.: World Bank, 1975.

Mosher, A. T. *Getting Agriculture Moving*. New York: Praeger, 1966.

Ruttan, Vernon W. "Induced Innovation and Agricultural Development." *Food Policy* 2 (1977): 196–216.

Subramaniam, C. "India's Program for Agricultural Progress." In *Strategy for the Conquest of Hunger: Proceedings of a Symposium*. New York: Rockefeller Foundation, 1968.

Wharton, Clifton R., Jr. "The Role of the Professional in Feeding Mankind: The Political Dimension." In *Proceedings of the World Food Conference of 1976*, edited by Frank Schaller. Ames: Iowa State University Press, 1977.

THE STRATEGY

Borlaug, Norman E. "National Production Campaigns." In *Strategy for the Conquest of Hunger: Proceedings of a Symposium*. New York: Rockefeller Foundation, 1968.

Cummings, Ralph W., Jr. "Defined-Area Campaigns: Principles Underlying Implementation." Mimeographed. New York: International Agricultural Development Service, 1977.

Lele, Uma J. *The Design of Rural Development: Lessons from Africa*. Baltimore: Johns Hopkins University Press, 1975.

Morss, Elliot R.; Hatch, John K.; Mikelwait, Donald; and Sweet, Charles F. *Strategies for Small Farmer Development: An Empirical Study of Rural Development Projects in the Gambia, Ghana, Kenya, Lesotho, Nigeria, Bolivia, Colombia, Mexico, Paraguay, and Peru*. Boulder, Colo.: Westview Press, 1976.

Mosher, Arthur T. *Creating a Progressive Rural Structure*. New York: Agricultural Development Council, 1969.

Mosher, Arthur T. "Reorganizing Regular Agencies and Procedures." Paper presented at an IADS Workshop, June 26–July 1, 1977. Mimeographed. New York: International Agricultural Development Service, 1977.

Mosher, Arthur T. *Thinking about Rural Development*. New York: Agricultural Development Council, 1976.

Mosher, Arthur T. *To Create a Modern Agriculture*. New York: Agricultural Development Council, 1971.

Nelson, Michael. *The Development of Tropical Lands: Policy Issues in Latin America*. Baltimore: Johns Hopkins University Press for Resources for the Future, 1973.

Waugh, Robert K. *ICTA: Four Years of History*. Guatemala City: Instituto de Ciencia y Tecnologia Agricola, 1975.

OPERATIONAL PRINCIPLES

Cochrane, Willard W. *Agricultural Development Planning: Economic Concepts, Administrative Procedures, and Political Process*. New York: Praeger, 1974.

Cummings, Ralph W., Jr. *Minimum Information Systems for Agricultural Development in Low-Income Countries*. Research and Training Network Seminar Report No. 14. New York: Agricultural Development Council, September 1977.

Galbraith, John Kenneth. "A Positive Approach to Economic Aid." *Foreign Affairs* 39 (1961): 444–57.

Gittinger, J. Price. *Economic Analysis of Agricultural Projects*. Baltimore: Johns Hopkins University Press, 1972.

Hopper, W. David. "Investments in Agriculture: The Essentials for Payoff." In *Strategy for the Conquest of Hunger: Proceedings of a Symposium*. New York: Rockefeller Foundation, 1968.

Mosher, Arthur T. "Reorganizing Regular Agencies and Procedures." Paper presented at an IADS Workshop, June 26–July 1, 1977. Mimeographed. New York: International Agricultural Development Service, 1977.

Pearson, Scott R., and Meyer, Ronald K. "Comparative Advantage among African Coffee Producers." *American Journal of Agricultural Economics* 56 (1974): 310–13.

Waterston, Albert. *Development Planning: Lessons of Experience*. Baltimore: Johns Hopkins University Press, 1965.

Land tenure and farm enterprises

Introduction

LAND TENURE is central in determining *who* benefits from increases in productivity. Land is an essential ingredient in agriculture and thus in rural life. It influences the amount of a farmer's production. It influences employment. It also influences status in the community. Together, wealth and status go a long way toward establishing a rural person's contribution to, as well as claims on, society. As Solon Barraclough states: "Farm size is a crucial development issue not because of economies or diseconomies of scale but because land ownership in traditional societies is practically synonymous with control of labor, wealth, social prestige, and political power . . . the ability to make others do one's will." Phillip Raup also puts the issue succinctly: "Land tenure institutions define a farmer's status. They create the framework of expectations within which hopes and fears motivate him to economic activity." Evidence from many nations suggests that rising agricultural productivity may be possible under a variety of land tenure conditions. However, a relatively equitable land tenure system is a requisite to ensuring *broad participation* of the rural population in the economic and political process of a country.

Perhaps no subject related to agricultural and rural development is more controversial than land tenure and related farm enterprise patterns. Rights to ownership of land have their roots in ages past and are cherished particularly by those whose properties, often extensive, have been in their families for generations. Although some large holdings are highly productive, many are not.

The agricultural difficulties of many nations have been aggravated by relentlessly growing populations and the subdivision of family lands among heirs to the point that holdings in some areas are tiny and fragmented. The increasing population raises demands for distribution of

271

"It is not the fault of the new technology that the credit service does not serve those for whom it was originally intended; that the extension services are not living up to expectations; that the panchayats are political rather than developmental bodies; that security of tenure is a luxury of the few; that rents are exorbitant; that ceilings on agricultural land are notional; that for the greater part tenurial legislation is deliberately miscarried; or that wage scales are hardly sufficient to keep body and soul together.

These are man-made institutional inequities. Correcting all of them within the foreseeable future is out of the question. On the other hand, even if only some of them are dealt with—security of tenure, reasonable rent and credit to sustain production needs—a measure of economic and social justice could be fused with economic necessity, thereby adding another dimension to the green revolution."

Wolf Ladejinsky
"The Green Revolution in Bihar"

arable land, making large private holdings especially visible. Political pressures mount. As a result, some feel that all land should be held by the state and that private ownership is obsolete or improper. Others argue that neither state nor individual or corporate ownership of large tracts is desirable, that lands should be divided at once among the tillers of the soil.

In many countries, changes in land tenure and farm enterprises are inevitable: the only question is whether they will be orderly or disorderly. The purpose of this chapter is to review the major issues involved and to answer questions likely to be raised by policymakers: Are there situations in which landholding and farm enterprise systems present such serious obstacles to the attainment of agricultural and rural development goals that land reform must be considered a prerequisite to progress? What are those situations and what alternative strategies can a government consider in attempting to create a system of farms and livestock operations and a land tenure structure that better supports rapid agricultural and rural development?

The impact of modernization on land tenure and farm enterprises

In traditional social settings characterized by underdeveloped product markets and supply systems, landholding arrangements have a pervasive influence. Mutual obligations exist: neither landlords nor tenants have the clear right to abolish one set of relationships and substitute another. For example, a tenant cannot easily switch landlords nor can a landlord easily dismiss tenants and hire laborers. Although the relationship between

"The greatest source of insecurity in most Asian villages is lack of ownership of house lots where rural families live. For example, in the Philippines less than one-half of all families own the lots on which their houses stand and, therefore, are discouraged from making even simple improvements like installing a water-sealed toilet. Where families own their house lots, they make the small and large investments in fencing, planting fruit trees and vegetable gardens and building better houses that make for a more attractive and richer rural life. Ownership of this house lot of 600 to 1000 square meters gives a family security of belonging in the community that encourages them to become responsible citizens. It also gives the family title to a piece of real estate with improvements that can be mortgaged should a loan be needed. For Asian governments the opportunity to carry through a land reform assuring every family of the ownership of a house lot affords the most dramatic widespread and cheapest means to rapidly achieving rural well-being and greater prosperity."

Ramon Magsaysay Award Foundation
Food Crisis Workshop

classes is often exploitative, it is not always despotic, for political and economic interdependence may give rise to mutually beneficial patron-client relations.

When a society begins to modernize, these custom-based social and economic relationships are fundamentally affected. New technology, with its impact on profitability, makes land more valuable. Those who are in a better position to acquire land do so; they attempt to shed customary social obligations to their clients; they take on the role of landlord; and they seek the influence of the government to secure property and contract rights. What benefits modernization brings then flow disproportionately to limited numbers of people—people who in many cases have contributed only indirectly to the agricultural production process. If this situation persists, the gap widens between larger landowners and others in the rural sector. Such a tendency is not only politically destabilizing but can be detrimental to production and income generation.

Large landholdings in densely populated developing countries have two common characteristics which are special sources of difficulties. First, the most visible deficiency is that large land resources often are underutilized for various reasons. Some owners hold land for speculative purposes. Absentee ownership is often accompanied by a lack of close supervision. Some owners of large landholdings have outside interests that have greater economic or social importance for them than farming. Government farms are frequently badly managed. Such an obvious waste of resources is difficult for local people to tolerate when so many are unemployed, food is in short supply, and people are destitute.

Second, because of real or imagined difficulties in hiring and managing a labor force or because of a fascination with automatic devices, there is a tendency for managers of large landholdings to substitute machinery for labor, which intensifies the unemployment problem. True, abundant labor is not always cheap. Minimum wage and social welfare laws may make the price of labor relatively high. A large unskilled labor force can be difficult to manage and may increase the risks of dealing with expensive machinery, improved livestock, and modern production practices, which require constant use of judgment. Machinery provides certain advantages in moving water, leveling land, and permitting more timely operations. However, by and large, highly mechanized (heavy machinery) operations are not required for higher yields per hectare.

In low-income countries, land must be viewed not merely as a resource for maximizing agricultural output but also as a vehicle for employing people and developing their skills and experiences. Introduction of large-scale, highly productive farming practices into areas of mixed landholding patterns tends to polarize economic opportunity, leading to displacement of small farmers from their insecure positions as tenants. One distressing consequence of rising agricultural productivity is the squeeze which reduces tenants to sharecroppers and eventually to landless laborers as more of the bigger owners mechanize.

Since most countries do not have enough jobs in the cities to employ the population, efforts must be made to increase employment in the countryside. Provision for the poor through welfare programs is unrealistic where so many are poor. There is often limited wealth to tax. Under these circumstances, land reform seems to many to offer one prospect for improving opportunities to increase productivity, incomes, and standards of living of the great mass of rural people.

Though this generalized description may not completely fit any particular country's experience, it serves to highlight the tendencies and pressures which usually arise in the modernization process in rural areas and to indicate the multidimensional role of land tenure in most societies.

The spectrum of farm enterprises

Nations have a wide array of land tenure and farm enterprise systems. The systems differ with regard to size of typical farm operation and degree to which incentives promote increased production and reinvestment. They vary in their effects on management of farms, on organization and synchronization of services (technical assistance, input supplies, credit, and marketing), and on distribution of benefits among operators and others in the rural areas. No attempt to provide a typology of farm enterprises can be inclusive. For agricultural development purposes, however, the more important farm enterprise types are corporate farms, state farms, group farms, family farms, and associations of family farms.[1]

CORPORATE FARMS

Corporate farms are often large-scale production units with associated processing facilities. They market primarily one or a few commodities through well-established channels. Usually their operations are highly synchronized (vertically integrated). That is, the entire system of research, production, harvest, postharvest handling, and marketing is usually controlled by a single organization. Properly managed, such systems are highly efficient. Production can be precisely scheduled to meet anticipated market demand. Research can be directed specifically to the solution of problems of importance, with research costs being a normal part of business expenses. Research results can be applied immediately by executive decision. Inputs can be purchased in quantity at considerable discount from retail. Financing is usually arranged through established commercial channels. Success (profitability) depends on the quality of management, and outstanding managers are scarce and usually well-paid. For many specialty products, access to foreign markets and the latest technology may require that an experienced company with assured market outlets be centrally involved.

STATE FARMS

State farms, often consisting of thousands of hectares, are operated by governments, usually with salaried managers who are responsible to a unit of the bureaucracy, and with employees who work for wages. In some societies, state farms are established for a specific purpose such as production of seed. In Communist countries, particularly the Soviet Union, state farms produce much of the crops and animals.

Major difficulties are often encountered with state farms, regardless of the ideology of the government. Production units are subject to management by departments of government far from the farm. Salaried managers and laborers who are paid wages lack incentives to take extra care in production practices, to be vigilant against outbreaks of disease or insects, and to watch quality and costs. Bad decisions and ill-timed

---

[1] The World Bank, in a Sector Policy Paper *Land Reform*, has identified six main tenure systems: the Asian feudal system (estates worked by small sharecroppers); the Latin American feudal system (large estates run by the owners or their managers who employ hired labor, sometimes sharecrop farmers); the traditional African tribal system (the land belongs to the community, which allocates it among the various families); the system of individually run farms in the market economies which is based on individual ownership; the socialist system, in which the land belongs to the state and is allocated in accordance with the goals set out in the plan; and the ranch and plantation system (managers and salaried staff).

services are common. Consequently, productivity and profitability are often low.

State farms may be useful in the initial stages of the development of remote regions—that is, in settlement programs—where labor is scarce and public services are not developed enough to permit the successful operation of owner-operated units. The People's Republic of China reportedly uses the state-farm technique in remote, thinly settled regions.

GROUP FARMS

Group farms are operated jointly by their members, who participate in management decisions. Individual income is based on each person's share of the income of the enterprise. Small plots for individual family use may be alloted. The success of group farms of any type depends largely upon (a) clear incentives for each member to increase productivity to enhance his personal income and for the entire group to reinvest in the enterprise to achieve higher productivity over the long run, (b) skill of management, (c) level of technology employed and its profitability, (d) availability of inputs, (e) access to markets, and (f) scale of the enterprise. The communes of China (Chapter 8), the collective farms of the Soviet Union, and the kibbutzim of Israel are prominent examples of this type of farm enterprise.

FAMILY FARMS

Family farms are operated by families or are subject to their management decisions. To be classified as "commercial," they must produce substantial amounts of products for sale. Such farms may vary greatly in size, in accessibility to markets, in skills of management. There are four general categories: owner managed, owner operated, tenant operated, and types related to communal land tenure.

Owner-managed, large-scale farms usually consist of extensive landholdings and are operated mostly with hired labor. Owners may reside on the farm or elsewhere. Paid managers may assist the owner. Examples include the haciendas of Latin America. Often the operations are quite labor intensive.

Owner-operated farms can be divided into two types. Larger owner-operated farms are mechanized and therefore capital intensive, commercially oriented, and usually involve a minimum of nonfamily labor. In addition to owning land, the operator may rent land to increase the size of his operation. Since the land may be used as collateral for loans, such farmers are generally good credit risks. Family income depends upon farm productivity so incentives to improve productivity and profitability are strong. This system predominates in North America.

In the case of smaller owner-operated family farms, landownership is held by families who provide the primary farm labor force. These include small subsistence farms as well as small commercial units. Cultivation is often labor intensive. Small-scale mechanization may be utilized. Small family farms can produce substantial surpluses for sale (as in Japan and Taiwan), land may be used as collateral for loans, and there are incentives to increase productivity and to reinvest in the enterprise. But many of these are subsistence farms: they are so small, farming methods are so traditional, and output is so low that much of the produce is consumed by the household. In areas of poorer soils and rainfall, and in more remote areas, these subsistence farms are numerous and the families are among the poorest in any country.

Tenant-operated farms differ widely in the role of the landlord in providing managerial and supply services, in security and rental or sharecropping arrangements, and in the quantity of land owned by a single landlord. The owner may or may not live in the vicinity. The tenants live on or near the farm and work it with family labor. Some tenants may have lease arrangements sufficiently satisfactory that they can afford to farm intensively and invest in farm improvements.

Tenants, however, are often beset with serious difficulties, such as high land rents, the obligation to give large shares of the produce to owners, and the risk that the owner will terminate arrangements. Tenants often have little incentive to invest in long-term improvements in land or facilities. If rents or shares to the owners are high, the tenant may see little point in trying high-input, high-yield systems. Consequently, productivity is often low. A high proportion of such farms are subsistence operations, where the families live in poverty.

The traditional communal system (not to be confused with communes of the Chinese type) is characterized by landownership vested in a collective body (a village, a tribe, an ethnic group) or the state, with individual families having the right to use part of the land in prescribed ways. There are numerous variations involving either shifting or reasonably permanent settlement. In some areas, lands are grazed by herds or flocks belonging to nomads. In other areas, common lands are grazed around boreholes which provide water. Slash-and-burn or swidden cultivation also falls into this category. Assets are largely represented by animals and tools the families possess. Because of the custom of moving animals, sometimes over long distances in remote areas, the problems of improving productivity through controlled grazing are especially difficult. Shifting cultivation often depletes the soil and exposes it to erosion.

ASSOCIATIONS OF FAMILY FARMS

Various mechanisms have been developed to enable family farms, especially the smaller owner-operated and tenant-operated farms, to secure better access to services, inputs, and markets to promote high productivity.

Corporation-managed contract farming is one way of associating family farms. Under this system a state or private corporation purchases products from individual farmers under contract, rather than producing them exclusively on its own landholdings. Processing and marketing remain the major functions of the corporation. The corporation is often responsible for local or operational research, for supply of inputs, for technical assistance to growers, and, through pricing systems, for control of quality. Farmers with small holdings produce products for the corporation and some food crops for home use. This system combines the benefits of synchronization with the incentives of individual landownership and assured markets. Increases in land values, if any, accrue to the farmers, not to the corporation, and there is individual pride of ownership—an important factor where rural people are becoming restless.

Family farms may also be associated in producer federations and cooperatives. In many countries, independent producers of a crop, or farmers in a region, form a commercial association to provide services and to otherwise promote their interests. The stronger, more profitable producer-controlled organizations may promote research by public agencies or even contribute to it financially. They may also arrange for supplies of inputs in bulk, facilitate marketing, and manage, or influence management of, irrigation schemes. They often have considerable political power, and use it to promote public action in their interest. While quality of farming may vary, well-managed organizations give individual producers many of the benefits of vertical integration.

MIX OF FARM ENTERPRISES WITHIN COUNTRIES

The incidence, and even existence, of each type of farm enterprise varies from country to country. For example, small tenant farms predominate in Asia, the large family farms predominate in North America, and a combination of large and nearby small units exist in many parts of the world, especially in Latin America (*latifundia* and *minifundia*). The mix depends upon the ideology of the government, its attitudes toward private enterprise, its policies or lack of them, its stage of development, the adequacy of public services, availability of competent personnel at all levels, and upon the national heritage.

The objective:
A commercial family farm economy

In densely populated agrarian countries or in thickly settled rural areas of any country, governments should seek to create a rural economy based primarily on commercial farms owned and operated by families (including group farms). Such farms would be operated by those who live on them and own (or lease) them, individually or collectively.[2] They would of necessity be small enough to be farmed by their owners, yet large enough to allow production of a significant surplus. They should be viewed as family businesses which are important components of a nation's domestic economy. Expansion of productivity and incomes from such family or group farms would be derived from increases in productivity per hectare, utilizing all possible advances of science and management to do so.

There are several reasons why governments might wish to adopt such a policy:

- To increase food and other agricultural production. Owner-operators of family farms have strong incentives to increase productivity since that is the primary way they can raise their incomes and standards of living. Intensive cultivation of small units can produce higher output per hectare than extensive management of larger farms. The farmers will promote long-term increases in productivity through on-farm improvements such as leveling land and providing irrigation, installing orchards for fruit, improved pastures for animals, and trees for fuel, as well as through cooperative efforts to improve drainage and to link farms to markets by constructing roads.
- To increase employment in rural areas. A high density of productive farms is essential to the support of rural trade centers, increasing opportunities there for employment as demand for goods and services expands. Also, on-farm employment for family members should increase, at least modestly.
- To improve standards of living in rural areas. Greater productivity will allow better diets for farm families. Higher incomes can be spent to improve housing and farm buildings and to provide potable water. Greater economic activity in the area will attract higher-quality social services such as schools and clinics.
- To expand domestic markets for products of urban industry, thereby contributing to employment in cities.
- To minimize restlessness in the countryside, by giving the majority of rural people the incentive to promote stability through productive employment as farm operators, in enterprises in the rural trade centers, or as laborers on farms.

For such a dynamic rural economy to emerge, public and private services must be tailored to the needs of such family-operated farms. And the synchronization of services stressed in Chapter 10 must be achieved, locality by locality.

---

[2] Ownership or lease arrangements vary. It is important that the farm operator have such secure use of the land that long-term improvements will be made.

Potential conversions

Enterprises or individuals who control large areas of land in densely populated areas of poor countries are likely to be targets of restless rural people who have been crowded into less productive, more remote areas. The most vulnerable land units are corporate farms, state farms, extensive family holdings, and large public or private holdings not organized into farms. Ways should be sought to convert those holdings to farms that are economically and socially more desirable—that is, commercial family or group farms—without sacrificing productivity, foreign-exchange earnings, or investment of local resources in development activities. A number of methods might be considered:

- conversion of corporate farms to corporation-managed contract farm operations by sale of lands to employees;
- conversion of extensive private landholdings to owner-operated commercial family or group farms, preferably through voluntary sale; or
- conversion of extensive public landholdings, including state farms, to owner-operated, commercial units.

The start of programs to increase yields and profits on all farms, large or small, need not wait for changes in ownership patterns, which are inevitably time-consuming and difficult. Several actions might be pursued:

- increased productivity and profitability of existing commercial family or group farms, whether owner managed or owner operated;
- organization of owner-operated farms into federations of producers;
- encouragement of industry to locate processing plants in rural areas and to contract with farmers for produce—offering farmers a market;
- conversion of subsistence farms to more productive owner-operated commercial farms, with conversion of tenancy arrangements to ownership and consolidation of fragmented holdings where applicable;
- conversion of shifting cultivation to more productive sedentary farming;
- improved management of grazing by animals of nomadic herdsmen.

However, success in increasing productivity should not be an excuse for delaying land reform where it is needed. In densely populated regions, failure of governments to move, quite visibly, toward a system of farms owned and operated by families or groups may invite rural unrest and militant efforts to redistribute land. Ways to bring about peaceful conversions must be found while there is time.

Reform

There are numerous ways to restructure the formal and informal rules governing access to productive resources and opportunities on the land. No approach is inherently superior to others. Nor are there simple prescriptions for size of landholdings to acquire and redistribute or for methods and amounts of remuneration. Ideally the changes will be carried out voluntarily. Where they are not, government must consider intervening.

REQUISITES

At least three factors are essential for any successful reform: government commitment, government power, and administrative organization.

Government commitment. Without question, the foremost condition needed for agrarian reform is firm resolve at the highest levels of government. No administrative structures and strategies will bring about reform without strong political backing. The sincerity of the national leaders' desire for effective land reform is often not in doubt. But the degree to which leaders are willing to take political risks and to incur costs that might compete with other favored programs is a more complex issue.

Government power. A second requisite of effective reform is the central government's possession of sufficient power to prevent enemies of land reform from overthrowing the government and to minimize landlord sabotage of the program. Except where a revolutionary peasantry has been strong enough to take land reform into its own hands, centralized power has proved essential. It is not surprising that most relatively successful land reforms have been carried out when the normal political process was suspended by direct intervention of outside political or military power (for example, Japan, Taiwan, South Korea), by a strong monarch or military ruler (for example, Iran, Peru), by a thorough socialist revolution (for example, China), or by an explosion of peasant unrest which threatened the political and social order (for example, Bolivia, Mexico).

Administrative organization. The administrative means for carrying out a reform program greatly influence the results. Successful reforms have combined administrative coordination and support at the center with close involvement of the beneficiaries in local decision-making and implementation. The precise strategy depends upon the respective strengths of the central administrative structure, large landowners, and peasant organizations.

Difficulties in generalizing

Because every country has unique characteristics, it becomes increasingly difficult to generalize as one moves from a discussion of the strengths and weaknesses of different land tenure and farm enterprise systems to the specifics of what to do about reform. First, land tenure arrangements are related to historical patterns of settlement and conquest, which in turn are derived from specific value systems grounded in religious, social, political, and cultural antecedents. Changes that work well in one setting may not succeed in another.

Second, an institution is not defined by its name but by the functions, procedures, rights, duties, and privileges associated with it. A farm corporation in Iran is not necessarily comparable to a farm corporation in California. A tenant farmer in the maize-soybean area of central Illinois has much more in common with a farm owner-operator in that area than he does with a tenant farmer producing maize in the Philippines. Tenants, sharecroppers, owner-operators, partnerships, corporations, or production cooperatives in various parts of the world (or even within the same country) are not necessarily comparable just because they are called by the same name.

Third, land tenure arrangements do not exist in isolation. The dimensions and future security of opportunities of rural people are critically affected by labor, capital, and product markets. Thus, land tenure arrangements interrelate with a wide range of the other factors.

Fourth, a country cannot be judged to have carried out land reform just because it has so declared, has legislation on the books, or has created institutions for that purpose.

Dividing and coordinating responsibility, power, and skills among peasants and the central government can result in mutually supporting complementarity. Local nongovernmental organizations can relieve the bureaucracy from routine administrative decisions. In turn the central bureaucracy will have access to the detailed local knowledge of land boundaries, land productivities, and ownership histories—knowledge superior to that obtainable by structured surveys and compilation of legal documents. Local administrative involvement can greatly enhance communication both within communities and between communities and the central administration. Assignment of responsibility and authority to local organizations of private citizens can stimulate local enthusiasm and help peasants develop political power to offset the usually overwhelming influence of large local landowners.

Determining the distribution of power and functions represents only the first layer of administrative decision in a reform program. Unsuccessful land reform programs generally display no lack of decrees or of sophisticated organization charts fleshed out with layer upon layer of bureaucrats. Such programs do not officially die; they just fade away into an administrative swamp of conflicting considerations and technical obstacles. Successful reform programs are built upon speed and decisiveness.

TENANCY REFORM

Attempts have been made to overcome the production inefficiencies and equity problems rooted in the tenure system by reforming the formal and informal rules regulating resource use without changing landownership patterns. This approach is probably more applicable in Asian countries, where tenancy with decentralized management is widespread and the man-land ratio is high. It can also be an important part of redistributive land reform when tenancy is expected to continue.

Examples of tenancy reforms include setting maximum share or cash rents, shifting completely to cash rent, requiring all lease agreements to be written and registered, and establishing security of tenure by regulating the length of leases and the circumstances under which tenants can be dismissed. These steps are aimed principally at overcoming the disincentives to efficient input use and long-term investment in the land. When accompanied by measures to facilitate access to credit and services as well, positive results might be expected. However, certain difficulties are associated with tenancy reform alone.

First, the form of tenancy that provides the best incentives cannot be decided in the abstract. For example, cash rental is more efficient theoretically, but tenants often prefer sharecropping for the risk insurance it provides. Therefore, unless the underlying risk problem can be directly addressed, it may be better to allow share tenancy with proper regulation. The landlord could be required to share costs in the same proportion as production and to compensate tenants for permanent improvements. Security of tenure could be safeguarded for a set period, with the tenant being given preference for renewal.

Second, rent control or legislation for tenancy protection without land redistribution is usually unenforceable and often works against the interests of tenants (leading to their displacement or to conversion to hired labor).

Third, specific attention must be given to the allocation of credit and access to services and technology. With proper regulation and incentive structures, landlords may be able to provide effective distribution of inputs; however, separate credit institutions are always preferable, in order to avoid the economic and social distortions that arise when a tenant becomes indebted to his landlord.

Finally, a well-enforced and effective tenancy reform may be just as difficult to achieve as land reform. Landlords may resist regulation by dismissing tenants and taking over managerial functions, perhaps with some hired labor. Or, under threat of dismissal, tenants may be forced to acquiesce in the continuation of harsh terms in disguised forms.

Commitment, power, and administration are the central issues. The aim of tenure reform is to regulate the power of the owners of land and other resources without totally neutralizing it. Therefore, tenants and rural laborers must have their own power base to confront that of the landlords. This can be achieved only through strong peasant or tenant organizations sanctioned and safeguarded by the central political power.

LAND REFORM

Land reform includes not only reform of tenancy conditions but also redistribution of land titles to tillers, abolition of tenancy by converting tenants into owners, expropriation of large holdings and distribution of land among the tillers either for individual ownership and operation or for collective use, or transformation of tribal and other traditional forms of tenure in the interests of productivity and equity.

Several operational elements are important in implementing extensive land reforms.

Land records. The land to be affected by the reform must be clearly identifiable. Records on sizes of ownership units in various regions as well as clear demarcations of public lands are useful. Lack of such records does not make reform impossible where a government has the will and determination, but their availability certainly facilitates the process. Certain people at the local levels will have a good unwritten record in their minds. Here it becomes particularly important to involve local people in the process rather than rely entirely on government agents.

Criteria for acquiring land. Clear and simple criteria are needed to determine exactly what land is subject to acquisition. It is often presumed that size of ownership units is a clear and objective criterion; this usually is not correct for at least two reasons. First, mere farm size is not the only pertinent factor.[3] Soils vary in quality; rainfall varies in quantity and distribution; a hectare of irrigated land has many times the productive potential of a hectare of nonirrigated land. Second, there are farm sizes below which a family cannot support itself from the output of the land alone. Some plots may be so tiny that additional expected returns from new practices are just too small to cause the farmer to adopt them.

[3] Gelia T. Castillo notes in *Changes in Rice Farming in Selected Areas of Asia*: "Farm size *per se* has little meaning, but acquires significance when viewed within the context of the community, the productivity of the land, infrastructure, and services available, intensity of land use, population pressure, tenure system, and the social and economic value attached to land ownership."

Simple methods for evaluating land. A relatively simple method for evaluating land must be established. Where one crop is dominant, and especially if land rent was previously based on a share of that crop, the simplest procedure is to base the value of the land on a certain multiple of the average annual harvest of that crop.[4] Where general cropping or mixed farming prevails, other means of land evaluation (other than basing it on the principal crop) must be used. Exactly what multiples should be used will depend on many factors. However, the reform will be unable to meet redistributive (and perhaps also productivity) objectives if the new owners must pay the full market price for the land. Most extensive land reforms have been substantially confiscatory.

Quick-taking procedure. There is need for a procedure which enables the reform agency to obtain possession of the land in the shortest time possible. Landowners can be provided legal remedies which could result in added or more favorable compensation if the appeal processes sustain their case. However, the appeal processes should not be able to reverse the decision of the reform agency or prevent the acquisition of land, provided it is being obtained under the criteria established. To the extent that criteria for acquisition are unclear or their application is delayed or haphazard, incentives for farm investments are weakened and productivity may suffer. This result can be minimized if the law is well formulated and the government states its intentions clearly and moves swiftly to carry out the reform.

Compensation. Ideally, owners of large tracts of land should be encouraged to sell parcels to would-be owner-operators. If land is expropriated, a compensation scheme must be established. This may involve a partial cash payment, with the bulk of the compensation in government bonds to be redeemed in future years. The cash payment often must be modest if the government is to have the financial resources to mount a large land expropriation. Bonds can have varying maturity dates and carry differential rates of interest to provide (along with varied cash payments) the necessary flexibility to treat different types of land or landowners appropriately. Various combinations of bonds and cash (and bonds adjusted for inflation and varying maturities) provide flexibility and can be used to counter some of the opposition to the reform.

---

[4] One hazard of using a "principal crop" as the basis for land valuation is that sometimes a goal of land reform is to shift land use from a traditional crop to a mixture of crops. This often involves a shift from an export or nonfood crop to locally consumed crops. Strict adherence to a "principal crop" standard may distort the land valuation or work against the goals of land reform by giving undue emphasis to past cropping practices.

Influence of former owners. If former owners are allowed to keep a portion of their land, they should not be allowed to select only the more improved, fertile areas, thus putting them in a position to gradually re-acquire resources from less well endowed competitors in the postreform period.

Distribution to new owners. When large estates are divided into small family farms, resident laborers are usually given first claim; off-farm wage and migrant workers should then be given opportunities to acquire land if any remains unclaimed.

Previous estate wage workers who receive small private plots often lack managerial skills and may create production problems for which there is no easy answer. (In the reform of a predominantly family size, tenant farm system, the beneficiaries have been farm managers all along, and the problem is generally less serious.) Good extension agents can be helpful, but rapid expansion of a high-quality extension service in a reform situation is usually difficult. Hence, in these situations especially, some cooperative arrangement among farmers (whether in group farming or some less collective format) should be considered in order to disseminate new skills, ideas, and techniques.

Realignment of fields and consolidation of small holdings. In the reform of a small-scale tenant system, the cultivator is usually permitted to retain land in amounts up to a ceiling. It is often desirable to realign fields and combine scattered plots. However, for rapid and smooth land transfer such efforts may have to be postponed until after redistribution is completed.

Payment by new owners. If the new owner is to pay for the land he receives, payments should be spread out and sufficient safeguards against crop failure enacted so that the land payments plus taxes and other charges do not exceed the previous rents and so that the payment schedule can be easily met at existing production levels.

Services. Land redistribution may rupture the system which provides credit, fertilizer, technical information, and marketing. The credit system which operates informally and formally is especially vulnerable. In the absence of these services, productivity and capital formation will decrease in the land reform areas. Both the power and resources of the new small owners tend to be dispersed. Therefore, both to avoid disruption of services and to ensure that the benefits of reform remain equitably distributed, a new system must be planned as part of the entire reform program. Former landlords can be encouraged to shift assets into financial or marketing activities. Group action, either to deal with private businesses and government agencies or to undertake direct operation of services, may be necessary to make these services responsive to the small farmers. Whatever the means employed, services must be synchronized locality by locality.

STRATEGY CHOICES

No magic formula for implementing land reform exists. Production losses occur primarily because of disruption, lack of services, or uncertainty about how the reform will be carried out. It is desirable to lay down clear criteria for reforms and to move quickly to minimize uncertainty. However, the task is complex. Special machinery often must be created. If action is delayed until all preparations are completed, the program may never start. Valuable lessons to improve results can be learned as the reform proceeds. A path must be found between the danger of immobility and the danger of provoking social conflict and perhaps derailing the whole reform program.

The sequence in implementing land reform is one strategic decision. The options are: (a) largest, foreign, or absentee landlords first; (b) region of most severe inequality first; (c) regions of most likely success first; (d) everybody; (e) regions where major crops are least productive.

The advantage of the big-holding-first strategy is its political impact and its immediate disarming of the most powerful opponents of land reform. The disadvantages include incentives for the large landlords to divide their properties, the complications of politics, and the administrative clumsiness of returning repeatedly to the same region for successive levels of reform.

The advantages of giving initial attention to areas of the most severe inequality include neutralizing potential dissidents and emphasizing the value of social equity. The principal disadvantage is that the areas of most severe inequality are frequently regions where success is most difficult to achieve.

The strategy of pursuing the easiest successes builds administrative experience and morale, creates a demonstration effect of what might be done, and stimulates peasant enthusiasm through such demonstration effects. The principal disadvantage is that some of the most visible excesses will be saved for last, and opposition can build in those areas that come last.

The principal advantage of trying land reform everywhere simultaneously is its tremendous positive political effect. The disadvantages are the possibility of catalyzing fierce political opposition and the possibility that administrative overextension will create a vicious circle in which failure begets failure.

Proceeding through land reform according to crop and to degree of modernization allows productivity considerations to be balanced against equity: modernized sectors can be protected, and political opposition can be minimized. The disadvantages include incentives to change crops, a series of administrative ambiguities wherever multiple cropping occurs, and the prospect of allegations of lack of government concern for equity.

A second strategic decision concerns the terms of the alliance between the central administration and the peasantry. An administration can utilize peasant capabilities if they are adequate, it can use the central bureaucracy to create and control a local organization, or it can gradually pass responsibilities to local groups on the assumption that responsibility will induce rapid learning. Whichever strategy is chosen, the implementing organization must be responsive largely to local peasants rather than to local elites or to the national government. But the local organizations must be able to rely on central power to disperse opposition and to back up local administrative decisions.

The final and most amorphous of the strategic political questions concerns the moral and cultural aspects of enthusiasm for land reform and resistance to it: whether it is possible to have conservative land reform, whether strong peasant organization is possible without radical changes of philosophical perspective, and whether the detailed administrative calculations are relevant when the basic psychology of the country is that of dominator and dominated.

The more delays there are and the more exclusions, the more difficult it will be to enforce and carry through land reform and the more difficult it will be to gain support for such a policy. Slippages, diversions, redefinitions, and regrouping of forces opposed to the reform are favored by lack of clarity, uncertainties, delays, and piecemeal efforts. The central problem is to create a self-reinforcing process by which the organizational capacities available are exploited to start land reform, and the land reform process itself then generates peasant enthusiasm, peasant organization, and an educational process—factors which strengthen the capacities of the system to continue land reform. The best way to develop such administrative infrastructure is to begin the reform. On the other hand, nothing fails like failure, so it is important to design some early success into the program, for instance by picking easy initial targets. But, again, much depends on a government's willingness and ability to make land reform a top priority and to supply the funds and manpower necessary to get the job done.

Summary

An equitable and productive land system is a necessary condition for initiation of agricultural development with widely distributed benefits. An important objective of national agricultural development in densely settled areas should be to encourage the formation of family-owned and family-operated farms as the primary means of increasing productivity and incomes of large numbers of rural people.

The size of holdings is only one element in land reform considerations. The conditions of tenure are equally important. In addition, the responsiveness of service organizations to the needs of farmers must be considered. The roles of these service organizations will be discussed in Chapters 12 and 13.

References

INTRODUCTION

Barraclough, Solon L. "Comment on the Economics of Farm Size by Bachman and Christensen." In *Agricultural Development and Economic Growth*, edited by H. M. Southworth and B. F. Johnston. Ithaca, N.Y.: Cornell University Press, 1967.

Ladejinsky, Wolf Isaac. "The Green Revolution in Bihar—The Kosi Area: A Field Trip." In *Agrarian Reform as Unfinished Business: The Selected Papers of Wolf Ladejinsky*, edited by L. J. Walinsky. New York: Oxford University Press, 1977.

Raup, Phillip. "Land Reform and Agricultural Development." In *Agricultural Development and Economic Growth*, edited by H. M. Southworth and B. F. Johnston. Ithaca, N.Y.: Cornell University Press, 1967.

THE IMPACT OF MODERNIZATION
ON LAND TENURE AND FARM
ENTERPRISES

Dorner, Peter. *Land Reform and Economic Development*. Baltimore: Penguin Books, 1972.

Ramon Magsaysay Award Foundation. *Food Crisis Workshop, February 7–9, 1977*. Manila: Ramon Magsaysay Award Foundation, 1977.

THE SPECTRUM OF FARM ENTERPRISES

Dorner, Peter, ed. *Cooperative & Commune: Group Farming in the Economic Development of Agriculture*. Madison: University of Wisconsin Press, 1977.

International Bank for Reconstruction and Development. *Land Reform*. Sector Policy Paper. Washington, D.C.: World Bank, May 1975.

REFORM

Castillo, Gelia. "Diversity in Unity: The Social Component of Changes in Rice Farming in Asian Villages." In *Changes in Rice Farming in Selected Areas of Asia*. Los Baños, Philippines: International Rice Research Institute, 1975.

Dorner, Peter. "The Experience of Other Countries in Land Reform: Lessons for the Philippines." *Land Tenure Center Newsletter* 48 (1975): 12–17.

International Bank for Reconstruction and Development. *Land Reform*. Sector Policy Paper. Washington, D.C.: World Bank, May 1975.

Kanel, Don. "Creating Opportunities for Small Farmers: The Role of Land Tenure and Service Institutions." In *Perspectives in Rural Development*, edited by

Lawrence J. Brainard and Ray Dumett. Lafayette, Ind.: Purdue University, College of Agriculture, 1975.

Montgomery, John D. "Allocation of Authority in Land Reform Programs: A Comparative Study of Administrative Processes and Outputs." *Administrative Science Quarterly* 17 (1972): 62–75.

Southeast Asia Development Advisory Group. "SEADAG Reports: Rural Development Panel Seminar on Land Reform in the Philippines, April 24–26, 1975, Pines Hotel, Baguio, Philippines." Mimeographed. New York: Southeast Asia Development Advisory Group, n.d.

Tai, Hung-Chao. *Land Reform and Politics: A Comparative Analysis.* Berkeley: University of California Press, 1974.

U.S. Department of State, Agency for International Development. *Spring Review of Land Reform: Findings and Implications for AID.* Washington, D.C.: Agency for International Development, 1970.

CHAPTER 12

Research with payoff

Introduction

It is time to reorient many agricultural research systems. Scientists must lead vigorously in establishing goals and developing strategies for swift and orderly increases in agricultural productivity at reasonable cost, and they must provide direct technological support to national agricultural development programs. Yet many research organizations in developing countries are still modeled after those of North America or Europe— which were not designed to support the fast pace of growth most countries must achieve. For sustained rapid agricultural development, nations must have a highly effective problem-solving agricultural research capability. The exceedingly high return to countries from investment in such research—the payoff from research—is well documented.

PAYOFF FROM COMMODITY PROGRAMS

The payoff from national coordinated commodity research programs is illustrated in Table 12.1, which gives data for several of the programs described in Chapter 8. As Schultz observes:

The available evidence strongly supports the inference that organized agricultural research has been a most profitable investment. The pioneer work by Zvi Griliches begins with his study of hybrid corn. He found that the accumulated past research expenditures on hybrid corn research, private and public, as of 1955, came to $131 million on which, for each dollar, the social return came to $7 annually or a 700 percent rate of return. Costly? Yes. Payoff? High indeed.

Japan initiated national coordinated crop breeding programs for wheat and rice in the 1920s. The efforts of the national experiment stations were linked with those of the many prefectural stations. Subsequently the coordinated research approach was extended to other crops and livestock.

Table 12.1. Internal rates of return to investment in agricultural research, selected countries and commodities

Commodity	Study[a]	Period	Annual internal rate of return (%)
U.S.			
Hybrid maize	Griliches (1958)	1940–55	35–40
All research	Griliches (1964)	1949–59	35–40
All research	Latimer (1964)	1949–59	not significant
All research	Evenson (1968)	1949–59	47
All research	Peterson & Fitzharris (1977)	1937–42	50
All research	Peterson & Fitzharris (1977)	1947–52	51
All research	Peterson & Fitzharris (1977)	1957–62	49
All research	Peterson & Fitzharris (1977)	1967–72	34
Japan			
Rice	Hayami & Akino (1977)	1915–50	25–27
Rice	Hayami & Akino (1977)	1930–61	73–75
All research	Tang (1963)	1880–1938	35
Mexico			
Wheat	Ardito-Barletta (1970)	1943–63	90
Maize	Ardito-Barletta (1970)	1943–63	35
Crops	Ardito-Barletta (1970)	1943–63	45–93
India			
All research	Evenson & Jha (1973)	1953–71	40
All research	Kahlon et al. (1977)	1960–73	63
Colombia			
Rice	Hertford et al. (1977)	1957–72	60–82

Source: Adapted from V. W. Ruttan, "Induced Innovation and Agricultural Development."
[a] See references at the end of this chapter.

Hayami and Akino note that "the Assigned Experiment System was an institutional innovation which economized on research resources—above all, knowledge and experience—while satisfying the requirement for location-specific agricultural research." The internal rate of return was 25–27 percent from 1915 to 1950 and 73–75 percent from 1930 to 1961.

In Mexico the annual rate of return from the hard-driving wheat research program was 90 percent, and, even for the supposedly less successful maize research program, the rate was 35 percent, according to Ardito-Barletta.

Kahlon *et al.* calculated economic returns to investments in research in India after 1960 at 63 percent.

Hertford *et al.* estimated the internal rate of return for Colombia's rice program during the period 1957–72 at 60–82 percent. Returns for Colombia's research on soybeans (1960–71) were also estimated at 79–96 percent, but for wheat (1953–73) the return was only 11–12 percent, and for cotton the annual return was zero. Hertford's study reveals the reasons for differences of such magnitude among the commodities.

Arndt and Ruttan summarized these results as follows: "there has been a proliferation of studies which indicates that returns to a great deal of investment in agricultural research have been two to three times higher than returns to other agricultural investment."

PAYOFF FROM DEFINED-AREA PROGRAMS

Returns to investment in area-development programs also can be high, even after only a few years of work, as data from the Puebla Project illustrate. Calculations of benefit-cost ratios for 1967–73 ranged from 1.77 (for direct gross benefits only, with additional labor charged at hired-labor rates) to 4.03 (for total benefits, with additional labor not charged).

Apart from the measurable returns, the project staff noted (in *The Puebla Project: Seven Years of Experience*) numerous indirect benefits:

An important intangible benefit derived from the Puebla Project is the progress that has been made in assisting farmers to organize in groups and resolve problems in a collective manner. Many farmers in the area are now aware of the advantages in working together in arranging for credit, transporting fertilizers, and petitioning governmental officials for changes in the operational procedures of service agencies.

The technical assistance program of the Project has provided the farmers with a better understanding of the agricultural service institutions. In 1967, for example, most of the farmers in the Puebla area did not know how to arrange for credit from official banks. Today, however, many farmers understand the procedures for requesting short-term credits for fertilizers, etc.; some also know how to apply for long-term credit to purchase equipment, animals, etc.

Over the long run, perhaps the most important intangible benefit attributable to the Puebla Project will be the favorable change that has occurred in the farmer's attitude toward modern technology and agriculture in general. Successful experience in the use of the new maize technology has given the farmers confidence that improved technology can be useful to them in other farming enterprises, and many have begun to seek new technical information about other activities, such as irrigation, improvement of fruit trees, and vegetable crop production.

Many subsistence farmers have received another intangible benefit in the form of greater certainty (because of the higher yields) that their family will have sufficient maize for the entire year. This represents an important contribution to the general welfare of the subsistence farm family, quite apart from the economic value of the increase in production.

Additionally, as a result of the action of the Puebla Project, problems in the operation of the credit banks and crop insurance company have been identified and studied. Operational procedures of these institutions are being changed so that greater use of these services can be made by the farmers in future years.

Qualifications

In reviewing estimates of financial returns—or payoff—four qualifications should be kept in mind:

Confounding. It is often difficult to separate effects of research from those of the many other factors which interact in complex ways to contribute to higher agricultural productivity. Among those other factors are roads and communications systems; education and training; inputs such as fertilizers, seed, and vaccines; irrigation and drainage; expertise of farmers; credit; and marketing systems. This confounding of the effects of many factors makes the estimates only rough approximations.

Catalytic effects. Provision of new technological components, such as higher-yielding varieties, means of soil improvement, or controls for crop or animal diseases and insect pests, often triggers investments in other factors necessary for progress. Solution of such technological problems is often a prerequisite to effective manipulation of production by means of pricing policy. Similarly, investment in experimental approaches to accelerated development (such as the Puebla Project) can reveal opportunities for replication in other areas, and so they too can be powerful catalysts. The value of any factor as a catalyst is difficult to isolate, and returns, if catalysts are involved, are likely to be greatly underestimated.

Indirect effects. Estimates of net returns generally exclude important noneconomic effects, both positive and negative. For example, it is not easy to include such results as (a) the impact on farmers who are not in the organized effort but who learn of new developments and adopt them; (b) the impact on activities not covered by organized programs—for example, a farmer learning to use fertilizer on one crop may begin to experiment with its use on others; (c) the value of initiation of change in areas previously neglected—that is, the replacement of a sense of hopelessness on the part of rural people with one of hope, which has both humanitarian and political values; (d) the contribution of increased income, if that occurs, to the vitality of rural trade centers, to reductions in population growth, to gains in employment, and to improved standards of living. One is thus forced to use judgment regarding the indirect value of these programs to the rural people and to society as a whole.

External factors. Returns to investment in national research programs are substantially dependent upon, and are enhanced by, a great variety of activities undertaken outside the country, much of them in earlier times.

A WORD OF CAUTION

One drawback of these cost-benefit studies is that most focus on reasonably successful research programs. There undoubtedly have been many programs for which payoff was nil or perhaps negative. Unsuccessful programs also deserve study to identify the reasons for failure. These qualifications notwithstanding, the estimates clearly indicate the large returns to investment which can be expected from effectively planned and implemented research programs. A better understanding by national authorities of the requirements for achieving these potentially high returns should increase support for agricultural research programs.

The roles of research

An effective national agricultural research system has at least six major functions:

- identifying national, regional, and local opportunities for advances in agricultural productivity and profitability, estimating their potential impact, and making the results available to authorities in understandable language;
- helping establish national, regional, and local goals against which progress can be measured, and elaborating strategies and tactics for reaching those goals quickly at reasonable cost;
- developing and testing components for improved production practices, better systems of harvesting, storage, transport, and marketing of produce, and more effective conservation of resources;
- combining components into profitable, high-yielding farming systems for each locality;
- identifying and making known improvements in supply of services— extension, input supply, credit, marketing, price policy, and other activities—that will substantially advance agriculture and the well-being of rural people; and
- training staff for research, extension, or educational institutions (see Chapter 14).

All of the above functions require either experimentation or the interpretation of agricultural research results or other evidence. Each has economic, social, or political implications. Most require consideration of engineering requirements because of involvement of transport, power, irrigation and drainage, land shaping, or mechanization. All have financial implications. Therefore, it is important that agricultural specialists and others work together in designing and implementing agricultural research.

IDENTIFYING OPPORTUNITIES

In *Creating a Progressive Rural Structure*, Mosher recounts traveling across the Indo-Gangetic Plain with a friend who asked, "Will this region ever be as productive as Iowa?" Although Mosher had lived and worked in that region of India for many years, he had not asked himself such a question: "I realized that I had been guilty of a common error. Too frequently we ask ourselves only 'what should we do next?' We do not look far enough down the years, visualize what should happen ultimately, then work backward to the present as well as forward from where we are now in developing our plans."

The national agricultural research establishment must take the lead in identifying, and making known in language that is understandable to others, potential long- and short-term advances in agricultural systems. And, if possible, it should go further, giving estimates of the benefits and costs (private and social) which can be anticipated.

Yields and areas of production of each commodity should be examined to compare current yields and production levels with what they could be. Requirements for each commodity for the future, with 10–20-year horizons, should be estimated, considering both likely local demand and opportunities for export. Then alternative strategies for reaching those goals should be developed. Technical or other barriers should be identified, and research and training needs for overcoming these barriers placed in order of priority. Research groups should also attempt to identify nonresearch barriers to be overcome, since the success of research as well as of the total national effort will depend on eliminating *all* major deterrents to progress. Entire commodity systems should be examined.

In a similar manner, attention should be given to crop or animal species not currently important in the country but that have potential value. This requires monitoring advances elsewhere in the world—in crop and animal science, in fisheries, in forestry, and in soil and water management—with consideration being given to opportunities for industrial as well as food or feed uses.

An equally important approach is to examine regions of the country to identify how their productivity might be enhanced by agriculture, alone or in combination with other activities. Mosher, in *Creating a Progressive Rural Structure*, suggested the need for a type of land classification which combines an estimate of the *inherent* capacity of each area for agricultural *production* with an estimate of the *immediacy* of its potential for agricultural *growth* (Mosher's emphasis). He proposed three categories:

- *Immediate growth potential.* Regions in which soils are good, rainfall is adequate or irrigation water is available, improved technology is available for at least one major crop of the region, and there is adequate market demand. Rapid diffusion is the most urgent need.
- *Future growth potential.* Regions where soils and climate are favorable but where irrigation, or highly productive technology, or communications, or transport systems are lacking. The most urgent need is research or investment in irrigation facilities or roads to convert the region to one of immediate growth potential.
- *Low growth potential.* Areas in which "farming never can be a highly productive occupation without major technological changes that cannot be foreseen."

Particular attention should be given to the status of technology which is or soon could be made useful in the region, to systems of input supply and marketing, to means of instructing the farmers—the basic requirements for adoption by farmers (see Chapter 10). The result will be a spectrum of opportunities requiring short to long periods to exploit, with projections of opportunities varying greatly in reliability. The important point is that through the judgments of informed people, bolstered by such data as are available, reasonably quick estimates of potential are possible and should be attempted.

Other considerations may influence the direction of agricultural research. In some countries deforestation is contributing to shortages of wood for fuel, to reductions in grazing land, and to serious erosion leading to loss of topsoil and silting of reservoirs. The research community should be looking for ways to alleviate such problems. Possibilities may exist to raise cropping intensity by growing more crops per year or through mixed plantings of various types. When research groups start asking, How can we best develop this region and this nation? they will have begun to make significant contributions to development.

ESTABLISHING GOALS

Establishing long-term (10–20-year) national agricultural development goals requires vision and strategic thinking about the agricultural potentials and problems of the country. Long-term goals, even if imprecise, provide a logical framework for short-term plans. And they offer targets against which a nation's progress can be evaluated.

To establish ambitious yet realistic goals, informed agricultural scientists must participate along with planning specialists. Agriculturalists can help make reliable judgments about where, how, and in what time span gains of a particular magnitude might be achieved.

Agricultural goals must also be stated in new ways. Usually, agricultural goals are expressed as desired increases in output (tons or percentage increases) or in numbers of hectares to be benefited. With such goals in mind, scientists and others will seek to achieve them in the most direct and rapid way possible, usually by working with larger farmers in more favorable areas. Such "production goals" may be appropriate when national authorities believe that their nations need maximum increases in output at minimum cost and in minimum time. But if, in addition to increases in output, the participation of large numbers of small farmers is needed, goals should clearly identify the number of farms or farmers to be benefited, and to what extent. Then scientists and others will begin to search for ways to raise productivity and incomes on large numbers of smaller farms.

Most governments plan in multiyear periods, commonly 5 years, for allocating resources. A 5-year horizon may be adequate for investments which can be scheduled with some degree of precision—for instance, construction of industrial plants, of irrigation or drainage systems, of sections of roads or railways, or of research facilities. However, planning only for the short range (up to 5 years) has two major disadvantages for setting objectives for agricultural research programs. First, short-term agricultural goals may fail to reveal the urgency and the magnitude of the task ahead (a short-term goal of increasing output 4 percent annually may not seem as difficult as the implied doubling of output in 18 years). Second, agricultural research is time-consuming. Developing a high-yielding cropping system requires at least 6–8 years if new varieties must be created.

Agricultural research programs must be geared to longer-range requirements as well as to shorter-term needs if the more ambitious goals are to be identified and attained. In *Creating a Progressive Rural Structure*, Mosher, in 1969, stated that he was "convinced that, in South and Southeast Asia, at least, each country could establish a dynamic and thoroughly modern agriculture throughout much of its territory in not more than 15 *years* if it planned both forward from where it is now and backward from where it hopes to be at the end of the period."

PRODUCING NEW TECHNOLOGIES

Farmers will respond rapidly to new technologies which promise clearly profitable production gains. These technologies can include new varieties or breeds, improved production practices, or both. Much is already known. Contributions from all sources—ranging from scientists outside the country to local farmers—must be evaluated. If progress is to be rapid, this calls for an orderly program of directed research.

The array of problems on which agricultural scientists can work is infinite, ranging from the merely interesting to those of critical importance. Agricultural teams should concentrate on problems requiring immediate attention, or on ones that will contribute significantly to their countries' progress, avoiding those that are not essential.

DEVELOPMENT OF LOCAL FARMING SYSTEMS

Discussions of building national research systems commonly bring to mind a vision of scientists in laboratories and on well-equipped field stations. Of course, that is where much of the work must be done. But if a nation's research is confined to central experiment stations and laboratories, it will be inadequate.

Agricultural technology is largely biological, and therefore must be developed for each season of each region of each country. Research will have to be done at regional stations and in farmers' fields to tailor the technology to existing farming systems. This demands decentralized field work by the nation's scientists.

In most developing countries, high proportions of the farmers are in remote areas and have extremely small holdings. They are generally not aware of the wide array of technological components available and are limited in their opportunities to put together profitable combinations for their own farm conditions. For this reason the scientists must help develop improved, locally adapted farming systems. Where extension services handle farm-level work, the agents must be trained in farm-level experimentation so they can work closely with scientists in testing new components and systems on farmers' own fields. Research and extension services, if administratively separate, must *function* as a unit.

The individual farm is *the ultimate experimental unit* in any national system. Thus the research system extends from central laboratories and field stations to the last and smallest of those experimental units.

IMPROVING POLICIES

Research aimed at improving pricing, marketing, input supply, and credit mechanisms can be conducted as part of commodity production or defined-area development programs, with individuals responsible for elements of the field agricultural work participating. All relevant agencies should consider that they have mutual interests in making the system work.

The spectrum of research

What is meant by agricultural research? What types of research should a government or an assistance agency support? What should make up a national research system? In small countries? In large ones? What should be the focus of research services, of extension organizations, of other entities?

CATEGORIES OF RESEARCH

The following five categories identify the important components of research. These categories are somewhat different from those conventionally used.[1]

[1] For example: *Verification trials* generally refer to on-farm tests, or our operational category. *Adaptive research* would encompass work done in specific regions to tailor technology to local conditions, or our tactical and operational levels. *Applied research* is a rather all-encompassing term which would include at least our strategic, tactical, and operational types. Some scientists might consider it to embrace our "supporting" category as well, as we do. Any research in the spectrum that is not basic is applied. We interpret *mission-oriented research* to include all work in support of specific objectives, usually developmental in nature, and therefore essentially equivalent to applied research. *Fundamental research* is by definition the same as basic research.

Operational or farm-level research. The identification, through experimentation on farms, of the combinations of crop and animal production practices that will provide higher productivity and profitability on those farms is called operational or farm-level research. Much of this research is done by farmers themselves, particularly those better-educated entrepreneurs involved in intensive agriculture. However, most farmers in developing countries have little education, have little income to fall back on in the event of failure, are often hesitant to take risks, and are uninformed about new technologies that they might employ. Consequently, they have limited ability to experiment with new systems. In the developing countries, therefore, scientists must help develop local farm systems, and for the most part they must do so on representative farms. *Perhaps 70 percent of a nation's technical agricultural manpower should be engaged in farm-level experimentation.*

Tactical research. In each country, technicians involved in farm-level research must be supported by work at local experiment stations—tactical research. Teams of scientists at local stations can test new varieties of many crops for the locality, compare fertilizer practices, test methods for controlling locally prevalent diseases and insect pests, identify improved crop or animal production practices, and determine other ways to increase farmers' incomes. Generally, tactical research—biological, engineering, or economic—aims to identify improved components of farming systems that operational people can combine to meet farmers' needs in a particular locality.

Strategic research. Biological, chemical, physical, or social science research aimed at solving major problems affecting several areas of a country or a region of the world, or at developing new approaches to improved production of a crop or animal species, is called strategic research. Such research should be in direct support of scientists engaged in tactical research in several regions of a country or in different countries. Most research at the international agricultural research institutes, at central experiment stations of the larger nations, and at major experiment stations in the industrialized countries is of the strategic type.

Supporting research. Investigations whose usefulness can be only partially foreseen might be called supporting research.[2] Examples are work

[2] The validity of the "supporting" category has been questioned by some on the grounds that it is little different from "basic" research. But U.S. agencies have, in fact, observed a difference. For example, the National Science Foundation reportedly has not funded many fundamental studies of economic species, on the grounds that they are "applied" and therefore the responsibility of the U.S. Department of Agriculture. USDA reportedly has not supported much fundamental work on economic species,

on nitrogen fixation and its potential applications to the grasses, on the genetics of economic species, on photosynthesis or the respiration processes of economic species, on the nature of organisms causing important plant or animal diseases, or on economic development theory. Much of the supporting research related to world food problems is undertaken by national agencies or universities in the developed countries.

Basic research. Basic research develops knowledge with no predetermined use necessarily in mind. This is an important category of research on which all supporting, strategic, tactical, and operational advances depend. Most basic research is undertaken in the more affluent countries. Examples would include studies of evolution or genetics involving non-economic species.

INTERDEPENDENCE

Any research center may be involved in several categories of research. But for any category of research to be effective it must be linked with other levels. Strategic, tactical, and operational research must draw on the findings of basic and supporting research to be effective. Conversely, basic, supporting, and strategic research have little value unless tactical and operational research are making their findings usable.

The growing cooperation between research institutes and laboratories in developed countries, international agricultural research organizations, and national research programs in low-income countries is leading to an increasingly efficient system of agricultural research in all categories (see Chapter 6).

PRIORITIES

All countries need operational and tactical research. The larger or more affluent nations may also find it advisable to have the strategic, supporting, or even basic types. But the highest priority for any nation in a hurry to produce results must be reserved for operational and tactical research.

AN EXAMPLE: WHEAT

Work on wheat illustrates the spectrum of research efforts. From *basic* work in the field of genetics came the capability of scientists to understand the mechanisms of inheritance of the several species of *Triticum*, to understand their relationships, and to devise plant breeding techniques for improving characteristics of wheats. From basic work in plant physiology came an understanding of nitrogen uptake, of requirements for

because it is considered "basic" and the primary responsibility of NSF. Therefore, one important area of research has been seriously neglected for perhaps a quarter of a century.

major and minor nutrients, and of factors affecting photosynthesis and respiration. The earliest work was undertaken primarily to extend knowledge, though it was undoubtedly hoped that results would somehow be usefully employed.

As the utility of basic work in genetics, physiology, and chemistry was recognized, efforts were intensified in many countries to improve the wheats by developing plant types that could more efficiently use sunlight, water, and nutrients. Attention was given to the nature of disease organisms (such as rusts), the nature of plant resistance, and factors affecting grain quality. These are but a few of many examples of *supporting* research on wheat. They are purposeful investigations of broad applicability and great importance.

Building on advances in many fields of basic and supporting research, it was possible in Mexico for scientists, through *strategic* research, to begin creating improved varieties and practices for low-latitude areas, as was being done concurrently by scientists of nations elsewhere. They found ways to incorporate wide adaptation to climatic conditions into new varieties, and to reduce danger from diseases.

In several wheat-growing countries, teams of scientists worked to identify improved wheat varieties adapted to local conditions and to determine effective practices related to fertilizer application or the control of locally prevalent diseases or insect pests. Such *tactical* research was undertaken with introduction of the semidwarf wheats into India and Pakistan in the mid-1960s. At the Indian Agricultural Research Institute and research stations elsewhere in India, experiments were conducted to determine appropriate rates, dates, and depths of planting; rates, dates, and placement of required fertilizers; and amounts and timing of irrigation water needed. Scores of experiments were installed, almost at a feverish pace, to find appropriate components for wheat production systems quickly. This was forced-pace, tactical research at its best.

The *operational* experiments carried on at the farm level, both by technicians and by farmers, to identify the combinations of components— the wheat-farming systems—for each locality completed the research spectrum, resulting in varieties and practices which could increase farmers' output by 50–100 percent and bring substantial increases in income.

PUBLIC VERSUS PRIVATE RESEARCH

At early stages of development most of a nation's ongoing agricultural research, from the solution of major problems by interdisciplinary scientific teams at central experiment stations through regional and local experiment-station testing, to work on farmers' fields, must be done by public agencies—usually the ministry of agriculture or colleges. The reason: private enterprise has few opportunities to become profitably engaged.

As a nation's agriculture intensifies, private companies become increasingly useful in developing and marketing hybrid seeds, in refining techniques of insect and disease control and fertilizer use, in developing farm machinery, and in other ways. However, most private companies cannot become so engaged until a substantial market for their products is fairly well assured. This often means there will be a time-lag between initiation of public-sector activities and entrance of private enterprise. It is unrealistic to expect private companies to undertake the massive task of development of technology and training of the technical personnel required to accelerate a nation's agricultural output. Many of them could contribute immensely but would need public financing.

Characteristics of effective research

While there is no blueprint for organizing and implementing national agricultural research systems, adherence to a number of principles will contribute to a high degree of effectiveness and improve the likelihood that returns to investment will be high.

ORIENTATION TO DEVELOPMENT GOALS

Development goals, as stated in the national development plan or elsewhere, provide a focus for the entire agricultural production program. Objectives for the research program should be related to broader agricultural and general economic goals.

In Chapter 10 three complementary approaches to rapid agricultural development of a country were identified: commodity production programs, defined-area campaigns, and reoriented and synchronized services. National research programs and services should be organized to directly support these approaches.

To do so, research planners must understand the national agricultural development plan: the regions on which to focus, the short-range and long-range production targets for each commodity (by region), and the possibilities of progress (as affected by soils, weather, status of technology). Research planners must also be able to identify important barriers to the success of either the commodity production approach or the defined-region approach. Only then can a research program be designed for achieving development goals.

Emphasis on yield per unit of time. The progress of research must be measured by improvement in crop or animal yield or decreases in cost of production per unit on farms. All research programs should include crop or animal yield trials under various conditions, and such yields should be continuously compared with yields obtained earlier or elsewhere. In

"The test of technology is yield. Unless scientists can produce on their experiment stations yields which are high by world standards, we can be sure that they have not yet mastered the technical problems confronting the producer. And, if the yields are high on the experiment stations but national average yields are low, we can be equally sure that the scientific advances are on the shelf and that for some reason the farmer is unable to make profitable use of them."

General Carlos P. Romulo
"Strategy for the Conquest of Hunger"

the tropics, where moisture is not limiting, the results of these trials should be expressed not only as the conventional yield per unit of area but also as yield per unit of area *per unit of time.*[3]

Measuring crop yield in kilograms per hectare, as is commonly the practice, tends to favor varieties that have a long growing season. If variety yields are compared in kilograms per hectare per day, varieties that use climatic and soil resources efficiently will be spotlighted. Varieties that perhaps yield less but mature faster may permit growing two crops a year. If a farmer can grow two fast-maturing varieties in succession, his total output and profit may be higher than if he grows one crop of a high-yielding but slow-maturing variety. For example, in some Asian rice-growing areas farmers have been able to switch from varieties that matured in 140–175 days to varieties that matured in 110–115 days. By doing so they were able to grow two successive crops of rice each year instead of one. Or they were able to grow a rice crop followed by some other crop such as a vegetable.

Yield in physical terms, while of importance to scientists, is of importance to farmers only if associated with increases in net income. The farmer, in the final analysis, measures yield in terms of income per hectare or for the farm unit as a whole, per season and per year. Consequently, costs and returns of new technology must be determined along with other measurements of "yield."

Use of maximum yield trials. As part of their agricultural research, biological scientists in each country should continuously test the limits of available technology as well as their ability to put together new technological components to achieve highest yields. Maximum yields may not be economically practical, but agricultural scientists should not, for supposed economic reasons—that is, the fact that economic conditions would make adoption by farmers unlikely—fail to attempt to raise the limits on productivity imposed by technology. Economic conditions can

[3] In some cases, emphasis should be on yield *per unit of time* per limiting factor. For example, water may be more limiting than land area in some areas or seasons.

Maximum rice yields

When research began at the International Rice Research Institute (IRRI) in 1962, researchers undertook to set new records for the amount of rice harvested per *year* from a single field. The object was to test the scientific team's ability to combine the best technology for maximum yield—the most efficient varieties, optimum spacing, maximum effective levels of fertilizer use, the best means of disease, insect, and rodent control, and optimum combinations of planting dates to allow the ripening periods to occur when light intensity and temperature would be most favorable for grain production.

By 1971, IRRI had achieved a yield of 25,650 kg/ha of rough rice in 1 year, or over 70 kg/ha/day. Yoshida, Parao, and Beachell, in "A Maximum Annual Rice Production Trial in the Tropics," stated that up to 28,000 kg/ha/year may be obtainable in IRRI's experimental fields.

Yields such as these are based on favorable field conditions and technologies which may be neither practical nor economically advantageous for the farmer. Nevertheless, such experiments do test the limits of technology and the ability of scientists of diverse disciplines to combine new materials and practices to achieve ever higher output.

Crop	Growth period[a]	Rice strain	Nitrogen applied (kg/ha)	Yield (tons/ha)[b] Crop	Cumulative
1	Jan. 18–May 7	IR8	130	8.78	—
2	May 10–July 22	IR747 B2	125	5.35	14.13
3	July 26–Oct. 6	IR747 B2	125	6.35	20.48
4	Oct. 11–Dec. 27	IR667–98	150	5.17	25.65

[a] Period in the main field. Seedlings were grown in a separate nursery area and transplanted when 20 days old.
[b] Rough rice at 14 percent moisture.

change. When the conditions do become favorable, the higher-yielding technology will then be available for introduction and rapid adoption.

Maximum yield trials have other advantages. They encourage interdisciplinary cooperation among researchers. They excite and motivate the scientists. They therefore stimulate better research efforts as well as provide an end product of the research: high-yielding technology adopted by farmers.

Orientation to small farmers. When agricultural goals are stated only in terms of production, researchers and technicians will naturally work in more favorable areas and with farms where the greatest gains can be obtained with the least difficulty. Many small farmers, especially in remote areas, will be left out. For this reason research programs may have slight impact on small-farm production. Research should be plainly oriented to benefit large numbers of small farmers quickly. Until a small-farmer orientation is achieved, they will continue to be by-passed at considerable social and political cost, and food-poverty-population problems will remain unsolved.

Accent on speed. In any research program—local, national, or international—the staff's sense of purpose and urgency can easily be detected. Are they growing two or three experimental generations per year of crops for which this would be feasible? Are they looking for simpler, faster, yet reliable ways to obtain measurements? Is speed of accomplishment a matter they talk about and in which they take pride? Are they in the field or laboratories early and late in the day? Are they in a hurry to get research results into use by farmers on a large scale? If so, the research program probably is in good hands. If not, changes either of personnel or of working conditions probably are in order.

TIMING OF RESEARCH

Substantial changes in the physical or economic conditions of any area are likely to make the prevailing agricultural technology obsolescent. Changes such as construction of major roads or irrigation systems or the start of land reform will generally require development of new agricultural technologies for the localities affected. Since agricultural research is time-consuming and requires continuity, the search for new technology must begin as soon as plans for construction or economic change are made. Delaying the start of the research, as is common, until the construction or change is complete will substanially reduce the payoff from the investment of public funds.

The payoff from research will be greatly improved if scientists participate in identifying the development potentials of each region and if government leaders insist that biological and socioeconomic research accompany engineering studies and construction.

CONTINUITY OF LEADERSHIP

Continuity of leadership of each research program—and of each major component—is extremely important. Technology, particularly biological components, must be *continuously* developed for each crop and animal species. It must be *continuously* tailored to local soil, climatic, and biological conditions.

The leaders of a nation's research on important commodities or regions should be the most competent technical people available. The must be in charge of the programs long enough to be held responsible for success or failure. The scientists can multiply their efforts by training substantial

"One of the tasks of the new [agricultural] strategy should be to trigger a continuing search for new possibilities of change. This means that scientific research workers should be more and more closely associated with the central problems of implementation, so that there is proper understanding of problems in the field. In fact, the massive introduction of imported seed and the associated shortening of the period normally involved in the introduction of a new crop gave rise to many problems. This was a new type of involvement for our scientists. We were compressing the time span of change. Problems of pests, proper fertilizer mix, correct tilling practices had to be tackled on farms instead of on pilot projects. This direct involvement gave many of our scientists a sense of belonging and as a result helped to enrich the nation's agriculture as well as science generally. I hope this trend will continue."

C. Subramaniam
"India's Program for Agricultural Progress"

numbers of young people in the use of new technologies; this can be done only if the scientists can stay with their work long enough to provide that training. If leaders are provided from other countries, they should not be short-termers; a succession of leaders, whether national or foreign, on 1-year or 2-year assignments rarely helps.

Each nation should develop *national authorities* in each important commodity or problem area. These individuals must understand the ways in which their specialty could contribute to national development; they must develop sufficient expertise and stature to interact effectively with international authorities; and they must be able to communicate their knowledge to national leaders. Governments can foster the emergence of national authorities by:

- offering competitive salaries to attract outstanding young people to agricultural research services;
- allowing commodity or problem-area specialists to remain in their specialties for extended periods of time and by not requiring that individuals move to administrative posts or other lines of work to qualify for advancement; and
- arranging for national personnel to train or work at international institutes or other centers, and to participate in relevant international conferences or workshops, as a means of establishing relationships with authorities elsewhere.

WELL-TRAINED STAFF

An especially high degree of training is required to carry out agricultural research; understanding must be acquired in basic biology, practical crop and animal husbandry, and in scientific principles and procedures.[4] Scientists at every level of research, particularly those who work directly with farmers, should have thorough schooling in each aspect.[5]

Governments can increase the competence of their research staffs by:

- staffing research services with personnel whose technical competence is high in areas relevant to their responsibilities.
- assigning scientists with substantial training and experience to regional (tactical) stations or farm-level operations, where the need for imagination and talent is great and opportunities for training young people are large.
- providing facilities of high quality, with adequate equipment, especially at schools and colleges of agriculture, and in each of the agricultural regions. Agricultural research stations are as important as teaching hospitals; if agricultural facilities are not comparable to those in medicine in any country, they should be upgraded to allow them to become the professional centers they should be.
- providing salaries to professional agriculturists which are comparable to those of professionals in medicine, engineering, or law.
- accepting only highly qualified personnel from technical assistance organizations.

ON-THE-JOB TRAINING

Training should not stop once staff join the research program; it should be a continuing activity.

Central, regional, and local experiment stations, production centers, and operational or farm-level research programs are superb places to train young people. Field skills can be learned in a setting which is not uncomfortable to new college graduates, particularly if their work is at the side of senior scientists they respect. Under the guidance of professionals, the trainee or intern can be given increasing responsibility as quickly as is justifiable. Moreover, these in-service trainees contribute importantly to implementation of the research program as they learn. Whether they are destined for research, extension, agribusiness, or educational careers, such training is of fundamental importance to both the individuals and the country.

Some scientists do not wish to be bothered with trainees as their assistants, preferring instead to have permanent and trusted aides whom they need not retrain at frequent intervals. This reluctance must be overcome, and the nation's needs placed ahead of the scientists' convenience. Once scientists find that trainees can learn quickly and accept respon-

---

[4] See Chapters 3 and 7 for a more detailed discussion of the complexity of agricultural production and research.
[5] Training is discussed in Chapter 14.

sibility early in the training period, much of the antagonism vanishes, and they begin to take pride in their protégés. They also realize that their former trainees, as they go into jobs in society, can do much to support the research effort.

TEAM RESEARCH

The rapid increases in wheat and rice production in Asia, the quick acceptance of better practices by farmers, and the enthusiasm developed among national leaders, could occur only after the scientists had assembled locally adapted cropping systems involving high-yielding varieties and production practices (including rodent control) and made them available to farmers. The "packages" could only be developed by a team of scientists whose interests spanned the several disciplines involved. That approach is essential for rapid and efficient research advances.

Research institutions are often organized by discipline. This is far less effective than organization into multidisciplinary teams to implement commodity-, area-, or problem-centered operations. Too often, for example, research in veterinary medicine (animal health) is separated from research on animal production, and researchers in the two fields are frequently unwilling to work together in pursuit of the nation's development goals. Moreover, animal productivity depends not only on animal health and management but on productivity of pastures and availability of feed during winter or dry seasons. Similarly, in the crop sciences, research in plant breeding, soils, plant pathology, and entomology is commonly oriented to quite separate goals. And in both crop and animal sciences the separation of work from that in economics is frequent. Cooperative work in animal sciences, soils, crop science, and economics not only is desirable but is essential to rapid progress.

Institutional or administrative separation is not necessarily bad; it is the failure of scientists to work in concert that seriously impedes progress. The type of cooperation that counts most is that at the regional and farm levels, and usually that is the most difficult to achieve. Lack of necessary cooperation, at any level, can be expected to slow progress and lower returns on investments.

INTEGRATION WITH OTHER ORGANIZATIONS

For maximum efficiency and speed of agricultural and rural progress, each nation must find ways to weld together the activities of research and extension services and of colleges and schools of agriculture. These organizations must in turn be linked closely with planning agencies, ministries other than agriculture, and the private sector. This complex task can be eased by orienting all agencies' activities to development of commodity production programs, to area development campaigns, and to synchroni-

"The recent trend away from identification of research and extension as separate functions and toward the concept of agricultural technology as a continuum should help to strengthen national organizations. National capabilities will be improved by the systematic development and use of improved technology, through the sequential steps of research, field station evaluation, farm-field testing, and demonstration/promotion. This operational continuum could easily be linked to inputs of seed, fertilizer, and crop protection materials and to credit sources and markets."

A. H. Moseman
Building Agricultural Research Systems
in the Developing Nations

zation of supporting activities; opportunities for all relevant organizations to become involved soon become obvious.

EXPLOITING INTERNATIONAL RESOURCES

The international cooperative scientific and technological system (Chapters 6 and 7) comprises strengthened national research and production systems, a network of international research and training centers, and centers of specialization in the higher-income countries. For many commodities or problem areas, there are outside institutions to which nations can turn for help in solving problems or training personnel, *if the nation has the capability to use that help.*

To take advantage of new opportunities, the national research effort must be so organized and staffed that it can establish continuing contacts with foreign sources of expertise. With strong commodity programs involving important crop or animal species, nations will be able to effectively pull in from the outside new crop germ plasm, animal breeding stock, and knowledge of more productive practices.

REPORTING RESEARCH RESULTS

There is one common weakness in reporting research findings which the scientific community should seek to correct. It is the failure to make the importance and implications of scientific, technological, or other advances known to nonscientists in nontechnical language. There are two main categories of nonscientists who must be reached—the politicians, planners, and bureaucrats who provide support for developmental programs, and the farmers and technicians who must implement them.

In an address at the 1976 World Food Conference, Clifton Wharton noted that politicians are professionals, as are scientists, but their perspectives often differ from those of the agricultural development professionals. He pointed out that "there are two political requirements (among others) for achieving significant sustained agricultural development:

First, that the political leadership have a genuine *commitment* to the goal of agricultural development; and second, that they have an understanding of the process."

In 1973, A. T. R. Rahman made a similar appeal to scientists:

What is needed and what should perhaps receive very high priority is that the research needs, the research findings, and the implications are to be spelled out in propositions and terms which politicians can understand. Research leaders and organizations have to put very high priority on making or creating this awareness among the top policy-makers and to generate such awareness; they have to spend time and energy to learn to talk in the language of the politicians. When political leaders see the payoffs from agricultural research, they pour more resources and their support into it.

Given the urgency of agricultural development in most countries, one must hope that leading scientists will review the arrays of scientific and technological publications emanating from their institutions to determine if they satisfy the needs for information of persons in other disciplines and of those nonscientists in authority who wield power in the development process. Are the facts and the implications for national development clearly, concisely, and interestingly presented? Or would national political leaders need to search through various publications (for which they usually have neither the time nor the expertise) to learn the implications of scientific work they are expected to support financially?

Getting reliable technical information to farmers and to those who work with them is a second important responsibility of scientists, in any country. Among the major techniques are on-farm experiments and demonstrations, field days for farmers and for personnel of agencies or industries serving farmers, radio shows, movies or slide presentations, mini-kits, and publications.

In 1974 the Philippines Council for Agriculture and Resources Research initiated a series of "Philippines Recommends" manuals, written in semitechnical language, to get up-to-date information to "extension workers, production technicians, mass media workers, provincial governors and other officials, and small farmers' leaders, to name a few." The series covers over 20 subjects ranging from maize to pineapple to grapes to fish farming. The manuals are updated by interagency and interdisciplinary technical editing panels who replace obsolete data and adjust recommendations to conform with the latest research results. Brazil has produced a similar set of publications.

Bringing research to the farmer

The research process is not complete until adoption of new techniques by farmers results in higher yields and increased incomes.

Adoption requires that the farmers be made aware of a new practice, become interested in it, try it out, and then adopt. At least the first two of these steps depend on the availability of information to the cultivator: without information, adoption cannot occur. In some research systems the researcher is directly responsible for development of technology through the final steps of adoption by farmers. Usually, however, the communications steps are carried out by extension agents.[6] Thus, research institutions must cooperate with extension and production personnel in tactical and operational or farm-level research, developing technical information and materials that are understood by both extension personnel and farmers, and training field agents. If research and extension services are separate they must work in closest cooperation.

Where a new technology is obviously superior to existing practices, the diffusion process almost takes care of itself. As initial groups of farmers obtain access to the technology, their successes demonstrate the benefits to neighboring farmers. To a large degree each of the rapid adoption patterns described in Chapter 8—for example, maize in the U.S., wheat in Mexico, wheat in India, maize in Kenya, and rice in the Philippines— occurred in this fashion.

The economic profitability of the new technologies is not always so obviously superior, however. In addition, the cultivator may be reluctant to try the new practices for numerous good reasons. Farmers are generally cautious and like to experiment themselves. They often only partially adopt recommended practices, they employ some types of practices more readily than others, and they tend to use new technologies initially on only part of their land.

The small farmer, in particular, is likely to be left out unless someone takes the initiative to assist him. He is not easily reached by radio, television, newspapers, or farm magazines. Nor does he have ready access to other information sources, such as experiment stations, local input distributors, or supervised credit advisors, that are available to the better-educated farmers. If the production specialist cannot competently respond to farmers' questions or if he gives the wrong advice, these traditional farmers suffer.

---

[6] The terms "extension service" and "extension agents" refer to the agency and its technical personnel responsible for helping farmers improve the productivity and efficiency of farm operations. In some countries the term "extension" is being replaced by "production." We consider the terms "extension agent," "production specialist," "farm-level worker," "change agent," and "operational research technician" to refer to essentially the same types of people, and we use the terms interchangeably.

New research ideas will spread farther and faster if they are clearly more profitable, if farm-level agents are competent, if on-farm trials are widely used, if production specialists' credibility is established early, if local people are recruited to help, if the available media are used, and if barriers to adoption of innovations are surmounted.

Governments should provide support to extension organizations wherever necessary, to allow them to upgrade competencies to the level of research workers and to establish close working relationships with research organizations.

COMPETENT EXTENSION WORKERS

To gain the confidence of farmers, the extension worker or production specialist must be competent in technology, in economics, in farming, and in reaching farmers.

Technical competency. The extension worker must have a basic understanding of agricultural science and be able to conduct field experiments to test whether innovations would be feasible and profitable for the farmer. He must also be able to diagnose common problems and abnormalities and to prescribe proper solutions.

Economics competency. He must be able to help farmers estimate (calculate costs and benefits) the profitability of choices such as combinations of inputs, cropping or animal husbandry practices, or alternative markets.

Farming competency. The production specialist must be capable of performing all physical tasks that a farmer does in producing crops or animals. As mechanization advances, the agent must learn to operate and maintain various machines.

Communication competency. The agent must be able to describe new advances to rural people and to help them try new ideas. The agent must be able to plan, prepare, and present *appropriate* information for the relevant audiences *and* to obtain feedback from them. The audiences include farmers, landlords, credit agency personnel, input distributors, wholesalers, retailers, or even consumers.

CREDIBILITY

Extension agents must establish their credibility early in any production program to get momentum. Community leaders can help the program if they are brought in at the beginning. Other prominent individuals who would not be useful in forwarding the program may nevertheless have to be consulted so that they do not obstruct the program out of a feeling of neglect. Face-to-face communication is therefore important in establishing initial rapport with the farmers. Team members should be of local origin, or at least fluent in the language of the area. Continuity of any technical assistance personnel in the early period will help build farmers' trust.

USING LOCAL PEOPLE

Local farmers can help technical assistance agents reach other farmers. As a rule, farmer-to-farmer communication is the most effective means of transferring information. A farmer knows which of his neighbors is credible, and he can easily relate trials conducted on a neighbor's farm to conditions on his own farm. The participating farmers must be trained, and new information must be provided to them on a continuing basis. If this link can be established, it will significantly reduce the number of professional staff members required for the project.

USE OF ON-FARM TRIALS

For farmers the most convincing new idea is one they see demonstrated as being successful under conditions they know—on their own farm or a neighbor's farm. Extension agents should conduct many widespread on-farm experiments.

Four types of benefits can be derived from a large program of on-farm trials. First, the experiments provide information from which scientists and others can devise recommendations for farmers of the area. Comparisons with the levels of production of farms without improved technology should be noted in the recommendation.

Second, the experiments allow farmers to see the effects of inputs and practices on production and even to begin to understand the payoff from using the entire combination of practices and materials recommended. Experiments, even more than demonstration plots, serve to attract the attention of farmers and to interest them in production campaigns when they get under way. Moreover, as occurred in Mexico's Puebla Project, on-farm experiments can help fertilizer distributors and credit bank personnel understand new agricultural technology. Experiments also help influence personnel of official agencies or private companies.

Third, on-farm experimentation provides a means of training new production specialists. For those production specialists who are more experienced, a continuing process of on-farm experimentation allows them to keep up with new technological developments.

Fourth, the on-farm tests provide a way for scientists to find out what weaknesses the new technology has under farmers' conditions. They may also reveal the mixtures of fertilizers most appropriate in the particular region, supply information on the probable economic returns to investment, and provide other significant information needed by the various unofficial and private agencies which may be involved in a production campaign.

PAYING THE EXTENSION AGENT

Local farmers may get better services if the extension agents have a vested interest in providing services to them. One way to do this is to require that part of the extension agents' salaries come from local sources —for example, provincial or district governmental units—who then will feel justified in demanding high-level service in return for their money.

USING MASS MEDIA

A wide range of media, including radio, pamphlets, village meetings, field demonstrations, meetings with farmer groups, and field days at harvest, can be effective in transferring information. While mass media may not be of primary influence in diffusing technological innovations (although their potential for doing so is high), they can create a climate for modernization among villagers. Mass media are most effective when combined with direct personal contacts. The traditional mass media, such as the village theater and traveling storytellers, have an important potential for development purposes, especially when they are combined with electronic and print media.

HELPING BREAK BOTTLENECKS

Extension agents must do more than merely increase the flow of information to farmers. A vast gap lies between having a farmer accept an idea in principle and having him begin to use it on his farm. Too often supplies or credit are not available in the quantity the farmer needs or when he needs them. Too often markets and storage facilities cannot successfully handle an increased volume of agricultural products.

Inadequate delivery systems, supporting institutions, and public policies are often major barriers to the adoption of new technologies. Furthermore, the agent must help the small farmer get fair access to the inputs and services necessary to make him competitive with larger farmers. Special programs must be set up to train technical assistance agents in the skills to break these bottlenecks.

Organization of research

The principal approaches for accelerating agricultural development are commodity programs, defined-area campaigns, and synchronization and reorientation of services. Research should be deliberately organized to lead and support them. Research personnel, then, will participate in teams concerned with improvement of commodity systems, with development of defined regions or with problem-centered research (solving problems or developing the information necessary for rapid progress of either commodity or defined-region programs).

COMMODITY RESEARCH SYSTEMS

The commodity-oriented research approach is not new. One of the earliest national coordinated commodity research programs was that for maize in the U.S. A. H. Moseman, in *Building Agricultural Research Systems in the Developing Nations*, traces the impetus for the practical development of hybrid maize in the U.S. to

the establishment, in 1925, of the cooperative research program of the corn belt state experiment stations and the USDA under the Purnell Act. This program, coordinated under the leadership of Dr. F. D. Richey of the USDA and with federal and state research workers participating, fostered the exchange of materials and ideas, the planning of uniform experiments that furnished information from many locations in a given year, and the prompt availability of data or experimental results to all cooperators.

That philosophy continues to be basic to successful national commodity programs as the following examples, covering several countries and commodities, demonstrate.[7]

India. Among the developing countries, India has perhaps the strongest agricultural research organization. The beginnings date to the turn of the century, but the building of a modern system, responsive to the needs of agricultural development, can be traced to a few significant steps over the past 20 years.

The Indian Agricultural Research Institute (IARI), especially since 1950, has grown into an organization strong in many disciplines. It integrates and coordinates research among the different divisions and among the sections of divisions through a research council which meets regularly to discuss progress. New projects are brought before the council before they are implemented to ensure maximum involvement of all relevant divisions. In 1958, IARI set up a postgraduate school which is a pace setter in research and a center for postgraduate training at the highest level, feeding the other institutions of research and education in the country.

The next factor in the transformation of research was the emergence

[7] The national cooperative commodity research approach, adopted by Mexico in the 1940s and 1950s when that country initiated programs with wheat, maize, potatoes, beans, vegetables, beef, and poultry, and Kenya's maize program are described in Chapter 8.

of state agricultural universities after 1960. Some have already achieved remarkable success through the integration of research, teaching, and extension (Chapter 14).

Another step toward more efficient research programs occurred in 1966 when the central (national) research institutes were brought together under the Indian Council of Agricultural Research (ICAR), which was given power to finance and implement research.

India did not lack trained scientists. The major problem was to reach agreement on research priorities and then to find a way to focus work on them. Creation of the All-India coordinated research schemes, beginning with maize in the late 1950s, provided one way to achieve those objectives while permitting institutions to retain their autonomy. The All-India schemes showed that multidisciplinary research was possible on a cooperative basis. Uniform trials were conducted throughout the country by local researchers. Varieties or new practices could be quickly identified for India's many regions. The All-India schemes have several important characteristics:

• Adminstrative control of each research center—whether main center or substation—remains with the authority that had previously controlled the station. This step removes the main impediment to cooperation among scientists working in the central institutes and the state institutes. It ensures that autonomy is not disturbed, but permits scientists to work together.

• Although land and laboratory facilities used in the All-India schemes are provided by the central government or the state government, depending on where the center is, ICAR supplies funds to cover additional staff plus necessary laboratory and field equipment.

• A senior scientist is named to coordinate each program. This mechanism permits trials of varieties and practices to be conducted on a comparable basis. In addition, visits of project coordinators to the centers help to identify and remove bottlenecks in cooperative work. A world collection of genetic material has been assembled for each commodity. Some plant breeding projects in India had previously suffered from the meagerness of germ plasm available. Sharing of the germ plasm especially helps project scientists working in states and universities.

• Finally, for each scheme there are annual workshops involving key individuals from all institutions to review results from the various centers and plan programs for the next crop season.

The first nationwide cooperative commodity research program in India was the Coordinated Maize Improvement Scheme, launched by the Indian Council of Agricultural Research (ICAR) in 1957. By 1971 it included 16 research stations in the four major maize-growing regions.

The All-India Coordinated Wheat Improvement Project was initiated in 1961, building on a half-century of scientific work in the country. Previously, wheat improvement was carried out at the India Agricultural Research Institute's six breeding centers and 18 state stations. Research on the IARI centers had been coordinated, but state stations operated independently. In 1971, S. P. Kohli, an early coordinator of the project, noted its benefits: "Both the speed and quality of wheat breeding have improved" and "the strengthening of the All-India Coordinated Wheat Improvement Project in 1965 and the introduction of the high yielding 'Mexican Wheat' germ plasm helped to make it possible for India to increase wheat production from about 10 million tons in 1965–66 to over 20 million tons in 1969–70."

In 1946 the central government became involved in rice research with the establishment of the Central Rice Research Institute (CRRI) at Cuttack. The All-India Coordinated Rice Improvement Project (AICRIP) was initiated in 1965 when its National Coordinating Center was established at Hyderabad. While CRRI remained the center for in-depth research on rice, AICRIP by 1970 was responsible for coordinating research at over 100 rice experiment stations. As S. V. S. Shastry, the first coordinator, has pointed out:

The underlying objective of the AICRIP is to promote a spirit of involvement by all rice scientists of the country in a common program. The provision of extra personnel and facilities is merely an augmentation of inputs. The testing program of AICRIP is not limited to 24 research centers receiving ICAR assistance, but includes 108 research stations throughout the country. Two central institutes, the IARI and the CRRI, nine agricultural universities, and several state departments of agriculture are involved in the program of multi-location testing. Rice workers from most of the cooperating centers participate in two AICRIP workshops each year to review the research results of the preceding season and to draw up the program for the following season.

India now has expanded the system of All-India coordinated research projects to cover most crops, all animals of economic importance, soils, water management, agronomic experiments, dryland farming, and others —perhaps the best evidence of the value of the approach as viewed by India's authorities.

Cooperation among different agencies in government is being fostered to prevent delay in carrying the fruits of research to farmers. ICAR and the Ministry of Agriculture operate a system of national demonstrations on farmers' fields. These demonstrations convince many farmers of the merits of the new technology because they see it being used by other farmers. Formation of the National Seeds Corporation facilitates the multiplication and distribution of seeds, which could otherwise be a serious bottleneck. Finally, the administrative machinery both at the center and at the state level coordinate activities to ensure that large supplies of seed, fertilizers, and other inputs are successfully distributed.

The Philippines. In 1972 the Philippines established an agency "to improve agricultural research in the country with authority to weld together the country's agricultural research resources into an effective and functional tool for national development." (The Philippines' production of rice is described in Chapter 8.) The agency, the Philippine Council for Agriculture and Resources Research (PCARR), has been assigned to: (1) define the goals, purpose, and scope of research in agriculture and natural resources; (2) develop a national research program based on a multidisciplinary, interagency, and systems approach; (2) establish a system of priorities for agriculture and natural resources research and a means of updating these priorities; (4) establish a system to generate funds for agricultural research; (5) program the allocation of all government revenues for agricultural research; (6) provide a mechanism for updating the national research program; (7) establish, manage, and fully support a national network of centers for the various commodity research programs; (8) identify, evaluate, and review agricultural research programs; (9) develop full communication among workers in research, extension, education, and national development; (10) establish a repository of research information in agriculture and natural resources; (11) provide for incentives to keep competent research scientists in the system; (12) have authority and responsibility, as part of its scope of operations, over all government-supported and -funded research on mineral resources except petroleum and other mineral oils; (13) enter into agreement or relationships with other similar institutions and organizations, both national and international, in furtherance of the above purposes; and (14) have the power and authority to call on any department, bureau, office, agency, state university or college, commodity institute, and other instrumentalities of the government for assistance in the form of personnel, facilities, and other resources as the need arises in the discharge of its functions.

PCARR is organized into three main bodies: Governing Council, Secretariat, and Technical Program Planning and Review Board (Fig. 12.1).

The Governing Council formulates policies for operating PCARR. It is composed of the chairman of the National Science and Development Board as chairman, the secretary of agriculture, the secretary of natural resources, the budget commissioner, a representative of the National Economic and Development Authority, the president of the Association of Colleges of Agriculture in the Philippines, the chancellor of the University of the Philippines at Los Baños, the director-general of PCARR, and two leaders in agricultural business.

The composition of the council links the national science structure of the country, educational institutions, and the private sector; it ensures

Fig. 12.1. Organizational structure of the Philippine Council for Agriculture and Resources Research

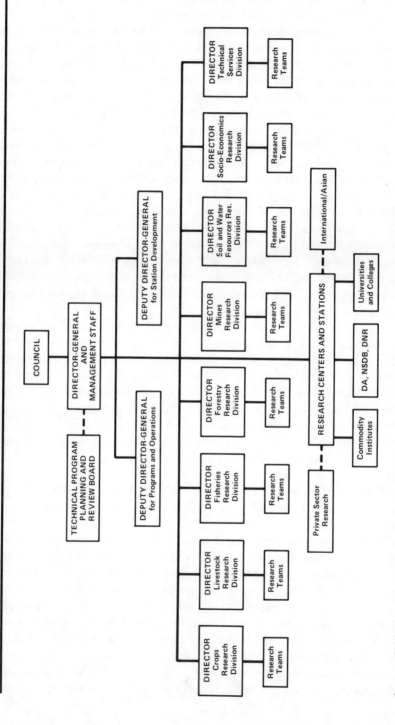

Source: Philippine Council for Agriculture and Resources Research, *Research for National Development.*

that PCARR is responsive to problems of agriculture and natural resources; and it ensures relevance to national development goals.

The Secretariat implements the policies set by the Governing Council. The Secretariat is composed of the director-general; the deputy director-general for programs and operations; the deputy director-general for station development; the research directors of the seven research divisions —crops, livestock, fisheries, forestry, soil and water, socioeconomics, and mines; the director for technical services; the director for administrative services; and the field research directors.

The research administrators at PCARR see to it that the nation's 2,200 researchers implement the national research program in agriculture and natural resources. They are assisted by 100 full-time program specialists, research assistants, technical specialists, and administrative staff.

The divisional research directors formulate the national research programs for their respective commodity areas. They plan, coordinate, and evaluate the research programs together with leaders and members of the 33 commodity teams, all of whom serve part-time with PCARR.

Scientists who are commodity research team leaders serve an average of 1 day a week or about 50 days a year. The 350 scientists who are members of the teams serve for approximately 10 days a year.

The members of each commodity research team are specialists. The National Corn and Sorghum Research Team, for instance, consists of a plant pathologist, grain processing specialist, weed control expert, marketing economist, animal utilization specialist, food expert, extension-education specialist, plant breeder, entomologist, crop physiologist, agronomist, and production economist.

The field research directors oversee conduct and implementation of research projects in the national network of agricultural centers and stations.

The Technical Program Planning and Review Board reviews the national programs of the 33 commodity groups. It is composed of the director-general of PCARR as chairman, the executive director of the National Food and Agriculture Council, and the PCARR deputy director-general for programs.

Malaysia. Throughout both the developed and developing worlds, there have been successful experiences in organizing research programs on estate crops, experiences which can be adapted to food and other commodities.

One model in the developing regions is the Rubber Research Institute of Malaysia, established in 1925. It has two experiment stations totaling about 3,000 hectares and a staff of 200 professional and 1,200 supporting employees, plus about 1,000 laborers.

The board of directors is composed of representatives of the Ministry of Primary Industries, the Ministry of Finance, the Department of Agriculture, and the Malaysian rubber industry, plus the institute's director.

Research planning, a staff function, is done annually. Proposals are prepared in line with policies of the board of directors. The institute's panel of consultants, internationally recognized authorities in their fields, make recommendations and the proposals are placed in order of priority. They are then reviewed by the institute's board, where views of the government and the rubber industry are taken into account, and by the Malaysian Rubber Research and Development Board, which decides on the research program to be supported by a levy of 1 Malaysian cent per pound of rubber.

The deliberate direction of research and the joint review of priorities and of research progress by both qualified scientists and users of the information are principles worthy of wide application to research activities in both public and private sectors.

Bangladesh. Rice, the major food crop of Bangladesh, is grown under irrigated, rainfed, and deepwater conditions and in three quite distinct seasons. Yields have generally been low, production has not met needs, and the nation has been forced to make large imports of rice.

The forerunner of the Bangladesh Rice Research Institute (BRRI) was established in 1970. It was given the present name and status of a fully autonomous institute by an act of the Parliament of Bangladesh in 1973.

Its 11-member board of governors consists of the minister of agriculture (chairman); two members of Parliament appointed by the government; the secretary of the Ministry of Agriculture; the secretary of the Ministry of Finance; the secretary of the Ministry of Planning; the chairman of the Bangladesh Agricultural Development Corporation (BADC); the director of agriculture for extension and management; the director of agriculture for research and education; a representative of the International Rice Research Institute; and the director of BRRI.

Among the functions of BRRI are (1) research on rice improvement and production at its laboratory, its 68-hectare central experiment station, and several substations; (2) establishment of project areas (about 140 square kilometers) for demonstrating new rice technology and for training farmers; (3) training extension officers and farmers in improved techniques of rice production, as well as giving short courses in rice production to district agricultural officers, plant protection inspectors, BADC farm superintendents, officers of the Soil Fertility and Soil Testing Institute, and instructors of the agricultural extension training institutes; and (4) maintaining a library and issuing publications.

BRRI is organized into several divisions: administration, rice breeding, agronomy, entomology, plant pathology, plant physiology, soil chemistry, rice technology, agricultural engineering, agricultural economics and

"When we are thinking at a national level there has to be a considerable amount of flexibility in the research system itself to embrace the combination of major problems. A strategy is devised related to the total national requirements. Once the end point or objectives are clear and precisely defined, much of the problem of the research director, and of the research worker, is resolved. The major issue is then to determine the type of strategy to adopt to achieve the overall objectives."

M. S. Swaminathan
"The Planning and Implementation
of National Research Programmes"

statistics, communication and training, and farm management. Of its 200 employees in 1975, 64 were scientists.

Financial support in 1975 was provided by the government of Bangladesh, for operating expenses; the Ford Foundation, for support by IRRI, advanced training of scientists, and purchase of equipment; U.S. Agency for International Development, for training of scientists; International Development Research Centre of Canada, for work on multiple cropping; and the Agricultural Development Council, a U.S. nonprofit corporation, for development of agricultural economics. The International Rice Research Institute provides a resident team of four scientists, and the Agricultural Development Council supplies an agricultural economist.

By 1975, BRRI had already released five of its own varieties plus two developed at IRRI for farmer use.

BRRI embodies many features of value to national commodity-oriented production programs. Its board of directors brings together representatives of agencies and organizations which must work in concert to raise rice production. It frees the research institute of some of the "civil service" constraints on salaries and promotion of talented staff. It attempts to deal with the entire technical system underpinning rice production—from central planning and research to development and promotion of improved cropping systems at the farm level. And it is production-oriented, being motivated by a central purpose: to raise rice production.

Based in part on experience with BRRI, the government is reorganizing and strengthening the Bangladesh Agricultural Research Institute, which has responsibility for most crops other than rice.

Botswana. The agriculture of Botswana, a country the size of France with a population of only 750,000, is dominated by beef cattle production. The nation's 3.5 million cattle are maintained under two systems: a traditional cattle-post management system and a fenced-ranch system. Most of the beef is shipped chilled to Europe from a single well-managed slaughter house.

Livestock research in Botswana dates from the 1930s. Since 1970 an integrated program of beef cattle and range research has been carried out within the Division of Research of the Ministry of Agriculture. The basic objective of this research has been to understand the differences between the two husbandry systems and to find ways to upgrade the traditional system to the level of the improved system (fenced ranches).

A policy review committee consisting of senior staff in the Ministry of Agriculture determines policy. However, since the population of Botswana is small and livestock is so important, almost every citizen has a means of making his feelings known, either directly through personal contacts or indirectly through parliamentary representatives in policy determinations.

The research team consists of a coordinator and specialists in animal breeding, nutrition, production economics, range research, data handling, field investigation (communal management), and range ecology, as well as management personnel for government ranches. Due to a shortage of trained personnel, the research program has been staffed largely by expatriates, some hired directly, others supplied by the United Kingdom, Sweden, and FAO.

Seventeen government research ranches, broadly covering the major cattle areas, have gradually been developed. The total area of the ranches is almost 50,000 hectares. The research has led to the introduction of the Tribal Grazing Land Policy, which is the government's major policy for increasing total production, distributing the benefits of the production widely, and reversing the deterioration of the range.

Guatemala. In 1970, three factors caused the government of Guatemala, a country of 6 million people, to examine its agricultural production efforts closely. First, food production was not keeping up with increases in demand. Second, with the exception of rice, yields of the basic food crops were increasing only slightly or not at all. Third, small farmers (cultivating 7 hectares or less), accounting for over half of food production, were not benefiting much from Guatemala's economic development efforts.

In 1971 the Ministry of Agriculture was reorganized. Separate organizations were created to have responsibility for marketing, agricultural credit, and general services—that is, development, training, and education including extension, irrigation, and research. Specific goals were to increase food production, especially of the basic food grains, and to stimulate rural development. Small and medium-sized farmers were identified as the main target group.

In 1973 the Institute of Agricultural Science and Technology (ICTA: Instituto de Ciencia y Tecnologia Agricolas) was created by legislation as a separate organization within the Ministry of Agriculture to generate and promote the use of science and technology within the agricultural sector of Guatemala. Its activities are (1) to conduct research on the agricultural problems of the country related to social welfare: (2) to produce materials and find ways to increase agricultural production; and (3) to promote the use of technology. ICTA was assigned to do research related to agriculture, to carry out programs of training and promotion directed toward the application of results obtained from research, to formulate training programs for scientists, and to distribute information and materials related to research.

As a decentralized (semi-autonomous) institute of the government, ICTA is governed by a board of directors (Fig. 12.2). The minister of agriculture is president. Other members are the minister of finance, the minister of economics, the secretary for national planning, the dean of San Carlos University, and one citizen-at-large named by the other members of the board. The heads of marketing, credit, general services, and the agrarian transformation institute are permanent advisors to the board and are usually invited to the sessions of the board.

Technical activities are carried out within the Technical Unit for Production. National programs for the major commodities—maize, sorghum, beans, wheat, rice, horticulture, and livestock—are each headed by a coordinator. Disciplines such as soils or socioeconomics support the commodity programs and also are headed by coordinators. Regional testing of the technologies is done within designated zones. All regional activities, including operation of production centers (experiment stations) and projects of the national commodity programs, are under a regional director.

ICTA Headquarters are in Guatemala City. Production centers are located in five of the seven regions into which the country is divided. In all, there are nine centers and subcenters.

The Guatemalan government supports most of the work. Foreign contributions have been made by the U.S. Agency for International Development, The Rockefeller Foundation, the International Center of Tropical Agriculture (using Rockefeller Foundation funds), and the Inter-American Development Bank.

The ICTA program has four notable features:

First, maximum use is made of the international agricultural institutes' basic breeding work. ICTA makes selections from the experimental varieties provided by the institutes and develops agronomic recommendations for the areas in which the crops will be grown. The success of this division of responsibility depends in large part on ICTA's skill in identifying and communicating its technical problems to the institutes and, in turn, on the ability of the institutes to respond.

Second, a socioeconomic team, with the collaboration of agronomists, studies the conditions under which farmers operate and works closely

Fig. 12.2. Organization of ICTA

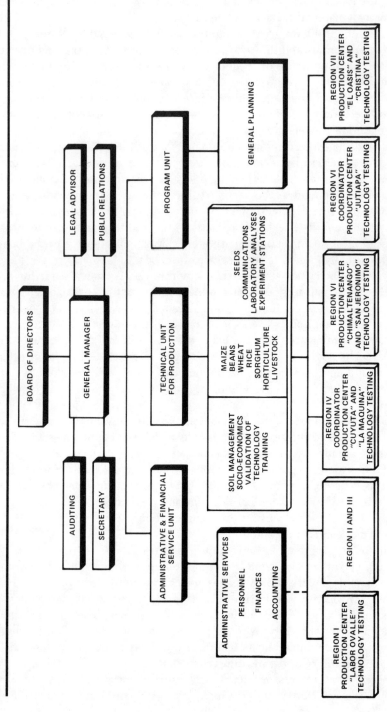

Source: Astolfo Fumagalli and Robert K. Waugh, *Agricultural Research in Guatemala*. Reprinted by permission of Instituto de Ciencia y Tecnología Agrícolas (ICTA), 5a. Avenida 12–31, Zona 9 Edificio El Cortez, Guatemala City, C.A.

with the technicians in devising production practices which are compatible with these conditions.

Third, the research activities are decentralized as much as possible to the regions and, within the regions, to the farmers' fields. Farmer participation is encouraged. Research stations are intentionally kept small and used only for essential activities.

Fourth, ICTA works with private groups to introduce and test technology at the farm level whenever feasible.

The ICTA program is new, and optimism is based more on promise than on actual experience. The extension, credit, and marketing activities, carried on by other government institutions, are still relatively weak. Links between ICTA and these complementary agencies must be strengthened.

Principles of organization. No single model can be proposed for organization of national commodity research systems. To be effective, commodity research systems must be structured to fit national institutional arrangements and resources. They will be influenced by the previous history of research in the country, particularly the relative degree of involvement of the national and local governments, educational institutions, and private bodies. The number of trained persons available has an important influence. These qualifications notwithstanding, several principles appear to be widely applicable to organizing commodity research systems:

- There should be a coordinated, continuing program of work dealing with the most important aspects of each commodity system. Research objectives should be ambitious and clear. The program should be headed by individuals who become increasingly expert on that commodity and are able to lead the nation's effort to improve output and profitability.
- Policy guidance should be provided by a body representing the diverse interests of the government and the private sector. Scientists should be represented. A single, high-level governing body can oversee an array of different commodity programs, as well as work on other problems.
- Some degree of autonomy from regular government rules and regulations is often desirable to provide freedom of action and to attract and stimulate good researchers. There are disadvantages associated with such autonomy; for example, rivalry among institutions rather than cooperation may limit effectiveness in accomplishing the main goal of increasing commodity production.
- The size, nature, and funding for each commodity research program should be dictated by the current or potential importance of the commodity to the economy; its importance to the livelihood of small farm-

ers; by the need for research to permit productivity and profitability to be increased, or costs decreased; by the array of ecological conditions for which technology must be tailored; and by the human and financial resources which can be committed.

• The expertise required on each commodity team will also be determined by the array of problems requiring resolution within the country as identified in situation papers (Chapter 10) and as later uncovered by the work of the research group itself. The team may consist of a single specialist with a modest support staff working in a few locations or of a larger group working in several regions. In nationwide cooperative programs, many research teams at many institutions might be directed from a central institute or major research station.

• Not all scientists working with a commodity team must be full-time researchers on that commodity. Some may be involved in work on several crops or animal species, especially specialists in plant pathology, soils, entomology, irrigation and drainage, engineering, economics, sociology, veterinary medicine, animal nutrition, pastures, and forage crops.

• Activities should be organized to promote a continuous flow of experimental results to and from experiment stations and farms. New strains of plants and animals, new agricultural chemicals, new feed supplements or vaccines, etc., should be introduced and tested down to the farm level, and previous, less useful types should be replaced. Cooperating farmers should participate year after year, ensuring that reasonable research requirements are satisfied even at the farm level; the extension process should be included in research activities, and the spread of innovations should be promoted.

Work on each commodity should normally be headquartered at a station in a region where the crop is important, with additional activities being carried out at those stations in the national network where research would be relevant, supplemented by on-farm testing. One experiment station may be the headquarters for a single important commodity, or for several of lesser significance.

Regional farm testing can be carried out by cooperating farmers on their own lands. Each farmer becomes involved in selecting superior crop varieties and evaluating crop or animal management practices. Each farm is then viewed as an experimental unit in the national system, and the farmer as a participant. Field days at harvest time facilitate the process and speed the relay of information to neighbors. Extension personnel should be active in such activities.

• Where educational institutions and private bodies also are active in commodity research, means must be instituted to ensure that *all* parties can and will work together toward achieving agreed upon, common goals. Respected intellectual leadership at the national level, required in all cases, can contribute discipline to total efforts. Central control of funding of cooperative (for example, interministerial) activities is a second, even more effective, means of ensuring coordination. Provision of national staff for key positions in cooperating institutions (for example, full-time research leaders at universities or colleges) is an even more effective means of ensuring cooperation.

DEFINED-AREA RESEARCH SYSTEMS

The defined-area approach to agricultural development allows attention to be given to any commodity or service which could improve income and employment on-farm or off-farm in a specific area. Research which is a part of the national program, including on-farm trials under a wide range of soil, fertilizer, and climatic conditions within the project area, is a necessary component in developing farming systems which offer substantially higher profits to the small farmer.

Improved farming systems. A first step, as suggested in Chapter 10, is to study the technology farmers in the area are using, as well as to search for technologies that, while not in use, might be applied locally with few modifications. Existing technology should be analyzed for changes that are likely to increase output and net incomes. The technological questions should then be listed in order of priority. Based on these priorities, field trials should be carried out.[8] These trials should be simple but well-designed experiments on farmers' fields in representative agro-climatic zones of the region. For crops, they should test variables such as varieties, date and rate of planting, date and rate of fertilizer application, etc., and should include measurement of economic return. The risks farmers face in using different levels of costly inputs should be estimated from information on weather variability and fluctuations in prices.

Recommendations can then be developed for different levels of investments in inputs and for different ecological conditions, taking into account the expected risks in production and marketing.

Tests should be continued until researchers understand the variability of weather conditions which farmers face.

In general the amount of agronomic research required before recommendations are made is proportional to the ecological variability in the area. In regions of irrigated farming or with favorable rainfall, recommendations derived at several locations after 1 or 2 years of research may have a useful level of precision. For nonirrigated regions where

[8] The credibility of the farm trials will be increased if farmers, scientists, and technical assistance workers jointly plan this research.

drought frequency and intensity vary within and among years, agronomic research at a number of locations for 2 or 3 years may be necessary.

Instruction of farmers. Effective communication is the product of comprehensive analysis and planning in which those involved seek answers to such questions as:

- Who needs to know about what, if the program is to achieve necessary levels of attention, understanding, acceptance, and action?
- Who has the information and skills to be shared or communicated? Are these sources readily available, or do they require processing, interpretation, or translation?
- What opportunities and means exist for processing and transmitting information readily, economically, and without undue distortion? What new means are needed?
- In what form must specific items of information be presented to ensure that the objectives are achieved with specific audiences?
- Does the communication plan provide adequate ways for the project staff to obtain information from farmers and others involved in the campaign?
- How competent is the project staff in analyzing information, preparing written materials, presenting ideas orally, making and using photographs and recordings, arranging displays and exhibits, organizing and leading group discussions, planning and conducting demonstrations, and asking questions of and listening to people? If the project staff is weak in some of these skills, what can be done through training, consulting, or arranging for special expertise where needed?

Staffing. A capable, highly motivated, multidisciplinary staff must be organized as a single team to handle production research, technical assistance to the farmers, and socioeconomic evaluation. Strong leadership is essential, but there should be no escape from team responsibility for achieving the goals of the project.

Staff size for a defined-area campaign will be influenced by the size and diversity of the agricultural area, the number of commodities or other problems to be addressed, the number of farmers to be serviced by the program, and the quality of transportation.

The number of research technicians will be determined first by the size of the area to be served. For a given size of area, more agronomic research technicians will be required in areas that have greater diversity in soils, physiography, temperature, and rainfall.

The number of technical assistance agents, however, will be determined more by the number of farm families than by the amount of cultivated land. In Mexico's Puebla Project, each technical assistance agent, assisted by one or two aides, was responsible for about 10,000 farm families. Localities there were relatively accessible. A technical assistance agent could reach the most remote village in his area in about an hour. For areas with poor roads or poor means of transportation, relatively larger technical assistance staffs will be needed.

The experience of the Puebla Project, as analyzed in *The Puebla Project: Seven Years of Experience, 1967–1973* (see Chapter 8 for details), suggests the following staff sizes for projects of similar types in other areas:

- 25,000 hectares and 10,000 farmers would require a coordinator, one technical assistance agent, one technician responsible for agronomic research, and one technician in charge of socioeconomic evaluations;
- 50,000 hectares would require a coordinator, three technical assistance agents, one agronomic research technician, and one evaluator;
- 100,000 hectares would require a coordinator, five technical assistance agents, two agronomic research technicians, and one evaluator;
- 200,000 hectares would require a coordinator, an assistant coordinator, 10 technical assistance agents, three or four agronomic research technicians, and one or two evaluators.

The project staff will normally have a basic education and general knowledge of agriculture, but will have had limited specialized training or previous experience. The guidance of specialists from outside the project will be required in setting up and analyzing surveys and experiments, in planning operations, and in resolving social and technical problems that arise during the campaign. The project staff should be in frequent contact with experienced specialists in such fields as agronomy, plant protection, animal science, veterinary science, economics, and communications.

Production and training centers. One means of synchronizing efforts among agencies and of speeding farm-level progress in defined areas is to establish strategically located production and training centers, each responsible for leading the development of an area. A "production center" should have an experimental farm staffed by a small number of agricultural scientists, economists, and others, with the primary objective of developing more profitable agricultural systems for its area. One function of the production center should be to test varieties, agronomic practices, or animal management techniques, for all crops and animal species important (or potentially so) in the region, in cooperation with scientists elsewhere in the national system. These experimental farms become the local testing stations in the national network. They undertake "tactical" research (described earlier). Second, the production center should serve as a headquarters and training center for technicians undertaking farm-level or "operational" research, and for training selected farmers. Third, it can serve as a center for initial increases of improved varieties or animal stocks. Fourth, for individuals from other agencies (credit, fertilizers, seed, home economics, etc.), the center could serve as a base for operations in the region.

These "tactical" production and training centers are important components of a defined-area research program. They should have adequate land and facilities for field tests and for training. The centers should be visited frequently by senior scientists whose tests are at the station, and by authorities of other cooperating agencies.

To undertake such broad activities, the station's resident staff should include an agronomist, an agricultural engineer, an entomologist, an animal specialist, an agricultural economist, a communications specialist, and a director or manager. These individuals should be highly capable and versatile. They should be able to install and maintain experiments of high quality and they should be dedicated to in-service training of younger people.

For the most part, the experimental program should be carried out by young persons *in training*, under the guidance of the small, permanent team of professionals. The trainees, who would remain at the production centers for 1–2 years, should be intensively trained in the skills of farming and in installing and managing experiments, and they should be given increasing responsibility as rapidly as possible. By the end of the first year, the better trainees should be in charge of major lines of work and be supervising and training newer trainees.

Centers should be a part of the national agricultural research system. However, they can also serve simultaneously as part of an extension system. A center should, as feasible, be established at each college or school of agriculture, with students as trainees, and with senior staff supplied, if necessary, by the research or extension services. All trainees should participate in farm-level activities with farmers. The trainees may be individuals from extension services who are rotated to a production center for training.

To support the production centers, other facilities will be required for commodity-oriented and problem-centered research, with locations determined by the requirements of the main lines of work for which each is to be used.

Above all, the mandate of the center should be clear: rapid development of the defined region while training substantial numbers of younger people. The success of the center should be measured by the speed of development of the region (effects on crop and animal yields and farmers' incomes) and by the quality and number of people trained.

PROBLEM-CENTERED RESEARCH

Behind national efforts to increase productivity and output of commodities and to develop regions, a wide array of supplementary research activity will be needed.

Research which transcends single commodities or regions should be organized and funded on a problem basis. Each nation should establish mechanisms for identifying those problems of greatest importance and for marshaling personnel in public agencies, universities, and the private sector to work on each problem on a sustained basis. Smaller, poorer countries may have to rely on outside organizations for help with certain problems, since they will not be able to afford comprehensive research systems. Some examples of problem-centered research which most nations will find to be important are:

Price policy, taxes, credit, marketing. Questions of agricultural prices that are profitable for farmers and reasonable for consumers, of how much credit will be required to catalyze use of new farming systems, of how to design and transport systems to facilitate movement of commodities into and out of rural areas, of how marketing can be made more efficient, and of how agricultural and rural development programs can be financed will require sustained attention by researchers who understand agricultural and rural problems as well as economic and social principles. While a central group must bear the major responsibility, individuals in a number of agencies and educational institutions can usefully participate if flexible funding is available.

The concept of a national coordinated research program can be applied to this set of issues as well as to commodities or other problem areas. Authorities in agriculture, in energy, in transportation, in business aspects of input supply and marketing, must be included if studies are to be most useful. Individuals doing research on policy matters must participate in units implementing commodity production or defined-area development programs.

Soils and land use. A nation's soils are among its most important resources. Each country should take steps to understand, develop, and preserve its soils.

Accurate soil inventories and land-use classification should accompany collection of hydrological and meteorological data, as a basis for planning agricultural development or conservation programs. Soils should be classified on the basis of fertility as well as physical properties.

Fertilizer requirements, including use of minor nutrients, must be determined crop by crop, locality by locality, farm by farm, and often field by field within farms. This requires on-farm trials, at least in representative locations.

Erosion of soils is a major problem in many countries. Valuable topsoil is being lost and reservoirs are being filled with silt. Each country faced with such difficulties should without delay develop plans for dealing with them; this will require joint efforts by experts in agronomy, forestry, and engineering.

Water management. Irrigation and drainage offer major opportunities to increase and stabilize crop yields, but such programs are costly. Most governments must set up a unit concerned with developing such systems. To achieve optimum payoff, the unit must study not only construction of major works but also maintenance and management of irrigation and drainage, development of appropriate farming systems, and reorientation of input supply and marketing. Attention should also be given to water rights laws, which may be inappropriate or ineffective, and to systematic collection and analysis of hydrological records of stream runoff and river flows, of meteorological data by region and locality, and of information on underground water resources. Researchers working on irrigation should be integrated with researchers working on nonirrigated areas to ensure that development of underground sources (tube wells) as well as surface waters is planned, to maintain a balance of investments between irrigated and rainfed agriculture, and to better coordinate construction of major works with developing farming systems.

Harvesting, threshing, and storage. As agricultural production is intensified, labor is often in short supply at harvest time, even in densely populated areas. There is need to improve the small-scale harvesters and threshers which can be manufactured in shops in most developing countries.

The drying procedure can markedly affect the quality of the dried product. There is an increasing need for simple and inexpensive mechanical dryers which can be manufactured or assembled in developing countries, and which use solar energy or other locally available sources of power.

Ways are needed to extend the storage life of agricultural products, to reduce bulk and weight, and to reduce spoilage or contamination of products. New storage methods are needed for many commodities in many regions, using structures or containers fabricated locally.

Small-farm research. Too little thought appears to have been given by the scientific community to research to meet the needs of small farmers, except in Asia, where farms are small. Opportunities for small-farm research exist in several areas:

- For crops such as beans and peas, there are climbing types which, properly grown with supports, will give much higher yields per square meter than conventional bush types.

• Intercropping and relay planting of crops in selected combinations can keep virtually all of the soil surface covered with plant growth year-round, with minimum waste of sunlight. Annual crops can be grown among trees in orchards. Sometimes three or four tiers of trees or crop plants can be grown on a single plot, with shade-tolerant plants in the lower layers.
• Many high-value crops such as vegetables, nut crops, and flowers have a high labor requirement and are well suited to small farms.
• Diversified farming systems, involving associations of crops and animals, are particularly useful on small farms.
• Terracing of hillsides, so widely practiced in Asia, is of course labor intensive, but has not been extensively employed elsewhere.
• The system of small-farm milk and cheese production and collection— as developed by Indian cooperatives—can be highly successful.

FIELD STATION SYSTEM

Every nation needs a system of strategically located research and training centers to support the commodity-oriented, defined-area, and problem-centered components of the research system.

In addition to a central station and laboratories, preferably close to the seat of government, one experiment station should be located in each area of distinct soil and climatic factors and be representative of the region served. Through land shaping and cropping practices, soil conditions should be made more uniform to improve the precision of experiments.

Certain of these stations should be designated as the headquarters for one or more commodity programs, with substations serving as testing sites and staff serving as cooperators in relevant national commodity programs. Some units should be multipurpose research production and training centers contributing to defined-area campaigns. Facilities at other stations should permit work on problem-centered research. Some stations might serve all three needs. Ideally there should be a single national network of stations, with those serving defined areas as basic units. The network should be sufficient to accommodate the indicated array of complementary commodity-oriented, defined-area, and problem-centered research efforts. Establishing stations to serve narrow political or scientific interests (often resulting in many small, ill-equipped, and poorly located facilities) should be avoided.

Research administration

We have not dealt with procedures for the administration of research organizations, except insofar as we have described the characteristics of effective research. There is considerable literature on the subject. I. Arnon has prepared an extensive review of research planning, formulation of agricultural research policy and programs, and evaluation methodology, with a comprehensive list of references. A. T. Mosher has dealt with the organization and planning of modern agriculture and with the role of the administrator. T. L. V. Ulbricht has reported on contract research and its effect on management in the United Kingdom. Numerous authorities have published papers in *Institutionalizing Research Management in Asia*, the proceedings of a symposium held in 1973 by the Southeast Asian Regional Center for Graduate Study and Research in Agriculture. Finally, A. H. Moseman edited *National Agricultural Research Systems in Asia*, which includes papers on research orientation and management, and he has contributed other important papers of his own.

Leadership by scientists

A major barrier to progress, particularly in countries that have not as yet mounted dynamic agricultural development programs, has been the conservatism of some agricultural scientists and educators. Their conservatism is manifested by a reluctance to think in strategic terms about the country's needs and to place those needs before personal interests in determining priorities for research. For some, the cause can be traced to the narrowness of their training, their high degree of specialization. Some exhibit an aversion to change or to risk and an unwillingness to work at the field level and at a speed which the urgency of problems may demand.

At the time when India was considering the initiation of its High Yielding Varieties Program, there was conservatism among India's scientists with the exception of a relatively small number of men of vision, according to C. Subramaniam, then the minister of food and agriculture:

When it came to a question of *forcing the pace* of the introduction of the new varieties after their tested release, there was considerable flutter in scientific and other dovecotes. "This has never been done before," went the argument, "and so it should not be tried now." When we consider the extent to which modern agriculture in many countries depends on introduction of once-exotic plants—potato, tobacco, tea, coffee, rubber—it seems all the more surprising that there was so much resistance within the scientific community itself. Those scientists, like Dr. B. P. Pal, Dr. M. S. Swaminathan, and Dr. D. S. Athwal, who pleaded for a bold step forward, were targets of intensive and almost abusive criticisms by proponents of tradition, both lay and academic. We were not unaware of the risks involved, but nonetheless we went ahead on the basis of the confidence of our scientists. . . . Fortunately, like the proverbial bumblebee which confounds the theorist by flying, in spite of his protestations that in theory it cannot, the farmers of India did accept and adapt the new strategy, despite advice against it and acerbic denunciations of its potential.

Overcoming conservatism in Turkey

In Turkey in the mid-1960s, seed of Mexican wheat varieties was brought into the country and given to a farmer on the Mediterranean coast to try (see Chapter 8). Yields were more than double those previously obtainable. Farmers in the region petitioned the government to allow a commercial importation of 60 tons of seed of the variety Sonora 64 from Mexico, so that a hundred farmers could test the new varieties on their own farms. Reportedly the agricultural scientific community objected, since the varieties had not been through the routine field tests in that country. Nevertheless, the seed was brought in and most farmers obtained exceptionally high yields. Then the minister of agriculture decided to import some 50,000 tons of seed. The agricultural scientists objected strongly, reportedly on the grounds that a failure could be devastating to the country. The Rockefeller Foundation was consulted on the wisdom of such large imports given the limited testing in the country. Turkey was advised to hold the import to 5,000 tons. The reason was not that there was concern about the performance of the varieties, for they had by then been tested extensively in nearby countries having conditions similar to those of the Turkish coast. Rather, it was because the varieties were "dwarf below ground as well as above" and needed to be precision planted with grain drills at a depth of less than 5 centimeters, not at almost 10 centimeters as then commonly practiced by Turkish farmers. The concern was that in the few months remaining before the next planting season it would be difficult to instruct many farmers in precision planting with grain drills. The minister compromised to a degree, bringing in about 22,000 tons of seed from Mexico and the northwestern U.S. With the assistance of experienced extension agents and farmers from the northwestern U.S., organized and financed by USAID, Turkish farmers were trained and some 19,000 tons were successfully planted.

The minister is reported to have commented later that he could not understand the conservatism of the scientists. After all, Turkey planted 1.25 *million* tons of wheat seed each year; surely the country would not be wrecked by bringing in only 50,000 tons. To the scientists, who normally start the variety-testing process with a few hundred grams of seed, 50,000 tons must have seemed like a vast and dangerous amount. To the minister, 50,000 tons was only a small fraction of 1.25 million.

Norman E. Borlaug made a blunt comment in 1968:

The most conservative man in traditional agriculture is the scientist, and sometimes I am not proud to be one of them. This is most discouraging. The scientist is a privileged person, the man who should lead us out of the wilderness of static, underproductive agriculture, and yet by his apathy and failure to exercise his unique vision, he keeps us in the swamp of despair.

The scientist fears change because he is in a relatively privileged position in his own society. If there is no breakthrough in yield, he will not be criticized. But if he makes a recommendation and something goes wrong, he may lose his job.

In many different countries there is no faith or understanding between the farmer and the scientist. Almost without exception the farmer says, "This man is a theorist. He is not a doer, and he can't help us." In the past, this complaint was all too often valid, but today the situation is rapidly changing.

The important part of this statement is "the situation is rapidly changing." At least that is true in countries where progress is now rapid.

The gap in perspective between scientists and national political leaders remains large in many countries. The agricultural research community of each country must develop the capability to view technological problems and potentials from strategic national and international standpoints. Given the generally narrow training of most agriculturists, this will not be easy. But national political leaders should expect their scientists to participate with planners in thinking and planning on a scale commensurate with the scope of national development needs.

Summary

Payoff from investments in agricultural research can be very high if research is organized to achieve ambitious development goals. In many countries a revolution is needed in concepts of research roles, scope, and implementation. Research should be an important catalyst of rapid agricultural development. Wherever agricultural progress is slow, scientists should take the lead in devising strategies for development which respond to the urgency of their nation's needs.

An overall strategy should comprise commodity production and defined-area research programs, undergirded by strong problem-centered research and in-service training of young people. The organization of research should allow direct support of these three major approaches to development, in cooperation with relevant agencies of government, universities, and private industry.

References

INTRODUCTION

Ardito-Barletta, N. "Costs and Social Benefits of Agricultural Research in Mexico." Ph.D. dissertation, University of Chicago, 1970.

Arndt, Thomas M., and Ruttan, Vernon W. "Valuing the Productivity of Agricultural Research: Problems and Issues." In *Resource Allocation and Productivity in National and International Agricultural Research*, edited by Thomas M. Arndt, Dana G. Dalrymple, and Vernon W. Ruttan. Minneapolis: University of Minnesota Press, 1977.

Centro Internacional de Mejoramiento de Maiz y Trigo. *The Puebla Project: Seven Years of Experience, 1967–1973.* El Batan, Mexico: Centro Internacional de Mejoramiento de Maiz y Trigo, 1974.

Evenson, R. E. "The Contribution of Agricultural Research and Extension to Agricultural Production." Ph.D. dissertation, University of Chicago, 1968.

Evenson, R. E., and Jha, D. "The Contribution of Agricultural Research Systems to Agricultural Production in India." *Indian Journal of Agricultural Economics* 28 (1973): 212–30.

Gittinger, J. Price. *Economic Analysis of Agricultural Projects.* Baltimore: Johns Hopkins University Press, 1972.

Griliches, Z. "Research Costs and Social Returns: Hybrid Corn and Related Innovations." *Journal of Political Economy* 66 (1958): 419–31.

Griliches, Z. "Research Expenditures, Education, and the Aggregate Agricultural Production Function." *American Economic Review* 54 (1964): 961–74.

Hayami, Yujiro, and Akino, Masakatsu. "Organization and Productivity of Agricultural Research Systems in Japan." In *Resource Allocation and Productivity in National and International Agricultural Research,* edited by Thomas M. Arndt, Dana G. Dalrymple, and Vernon W. Ruttan. Minneapolis: University of Minnesota Press, 1977.

Hertford, R.; Ardila, J.; Rocha, A.; and Trujillo, C. "Productivity of Agricultural Research in Colombia." In *Resource Allocation and Productivity in National and International Agricultural Research,* edited by Thomas M. Arndt, Dana G. Dalrymple, and Vernon W. Ruttan. Minneapolis: University of Minnesota Press, 1977.

Kahlon, A. S.; Saxena, P. N.; Bal, H. K.; and Jha, D. "Returns to Investment in Agricultural Research in India." In *Resource Allocation and Productivity in National and International Agricultural Research,* edited by Thomas M. Arndt, Dana G. Dalrymple, and Vernon W. Ruttan. Minneapolis: University of Minnesota Press, 1977.

Latimer, R. "Some Economic Aspects of Agricultural Research and Extension in the U.S." Ph.D. dissertation, Purdue University, 1964.

Peterson, W. L., and Fitzharris, J. C. "The Organization and Productivity of the Federal-State Research System in the United States." In *Resource Allocation and Productivity in National and International Agricultural Research,* edited by Thomas M. Arndt, Dana G. Dalrymple, and Vernon W. Ruttan. Minneapolis: University of Minnesota Press, 1977.

Ruttan, Vernon W. "Induced Innovation and Agricultural Development." *Food Policy* 2 (1977): 196–216.

Schultz, T. W. *Investment in Human Capital: The Role of Education and of Research.* New York: Free Press, 1971.

Tang, A. "Research and Education in Japanese Agricultural Development." *Economic Studies Quarterly* 13 (February and May, 1963): 27–41, 91–99.

Wortman, Sterling. "The Impact of International Research on the Performance and Objectives of National Systems." In *Resource Allocation and Productivity in National and International Agricultural Research,* edited by Thomas M. Arndt, Dana G. Dalrymple, and Vernon W. Ruttan. Minneapolis: University of Minnesota Press, 1977.

THE ROLES OF RESEARCH
Mosher, A. T. *Creating a Progressive Rural Structure.* New York: Agricultural Development Council, 1969.

THE SPECTRUM OF RESEARCH
Wortman, Sterling. *The World Food Situation: A New Initiative.* New York: Rockefeller Foundation, 1975.

CHARACTERISTICS OF EFFECTIVE RESEARCH
Galt, Daniel Lee. "Economic Weights for Breeding Selection Indices: Empirical Determination of the Importance of Various Pests Affecting Tropical Maize." Ph.D. dissertation, Cornell University, 1977.

Hildebrand, Peter E. *Generating Small Farm Technology: An Integrated Multidisciplinary System.* Paper prepared for presentation at the 12th West Indian Agricultural Economics Conference, Caribbean Agro-Economic Society in Antigua, April 24–30, 1977. Mimeographed.

Madamba, Joseph C. "Institutional, National, and Regional Research Relations." In *Institutionalizing Research Management in Asia.* College, Laguna, Philippines: Southeast Asian Regional Center for Graduate Study and Research in Agriculture, 1974.

Mann, Charles K. *Factors Affecting Farmers' Adoption of New Production Technology: Clusters of Practices.* Paper prepared for presentation at the 4th Regional Winter Cereals Workshop: Barley, April 4–28, 1977, Aman, Jordan. Mimeographed.

Moseman, Albert H. *Building Agricultural Research Systems in the Developing Nations.* New York: Agricultural Development Council, 1970.

Pal, B. P. "The Indian Agricultural Research Institute, the Indian Council of Agricultural Research, and the All-India Coordinated Agricultural Research Program." In *Strategies for Agricultural Education in Developing Countries: Agricultural Education Conference I.* Working Paper. New York: Rockefeller Foundation, 1974.

Rahman, A. T. R. "An Overview of Research Management in Southeast Asia." In *Institutionalizing Research Management in Asia.* College, Laguna, Philippines: Southeast Asian Regional Center for Graduate Study and Research in Agriculture, 1974.

Romulo, Carlos P. "Strategy for the Conquest of Hunger." In *Strategy for the Conquest of Hunger: Proceedings of a Symposium.* New York: Rockefeller Foundation, 1968.

Subramaniam, C. "India's Program for Agricultural Progress." In *Strategy for the Conquest of Hunger: Proceedings of a Symposium.* New York: Rockefeller Foundation, 1968.

Wharton, Clifton. "The Role of the Professional in Feeding Mankind: The Political Dimension." In *Proceedings of the World Food Conference of 1976,* edited by Frank Schaller. Ames: Iowa State University Press, 1977.

Wortman, Sterling. "The Technological Basis of Intensified Agriculture." *Agricultural Development: Proceedings of a Conference.* New York: Rockefeller Foundation, 1969.

Yoshida, S.; Parao, F. T.; and Beachell, H. M. "A Maximum Annual Rice Production Trial in the Tropics." *International Rice Commission Newsletter* 21 (September 1972): 27–32.

BRINGING RESEARCH TO THE FARMER

Benor, Daniel, and Harrison, James Q. *Agricultural Extension: The Training and Visit System.* Washington, D.C.: World Bank, 1977.

Byrnes, Francis C., and Byrnes, Kerry J. "Agricultural Extension and Education in Developing Countries." In *Rural Development in a Changing World,* edited by Raanan Weitz. Cambridge, Mass.: M.I.T. Press, 1971.

Centro Internacional de Mejoramiento de Maiz y Trigo. *The Puebla Project: Seven Years of Experience: 1967–1973.* El Batan, Mexico: Centro Internacional de Mejoramiento de Maiz y Trigo, 1974.

Rogers, Everett M. "Communication in Development." *Annals of the American Academy of Political and Social Science* 412 (1974): 44–54.

ORGANIZATION OF RESEARCH

Centro Internacional de Mejoramiento de Maiz y Trigo. *The Puebla Project: Seven Years of Experience: 1967–1973.* El Batan, Mexico: Centro Internacional de Mejoramiento de Maiz y Trigo, 1975.

Fumagalli, Astolfo, and Waugh, Robert K. *Agricultural Research in Guatemala.* Guatemala City: Institute of Agricultural Science and Technology, 1977.

Golden, William P., Jr. "Sri Lanka's Agricultural Extension Service." In *Strategies for Agricultural Education in Developing Countries: Agricultural Education Conference I.* Working Paper. New York: Rockefeller Foundation, 1974.

Indian Council of Agricultural Research. *Agricultural Research and Education: Recent Progress.* New Delhi: Indian Council of Agricultural Research, 1977.

Kanwar, J. S. "Soil Research Organizations in India." In *National Agricultural Research Systems in Asia,* edited by A. H. Moseman. New York: Agricultural Development Council, 1971.

Kohli, S. P. "The All-India Coordinated Wheat Improvement Project." In *National Agricultural Research Systems in Asia,* edited by A. H. Moseman. New York: Agricultural Development Council, 1971.

Laird, Reggie J. *Investigacion Agronomica para el Desarrollo de la Agricultura Tradicional.* Chapingo, Mexico: Colegio de Postgraduados, Escuela Nacional de Agricultura, 1977.

Madamba, Joseph C. "Institutional, National, and Regional Relations." In *Institutionalizing Research Management in Asia.* College, Laguna, Philippines: Southeast Asia Regional Center for Graduate Study and Research in Agriculture, 1974.

Mahapatra, I. C. "The All-India Coordinated Agronomic Experiments Scheme." In *National Agricultural Research Systems in Asia,* edited by A. H. Moseman. New York: Agricultural Development Council, 1971.

Mahapatra, I. C. *Bangladesh Rice Research Institute.* Dacca: Bangladesh Rice Research Institute, 1974.

Menon, K. P. A. "Building Agricultural Research Organizations—The Indian Experience." In *National Agricultural Research Systems in Asia,* edited by A. H. Moseman. New York: Agricultural Development Council, 1971.

Moseman, Albert H. *Building Agricultural Research Systems in the Developing Nations.* New York: Agricultural Development Council, 1970.

Moseman, Albert H., ed. *National Agricultural Research Systems in Asia.* New York: Agricultural Development Council, 1971.

Mosher, A. T. *Creating a Progressive Rural Structure.* New York: Agricultural Development Council, 1969.

Philippine Council for Agriculture and Resources Research. *Research for National Development.* Los Baños, Philippines: Philippine Council for Agriculture and Resources Research, n.d.

Ramon Magsaysay Award Foundation. *Food Crisis Workshop, February 7–9, 1977.* Manila: Ramon Magsaysay Award Foundation, 1977.

Shastry, S. V. S. "The All-India Coordinated Rice Improvement Project." In *National Agricultural Research Systems in Asia,* edited by A. H. Moseman. New York: Agricultural Development Council, 1971.

Singh, Joginder. "The All-India Coordinated Maize Improvement Project." In *National Agricultural Research Systems in Asia,* edited by A. H. Moseman. New York: Agricultural Development Council, 1971.

Sprague, Ernest W. *National Production Programs for Introducing High-Quality Protein Maize in Developing Countries.* Translations and Reprints No. 13. El Batan, Mexico: Centro Internacional de Mejoramiento de Maiz y Trigo, January 1975.

Swaminathan, M. S. "The Planning and Implementation of National Research Programmes." In *National Agricultural Research Systems in Asia,* edited by A. H. Moseman. New York: Agricultural Development Council, 1971.

Wahab bin Abdullah, Abdul. "The Rubber Research Institute of Malaysia." In *Institutionalizing Research Management in Asia.* College, Laguna, Philippines: Southeast Asia Regional Center for Graduate Study and Research in Agriculture, 1974.

RESEARCH ADMINISTRATION

Arnon, I. *Organization and Administration of Agricultural Research.* Amsterdam: Elsevier, 1968.

Arnon, I. *The Planning and Programming of Agricultural Research.* Rome: Food and Agriculture Organization, 1975.

Indian Council of Agricultural Research. *ICAR: Agricultural Research Service.* New Delhi: Indian Council of Agricultural Research, 1977.

Moseman, Albert H. "Coordinated National Research Projects for Improving Food Crop Production." In *Resources Allocation and Productivity in National and Inter-*

national Agricultural Research, edited by Thomas M. Arndt, Dana G. Dalrymple, and Vernon W. Ruttan. Minneapolis: University of Minnesota Press, 1977.

Moseman, Albert H. "Organizational Structures for National Agricultural Research Systems." In *Agricultural Research Management (Asia),* Vol. 2. College, Laguna, Philippines: Southeast Asian Regional Center for Graduate Study in Agriculture, forthcoming.

Moseman, Albert H., ed. *National Agricultural Reseach Systems in Asia.* New York: Agricultural Development Council, 1971.

Mosher, A. T. *Serving Agriculture as an Administrator.* New York: Agricultural Development Council, 1975.

Mosher, A. T. *To Create a Modern Agriculture.* New York: Agricultural Development Council, 1971.

Southeast Asian Regional Center for Graduate Study and Research in Agriculture. *Agricultural Research Management (Asia),* Vol. 1. College, Laguna, Philippines: Southeast Asian Regional Center for Graduate Study and Research in Agriculture, 1976.

Southeast Asian Regional Center for Graduate Study and Research in Agriculture. *Agricultural Research Management (Asia),* Vol. 2. College, Laguna, Philippines: Southeast Asian Regional Center for Graduate Study and Research in Agriculture, forthcoming.

Southeast Asian Regional Center for Graduate Study and Research in Agriculture. *Institutionalizing Research Management in Asia.* College, Laguna, Philippines: Southeast Asian Regional Center for Graduate Study and Research in Agriculture, 1974.

Southeast Asian Regional Center for Graduate Study and Research in Agriculture. *Proceedings of the Seminar-Workshop on Institutionalizing Research Management in Asia, Dec. 10–19, 1973.* College, Laguna, Philippines: Southeast Asian Regional Center for Graduate Study and Research in Agriculture, 1974.

Ulbricht, Tilo L. V. "Contract Agricultural Research and Its Effect on Management." In *Resource Allocation and Productivity in National and International Agricultural Research,* edited by Thomas M. Arndt, Dana G. Dalrymple, and Vernon W. Ruttan. Minneapolis: University of Minnesota Press, 1977.

LEADERSHIP BY SCIENTISTS

Borlaug, Norman E. "National Production Campaigns." In *Strategy for the Conquest of Hunger: Proceedings of a Symposium.* New York: Rockefeller Foundation, 1968.

Subramaniam, C. "India's Program for Agricultural Progress." In *Strategy for the Conquest of Hunger: Proceedings of a Symposium.* New York: Rockefeller Foundation, 1968.

CHAPTER 13

Inputs, finance, marketing, and prices

Introduction

To TAKE MAXIMUM advantage of technological advances in farming systems, farmers must have:

- access to recommended production inputs at the specific times and places and in the quantities and qualities needed;
- access, if necessary, to outside sources of finance to purchase these inputs;
- access to markets in which to sell products;
- economic incentives to use the recommended practices through favorable relationships of prices of inputs and products.

While new agricultural technologies, particularly biological components, tend to be scale neutral—that is, equally profitable on farms of any size—they are often adopted earlier and more rapidly on larger farms because of better accessibility to roads and markets or because the service institutions favor these groups. Thus, supply and marketing organizations influence both the pattern and the pace of agricultural development.

Input availability and distribution

Increases in crop production through intensive agriculture require the use of such manufactured inputs as chemical fertilizers, pesticides, herbicides, and sometimes supplementary irrigation and mechanical power. In animal production there are needs for chemicals to control diseases and pests, for supplemental minerals or nutrients, and for supplementary feed.

In contrast to some markets for crops and animals which have had long histories of evolution, systems for delivering farm supplies to small farmers are rare in most areas. While consumer products like cigarettes, soft drinks, or beer can be purchased in remote parts of most countries, seed or agricultural chemicals often cannot.

This contrast in accessibility between popular consumer goods and agricultural supplies is understandable. Some materials, especially fertilizers and seed, are bulky. Several hundred kilograms of fertilizer materials may be required per hectare. Dealers need substantial storage space. Moreover, to order and sell the new agricultural inputs intelligently, they must keep up-to-date on technical information if farmers are to get the returns which justify subsequent purchases. In countries in which even technical assistance personnel have little information, this is a demanding requirement for small store owners. It is difficult to establish a decentralized system which can deliver both information and materials to outlets that often must be within a few kilometers of farmers with limited mobility.

FERTILIZER

Nitrogen (N), phosphate (P_2O_5), and potash (K_2O), as well as many minor elements, are essential to plant growth. These nutrients can be derived from several sources, including the natural fertility of the soil and animal and plant wastes. Additionally, plantings of legumes have the ability to fix nitrogen from the air. In intensified agriculture, these natural sources of nutrients must often be supplemented with chemical fertilizers to increase the quantities and to provide the precise mixtures needed for normal plant growth.

For maximum benefit, fertilizer must be available to the farmer when and where he needs it, in the quantities he needs, and at a reasonable price. There are four stages in achieving this objective: establishing recommendations to the farmer, setting prices, ensuring that the supplies in the area will satisfy demand, and seeing that supplies are distributed effectively.

Farmer recommendations. Table 13.1 shows the production response of wheat to two fertilizers at a location in India. It illustrates two important points. First, if the level of either P_2O_5 or N was held constant, the returns to the additional units of the other nutrient were diminished.[1]

---

[1] In this case, with no applied nitrogen (and no phosphate) a yield of just over 500 kg/ha of wheat was obtained (with soil nitrogen or phosphate as the source of nutrition). The first 20 kilograms of applied nitrogen increased yield by 218 kg/ha, giving a marginal response of 11 kg/ha of wheat per kilogram of nitrogen. Each successive 20 kilograms of nitrogen added a decreasing increment to yield until a top yield of over 950 kg/ha of wheat was reached with just over 60 kg/ha of nitrogen. The next 20 kilograms of nitrogen actually decreased yield.

Table 13.1. Wheat yield after application of different levels of N and P_2O_5 at the experiment station in Powerkheda, Hoshangabad (M.P.), India, 1961 (kg/ha)

Nitrogen applied (kg/ha)	P_2O_5 applied (kg/ha)								
	0	10	20	30	40	50	60	70	80
0	550	785	957	1,064	1,108	1,088	1,004	857	646
20	768	1,042	1,253	1,400	1,438	1,502	1,457	1,349	1,178
40	903	1,216	1,467	1,652	1,774	1,833	1,827	1,759	1,626
60	954	1,307	1,597	1,821	1,983	2,080	2,114	2,085	1,991
80	923	1,315	1,643	1,907	2,108	2,245	2,318	2,327	2,273
100	808	1,244	1,612	1,915	2,155	2,331	2,443	2,492	2,477
120	610	1,080	1,487	1,830	2,108	2,324	2,475	2,563	2,588
140	329	838	1,285	1,666	1,984	2,239	2,456	2,557	2,620

Source: D. W. Hopper, "The Economics of Fertilizer Use."

Second, if the levels of *both* N and P_2O_5 were increased, they interacted favorably, resulting in improved yields.[2] This concept of *interaction*, the complementary relationship among inputs, is important in developing recommendations of *packages* of practices.

The farmer attempts to maximize profits, not yield. Theoretically he will increase fertilizer use to the point at which the value of the additional product just exceeds the cost of the final increment of fertilizer. From the experimental data in Table 13.1, it can be determined that if the price of nitrogen were five times the price of wheat (per kilogram) and the price of phosphate three times the price of wheat, the economically optimum dosages would be 103 kg/ha of nitrogen and 69 kg/ha of phosphate.[3]

In practice the task of making recommendations to farmers is more complex. First, even under experimental conditions, yield response differs from year to year, season to season, and location to location (Fig. 13.1). This variability is due to factors such as soil type, temperature, rainfall, solar energy, time of planting, previous crops, and management. Therefore, not one but a series of relationships exists.

Second, the response on farmers' fields may differ significantly from responses obtained under experimental conditions. The farmer may have different and nonuniform soil. He may not provide close supervision of

[2] Sixty kilograms of nitrogen applied with 40 kilograms of phosphate gave a yield of nearly 2,000 kg/ha of wheat compared with 954 kg/ha of wheat from application of 60 kg/ha of nitrogen alone, or 1,108 kg/ha of wheat from 40 kg/ha of phosphate alone.

[3] Economically optimum dosages are derived by setting the marginal products for nitrogen and phosphate each equal to the ratio of their price to the price of wheat and then solving the two simultaneous equations (the prices of nitrogen, phosphate, and wheat being known).

Fig. 13.1. Effect of season, year, and location in the Philippines on the response of two rice varieties to application of nitrogen fertilizer, 1968–71

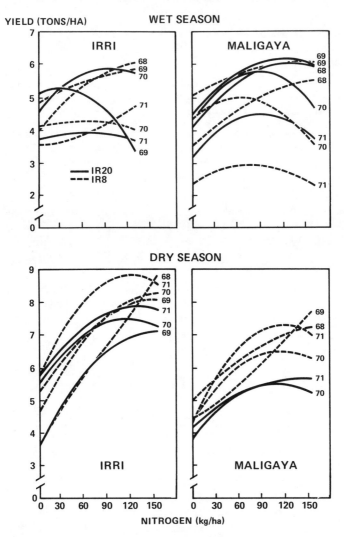

Source: Randolph Barker, "The Economic Analysis of Experimental Results in Yield Response on Rice," International Rice Research Institute.

weeding. He may not have control over water or other factors to the same degree that experimental facilities do. Therefore, researchers must test fertilizer response in a wide range of farmers' fields as well as at research stations.

Third, the farmer may not be able to buy the optimum amount of fertilizer. Because he lacks sufficient cash or credit or because of shortages, the farmer may cut back on one nutrient relative to others and lose the benefits of interaction.

Fourth, prices of both fertilizer and the crop change from year to year. When the fertilizer response curve is relatively flat—that is, when the marginal response declines gradually—the economically optimum level (to be recommended) is much more sensitive to price changes than when the response curve is relatively steep. Projections of expected crop prices must be made. These price expectations must be considered carefully before making fertilizer recommendations to the farmer.

Finally, farmers seldom use fertilizer at the optimum level. They generally leave some gap to account for production risks in the expectation that conditions will be less favorable than average.

To the extent possible, recommendations should be rounded to convenient amounts related to sizes of sacks or packages being marketed.

In summary, for each variety of each crop, for each major ecological area, and for each season in the tropics there may be different fertilizer recommendations. These must be adjusted from time to time to reflect changing physical or economic conditions. In actual practice the decision-making process will be less complicated than this seemingly endless number of potential recommendations would imply. Conditions in many areas will be similar. Moreover, farmers can be expected to make adjustments on their own.

Pricing. Under most conditions the extra yield from added amounts of fertilizer shrinks rapidly at the point at which profits are highest. At high yield levels even halving the price of fertilizer is not likely to change the optimum dosage greatly. From this viewpoint, fertilizer use is relatively insensitive to price changes.[4]

However, the farmer looks at fertilizer price from another viewpoint: the total cost he must pay at the time of purchase. Especially before the farmer has first experienced financial gains from fertilizer use, total cost may seem particularly formidable to him.

There are several ways to relieve the cost burden to the farmer. Credit permits the farmer to postpone his payment. Technical advice enables him to make more effective use of the fertilizer, thereby increasing output per amount used. Commodity prices supported at high, stable levels give him an assured return. Generally, subsidies of fertilizer prices should be resisted unless other ways to increase yields are clearly less effective.

Estimating demand. The record of individual countries or of the world collectively in estimating future fertilizer demands has not been good. In

[4] The section "Input Subsidies or Higher Product Prices?" later in the chapter covers this issue generally.

part this has been due to reliance on trend projections—that is, the assumption that what has happened in the recent past will continue into the near future. While this method is simple and better than none, it does not take into account changes in technologies, credit availabilities, prices, or other factors which affect demand.

A more sophisticated projection method is to gather fertilizer-response data for various crops, estimate the rate at which the new varieties will spread over the countryside and the average dosage which will be used on each, and then estimate requirements or demand from this information. This method too has limitations. The difference between "requirements" and "demand" must be recognized. In estimating "requirements," one works backward from a production target to calculate the amount of fertilizer which would be needed to achieve that target. In estimating "demand," one calculates the amount likely to be used, taking into consideration such variables as types of crops, the fertilizer-yield response functions of each, prices of the products, extent of dissemination of technical knowledge to the farmer, amount of credit, and adjustments for constraints to fertilizer use. This exercise requires good data and exacting analyses which are beyond the capabilities of most countries, but to which they should aspire.

No one method of estimating demand is superior on all counts. Especially in countries where data are not reliable, the best approach is to project future use based on an extrapolation of past experience. Adjustment should then be made for introduction or spread of new varieties or changes in price relationships based on experienced judgments.[5]

Distribution to the farmer. Not only must enough fertilizer be in the country, but it must be located where it is to be used at the time it is needed. Planning must begin well in advance of each cropping season. The product must be in the country on time. Expected requirements must be divided regionally and subregionally by seasons. Fertilizer should be packaged in amounts convenient for farmers with small holdings. Finally, there must be an inventory system which promptly reports data into a central location where it can be analyzed so that shortages and surpluses can be adjusted during the year.

Promotional efforts by private fertilizer dealers are an extremely important determinant of fertilizer distribution. The distributor, if credible (as shown by his knowledge of the product and of its value to the farmers), may be the primary source of the farmer's information on fertilizer. Information on high returns from use of fertilizers, along with the expe-

---

[5] The International Fertilizer Development Center (U.S.) has made comprehensive fertilizer requirement projections for a number of countries which can serve as models for others (see the study by Free, Kresge, and Foster for an earlier example).

rience of other farmers, will be the main stimulants to use, particularly by those who have had limited experience with fertilizer in the past.

Planning an effective fertilizer procurement and distribution program is a complex process. However, the payoffs in terms of increased production justify much attention to this subject.

SEED

Seed of high-yielding varieties is usually among the least costly of the important modern agricultural inputs. Yet in many countries few farmers have access to seed of established identity and of high viability and purity.

It is easy for governments to get into the seed business because they often own farms, recognize a need, and are not aware of other alternatives. Developing a seed production and supply system can rarely be done without some government involvement—especially when attempts are being made to make seed available quickly. However, private organizations can often be much more effective. Therefore, at an early stage a government should clearly identify the roles of other organizations and develop policies that will help them to fill those roles.

A brief listing of some major components of national seed supply efforts will reveal the nature and complexity of delivering to the farmers high-quality seed of improved varieties:

- *Identification of superior varieties.* Plant breeders in many countries are continually producing new varieties of scores of crops while countless farmers are selecting new strains of some crops, multiplying them, and distributing them to neighbors. One task of government is to test the performance of new strains in each season and in diverse regions. The task is complicated since time of planting, season, level of fertilizer use, and other factors affect performance. Resistance to diseases or insect pests may break down as new, more virulent strains of pathogens appear. The testing of varieties, a never-ending process, requires skill and judgment.
- *Production of breeder's and basic seed.* In the case of varieties recommended for farmer use, special efforts must be made to increase the "breeder's" seed (seed from the experiment station) in weed-free fields under conditions that allow highest yields, since rapid increase at this point is necessary. This seed must be carefully dried, treated against insect pests, and stored in moisture-proof containers. When a national program is at an early stage of development, most of this seed, especially that of cereal crops, can move directly to farmers for multiplication. Introductory techniques like mini-kits are often the start of such "seed increases." As later stages are reached, more seed is needed and additional multiplications are required; at this point, breeder's seed is

used only to give growers a source of new supplies of seed of assured identity and purity.

- *Production of seed for farmers.* Next the breeder's seed is sold or given to private growers or official seed farms for multiplication and sale to farmers.
- *Monitoring quality.* The farmer is vulnerable to purchases of crop seed of the wrong variety, seed that is old and will not germinate, and seed that is carrying weed seed or disease organisms. Good and bad seed may look much alike. If unscrupulous or careless sellers deliver a poor product, the farmer may not become aware of it until the crop fails to germinate or reach maturity. To protect farmers, governments should arrange for agencies independent of the seed producers to inspect the growing and processing of seed and to test seed for germination and purity—that is, to "certify" it as to identity and quality. In addition, many governments control quality at the marketing level. This can be done through legislation and, if administered well, can have a desirable effect on the quality of all seed sold and provide a double check on the quality of the certified seed. (Farmers of course will try to protect themselves by saving their own seed or buying from a trusted source.)
- *Getting seed to farmers.* Like fertilizers or pesticides, seed must be available to farmers on time and in the quantities required. A range of methods should be considered, including using trucks as mobile outlets, mini-kits, and supplying small farmers in groups.

Government or private seed industry? The relative role of public and private bodies will change as the seed industry evolves.

In the initial stages of development, identifying superior varieties is usually the task of plant breeders in universities or government agencies. In later stages, when private research is undertaken and private varieties are introduced, the relationships between government and private testing programs and use of results must be clarified.

Increasing breeder's or basic seed is the responsibility of the plant breeder when the seed program is in its early stages. As the nation's capability moves ahead, the plant breeder may find it desirable to share this responsibility with a special seed maintenance and multiplication unit or enterprise which handles publicly developed varieties.

Producing seed for farmers is not an activity in which government agencies normally have an inherent advantage. This step can be taken over by private producers or shared by them with public institutions. However, potential private producers have to be found, stimulated, informed, and sometimes financed. They must see some benefit to themselves before they become involved.

Monitoring seed quality and operating education and information programs is generally a government responsibility at all development stages.

Finally, getting seed widely used by farmers requires a decentralized delivery system or a series of systems. Wherever possible, that seed should be produced and sold on a competitive basis by private seed producers. They can be expected to maintain the quality of their products to obtain subsequent sales. The more successful seed enterprises work through a large number of distributors and dealers. These people get information to farmers about the advantages of the new varieties as well as about practices for achieving high yields. Marketing includes the entire range of activities from assessing demand to selling and delivering seed to farmers, a process with which many governments have difficulty. Too often government authorities misjudge demand, fail to arrange for the right amounts of seed of the best varieties to be produced, and do not get seed to each locality on time. They do not ordinarily have incentives to give seed supply the close attention it requires. Private companies do.

The seed industries of different countries range from mostly private to mostly public seed enterprises. Enterprises with varying degrees of involvement by private companies can, if well managed, ensure the successful production, processing, and marketing of an increasing quantity of good seed of improved varieties. International seed companies can strengthen national seed activities through distributorships, franchise arrangements, and joint ventures with local seed enterprises. This component is extremely weak in many countries.

The question of hybrids. For some crops, such as maize and sorghum, uniform, high-yielding hybrids can be produced. Seeds of hybrids are obtained by a complex breeding process which farmers cannot easily carry out. To maintain the potential yield advantages of hybrids, the farmer must plant new hybrid seed each year. If a farmer saves and plants seed harvested from his hybrid, his subsequent planting will be variable and lower in yield than the original hybrid. In Europe, North America, and some countries elsewhere, virtually all hybrid seed is produced and marketed by private companies (Chapter 8). They have been major forces in promoting both improved hybrids and better agronomic practices (to promote still greater sales of seed). These seed companies have been important catalysts of modernization.

Major difficulties appear with hybrids in some developing countries. The inbreeding and cross-breeding process is highly complex, requiring careful technical control. Many maize and sorghum producers have small holdings and are located in remote areas. Private companies often have difficulty selling large numbers of small lots of seed profitably since the cost per sale is high, but some, as in Kenya, have been successful (Chapter 8). Whenever hybrids are superior and farmers are willing to pay the price for them, seed enterprises that wish to develop and distribute hybrids should not be hampered by overregulation.

As an alternative to hybrids, high-yielding, open-pollinated varieties or synthetic varieties (composites) can be developed. Farmers can save and plant their own seed from these varieties. Synthetics and open-pollinated varieties are especially useful for farmers in remote areas. Even with these varieties some seed multiplication system is needed, not only for the initial introduction but also for the replacement of seed that has become mixed, destroyed, or consumed.

Quarantine agencies: Help or hindrance? Scientists often know the possible benefits to a country of introducing varieties or experimental strains of seed produced elsewhere. They usually are also aware of the dangers of bringing into the country new and serious plant and seed-borne diseases or insect pests. Thus they establish quarantine services to regulate the introduction of biological materials.

Quarantine services should be a help, not a hindrance, however. Too often, persons in charge of quarantine services view their mandate only as the protection of the country against unwanted organisms. Much more must be expected of them. Quarantine services, or the agencies of which they are a part, must be held responsible for safely and speedily introducing plant and animal materials important to the country. The services must not be allowed to take satisfaction from the amount of material they have destroyed (which is the easier course for those in charge); rather, they should be encouraged to take pride in the number of important stocks they have safely introduced. A panel of scientists, private seed producers, and government officials should review the actions of quarantine agencies regularly to be sure that these actions support rapid development.

Subsidize seed? Many official seed agencies produce seed and sell it to farmers at or below cost. If official seed sales are subsidized, the private sector cannot easily compete, and a deleterious public seed monopoly is encouraged. Seed costs should not be subsidized.

PESTICIDES AND HERBICIDES

With the use of high-yielding varieties, heavy fertilization, higher plant density, irrigation, and good management practices, plant growth usually is lush, providing a favorable environment for pests and pathogens. Weeds also respond to the high levels of fertilization and irrigation. While chemical control of pests or weeds may not be profitable at the low yields obtained through traditional practices, applications to intensely managed crops often pay handsome dividends (Chapter 7).

Insects can be controlled with pesticides in two general ways. The first approach, usually not recommended, is preventive or prophylactic treatment—applying insecticide at regular intervals regardless of whether there is an imminent or actual insect attack.

The second, and recommended, approach involves the application of insecticides known to have specificity to the target insect pests and minimum adverse side effects, but only when a serious infestation threatens. To be most effective, application must be made at the proper growth stage of the plant and at the appropriate life cycle stage of the insect.

When there are many small holdings growing photoperiod-insensitive varieties, as happens in the rice areas of Asia, planting and harvesting on adjacent fields are not likely to be uniformly timed. In these conditions, the effectiveness of blanket spraying of large areas is reduced.

On most small farms, capital is short. Pesticides or herbicides are usually expensive. Experiments indicate that chemical treatments vary greatly in effectiveness, being influenced by variety, season, and differences in cultural practices. Furthermore, the high variability of experimental results indicates that, with the little information now available in most developing countries, it is difficult to give farmers economically sound recommendations about insecticide application. In the absence of adequate data, the farmer must rely largely on previous experience. However, previous experience may not be a reliable guide if he is using new varieties and if higher levels of fertilizer application result in increased insect activity. For these reasons small farmers are understandably cautious in using insecticides.

Herbicide use will be influenced by its effectiveness and the relative cost of labor for hand weeding. Herbicides generally must be applied at particular times to be effective.

Pesticides and herbicides can have drawbacks. Some are toxic to animals and humans. This has particularly serious implications in those areas where fish are grown in combination with rice. By killing insects which are beneficial to agriculture, broad-spectrum pesticides disturb delicate ecological balances. Application often requires mechanical equipment, which is expensive to buy and difficult to maintain. Some pesticides tend to decompose slowly in soil and water.

Pesticides will, in spite of their shortcomings, be essential for high yields of crops in many regions for some time. In the long run, however, farmers will increasingly combine judicious chemical application with resistant varieties, steps to encourage insect predators, and careful tillage practices to repress harmful insects. This technique, called integrated pest control, will advance rapidly as scientists gain a better understanding of the vulnerable stages in insects' life cycles and as better, more specific chemicals are developed. Integrated pest control will greatly reduce the amount of toxicants the farmer applies each season.

Improvements in several other areas will permit farmers to use pesticides more effectively. Application techniques must be improved. Reliable, inexpensive hand applicators that can be manufactured domestically are needed. Early warning systems to spot increasing build-ups of pests and diseases should be organized (regional surveillance of wheat diseases in the Mideast is already under way).

As in the case of crop varieties, large numbers of new pesticides and herbicides continue to be produced by the world's laboratories. The value of such materials can be determined only by field tests, which are not easy to install or interpret. The role of government in ensuring safe use of farm chemicals should embrace:

- prompt field testing of materials for effectiveness and safety, and developing recommendations for farmers crop by crop, region by region;
- regulating the manufacture or import of materials; and
- encouraging the growth of decentralized delivery systems which will make approved pesticides and herbicides available when and where needed, in appropriate-size packages—together with fertilizers, seed, and other inputs—and with information on proper use.

The primary involvement of government with pesticides and herbicides should be to find ways to employ them safely and effectively to increase the productivity of the nation's agriculture. Field tests of chemicals normally will be the responsibility of scientists at experiment stations and production centers. Information on safety can be provided in part by manufacturers, who will have been required to file such information with the authorities of countries of manufacture, but safety should be confirmed in most cases in local experiments or through national or international research institutes.

IRRIGATION AND DRAINAGE

Water, like nitrogen, is one of the most limiting production factors in agriculture. There may be too little or too much, or it may be poorly distributed during the year. Availability of irrigation significantly influences the number and types of crops that are grown, the inputs that are used, and subsequently the total production achieved.

The basic strategy of water management for maximum agricultural production is to balance the supply of water available in the rooting zone with the moisture requirement of the crop. Crop water requirements often exhibit pronounced seasonality and are often out of phase with distribution of rainfall. During dry periods, the growing crop depends on moisture stored in soil near its roots. When water in the root zone is insufficient to meet crop needs, irrigation is required.

Crop varieties have specific water requirements. For example, the semi-dwarf wheat varieties are critically responsive to irrigation at two key periods: the crown root stage about 20 days after sowing, and the stage when grains are filling, during the usually hot, dry weather of later maturity. If needed, irrigation during either period can make a significant difference in yield. Rice varieties are quite sensitive to moisture stress, particularly during later stages of growth. Yield reduction can be expected whenever several weeks of drought occur. When water is inadequate, taller varieties with larger root systems may be better able to make use of available moisture in lower soil layers.

Most farmers understand well the importance of water. As the *Asian Agricultural Survey 1968* noted:

The component singled out by the Survey Team as being perhaps the most critical element for the future of Asian agriculture was the degree to which cultivators can control the water available to their crops on their own individual fields. This conclusion does not reflect the team's view alone. Asian farmers know it and wherever possible have invested personal capital in water lifting and spreading devices to provide better moisture control on their fields. But farmer action alone or with neighbors, cannot effect the construction of a system of ditches to remove excess water from river drainage areas, nor can it result in the building of a network of channels to bring water from canals and large reservoirs to individual fields. These are tasks that must be undertaken by the government.

The return to an investment in farm water control at the terminal point of a properly designed irrigation system can be very high. It will not come from the increased yield of a single crop that is obtained from precision irrigation and proper drainage, but far more from the capability it gives the cultivator to grow two or three crops per year. Water control at the farmer's field focuses attention on the yield per hectare per day, a concern that can be much more rewarding than the narrower stress on yield per hectare of a single crop.

The value which individual farmers place on irrigation is demonstrated by the large increase in privately financed tube wells that occurred along with the introduction of the new cereal varieties in the 1960s in northern India and Pakistan. Even in cases where canal water outlets ran to the fields, many farmers still invested in private wells. This investment indicated both the high returns available (often the tube wells would pay off in 2–3 years) and the inefficiency of public water distribution. Canal water is not available when rains are not adequate to fill rivers and reservoirs.[6] Furthermore, the distribution of public water is often characterized by favoritism and corruption. It is an advantage to have one's farm located at the beginning of the canal turnoffs, to know the gatekeeper or the person with the key to the tube well, or to have extra cash when water is critically needed. Therefore, farmers will often invest their own funds to ensure that they do not have to rely on others for water.

Drainage is equally important. Few crops can tolerate standing water

---

[6] Tube wells also may not always be a reliable source of irrigation when deficient rainfall lowers water tables or reduces the power generated by hydroelectric dams or when diesel fuel is not available or becomes very high priced.

for any sustained length of time. Even crops that can tolerate standing water require controlled levels in order to prosper. Periodic flooding and evaporation leave residues of salts which render soil useless for crop production. Removal of salty water requires subsurface drains. Standing water can serve as a breeding ground for mosquitoes or parasites.

Because drainage requires moving water from one field to land somewhere else, individual initiative is seldom effective in achieving more than shifting one person's problem to another. The government or affected landowners acting cooperatively must attack this problem on an area basis.

Design of systems. Definition of objectives is the first step in designing an irrigation and drainage system. In systems that have multiple goals, priorities must be assigned.

Five main factors condition the design and operation of an irrigation and drainage system: (1) the water sources available, (2) the topography of the land, (3) the nature of soils and climate, (4) the existing social structure and cultural values, and (5) the market opportunities for agricultural products. Available water sources will determine whether a public (dam or river) diversion or private (tube well or individual tank) scheme is to be employed. The topography of the land will dictate the ease with which the water could be delivered to and drained from the fields. The nature of soils, the amount and distribution of rainfall, and the temperature pattern will influence which crops are most suitable and what the most appropriate water delivery schedule will be. The social structure and cultural values will indicate the formal and informal patterns of farmer organization which might be employed and the cooperation and response to authority which might be expected. The market opportunities for agricultural products, in connection with the other factors, will influence the amount of expenditure which might go into construction of the irrigation system.

In the design of new systems, attention should be given to the full set of prerequisites for adoption of new higher-yielding agricultural systems by farmers. A frequent weakness of construction contracts for new dams and canals, designed by firms and water resources agencies, is that they pay only token attention to the other requirements for success. With the initiation of design of major dams and canals, work should also begin on field experiments to develop new cropping systems, on design of canals to deliver water to farmers' fields, on roads, on input and credit delivery and marketing systems, and on means of pricing water use. It may take as long (several years) to develop the agricultural systems and prepare other services as to build the dams and canals.

Redesigning or increasing the efficiency of an existing system is often more difficult. Farmers in the area have vested interests, and legal problems may be greater. Although the same series of questions might be asked as when designing a new system, the solutions could be quite different.

Pricing. In most countries, pricing policies for public irrigation water are economically unsound. Methods have been devised to provide rules for water pricing; in fact, there is a substantial body of literature on this subject. Furthermore, many physical and economic relationships in plant growth are well understood. Ways to minimize costs by not using too much water and to avoid reducing yields by applying too little water are known.

The problem of water pricing is largely that irrigation water is difficult to control and measure as it is delivered directly to the farmer's field. Systems in the humid tropics usually lack storage facilities; they often do not have enough water to adequately irrigate the entire area they are supposed to serve. In river diversion systems, the farmer irrigates when water is available. Those at the end of the turnoff are less likely to get water at all, and especially when they want it, than those at the head of the canal. Often, after the water leaves the canal it runs from one farmer's field to another, with availability being determined by the total amount of water and the relationships among farmers.

More control can be exercised in modern systems, allowing managers to allocate the limited water supply to the crops at their most vulnerable growth stages. However, to justify expenditures to pay for these systems, more effective ways must be developed to ensure that those who benefit most pay a greater share of the costs. There should be a high payoff from improving the efficiency of irrigation systems.

More importantly, water is a political subject. Long histories of low rates have been established. Farmer pressures make change difficult.

Government's role is threefold. First, it should seek to expand irrigation and drainage facilities, by itself or by encouraging private initiative, wherever this can economically lead to higher and more stable yields, giving attention to possibly adverse side effects such as salinization of the soil and increase in human diseases such as schistosomiasis. Second, it should ensure that construction of major works is accompanied by attention to all the other prerequisites for high payoff—the cropping systems and services—as well as by attention, where necessary, to stabilizing watersheds by reforestation. Third, wherever efficiency is low, delivery and drainage systems should be modernized.

LABOR AND MECHANIZATION

Mechanization of agriculture—the use of mechanical devices to replace human labor—is a controversial subject. It is not uncommon to find that large tractors, self-propelled combines, automated seed processing plants, and other "advanced" devices go unused in the countrysides of the poorer countries. Usually the machines were not suited to the small scale of the country's farms. Or the equipment lacked spare parts. Yet national governments continue to sanction imports, and assistance agencies, both bilateral and multilateral, continue to finance or otherwise supply them. The practice has derived in part from the widely held but erroneous assumption that large-scale mechanization, Western style, is desirable and even necessary for higher yields. After all, have not the U.S., Australia, and Canada developed the world's most productive types of agriculture through mechanized agriculture?

The issues. The traditional energy sources in rural areas have been human labor and draft animals. Some mechanization of farming is inevitable and desirable, and in fact is well under way in many areas. The fear is that mechanization will compete unduly with labor, leaving many rural people without employment. The real questions are how rapidly the process of mechanization should be allowed to occur and what types of mechanization will contribute most to rural employment and productivity of farming.

The technical argument for mechanization appears to be rather straightforward. It is claimed that the developing countries have low levels of horsepower per hectare and therefore have low yields. Increases in manpower and animal power will be gradual at best, and there is limited scope for introducing better animal or human tools. Budgeting studies often indicate that mechanization provides low-cost power and is profitable for farmers. Furthermore, the land released from growing fodder to feed draft animals can be used to grow other crops. Therefore mechanization must be encouraged.

The counterargument is usually based on present availability of both men and draft animals, their likely rates of increase, the importance of animals in the farming system, the presumably limited alternative use of labor in low-income countries, the high foreign-exchange costs of machinery imports, and difficulties in establishing domestic manufacturing.

Mechanization and productivity. Highly productive cropping systems, whether on small or large farms, multiple cropped or monocropped, can benefit from certain forms of mechanization. Careful field preparation, precise planting depths and fertilizer placement, and, frequently, timely cultivation and irrigation require mechanization. Mechanical threshers often give higher grain output. Artificial driers are needed when crops are harvested during wet seasons. Power is needed to permit the timely field preparation required for multiple cropping.

Small-scale modern farming. Many operations can be accomplished with small equipment. In some areas of the world, small farms produce high yields per hectare per year using "gardening" techniques. On these farms, with hand labor or two-wheel tractors and implements, farmers employ a wide variety of multiple-cropping practices to spread labor requirements and produce high annual yields and income per hectare. This type of agriculture is well developed in Japan, China, and parts of Europe. Since it is highly productive, it is modern.

Wherever opportunities exist for this type of high-yield agriculture, it is in the interest of the rural people, and of their governments, to stimulate it by encouraging mechanization tailored to the scale of the farming. The International Rice Research Institute, for example, has developed small harvesters, threshers, dryers, direct-seeding devices, pumps, and improved walking-type tractors. China and Japan have rice-transplanting machines. Such items can in large part be manufactured in most countries and are relatively easily maintained and repaired, creating opportunities for additional employment in rural trade centers. They are relatively easy to move in congested areas or on difficult terrain.

Large-scale modern farming. In some circumstances heavy machinery will be necessary. For example, in the prolonged dry season that occurs in parts of Southeast Asia, the hard soils cannot be plowed with animals or small tractors. Nor is subsoiling in any area possible with small implements. Land shaping is facilitated with land planes. Large irrigation and drainage systems may require high-volume pumps. In some countries, farmers may hire contractors who own heavy equipment to perform necessary services on a custom-servicing basis.

Medium- and large-scale mechanized farming gives high output per man-year and can also be highly productive per hectare. Farm operators with large holdings in developing countries often prefer to use labor-saving machinery, for a variety of reasons. First, it allows them to avoid dealing with large numbers of employees. Second, they can dominate large areas of land, achieving needed precision in operations. Third, they may be convinced it is the best and most productive way to farm. And fourth, some consider a mechanized farm to be an important status symbol. *But* the very large mechanized farm operation does little to enable large numbers of rural people to increase incomes, especially in densely populated poor agrarian countries. It may displace labor unnecessarily.

Mechanization and infrastructure. Heavy equipment is often also used for building roads, irrigation systems, and other rural public works. While efficient, it displaces labor. In densely populated poor areas, public works should when possible be constructed by labor-intensive methods to raise the purchasing power of the populace. Often the best solution will involve a compromise—some heavy equipment plus liberal use of labor.

Toward selective mechanization. Mechanization should be evaluated in terms of the needs of a country and the particular characteristics of a commodity; that is, it should be selective. Many variables should be considered in evaluating the impact on society of a single change in mechanization, including probable effects on area planted, crop mixtures and yields, costs of machinery and fuel, employment, saving of land previously used for animal feed, leisure, and income differences. None of the conclusions from the calculations will be certain until after they are carried out. While mechanization may substitute for labor in any single operation, an overall increase in demands for labor actually may occur due to increases in area cultivated, cropping intensity, or employment in small machine shops. When calculated in terms of costs and benefits to individual farmers, investments in tractors and other machines are often highly favorable. However, estimates of the impact on society (the social costs) may lead to quite different conclusions. Too often studies of mechanization, while using sophisticated techniques, rely on dubious data. Generalizations are too often based on isolated examples.

It is not our intention to argue against the use of large mechanized equipment when justified. Rather, for a country wishing to increase productivity and incomes of small farmers, the following questions should be asked each time imports of heavy farm equipment are proposed:

- Is the unit necessary to increase yield per hectare, or could the work be done as well with smaller, simpler units?
- Will it contribute to increased employment in rural areas, or is it primarily a labor-saving device?
- Can it be repaired in the country, and are spare parts readily available?

Only when there are affirmative answers to each of these questions should imports be encouraged.

Some general principles should be considered in designing a mechanization policy. First, the objectives of the policy should be clearly stated and be consistent with the more general agricultural development objectives of the country. Second, supporting data should be compiled from the country or region in which the mechanization is to take place, should cover a range of variables, and should reveal both short- and long-term effects. Finally, the full range of policies to guide the pace and nature of mechanization should be weighed. One obvious rule is that neither the exchange rate used to calculate the costs of parts or whole units nor the interest rate charged on loans to finance purchases should be subsidized.

Rural finance

Credit becomes important as a rural community moves from traditional toward modern stages of development—from a barter to a cash economy. Inputs must often be purchased with cash. A surprising amount of capital can be mobilized by the farmers themselves, either from their own funds or from informal sources—relatives or moneylenders—in response to profitable opportunities. However, many farmers, especially the smaller ones, may not have access to adequate financial resources. They must use other sources.

Credit should lubricate the production process for those unable to provide their own financing. Credit can also help people adjust to risk and uncertainty. The compelling incentive to borrow should be the expectation of higher profits—more than enough to cover the costs of the credit.

REQUIREMENTS FOR AN EFFECTIVE SYSTEM

There are *three* requirements for an effective rural financial system. First, farmers must have profitable investment opportunities. Such opportunities will exist if improved technologies, reasonably priced production inputs, attractive product prices, and accessible and stable markets are available (see Chapter 10).

Second, interest rates should be at or near levels in the commercial market. Interest is a cost—the cost of capital. The higher the interest rate, the higher the economic returns to cover this cost must be. The interest rate, like the cost of any other input, serves as an allocating mechanism, in this case encouraging or discouraging investments which have a capital component.

Third, financial services should be made available to all persons. Rules governing rural credit should be no different from those governing credit in general. The main differences are ones of degree—such as the nature of the risks (from weather, etc.), the seasonality of production, and the large numbers and small sizes of the borrowers.

Concessional rates? Credit rates are concessional if they are set at levels which are below those for alternative uses of the money or, if inflation is significant, at negative real levels. Highly concessional rural credit rates have numerous shortcomings. They shift credit away from agriculture in general and from small farmers in particular. They encourage relatively unproductive activity. They result in unfair competition with private sources. They reduce income opportunities for the rural poor.

Concessional interest rates often result in demands for credit which could exhaust available funds. Bigger borrowers take out a large proportion of these loans. They have numerous opportunities to invest funds at high returns, often in nonagricultural uses. They are often slow in repaying. Little is left for smaller borrowers, who are in weaker positions to compete because they have less influence.

Substantial amounts of savings can be tapped from the rural community, even from small farmers, if the appropriate incentives are given. Savings banks are one of the few alternatives the rural poor have available to increase their money. The poor may not use rural banks if they receive a rate of return that is lower than rates of inflation. As a result, they spend their money on consumption goods. The affluent have a greater range of alternatives for use of their surplus money.

The unproductive farmer usually cannot be helped by credit, concessionally priced or not. Once concessional rates are introduced, political pressures become strong to retain them. Flexible interest rates can be an effective antiinflationary measure when combined with a restrictive fiscal policy. The better ways to subsidize weaker farmers are through improved technologies, support prices for major products, technical assistance, and better access to markets—not through inflexible and concessional interest rates.

Biases against small farmers. Bankers fear that chances for default are higher for smaller farmers. Therefore rules are often instituted to husband the available funds, ostensibly to ensure that they are used to increase agricultural production and to increase the security of the loans. Borrowing is restricted to loans to increase production; that is, loans for consumption are denied. Loans are given in the form of vouchers redeemable for fertilizer or insecticides rather than in cash. Minimum loan levels are established. Collateral is required.

More subtle restrictive measures also are employed. The farmer may be required to file a farm plan. He may have to have his fields inspected periodically to receive advice from bank-employed technical assistance agents—and he may have to pay for the advice. He may have to fill out complex papers. He may have to make several trips to the bank. He may even have to pay bribes.

The common factor in all these restrictive practices is that they usually do not increase production. For example, loans in the form of production goods (fertilizer, seed, etc.) or vouchers can easily be converted to cash to buy consumer goods or invest in nonfarm businesses. The restrictive practices also generally work to the disadvantage of small farmers. Smaller farmers have limited collateral; tenants often have none. The noninterest "costs" of compiling farm plans, visiting the bank, etc., may be so large to the borrower as to negate the supposed advantage of concessional rates. Supervised credit often is not helpful to the small farmer. Farm plans, for example, are useful in theory but seldom are carried out seriously. Technical assistance should be a normal function of government; it should not be restricted to bigger farmers and should not be an additional cost attached to a small farmer's loan. Government loan insurance should be available to protect against production losses due to weather or insects.

If interest rates are flexible and more or less reflect market levels, and if the supply of funds is adequate, there is no need to ration funds to ensure that they are used for productive purposes or that small farmers have access. Funds will be used for purposes which promise to pay high returns—which would be agricultural production if the four requisites for adoption by farmers are operative. The bigger borrowers would be discouraged by market forces; that is, they would gain no special advantages by borrowing from the rural banks and overusing rural credit resources.

Default. There are two primary causes of default. Often the borrower is unable to repay because his investment turned out to be unprofitable. Sometimes, however, the borrower is unwilling to repay even though able to do so. The borrower may think that he is getting money from some vague source, such as the government, and may feel no obligation to repay. For political reasons, governments are often reluctant to press farmers for repayment. If, however, the savings that finance his loans come in part from his own funds and those of his peers, he may feel more obligated to repay and he would probably be subjected to considerable social pressure to do so. In short, if a good credit rating is worth something to him, the farmer will repay. One way to improve loan collection is to send mobile banks to the farmers' fields at the time of harvest; they reduce the costs to the farmer by facilitating repayment while he still has income from the harvest. Small farmers do not necessarily default at higher levels than large borrowers, and repayment is seldom related to collateral.

PUBLIC OR PRIVATE?

No type of operation, public or private, is demonstrably superior to others on all counts. Often private sources are able to supply most, if not all, of the credit necessary to achieve modernization. These private sources are flexible in operation and fit smoothly into the sociological and cultural realities of rural life. They may cost the borrower less than bank credit.

Government credit sources can improve credit markets by introducing another element of competition. Their presence can help to exploit the existing strengths and shore up the weak points in the private system. They can play this constructive role, however, only if they operate under conditions similar to those of other suppliers of credit, including the offering of credit at rates and with terms which reflect underlying economic conditions.

GROUPS

Credit can play another role in agricultural development programs by serving as the impetus for farmers to form groups. That role can be as valuable to total development results as use of the credit itself. Individually, small farmers have limited bargaining power with banks and other agricultural service organizations. Generally farmers place high priority on credit needed to gain access to the resources that will improve their livelihood. They are willing to work collectively to improve their bargaining power to obtain that credit. Groups reduce borrower costs. Groups provide means of pooling collateral. Group self-discipline can enforce better repayment of loans. Groups reduce lender costs. Once groups are formed, they provide a convenient way for technical assistance agents to reach many people quickly. Borrowers are generally receptive to technical advice because they must raise their incomes to repay their old loans and get new ones.

Groups soon realize that their bargaining power can be used to bring about changes in distribution of fertilizers and pesticides, in access to markets, in education and health care, and even in availability of longer-term loans to finance capital improvements on their farms.

There is no simple prescription for forming groups; in fact, formal or informal groups already exist in some areas. The nature of the organization must be dictated by the societal rules which prevail. Some rural societies are too individualistic and competitive, while others may be too permissive to enforce the discipline required.

In organizing groups, special attention must be paid to small farmers, who most need to be in groups. The more progressive farmers are often the ones who need least to be in groups. Once groups are formed, care must be taken to avoid having them captured by the elites.

One difficulty to anticipate is that groups may form the basis of political movements which may not be welcomed by the political powers of the country. If the ruling powers consider them a threat, groups will be difficult to organize. If the ruling powers use the groups for partisan political ends, their contribution to agricultural development can be severely diluted.

These difficulties notwithstanding, farmer groups organized initially to gain better access to credit represent a tremendous potential force for agricultural progress.[7]

---

[7] See the discussions of Comilla and Puebla in Chapter 8.

Rural finance in Asia

The 1976 Asian Agricultural Survey, conducted under the auspices of the Asian Development Bank, revealed that during the past decade "there have been many innovations and encouraging developments in the financing of agriculture."

First, national credit networks have expanded. From 1969 to 1975, India's commercial banks opened 5,000 new branches in rural centers. Branches of the Peoples Bank in Sri Lanka increased from 27 in 1967 to 340 in early 1976. Since 1965, 520 rural banks have been established in the Philippines, serving about 60 percent of the municipalities; since 1973 the Philippine National Bank has set up over 100 branches.

Second, lending for agriculture has expanded. During 1968–74 in India, such lending increased 32-fold, from 257 million rupees to 8,300 million. During 1965–75, rural banks in the Philippines increased lending 10-fold. During 1970–74, the Peoples Bank in Sri Lanka more than doubled its credits.

Third, there have been changes in the practices and policies of the credit agencies. Prior to 1970 most banks required collateral—usually land—for loans to farmers. This "discriminated against small and landless farmers, who consequently did not have much access to institutional credit." Now "status as cultivator is normally the only requirement to obtain short-term institutional credit." Institutions can now loan the full amount of money needed to cover production costs.

Fourth, since the early 1970s a number of governments have been designing credit strategies to benefit small farmers, and have provided incentives or mandates to banks to participate. Some banks are now required to lend a prescribed proportion of their funds to agriculture, or to open a certain number of rural branches for each new urban branch.

Marketing

While national authorities usually recognize that farmers need seeds, fertilizers, pesticides, and technical information, they sometimes overlook the need for vigorous markets. Production of a surplus makes sense for a farmer only if a market for the surplus exists, if he has ready access to that market, and if, with his income, he can purchase items that he desires. This commercial market place is different from one where subsistence farmers barter bits of surplus for a limited range of products. As increasing numbers of farms in an area are commercialized, the resulting output will usually exceed that which can be sold to other people in the same area.

A commercial farmer must be able to sell in a market which is reliable and which is connected with more distant consumption centers. Such a market should also offer commercial agricultural inputs and should be close enough to the farmer that he can reach it, do his marketing and purchasing, and return home within the day, using whatever means of transport is normal.

MARKET PLANNING

Economic development is accompanied by rising per capita incomes. Since some of the additional income is spent on food, the total demand for food rises more rapidly than the rate of population growth. Furthermore, since the increase in numbers and incomes of people is generally more rapid in urban centers than in rural areas, growth of urban demand for food is higher than the average for the country. Therefore, prices are bid up and incentives are created for farmers to sell more. Commodities will, if possible, be produced for sale in seasons when prices are highest. New facilities will be required, such as dryers for rice harvested during the rainy season in Asia. The presence of processing facilities can be a major influence on the introduction of new crops or products. The input and product marketing systems will be placed under mounting pressure to facilitate future growth in agricultural production.

In any country or region the question must be asked: Where will future bottlenecks appear and what can be done to reduce their interference with an orderly and increasing flow of goods? Needed facilities will involve large fixed capital investments. Projections of future regional cropping patterns and growth rates, which might guide the placement of these facilities, can only be approximate. Short-run changes must be made within a longer-run context to avoid practices or investments which, once adopted, would interfere with handling larger volumes and different types of goods and services than those currently marketed.

Effectiveness of the private market. Studies of marketing systems in Asia, Africa, and Latin America indicate that, at existing levels of production, private marketing systems are surprisingly effective. Prices in the markets appear to be influenced by aggregate supply and demand for the region and country. Price differences from one market to another infrequently exceed transportation costs by a large margin (when large differences occur they are usually due to the availability of small volumes during the off-seasons, during times of shortage, or when the government has artificially restricted commodity movements). While prices in the off-season are usually higher than at harvest time, the differences seldom exceed storage costs substantially (costs which include charges for the high interest rates and high rates of loss prevailing in low-income countries). On the average, the profits from holding commodities do not appear to be excessive for the management performed and the risk assumed. In markets that have large numbers of small traders, evidence of price rigging is remarkably rare, although there are some notable monopolies of some perishable products (for example, potatoes). Studies of marketing margins reveal that the share of the retail price going to the wholesaler (above transportation and storage costs and market fees) is usually small.

Thus, the private marketing systems appear to operate effectively *in the absence of monopolies.* Imperfections in the private marketing system seem to be largely due to inherent uncertainties of supply and demand and to seasonal scarcities of stocks. These uncertainties arise from forces over which private traders have limited control. However, even in normal times and especially in times of extreme shortage or of rapid growth in production, problems do appear which may require government intervention.

Information. Perhaps the first place for government intervention is to ensure that market information that meets reasonable standards of accuracy, timeliness, and coverage is widely available. In most countries, informal systems among traders provide market news, usually quite accurately. Some traders, however, are excluded from the informal systems, and therefore suffer a disadvantage. Moreover, market news often is not available to the farmers, so they have difficulty finding the best market and best time to get the highest price for their products.

Government crop reporting services in most developing countries must by necessity rely heavily on informed impressions rather than on precise data. Even national production and consumption statistics are often only approximate. Accurate data on marketing qualities, quantities, and prices can provide a proxy for production data and give a range of information which is necessary for formulating policy intelligently at regional and national levels. Information should be collected in each significant market and disseminated widely and frequently. It should include data on the amount of major commodities traded or available in the market place, with values (prices) given in standardized units and quantities.

Regulation. It is equally important to ensure that practices such as weighing and market charges are honest in every market. Such regulative action can often be carried out by committees composed of representatives of the different participants within the markets. However, government officials must ensure that these local regulatory committees do protect the rights of all participants and do carry out uniform practices from one market to another.

Managerial and institutional innovations. The marketing system, while functioning with large numbers of competitors and reasonably efficient prices, may be improved by managerial and institutional innovations. The wholesaling and retailing levels especially are subject to rapid technological change. Extension and education programs aimed at improving behavior and efficiency at these levels could have significant payoffs.

Storage. There are few accurate estimates of waste, including losses in storage and in marketing. Undoubtedly, rodent and insect damage is sizeable since much storage is unprotected. In low-income countries, however, estimates of waste must be interpreted with caution. Much of what is "wasted" is actually downgraded in quality and gleaned by humans or sold as animal feed. Many of the high estimates of waste are reported by self-serving persons anxious to promote their own programs. Moreover, many schemes that are suggested to reduce waste are not economical—they cost more than the losses. Nevertheless, modern storage is necessary in improving marketing systems. In fact, better storage is probably one of the fastest ways to increase food availability in the short run.

The private trade should be expected to build many of the required storage facilities. Farmers can be encouraged to construct small, inexpensive structures to protect grain from insects and molds on their own farms or cooperatively. This will improve their ability to take advantage of seasonal increases in prices. Technical assistance should be made available in construction. Credit should be made available to permit smaller farmers to build or purchase such structures.

Storage must also be provided by the public sector for buffer stocks and food distribution programs. Planning for public storage must take into account expected regional crop production patterns, seasonal peaks in procurement and public distribution, the expected normal uncertainties in foodgrain distribution, and expected private construction. The greater the availability of public storage and the potential competition by public stocks, the less the incentive will be for private construction. Therefore, the desired future balance between public and private stocks must be weighed carefully.

Transportation. To participate in market-oriented, intensive agriculture, each farm must be linked with the national transportation system of major roads, railways, and waterways. A. T. Mosher notes that "almost all discussions of transportation in developmental literature deal with highways connecting district centers with each other and to major cities and seaports." But, "by a large margin, the biggest task in achieving a Progressive Rural Structure whether in terms of the magnitude of the physical construction involved or in terms of cost, is the construction of rural roads." Accessibility of farms to markets, and vice versa, is a major influence on the adoption by farmers of new, more intensive farming systems and is perhaps even more important than other factors such as size of farm and educational level of the farmer. A farmer with only a few

"Roads are essential to agricultural growth but they also serve other aspects of rural welfare by increasing the ease of human mobility and the mobility of all types of governmental services. In addition, they broaden the market for industrially produced consumer goods, they encourage the dispersion throughout rural areas of small-scale industries, and they play a major role in national political and social integration. . . . And because so many purposes are served by a national transportation system, it is not justifiable to count all of the costs of rural roads as an investment in agriculture."

A. T. Mosher
Creating a Progressive Rural Structure

hectares may have to move *tons* of goods if he adopts new technology. Being within, say, a day's *walk* of a market is not enough. There must be roadways of some type and some means of moving produce over them.

A growing volume of inputs and products will require expanded road networks and better market-to-market transportation. Some observers believe that if farm-to-market roads are economically justifiable, they will be built and maintained by the villagers themselves. However, farms are also markets for products of urban industry, and the existence of rural roads can help lower costs of farm products in urban areas. In other words, roads benefit all of society. Market-to-market roads and, usually, farm-to-market roads should be public responsibilities. Transportation for agriculture is integral to overall economic development and must be evaluated accordingly. In numerous countries, investments in roads have greatly narrowed farm-retail margins.

Quality standards. Within a developing country the market place usually does not offer a large price premium for higher-quality domestically produced commodities. For example, consumers in a rice-producing nation pay little more for rice with 5 percent broken grains than they do for rice with 15 percent broken grains. In a country's export trade, however, quality standards may be highly important because buyers need to compare the products of many different sellers, who are often in different countries. In that case the differences in price from one grade to another can be large. Quality of final product can be influenced by drying, threshing, and cleaning practices before the product is marketed; for example, proper drying will reduce breakage of rice grain during milling. In such cases, price premiums can be offered to stimulate the producer to improve quality. Careful processing procedures, establishment of grades, and proper storage also can be important to provision of a high-quality final product.

Employment. The marketing systems in most developing countries can be labor intensive. While one objective of modernizing marketing is to lower costs, another objective should be to maintain or, better, to increase the employment opportunities within the system. Road-building projects should use the substantial amounts of labor available in rural areas. Increased market scale need not be achieved through capital-intensive methods. Losses in bag-storage facilities, which employ many workers, can be kept as low as those in giant mechanized grain silos. But there must be advance planning if labor is to be used effectively.

Comprehensiveness of reforms. The marketing system extends from the farmer's field through the various selling and processing levels, to the retail level, and finally to the consumer's table. While change at any level to improve operations should not be discouraged, the greatest returns will often result from comprehensive examination of the entire system followed by a planned program of changes at all levels.

Commodity price policy

Farmers require adequate economic incentives to produce agricultural commodities beyond their own subsistence needs. The costs of production, the amounts produced, and the prices received for production determine profits. Since the effects of weather, disease, and insects are not known beforehand, the farmer's expectations of production and prices received must be discounted for the risks he may face.

The basic forces of supply and demand, even in an adequate marketing system, may not be generating progress toward development objectives as fast as policymakers would like. Governments may therefore attempt to influence farmers' profits to improve production performance by manipulating: (1) the general level of aggregate agricultural prices, which influence input/output price relationships to producers and real income to consumers; (2) the relative prices among agricultural commodities, which influence the allocation of land and other inputs among crops; and (3) the stability of prices, which influences risk.

STIMULATION OF CHANGE

In traditional agriculture, where few inputs other than land, family labor, draft animals, and seed are used and little is marketed, prices of agricultural inputs and products do not influence total production greatly. Farm resources generally are fully employed. Exceptions include fallow land, which could be brought into cultivation, and the digging of shallow wells for irrigation.

"Whether in Taiwan, the Philippines, Thailand, Burma or other developing countries, farmers respond most of all to the price their produce brings. To assume farmers can be encouraged to expand production without it being profitable is one of the most serious miscalculations in government policy. Understandably, governments are anxious to protect the consumer by controlling the price of rice. And city dwellers are more articulate, organized, and closer to the center of decision-making than farmers. As prices of petroleum products, fertilizer and insecticides have escalated during the past 3½ years, farmers' costs have risen radically. Unless governments recognize promptly the diminishing economic margin available to farmers, Asia's grain production will be crippled. The alternatives of subsidy for farm inputs or gradually rising prices for consumers are neither one attractive. Yet, the controlling principle must be maximizing production."

Ramon Magsaysay Award Foundation
Food Crisis Workshop

When a new high-yielding technology (requiring inputs which must be purchased) is available, price policy becomes substantially more important in influencing farmers to increase output. Prices of farm products must be high enough to allow farmers to use purchased inputs profitably and stable enough to encourage long-term investments in land, water improvement, buildings, equipment, and transport.

In situations of prospective technological change, planners should analyze farmer profits to determine whether existing prices encourage farmers to use improved technologies. *If* the price levels are not adequate, *if* investigations yield reasonable assurances that the farmers will respond by adopting improved technolgies, and *if* the government is confident that it can withstand consumer pressures until the time that increased productivity brings down prices, then policymakers should consider raising the level and improving the stability of prices, or of providing input subsidies.

INPUT SUBSIDIES OR HIGHER PRODUCT PRICES?

The terms of trade for the producer may be changed by lowering input prices or raising product prices. Each course of action has positive as well as negative features.

The advantage of subsidizing inputs the farmer buys, such as fertilizers, pesticides, equipment, and livestock, rather than raising the prices of products he sells is that the cost of the former is directly related to the use of practices that increase productivity. The cultivator must buy and use inputs to reap advantage from input subsidies. The cost to the economy of increasing agricultural output through input subsidies is likely to be lower and can be borne through the tax system.

However, as purchasable inputs become more widely used, the costs of subsidies mount. A further disadvantage is that the impact of input price subsidies on different crops cannot be controlled. For example, a subsidy on fertilizer may ensure that more fertilizer is used, but it cannot direct the added fertilizer to a specific crop. Thus input subsidies are a dull policy tool.

Additionally, input subsidies discourage private dealers. In developed countries, one of the more effective methods of getting technical information to farmers is through private input distributors. If the price margin on input distribution is cut too narrowly, the input distributor cannot afford to spend the time and hire the assistance necessary to provide that technical information. Therefore, the quality of his services may suffer, and consequently the farmer's interest in buying inputs may diminish. Some people believe that promotional activities are much more important than price in stimulating farmers to use the new inputs.

Input prices are frequently "administered prices," which change only occasionally, while product prices fluctuate with market forces. Consequently the uncertainty facing cultivators is reduced more if product prices are supported. Also, inputs are purchased at the beginning of the production cycle, so their prices are known at the decision time, while product prices at harvest time can only be predicted. Offering input subsidies does not change this situation. If product price supports are offered, however, both input and product prices have a high degree of certainty at the decision time.

Furthermore, price support policy can help the government meet its responsibility for food supplies in urban areas. A food consumption policy which incorporates product price supports can contribute to meeting the objectives of increased production and increased supply to the towns and cities, with accompanying savings in scarce administrative talent.

For these reasons the weight of the argument clearly seems to favor product price supports coupled with continued efforts to reduce input costs through greater production and marketing efficiencies.

IMPLEMENTATION OF PRICE SUPPORTS

In food-deficit countries, if imports are restricted, market prices often rise enough to give remunerative returns and encourage farmer response. Greater price stability to counter the effects of production changes brought about by weather will be the primary requirement to provide price incentives to increase production. Government intervention to support prices at a minimum level may be desirable in years of bumper crops and to stabilize prices at a maximum level in years of poor production. Any price support and stabilization program should focus on only a few major crops and should be planned for the long run.

New technologies should lower costs per kilogram of production, so commodity price levels should eventually decline. Long-run price relationships should be formulated so that nonadopters in the initial stages, many of whom will be small farmers, are encouraged to participate later.

Once production does begin to rise rapidly, support prices should provide risk insurance (primarily to counter variations in weather), protecting only variable or cash costs of production rather than full costs of production. Acceptance of this long-run role for support prices will permit the price structure to move toward equilibrium as directed by basic supply and demand forces and permit the required transfer of resources into the nonagricultural sectors. This policy will ensure continuing pressure toward efficiency and introduction of cost-reducing technology and will lighten the otherwise growing load of supporting agricultural prices.

Prices influence the distribution of income of both producers and consumers, effects that sometimes are not obvious. For example, higher prices benefit farmers in relation to the quantities of produce they sell. Large farmers generally market far greater portions of their additional food-crop output than do smaller farmers. Higher prices reduce the real incomes of consumers, especially hurting low-income consumers (including small farmers who do not produce all of their consumption needs), who spend a large proportion of their income on food. Therefore, policies that raise prices in the short run above levels reached under normal market conditions are justified only if in the long run production can be expected to increase significantly.

Criteria for establishing price levels. Levels of support prices can be calculated in several ways. Each has advantages and disadvantages, so a combination of methods should be used. Several criteria can be used to evaluate the most appropriate combination. First, the technique should be forward-looking so that the price support can be calculated and announced in advance of cultivators' investment decisions (for example, before planting time). Second, the technique must be responsive to changes in production technology so that as new technology is introduced and unit costs of production fall, prices are not held artificially high. Third, the technique must be objectively defined so that no interest group gets a stranglehold on prices and so that prices can be revised to reflect economic changes.

A moving average, constructed by dividing the most recent few years of prevailing market prices by input costs, provides a simple parity index when related to a suitable base period. Statistical surveys or synthesized farm budgets can provide additional information on farmer costs. World prices corrected for exchange rates provide a check against price levels in other countries. Finally, the cost to the national budget must be evaluated.

Timing. To be effective, the support prices should be set each season before crops are sown and they should be maintained for the entire season. If supply begins to build up, this may be an economic signal to lower the support price; the reverse might be indicated by a depletion of stocks. But any adjustments must be made for the *next* crop season, not for the one in progress. The penalty for failure to observe that principle is loss of faith in government.

Regional price differentials. A basic national support price should be set with allowances being made for regional price differences based on transportation costs. In this way, economic forces will be free to allocate the area sown to various crops over the country depending on the relative profitabilities in different locations.

UPPER LEVELS

Perhaps the safest thing that can be said regarding increases in crop prices is that flexibility must be permitted. If a rigid upper limit is maintained at harvest time (for example, the level of the previous year) and supply falls by 20 percent, then producers' incomes will fall by 20 percent. The other extreme, allowing prices at harvest time to rise 20 percent above the "normal" level, would increase producers' incomes and shift the whole burden onto consumers, whose real incomes would suffer. In the long run in a period of rising production, some of the gains in productivity should be passed on to consumers. Therefore, some trade-off between producer and consumer interests is required.

Seasonally, prices must be allowed to rise above the harvest price at least enough to cover holding costs—storage, interest, etc. An adequate adjustment for risk should be added to these holding costs. Traders have difficulty estimating how much they should store. Some years the seasonal price increases do not cover storage, and traders suffer losses. They must balance these losses with larger-than-minimum profits in other years to at least break even over time. Otherwise, private traders will be driven from business, and government will be forced to assume the entire burden of distribution.

BUFFER STOCKS

A buffer-stock program operated in conjunction with price supports and a public foodgrains distribution system can be a major instrument of food and agricultural policy in a developing country's struggle for freedom from hunger.

To encourage responsible development of the private market, the government should function as the buyer of last resort. If the support price is too high, the government will buy most of the foodgrains marketed; if it is set too low, the government will purchase little. Therefore, the support price should be used primarily for production incentives, and another policy tool may be needed to procure necessary volumes of foodgrains for distribution. Imports are one option, especially for smaller countries. Expecting support prices to fulfill too many objectives has led to unwarranted frustration with the price support concept, some undue conservatism in recommended price support levels, and a reliance on compulsory levies to procure food required for public distribution.

Similarly the government should be the supplier of food to consumers only as a last resort. Supplementary feeding programs to improve nutrition among groups whose incomes are too low to purchase sufficient food are needed in most developing countries. Such programs can provide a reasonably predictable and steady means for reducing excess stocks accumulated under price support programs. Distribution to stabilize prices, primarily in cities and towns, should increase only during periods of shortage.

A public buffer-stock scheme in any country is costly and complex to operate. Coordination is essential. One group must have overall authority to produce, import, transfer, stock, and distribute foodgrains as needs dictate. An effective information system must be developed to report production prospects, daily market arrivals, dispatches, prices, transport availabilities, and storage at key points. It will strengthen the basic marketing system. That is an additional advantage of a buffer-stock scheme.

Rural centering

The economic landscapes of subsistence and commercial agriculture are significantly different. Subsistence agriculture consists largely of similar villages, periodic markets at which farmers exchange their small surpluses, and a few large cities at export/import points or government centers. In commercial agriculture, there must be a central market in each agricultural area around which cluster other activities such as agricultural processing, motor vehicle servicing, schools, health care facilities, and commercial stores of various types. The central market town is clearly different from villages in that it provides a location for most of these activities. The central town is also the only likely alternative to the cities for people who move out of agriculture. As the rural areas become increasingly prosperous, the towns provide numerous occupations not available in the relatively undifferentiated villages, where almost everyone works in agriculture.

The development of the central town in each agricultural area is a natural phenomenon, but it is also one which can be encouraged by government action. As the central place achieves a certain mass, new activities become economical and the process of growth can be self-generating. If the government knows which are most likely to be the central towns, it can locate government service facilities there. This will encourage the private sector to invest in a wider range of activities in the town.

Numerous studies of Western experience have revealed a close relationship of areas of high agricultural progress to industrialization and urbanization. Proximity to urban/industrial areas provides the agricultural activity with several advantages. Commercialization is hastened. There are ready cash markets. Production inputs are more likely to be available to the cultivator at the time and place and in the quantity he needs.

The market is a convenient place to mobilize labor. The agricultural sector is the residual employer. People move from farm to market frequently. If markets are conveniently located, a large potential labor force which resides on the farms is readily available for nonagricultural employment in market centers on a seasonal, if not year-round, basis. Dispersion of small agro-industries, factories, and other labor-intensive activities to market towns is a way to employ either year-round or seasonal surplus labor. This labor can also be used for rural works in the immediate area.

The market is also a convenient place to mobilize financial capital. It is where goods are exchanged for money. Vigorously led financial institutions in market towns can provide a place for rural people to invest their money. They can provide credit to finance needed agricultural purchases. Furthermore, these institutions can channel financial resources to nonagricultural activities when that is appropriate.

Finally, the market town, because it has a high population density, is a convenient place for a variety of services. Availability of credit can permit purchases to be made before production begins. Technical information may be supplied, either through commercial or government channels. Other services including education, health, family planning, and entertainment induce the cultivator to participate in town activities.

A basic objective of agricultural development is to increase the commercialization of agriculture. The concept of market planning integrates input supply, product sales, credit, extension, industrial and commercial activity, and services. Distance dictates the growth patterns of markets. Each market's influence radiates outward. As the distance from one market increases, competition from other markets increases. Field studies can identify key locations for building centers of activity to promote a multiplier effect on growth.

Ludhiana and Coimbatore in India, although obviously not planned for such a purpose, are examples of this process of rural centering. Towns radiating outward from these larger cities serve as intermediate links to rural areas.

This approach to market planning might be integrated into a policy to attack the broader spatial dimension of agricultural development. Interregional equity is often explicitly stated as a development target. Road construction, transportation structure, urbanization policy, price support programs, and location of irrigation, storage, and processing facilities all influence future regional growth patterns. For example, sugar-crushing and -refining mills in one part of a country ensure that a substantial volume of sugar will continue to be grown in that area in the future. The location of starch industries can influence maize production. The presence of an oilseed-solvent plant affects the concentration of soybean plantings.

In view of inevitable changes in market development, great opportunities exist to strengthen market towns as part of an integrated agricultural development strategy.

Summary

Production of a marketable surplus is sensible for a farmer only if there is a market offering incentive prices for that surplus, if he has ready access to that market, and if he can purchase items that he desires with his income in that market. The private sector generally carries out marketing functions remarkably effectively. The government can substantially improve the effectiveness of private marketing by regulating practices, improving information, encouraging construction of private storage facilities, and investing in roads, markets, and storage.

Technological advances alone cannot secure the sustained agricultural change which will benefit large numbers of the rural poor. Institutional framework and economic incentives must encourage adoption of improved technologies to the point of achieving the full potential gain.

Agricultural service organizations must be responsive to the needs of producers and, in the case of the marketing system, to the needs of consumers. Price policies must be development oriented.

The means by which to achieve a proper economic environment will differ from country to country and from time to time. In this chapter we have attempted to identify the major considerations for promoting such an environment.

References

INPUT AVAILABILITY AND DISTRIBUTION

Asian Development Bank. *Asian Agricultural Survey 1968*. Manila: Asian Development Bank, 1968.

Centro Internacional de Mejoramiento de Maiz y Trigo. *The Puebla Project: Seven Years of Experience (1967–1973)*. El Batan, Mexico: Centro Internacional de Mejoramiento de Maiz y Trigo, 1975.

Dalrymple, Dana G. *Evaluating Fertilizer Subsidies in Developing Countries*. AID Discussion Paper No. 30. Washington, D.C.: U.S. Agency for International Development, Bureau for Program and Policy Coordination, 1975.

Free, Joe; Kresge, Conrad; and Foster, Thomas H. *Dominican Republic Fertilizer Situation*. Bulletin Y-103. Muscle Shoals, Ala.: National Fertilizer Development Center, Tennessee Valley Authority, January 1976.

Gemill, Gordon, and Eicher, Carl. *The Economics of Farm Mechanization and Processing in Developing Countries*. Research & Training Network Seminar Report No. 4. New York: Agricultural Development Council, December 1973.

Harre, E. A.; Livingston, Owen W.; and Shields, John, T. *World Fertilizer Market Review and Outlook*. Bulletin Y-70. Muscle Shoals, Ala.: National Fertilizer Development Center, Tennessee Valley Authority, March 1974.

Hopper, W. David. "The Economics of Fertilizer Use—A Case Study in Production Economics." *Indian Journal of Agricultural Economics* 17 (1962): 12–22.

Lazaro, Rogelio C.; Taylor, Donald C.; and Wickham, Thomas H. *Irrigation Systems in Southeast Asia: Policy and Management Issues*. Singapore: Singapore University Press, 1977.

Levine, G.; Capener, H.; and Gore, P. *The Management of Irrigation Systems*. Research & Training Network Seminar Report No. 2. New York: Agricultural Development Council, August 1973.

Merrill, William C. *The Impact of Agricultural Mechanization on Employment and Food Production*. Economics and Sector Planning Division Occasional Paper No. 1. Washington, D.C.: U.S. Agency for International Development, Technical Assistance Bureau, September 1975.

Perrin, Richard K.; Winkelmann, Donald L.; Moscardi, Edgardo R.; and Anderson, Jock R. *From Agronomic Data to Farmer Recommendations: An Economics Training Manual*. El Batan, Mexico: Centro Internacional de Mejoramiento de Maiz y Trigo, 1976.

Ruttan, Vernon W. "Agricultural Product and Factor Markets in Southeast Asia." *Economic Development and Cultural Change* 17 (1969): 501–19.

Shields, John T. "Estimating Fertilizer Demand." *Food Policy* 1 (1976): 333–41.

Timmer, C. Peter. "The Demand for Fertilizer in Developing Countries." *Food Research Institute Studies* 13 (1974): 197–224.

RURAL FINANCE

Adams, D. W. "Policy Issues in Rural Finance and Development." Mimeographed. New York: International Agricultural Development Service, 1977.

Adams, D. W., and Nehman, G. I. *Borrowing Costs for Agricultural Loans in Low Income Countries*. Economics and Sociology Occasional Paper No. 438. Columbus: Ohio State University Agricultural Finance Center, 1977.

Asian Development Bank. *Asian Agricultural Survey 1976*. Manila: Asian Development Bank, 1977.

Blair, Harry W. *The Elusiveness of Equity: Institutional Approaches to Rural Development in Bangladesh*. Special Series on Rural Local Development No. 1. Ithaca, N.Y.: Cornell University, Rural Development Committee, 1974.

Diaz-Cisneros, Heliodoro. "An Institutional Analysis of a Rural Development Project: A Case of the Puebla Project in Mexico." Ph.D. dissertation, University of Wisconsin, 1974.

Donald, Gordon. *Credit for Small Farmers in Developing Countries*. Boulder, Colo.: Westview Press, 1976.

Miller, Leonard F. *Agricultural Credit and Finance in Africa*. New York: Rockefeller Foundation, 1977.

MARKETING

Breth, Steven. "Asian Farmers Can Adopt Guatemala's Low-Cost Metal Silos." *Modern Agriculture & Industry—Asia*, April 1976 p. 10.

Cummings, Ralph W., Jr. "Effectiveness of Pricing in an Indian Wheat Market: A Case Study of Khanna, Punjab." *American Journal of Agricultural Economics* 50 (1968): 687–701.

Cummings, Ralph W., Jr. *Minimum Information Systems for Agricultural Development in Low-Income Countries.* Research & Training Network Seminar Report No. 14. New York: Agricultural Development Council, September 1977.

Harrison, Kelley; Henley, Donald; Riley, Harold; and Shaffer, James. *Improving Food Marketing Systems in Developing Countries: Experiences from Latin America.* Marketing in Developing Communities Series No. 6. East Lansing: Michigan State University, Latin American Studies Center, 1974.

Jones, William O. *Marketing Staple Foodstuffs in Tropical Africa.* Ithaca, N.Y.: Cornell University Press, 1972.

Lele, Uma J. *Food Grain Marketing in India: Private Performance and Public Policy.* Ithaca, N.Y.: Cornell University Press, 1971.

Lewis, John P. "Designing the Public Works Mode of Anti-Poverty Policy." In *Income Distribution and Growth in the Less Developed Countries,* edited by Charles C. Frank and Richard Webb. Washington, D.C.: Brookings Institution, 1977.

Mosher, A. T. *Creating a Progressive Rural Structure.* New York: Agricultural Development Council, 1969.

Thomas, John W. "Rural Public Works and East Pakistan's Development." In *Development Policy II—The Pakistan Experience,* edited by Walter P. Falcon and Gustaf F. Papanak. Cambridge, Mass.: Harvard University Press, 1971.

Wharton, Clifton R., Jr. "The Infrastructure for Agricultural Growth." In *Agricultural Development and Economic Growth,* edited by Herman M. Southworth and Bruce F. Johnston. Ithaca, N.Y.: Cornell University Press, 1967.

COMMODITY PRICE POLICY

Cummings, Ralph W., Jr. "Buffer Stocks." In *Seminar Report on Foodgrains Buffer Stocks in India.* Seminar Series 8. Bombay: Indian Society of Agricultural Economics, 1969.

Krishna, Raj. "Agricultural Price Policy and Economic Development." In *Agricultural Development and Economic Growth,* edited by Herman M. Southworth and Bruce F. Johnston. Ithaca, N.Y.: Cornell University Press, 1967.

Mellor, John W. *Agricultural Price Policy and Income Distribution in Low Income Nations.* World Bank Staff Working Paper No. 214. Washington, D.C.: World Bank, September 1975.

Mellor, John W. *The Basis for Agricultural Price Policy.* Agricultural Development Council Teaching Forum No. 22. New York: Agricultural Development Council, November 1972.

Ramon Magsaysay Award Foundation. *Food Crisis Workshop, February 7–9, 1977.* Manila: Ramon Magsaysay Award Foundation, 1977.

CHAPTER 14

Expediting training

Introduction

A NATION'S SUCCESS in extending the agricultural revolution to all its regions will depend in large part on its ability to produce substantial numbers of people who understand national goals and objectives, who command basic farming skills, who are well grounded in agricultural science and technology, and who are oriented to acting fast. In particular, individuals are needed who can direct and participate in commodity production programs and defined-area campaigns and who are capable of drawing public and private institutions into these development activities in a concerted way.

Most countries already have a variety of institutions, some with impressive academic programs, that prepare people for agricultural careers. Strong training in academic disciplines (for example, crop or animal sciences, including basic chemistry and physics, or economics, or sociology) is highly desirable for agricultural college graduates. However, one basic question is how to make the existing educational institutions, the schools and colleges of agriculture, contribute more effectively to agricultural development and how their efforts might be supplemented. In other agricultural agencies, new ways to accelerate training for faster agricultural development are being tried. While no universal recipe exists, several principles and techniques have wide applicability. This chapter describes some of them.

Training strategy

Competent, confident, action-oriented agricultural workers and leaders can be produced rapidly and at reasonable cost:

- if educational institutions of all types—schools for rural youth and adults, secondary schools, universities, postgraduate schools, and various nonformal educational groups—are involved in the development of the region they serve (that is, if they conduct development activities as they educate);
- if all agencies involved in agriculture—including research and extension organizations—are engaged in training (that is, if they train while performing their duties);
- if training activities have as their three major objectives (1) providing opportunities for individuals to acquire relevant skills, knowledge, understanding, and attitudes, (2) enabling young people to assume responsibility early in their careers, and (3) inspiring individuals to work diligently and purposefully to devise new ways to speed progress; and
- if the training of individuals is systematically upgraded and broadened so that their increasing abilities permit them to assume greater and different responsibilities as agricultural development progresses.

DUAL-PURPOSE TRAINING

This strategy of training rests on a dual-purpose concept: that the training of individuals should be an integral part of development programs or directly support them, and particularly that education and training institutions should be involved substantially in the development of their regions or countries.

As nations organize commodity production programs, defined-area campaigns, or other problem-centered activities, most activities can be carried out by people in training who work with a small cadre of senior professionals for 1–3 years.[1] These interns will learn on the job as they contribute to development efforts. Even though many of the participants may be quite young, they should be considered staff members rather than students, and their responsibilities should be increased as rapidly as circumstances permit.

Cooperation among agencies and institutions to systematically upgrade the capabilities of staff members will benefit the nation as well as the organizations involved. Research and extension services can provide in-service training in field experimentation for staff members of colleges, schools, and extension services. Research personnel can help colleges and other agencies by involving them in cooperative programs and by giving seminars to faculty and students. In these ways, costs of training can be justified not only by the improvement of individual capabilities but also by the value of concurrent contributions to development. Opportunities

[1] This is called "on-the-job" or "in-service" training; the people in training may also be referred to as interns.

to use this dual-purpose approach obviously depend upon the existence of commodity production programs, defined-area campaigns, and problem-centered activities—another justification for their implementation.

Dual-purpose, in-service training should be a central component of each nation's agricultural development effort.

SKILLS, KNOWLEDGE, AND COMPETENCY

Training should ensure that each individual has opportunities and motivation to learn in three interrelated areas. First, every agricultural worker, no matter what his assignment is, should have basic *farming skills*. Second, each worker should acquire the *specialized knowledge* necessary to make him effective at his assigned duties. Third, each worker should have *management competency* to enable him to organize his own efforts and, in appropriate situations, to assist in organizing commodity production programs, defined-area campaigns, or other problem-centered activities.

Basic farming skills. The developing world has too few agricultural professionals who understand farming. One reason is that a higher proportion of students finish secondary school in urban areas than in rural areas. More urban students then go on to colleges and universities where they obtain agricultural degrees. They have not grown up on farms. They are often taught by professors who also have little or no farming background. Unskilled faculty teaching unskilled students persists in a self-perpetuating cycle.

Francis C. Byrnes, who helped establish practical crop and animal production training courses at the International Rice Research Institute (IRRI) in the Philippines and the International Center of Tropical Agriculture (CIAT) in Colombia, has noted that:

- Many scientists, extension specialists, and educators teaching crop production courses are not themselves able to grow crops to obtain high yields; they simply have not had an opportunity to learn.
- Most animal science and veterinary medicine graduates who enter the CIAT training courses are unable to handle and restrain animals for diagnosis and treatment.
- Animal specialists often resist taking production-oriented examinations and are apprehensive about living and working on ranches. Usually trainees need at least 2 months to become adjusted and begin building self-confidence; thereafter, they become effective learners, using theoretical training in conjunction with practical training.
- The greatest barrier to effective production training is the low prestige the participants associate with working on farms or ranches.

Some agricultural scientists and educators (persons who often do not have basic farming skills) claim that basic skills are unimportant because they would rarely be used. This viewpoint must be countered. Farming "experience" is essential in order to acquire an understanding of agriculture and an empathy for farmers and farming. People who are not confident of their farming skills are reluctant to work with farmers. Therefore, to transform agriculture, nations need large numbers of technicians and scientists in agriculture who are *competent* to deal with diverse farm problems and who are, more importantly, *confident* in their own competence.

Specialized knowledge. As agencies or industries become involved in commodity production programs, defined-area campaigns, or efforts to synchronize and reorient services, demand will develop for individuals who have, in addition to basic farming skills, special knowledge of commodities or agricultural operations. These capabilities are so diverse that they usually must be acquired as the individuals work with the agencies or industries concerned.

There is an extreme deficiency of this specialized knowledge among agriculturalists in the developing world. For example, before taking an intensive short course at IRRI, rice production workers (college graduates) have been examined regarding their knowledge of common rice diseases, production practices, insect pests and their damage, nutritional disorders, and the chemicals used by farmers. On the average, Asian rice extension workers scored 25 percent correct answers on the tests. Prior to 6-month rice production training programs at IRRI, professional agronomists from 30 countries averaged only 32 percent correct answers. Similar test results with rice workers have been obtained at CIAT in Colombia. Also at CIAT, the mean score of a practical test of 34 agronomists on diagnostic and management skills with diversified crops given at the beginning of a year of training in the field was only 36 percent. In other words, these agricultural workers were right only one time out of three or four in identifying farmers' problems.[2]

Emphasis must be placed on producing individuals whose technical knowledge (of such subjects as soil testing; precision application of fertilizers, pesticides, and herbicides; improved water management; more effective animal disease and pest control; and farm record-keeping techniques for determining economic implications of improved production practices) deepens as the level of their training and responsibility rises, and who are therefore increasingly competent and confident. Training ought to begin as early as possible, and certainly no later than the

---

[2] After completion of the training courses, average scores at both IRRI and CIAT have been raised to 85–90 percent.

secondary-school level. Individuals need to be able to acquire specialized knowledge systematically as they move through schools and colleges of agriculture into public agencies and commercial organizations.

Management competency. Intensified agriculture depends on a wide range of services such as credit, chemical fertilizer distribution, and marketing. Both public and private agencies are often involved in these services. Therefore, as efforts to force the pace of agricultural and rural development are undertaken, individuals must be trained to manage institutions and programs to carry out these responsibilities.

Some institutions, in the developing world as well as in developed countries, offer management courses relevant to agricultural activities in developing countries. However, there is great need for innovation in agricultural management training. In particular, individuals involved would benefit from more knowledge of successful strategies for action and of means for implementing them. These can perhaps be obtained effectively by review of case studies, more of which need to be developed. Management and financial techniques also need to be adapted to agricultural situations in developing countries.

ORIENTING ATTITUDES TO RAPID DEVELOPMENT

Attitudes are as important as operational techniques or skills, knowledge, and competencies in achieving success in development programs.

Promotion of "importance." At every level of training, individuals should be enabled to understand the importance of the work they are doing. This can be accomplished by acquainting them with national needs and goals, the relation of their own activities to those needs and objectives, and the importance of their activities. From a sense of the importance of one's work, dedication is derived.

Sense of urgency. At every level of training, the need for fast action— a sense of urgency—should be stressed. No time should be lost in beginning the training of local staff to direct and implement agricultural development programs. Upgrading personnel by involving them in development activities, largely through on-the-job internships, is generally speedier, more effective, and less costly than independent training programs or education at institutions that are not directly involved in national development efforts.

Estimating requirements for agricultural graduates. In many countries that have unemployed and underemployed agricultural graduates and in which agricultural salaries are low relative to those of other professions, governments have become disillusioned with many of their agricultural institutions. They have concluded that investments in these institutions have not resulted in expected agricultural advances.

Low performance of agricultural graduates can usually be traced to the lack of programs and institutions organized to increase productivity commodity by commodity, region by region, with the necessary synchronization and orientation of services by government and industry. In addition, poor performance results when teachers of the agricultural personnel themselves lack technical or managerial skills and have narrow, superficial, and impractical educations.

Experience indicates that as governments embark on significant new agricultural initiatives, demands for well-trained agriculturists and economists will expand both among public agencies and in the private sector, and demands are likely to be underestimated by wide margins.

Gaining experience in rapid agricultural development. Many scientists and educators in the developing countries have advanced degrees in agricultural sciences and economics from universities in Europe or North America. In the industrialized countries—the U.S. at least—there has been little incentive since World War II, as a result of intermittent agricultural surpluses, to accelerate agricultural production. Funds for production-oriented research have been hard to obtain from legislatures reluctant to increase capacity to produce greater surpluses. Scientists and faculty members have not been challenged in recent decades to seek strategies for accelerated agricultural development. Graduate students now tend to specialize narrowly. Most are not taught to think strategically about ways to speed agricultural advance. Consequently, students from developing nations often return home unprepared to become involved effectively in urgent national programs.

The low-income countries can no longer rely on the developed countries alone to satisfy their training needs. Countries that send large numbers of students to the industrial countries for advanced training must choose study posts and advisors carefully and, even then, be prepared for a corps of returning specialists who are academically well prepared but who may be narrowly specialized and have not developed the skills required for forced-pace development.

Agreement on the comprehensive strategies by which poorer countries are mostly likely to achieve fast progress at low cost (discussed in Chapters 10–13), and training of young people for roles in the necessary programs (discussed in this chapter) are high-priority items for educators and scientists in developing and developed countries alike.

Roles of institutions

Past agricultural successes in developing countries could not have occurred without trained agricultural leaders. Education and training institutions, however, can be so isolated from development activity that they are frequently ignored by authorities concerned with development. This is distressing since professionals at these institutions could contribute importantly to agricultural and economic progress in their regions. The training strategy just described can be applied to these institutions.

COLLEGES OF AGRICULTURE

Colleges of agriculture have several clear-cut roles: transmission of skills, knowledge, and competencies to students (instruction); acquisition and generation of knowledge and skills (research); and the application of these skills for development purposes (extension). A related role is the preservation of knowledge, primarily via libraries.

Instruction. The historical and classical mission of colleges of agriculture is to teach. Instruction is frequently limited to lectures, assigned readings, and examinations. Yet agriculture is a problem-solving science; classes must be taught with reference to experimentation and must be supplemented by field work.

In some developing countries, making concerted development a major objective has been the impetus for reexamining the quality and relevance of college instruction. Ajibola Taylor, commenting on the University of Ibadan in Nigeria, noted in 1975:

By the early 1950's it was clear that adaptations of the existing curricula were not enough: the entire structure had to be revised. In the reviews that followed, broad objectives were defined for training in agriculture for development. These included: training in plant, animal, and soil sciences so that the interaction of these as applied sciences was thoroughly understood; emphasis on scientific method so that students would be able to undertake basic investigations for crop and animal improvement; and an orientation of students toward the *dissemination* of their knowledge and techniques to lay farmers. In other words, curricula development and training were to become largely production and research oriented—with research sharply focused on improved methods of production.

Taylor cautioned:

The government sees agricultural research in universities as upgrading knowledge—simply. But we see it as more applied. We must have an impact in the rural areas.

We must be on guard against an unconscious neglect of production practices

"The Western educational system, which serves as the model for most [Developing Member Countries of the Asian Development Bank] is highly discipline oriented. Researchers are rewarded for achievements within the narrow context of their discipline. The result is not only a lack of pragmatism in research, but also an extraordinary lack of communication among disciplines. The lack of communication and understanding is reflected in the distrust between biological and social scientists, and even within these broad categories the distrust among the disciplines. The lack of communication exists not only horizontally among disciplines, but also vertically among research workers, extension specialists, and farmers. The problem goes to the very roots of the educational system, and suggests the need for major reforms. Part of the problem seems to lie in the neglect of adequate training for extension and lower level research workers."

Asian Development Bank
Asian Agricultural Survey 1976

—a situation in which the student becomes knowledgeable but remains unsure of his ability to *apply* that knowledge.

Gil Saguiguit, formerly of the University of the Philippines, put the issue another way: "It should not be a matter of splitting practical from academic work. We need instructors who can describe *principles* as they are *applied*. Students should see the practice as they hear about the theory."[3]

Courses are more exciting and useful if instructors can relate principles to local practice. The faculty should be helped to become involved in development programs and experienced individuals should be brought to the campus to lecture or give short courses.

To complement classroom teaching, various techniques can be employed to help students gain an understanding of agriculture and acquire farm skills:

- Provision may be made for farm "practice." This involves time in the fields at manual labor. However, learning to get one's hands dirty in such ways is, by itself, insufficient; it is comparable to limiting the experience of medical students to cleaning hospital corridors.
- Colleges can arrange for students to grow crops or manage animals on a plot of land with responsibility for making decisions and keeping cost accounts, perhaps permitting students to keep the profits. Some institutions have had success with such arrangements and report that students often exhibit considerable ingenuity.
- Students may live and work in villages or on farms for short periods. Reportedly this is especially useful for students from urban areas.

[3] Quoted by Smeltzer in "Farm Practice Training for College Students."

• Experience on the experiment station or with nearby on-farm trials allows students to become familiar with tactical and operational (on-farm) research techniques. This helps them appreciate the interactions which influence crop and animal yields and prepares them for work with farmers or as farmers. This approach is feasible only if the college has a research program geared to development goals.

Research. Each college of agriculture should participate in a system of national and local research efforts, conducting investigations on its experiment station as well as field investigations in the region served.

The experiment station is as vital to a college of agriculture as a teaching hospital is to a medical school. On an experiment station the student can master technical agriculture under the guidance of professionals. It is here that the student can learn to produce crops and handle animals, to diagnose agricultural problems, to examine the results of experimental treatments, to handle laboratory aspects of diseases and insect problems, to put together complex production practices to obtain high economic yields of crops or animals, and to tailor systems of agricultural production to localities. Agricultural students, like those in medicine, must be prepared broadly enough to apply their knowledge as general practitioners; specialization, if any, can come later.

A dynamic on-farm research program has similar benefits. It permits faculty members to improve their capabilities and to acquire local information needed to make their courses exciting and relevant to progress in the area served. Faculty talent can contribute to the solution of important problems and help identify strategies and techniques of development. Students can acquire skills and an understanding of technical agriculture as they contribute to research progress through field experimentation.

Establishment of research priorities at colleges and universities can be controversial. One view is that university researchers should be supported in whatever work they choose. Another view is that research efforts should be directed exclusively to problems of high priority, with objectives imposed by government if that is the source of financial support. Neither extreme is desirable. Rather, scientists and educators should take the initiative in working with government agencies and the private sector to identify and implement lines of work of greatest importance. It must be both feasible and mutually desirable for any work to be undertaken at the college, either by college staff or by scientists assigned to the college experiment station by other agencies. As examples of activities which might have mutual benefit, particular attention can be given to the following:

• The college farm could function as a production or tactical research center for the area in which it is located. By carrying out field and laboratory experiments on commodities and problems relevant to local development as part of a cooperative national effort, faculty and students will be able to observe and to participate in up-to-date and dynamic agricultural activities. A dual purpose is served: useful data are generated and the instructional program benefits. Since the results of the experiments will be of immediate interest to farmers of the vicinity, farmers can be attracted to the campus for field days, thus elevating the importance of the college in the minds of rural people and political leaders and keeping the college in touch with the people it serves. *A college should have this basic set of tactical research activities, even if no other.* Guidance should be provided by full-time research personnel, as discussed under "Production Centers" in Chapter 12.

- Some national commodity research programs can be centered at colleges, with some faculty members participating part-time. This may require the national research agency to provide funds and assign full-time research leaders to the college.
- The college could participate in defined-area development campaigns in its vicinity; a strong college should have full responsibility for at least one large region. This gives faculty and students the opportunity to learn about rural people and their problems while helping to identify strategies and techniques for achieving progress. In carrying out such a program, the college should have clearly stated goals, responsibilities, and authority, together with freedom to innovate in cooperation with local leaders and other agencies.
- Problem-centered research—related to the four sets of requisites for adoption by farmers described in Chapter 10, or other important topics as suggested in Chapter 12—can be undertaken by college faculty and students if funds are made available. To qualify for financial support, the *importance* of the activity to the success of either national commodity or area-development efforts should be demonstrated.

The failure of a college to undertake significant research on experiment stations or on farms can usually be related to the faculty's lack of confidence in their farm skills, to the inability of faculty members with heavy responsibilities for classroom teaching or administration to handle research programs, or to inadequate funds for laboratory or field work. The second reason deserves special attention because the requirements of agricultural research in the tropics are often not fully recognized.

Agricultural research in tropical countries involves year-round field activity. By contrast, in temperate climates, faculty members in fields such as agronomy, plant breeding, and plant pathology can teach during the fall, winter, and spring quarters, yet be involved full-time in field research during the single summer cropping season. In tropical areas, if teaching faculty are to participate in continuing research programs on a part-time basis, the long-term programs must be under the guidance of full-time scientists—specialists in major commodities or other lines of research. These full-time scientists may be research professors of the college faculty or they may be assigned to the college by the nation's research or extension agency. The university should have responsibility for at least one major defined-area program. Some of the faculty should lead or participate in national commodity programs.

Colleges of agriculture can be reoriented quickly with imaginative leadership and flexible support. In the mid-1960s, Makerere University College in Uganda was primarily a teaching institution with relatively poor facilities and a "farm" little better than the subsistence farms around it. Graduates had few agricultural skills, and there was little demand for their services. The system of national research stations, under the Ministry of Agriculture, also was languishing. In 1966 the university installed a full-time dean who was dedicated to development of the country. Using limited grant funds for research of high priority, the faculty started a vigorous field research program assisted by a professor working full-time at the field station. Within 3 years the program was attracting national attention. The imagination and the energy of both Ugandan and expatriate staff had been unleashed. The president of Uganda attended a field day and was so impressed that he requested the university to review the national agricultural research program and recommended improvements.

At Kasetsart University in Thailand, research was expanded in 1966 with the establishment of the National Corn and Sorghum Program, a cooperative undertaking of the university and the Ministry of Agriculture. A central research and training center, established at the university's Farm Suwan 150 kilometers northeast of Bangkok, was jointly staffed and funded by the university and the ministry. The program permitted faculty and students in diverse disciplines to participate in research on a part-time basis while a few full-time researchers provided program continuity.

Maize and sorghum, the commodities around which to start cooperative activity, were important to Thailand, the work was needed, and interested and trained staff were available to work on the crops. Dale Smeltzer, who was in charge of the training for Kasetsart University, noted in 1975:

Students are required to have 300 hours of agricultural work experience. Most students meet this requirement by participating in programs given at student training farms operated by the university. In addition, students may volunteer to spend 8 or 10 weeks of their summer vacation at Farm Suwan. . . .

Students in the Department of Agricultural Economics at Kasetsart have used a slightly different method. They have served as interviewers in farm survey research under leadership of faculty members, assisting also in the tabulation and analysis of data.

Kasetsart University has used several other devices to enable faculty and students to engage in significant research.

- Research leadership positions allow outstanding faculty members, most of whom would otherwise have to work at two or more jobs, to take on full-time teaching and research. These 5-year positions recognize people who have already demonstrated unusually high competence.
- Research assistantships permit younger faculty and senior students to engage in part-time farm-level research.
- Graduate assistantships focus on field work to encourage young agriculturists to concentrate on their country's problems from a university base.

Development activities (extension). There are growing numbers of colleges of agriculture involved in accelerating development.

During the 1960s, as India was pressing its High Yielding Varieties Program to increase cereal production on 13 million hectares in 5 years, some of India's new agricultural universities, as well as the Indian Agricultural Research Institute, played leading roles. The Punjab Agricultural University released several high-yielding wheat and rice varieties which were rapidly adopted by farmers (Table 14.1). It carried out studies of credit and marketing which contributed to improvements in these services, and it operated an extension training program that involved it directly in the agricultural development of the state. The Uttar Pradesh Agricul-

Table 14.1. Changes in area, production, and yield after introduction of new rice varieties, Punjab, India

Year	Area planted to rice (thousand ha)	Area planted to semidwarf varieties		Production of milled rice (thousand tons)	Yield (tons/ha)
		(thousand ha)	(%)		
1950	120	—	—	107	0.79
1955	149	—	—	107	0.72
1960	227	—	—	220	1.1
1965	292	—	—	292	1.0
1966	285	4	1	338	1.2
1967	314	17	5	415	1.3
1968	345	27	8	470	1.4
1969	350	72	20	535	1.5
1970	390	143	38	688	1.8
1971	450	311	73	920	2.0
1972	476	378	79	955	2.0
1973	498	450	84	1,140	2.1
1974	570	500	88	1,181	2.1
1975	566	500	91	1,445	2.6

Source: "The Highest Contribution," *Ceres.*

tural University participated in several All-India research programs, and was a primary force in promoting new technology among farmers, in organizing a seed company, in starting rodent control programs in rural areas, and in promoting the development of science-based agriculture in the state. At annual field days, producers (including small farmers) came long distances to learn of the work of the experiment station. These universities, each under development-oriented educators, have been given much credit for the rapid advance of their states in the production of diverse commodities and in raising the incomes of rural people.

Staff and students at the University of Ibadan in Nigeria have worked with 28 nearby villages and hamlets to accelerate rural development based on agricultural advance and to improve health and the welfare of women. Initiated in 1970, the Bedeku Expanded Pilot Project on Rural Development provided a field laboratory where university personnel can not only study but actually participate in rural development. The project staff members cooperate with the local people and their organizations as well as with government and other development agencies.

Colleges of agriculture are often under a ministry, such as the Ministry of Education, which is not responsible for agricultural development. Nevertheless, the college needs facilities and funds to permit faculty and students to participate in research as an integral part of national development. There are a number of administrative options by which to achieve this result within any organizational framework; the important point is to find one that works.

SCHOOLS OF AGRICULTURE

Schools of agriculture offer practical training at the level of the secondary school or early college years. For many persons, such training is the end of their formal education, and in some countries government agencies employ many of the graduates as technicians.

These schools should impart many skills of intensive farming, and of on-farm or operational research techniques, along with the usual courses of instruction. Establishing a "production" center (described in Chapter 12) at the school will permit students to work on a wide range of crops and animals, on soils, and on elementary farm economics. Field tests conducted at such schools, with maximum participation by students (a minimum of laborers) under the guidance of a small staff of full-time professionals (agronomist, animal husbandry specialist, entomologist, economist, agricultural engineer), will contribute valuable research results as they contribute to the training of students.

Graduates of the Escuela Agricola Pan-Americana in Zamorano, Honduras, have long been in demand for positions of responsibility in Latin America. The school has emphasized practical training in a 3-year, nondegree course, yet many people consider its alumni to be more competent than many graduates of 4-year colleges.

In the Dominican Republic, the Instituto Superior de Agricultura near Santiago is developing a solid reputation in preparing students for agricultural careers. Each student grows a crop or develops a farm enterprise for profit during his course of study. Standards are high, and applications for admission greatly exceed the number who can be admitted. The school is participating in a new program to help develop the hill areas in the western part of the country.

POSTGRADUATE CENTERS

Several colleges of agriculture in developing regions offer master's or doctoral degrees of high quality. Some of the most successful are the Post-Graduate College at Chapingo, Mexico; the University of Ibadan in Nigeria; the Graduate School of the Indian Agricultural Research Institute, the University of Uttar Pradesh, and the Punjab University in India; and the University of the Philippines College of Agriculture. There are several benefits to be derived from training students of the region at such centers: (1) training can be highly relevant to the needs of the students' home countries; (2) dissertations or research elements contribute directly to solutions of problems of the developing regions; and (3) costs are generally lower than at universities in industrialized countries.

In Mexico, the Post-Graduate College at Chapingo has led the development of strategies for defined-area campaigns, beginning in 1967 with the Puebla Project. It now works closely with the national research and extension agencies in intensifying work in other defined areas throughout Mexico.

The University of the Philippines College of Agriculture has pioneered in the organization of national commodity research programs in cooperation with several other colleges of agriculture, government agencies, and private industry. Numerous national research programs are now headed by university graduates. The college has initiated a program to upgrade the education of personnel from national agencies by enabling them to earn master of science degrees. It has organized numerous short courses and workshops. And it has initiated a communication program which includes publication of extension bulletins, radio programs for rural people, and newsletters. In part as a consequence of these activities the college has become a center for graduate training in agriculture for Southeast Asia, with students from many countries in residence.

The quality of training offered at such graduate schools depends on the experience and capabilities of the staff. It should not be surprising, then, that institutions that are deeply involved in national commodity programs, defined-area campaigns, and problem-centered activities in their own countries are emerging as international leaders in the field. It is at such schools that much of the innovation in rapid agricultural development is occurring today.

RESEARCH SERVICES

Research organizations offer remarkably good opportunities for training young people. Training on a substantial scale should be a required activity of each unit of every research organization.

In the nationwide agricultural program undertaken cooperatively from 1943 to 1961 by the Ministry of Agriculture of Mexico and the Rockefeller Foundation, activities in wheat, maize, sorghum, potatoes, beans, vegetables, and animal production, as well as in soils, plant pathology, entomology, experiment-station development, and other specialties, were each headed by one or two experienced scientists. All other work in these nationwide programs was done by trainees (interns) who were recent college graduates. From the first day on the job, these young people were full-time members of the staff, not students. Within a few months the better new staff members were already in charge of important elements of the work and by the second year they were in charge of stations or main lines of activity, directing their own staff of less-experienced trainees. Seven hundred young Mexicans received such training for 1–3 years. Some then went on to graduate studies, others took positions in government agencies, in educational institutions, in industry. At least one became a state governor. Another became minister of agriculture.

In the Philippines, early in the 1960s, arrangements were made with the Bureau of Plant Industry for eight rice specialists to spend 1 year at IRRI as in-service members of the research staff. They participated in field experimentation as well as in weekly seminars on diverse rice problems. They acquired higher levels of competence; experienced increasing responsibility; learned to install, maintain, and evaluate experiments; developed confidence in their own abilities; and established useful friendships with members of the research group. Each visiting specialist contributed to IRRI's research program, so much so that senior staff members were reluctant to have them leave. When they returned to their field posts, they soon found that their new competence made them much more effective in dealing with farmers and in fact they became so popular among farmers that they preferred to work at the farm level.

In Thailand from 1967 to 1975 training classes under the auspices of the Inter-Asian Corn Program were operated in conjunction with Thailand's National Corn and Sorghum Program. According to Dale Smeltzer:

A total of 193 trainees from 15 countries participated. Approximately two-thirds had research responsibilities at home, a bit less than one-third were primarily involved in extension, and five were teachers in universities or technical schools. Trainees were selected by officials in their national programs, often in consultation with IACP staff and advisors from various donor organizations. The 6-month training periods were held at Farm Suwan. Each trainee was expected to conduct at least one field project—preparing a project outline, reporting results, and interpreting their meaning. A wide range of projects were completed—variety trials, fertilizer trials, soil management trials, insect and disease control studies, mixed cropping experiments, and seed multiplication plots. The trainees worked together; *they did all the work except for basic land preparation.* The field activity occupied well over half the trainee's time. The rest was given over to lectures on basic crop production, soils and fertilizers, irrigation, marketing.

Smeltzer noted that the training was commodity focused, which had both advantages and disadvantages. One asset was that the entire class had a common interest; thus comprehensive coverage could be given to maize production, protection, improvement, marketing, and utilization. However, a major liability was that it often led to oversimplification, and staff were "at times tempted to avoid looking at the real world of diversified Asian farms."

Some scientists and extension agents object to conducting research with young people in training, claiming that training is not their responsibility. They insist that their research and extension activities require permanent technicians and staff. This is not true. Such attitudes usually represent attempts to avoid the added chores of training new people or reflect the limited experience scientists have had with trainees.

PRODUCTION OR EXTENSION SERVICES

Extension personnel, who are involved in on-farm tests and demonstrations or surveys as part of commodity production programs or defined-area campaigns, must continually improve their knowledge and skills. Farm testing and demonstrations provide a means of training new production specialists (as well as farmers) who need experience in practical farming as well as knowledge of technology and its application. For more experienced personnel, a continuing program of farm experimentation allows them to keep up with new technological developments.

Government extension services must go well beyond merely increasing the flow of technical information to the cultivator. Farmers often need assistance in obtaining the inputs necessary to take full advantage of the new technologies, including credit at reasonable rates of interest with reasonable procedures, and fairly priced, adequate amounts of fertilizers, pesticides, and herbicides when needed. Access to markets with stable crop prices is necessary to ensure favorable relationships between input costs and crop prices. These problems can often be resolved if they are fully understood and properly presented to the people with authority to do so. The extension agent should be sensitive to providing this type of

Table 14.2. Training programs and conference events offered by the international
agricultural research centers in 1976/77 or 1978

Program	Duration	IRRI
Individual training		
In-service internships		
Research (disciplinary)	growing season	•
Production (multidisciplinary)	growing season	
In-service internships in management of station operations	6 months	
Short internships on special research or production skills	1–2 months	•
Summer student trainees (undergraduates)	2–3 months	
M.S. thesis research	6–12 months	•
Ph.D. dissertation research	12–24 months	•
Advanced research fellowships (visiting research		
associates), post–M.S.	6–14 months	•
Postdoctoral fellowships	6–24 months	•
Visits by policy-makers & decision-makers	3–5 days	•
Crop training		
Research course	4–6 months	•
Research short course (specific subject)	1–4 weeks	
Production short course (multidisciplinary)	2–4 weeks	•
Production course (multidisciplinary)	4–6 months	•
Seed production course	2–6 months	
In-country short course (production or research)	2–6 weeks	
Conferences		
Presentation days	3 days	•
Scientific workshops (headquarters)	3–5 days	•
Decision-& policy-makers' workshops	3–5 days	
Regional workshops (in countries)	5 days	
Internal seminars	2 hours	•
National workshops	3–5 days	

Source: Fernando Fernandez, *Objectives and Content of Training at the International Centers of Agricultural Research.*

assistance in response to farmers' suggestions or on his own initiative. Much effective training to improve skills, knowledge, and competencies can be provided to extension personnel relatively quickly on an in-place, in-service basis at local production centers by personnel of production or extension agencies. More advanced technical training can be accomplished by rotating extension personnel into research services or other agencies for periods of on-the-job training.

There are growing numbers of experiences with successful approaches to instruction of both technicians and the small farmers. Some were mentioned in Chapter 8—the Puebla Project, the Maize Program in Kenya, the Masagana 99 Program in the Philippines, and the wheat program in coastal Turkey. The training and visit system of extension described by Daniel Benor and James Q. Harrison deserves study by those planning low-cost ways to help large numbers of small farmers increase the productivity of their major crops; it appears to incorporate the techniques known to be important to the success of such efforts.

CIMMYT	CIAT	IITA	CIP	ICRISAT	ILCA	ILRAD	AVRDC	IFDC
•	•	•	•	•	•	•	•	•
•	•	•	•	•	•			
	•		•	•	•	•	•	•
	•	•		•			•	•
•	•	•	•	•	•	•	•	
•	•	•	•	•	•	•	•	•
•	•	•	•	•	•	•	•	•
•	•	•	•	•	•	•	•	
		•	•					•
•	•	•	•				•	•
•	•	•	•					
•	•	•		•	•	•	•	•
•	•		•		•	•		•
•		•	•				•	•
•	•		•	•	•	•		•

FOREIGN INSTITUTIONS

Education and training do not necessarily have to be carried out entirely within one country. Sometimes the desired program may not be available, or it may be advisable to supplement training within the country with experience elsewhere.

For example, many colleges and universities in the developed countries have high-quality undergraduate and graduate programs. However, while they may be strong in providing methodological skills, they are often weak in relating training to the problems of the country to which the student will return. It is usually desirable, therefore, to limit foreign academic training to postgraduate levels when it is not available at home, and even then to attempt to see that much of the research phase of the training is carried out in the home country or region.

Many specialized programs, often of short duration, are available at educational institutions and organizations abroad. For example, the training of instructors for national centers can often be done at international agricultural research centers (Table 14.2).

Training in developed countries or at regional centers should be considered as only supplementary to training within each country and should not be used as an excuse to move slowly in developing adequate training systems locally.

A note on the U.S. experience

Many developing countries must find a way to break a system which perpetuates poor-quality agricultural training. The U.S. experience is instructive for understanding how one country educated a generally agriculturally literate population as well as a diverse array of competent scientists, administrators, teachers, technicians, businessmen, and farmers with a highly developed service orientation to agriculture.

PROMOTION OF SKILLS

Until recently a high proportion of the young people entering U.S. colleges of agriculture have come from farms and rural areas. Many rural youths in the U.S. begin helping on the farm at an early age. Working with animals and crops is a part of their routine activities. Agricultural skills are passed from parents to children, from neighbor to neighbor, and from local agribusiness enterprises to farmers. There also are organized efforts to teach farming skills to rural people. Millions of U.S. youths have been trained in agriculture through vocational agriculture available in secondary schools, the Future Farmers of America, and 4-H Clubs.

Therefore, most agricultural students have been somewhat proficient in crop or animal production. Moreover, many of the professors leading research and extension activities or teaching classes have farm backgrounds and are themselves skilled in the practices of agriculture. At the agricultural colleges, students have continued to learn principles and practice both formally and informally; as student assistants, they have worked in the experimental fields, in the shops, or on projects under the guidance of professionals. The farm backgrounds of both students and professors, plus the relevant information offered in course work (information often fresh from the associated state and federal experiment stations and on-farm tests), have been conducive to the development of student competence. The graduates have been well prepared professionally to serve as extension agents, as employees of agricultural industry, as teachers, or in other agricultural vocations.

Large numbers of youths with farm backgrounds have entered college to study subjects other than agriculture, such as business, banking, law, medicine, and education. As a result people familiar with intensive agriculture have been infused throughout American society. At many points in society, decisions regarding agriculture are being made by knowledgeable people.

DEVELOPMENT ORIENTATION

At the university experiment stations, at least until recently, the major efforts of most scientists have been directed quite specifically and deliberately at improving the productivity and profitability of the agriculture of the states served—that is, at defined-area development, commodity by commodity. The contributions of the universities to state agricultural development have largely been made possible by dedicated men of science, many of whom were both educators and researchers of note.[4]

Research financing has largely come from state sources or has involved relatively unrestricted funds from the federal government. Priority has been given to state problems because future appropriations depend on an appreciation by political and farm people of the importance of this work.

PROBLEMS IN THE SYSTEM

Not all U.S. experience should be replicated. Until a few years ago, some southern states had dual systems of education, one for black students and one for white, and dual extension systems. While white colleges generally had adequate facilities and budgets for agricultural research and related activities, black colleges did not. Black students in agriculture, who came mostly from small, traditional farms, acquired few modern skills at home and had few opportunities to develop them at college since black colleges rarely had field programs. Therefore, graduates who entered the black extension service had little to offer the black farmers they were sent out to assist. Unskilled students were taught by unskilled instructors to serve poor farmers. This system of neglect is disappearing, but it clearly contributed to the poverty of the rural black people of the U.S. South and to their movement out of agriculture.

In some states, including some outside the South, agricultural research and extension programs generally have not been well supported financially, have offered low professional salaries, and therefore have been staffed by inadequately trained and poorly motivated people. Sometimes

---

[4] Many of the agriculturists elected to the prestigious National Academy of Science are field research workers as well as strategists—E. C. Stakman, J. G. Harrar, and James Horsfall, plant pathologists; Norman Borlaug, who directs the International Wheat Improvement Program at the Centro Internacional de Mejoramiento de Maiz y Trigo (CIMMYT); G. F. Sprague, for years the leader of maize and sorghum investigations for the U.S. Department of Agriculture; Glenn Burton, the noted forage crop and millet specialist of the U.S. Department of Agriculture; and Jack Harlan, an authority on the evolution of crop plants, to name a few. All have been dedicated not only to research that is highly relevant to agricultural progress but also to the application of such advances to benefit American farmers.

university or state leaders have been apathetic about agricultural development, thereby causing low morale among agricultural faculty and making it difficult for the university to hold skilled professionals. Consequently, these states have had weak field research programs, have lagged behind other states in the modernization of agriculture, and have generally produced graduates who are poorly qualified for the better jobs.

Since World War I, and particularly in recent years, there has been a shift of research and extension programs and of federal and state policies toward the needs of the growing number of large-scale, capital- and energy-intensive farms. Such an orientation may not be useful in the less-developed countries.

Concluding comments

National institutions need capable people to staff accelerated agricultural development programs. Agricultural research and extension workers in developing countries often are not willing to work at the farm level. Frequently this reluctance is based on the individuals' lack of technical and practical skills and lack of confidence in their ability to work with farmers; they fear embarrassment. Even well-trained, confident agriculturists can become disillusioned with field assignments if they find that support is inadequate, if they are unable to get supplies, if they lack mobility, if they are burdened with administrative minutiae, if they are out of touch professionally, or if they receive lower salaries than similarly qualified professionals in other assignments (for example, in medicine, law, or engineering)—conditions which too often characterize agricultural programs in developing countries.

The skills, knowledge, and competencies useful to agriculturists—if only to give them confidence—are so diverse that training should begin early in each person's career, preferably at the secondary-school level, and continue through at least the first years of professional work. To the extent feasible, training should be combined with participation in research or development activities; that is, it should be dual purpose. This is the best means of rapidly training the substantial numbers required at minimum cost while achieving the added benefits of acceptance of responsibility and the linking of agency personnel.

References

TRAINING STRATEGY
Byrnes, Francis C. "Agricultural Production Training in Developing Countries: Critical but Controversial." In *Strategies for Agricultural Education in Developing Countries: Agricultural Education Conference I*. Working Paper. New York: Rockefeller Foundation, 1974.

Byrnes, Francis C., and Golden, William G., Jr. *Changing the Change Agent.* Los Baños, Philippines: International Rice Research Institute, 1967.
Gray, Clarence C. "Agricultural Curricula and Instruction for National Development: An Integrated Approach." In *Strategies for Agricultural Education in Developing Countries: Agricultural Education Conference I.* Working Paper. New York: Rockefeller Foundation, 1974.
Peabody, N. S., III, and Cornick, Tully R. *Teaching Agricultural and Rural Development Administration (TARDA).* Cornell International Agricultural Mimeograph 54. Ithaca, N.Y.: Cornell University, 1977.
Strategies for Agricultural Education in Developing Countries: Agricultural Education Conference I. Working Paper. New York: Rockefeller Foundation, 1974.
Strategies for Agricultural Education in Developing Countries: Agricultural Education Conference II. Working Paper. New York: Rockefeller Foundation, 1976.

ROLES OF INSTITUTIONS
Areekul, Sutharm, and Johnston, James E. "Kasetsart University, Thailand: The National Corn and Sorghum Program." In *Strategies for Agricultural Education in Developing Countries: Agricultural Education Conference I.* Working Paper. New York: Rockefeller Foundation, 1974.
Asian Development Bank. *Asian Agricultural Survey 1976.* Manila: Asian Development Bank, 1977.
Benor, Daniel, and Harrison, James Q. *Agricultural Extension: The Training and Visit System.* Washington, D.C.: World Bank, 1977.
Fernandez, Fernando. *Objectives and Content of Training at the International Centers of Agricultural Research.* Paper prepared for the CGIAR at the "Forum on Training," International Centers Week, September 1977, Washington, D.C. Mimeographed.
Fernandez, F. "Unorthodox Strategies and Methodologies for Agricultural Production Training: CIAT's Experiences in Colombia." In *Strategies for Agricultural Education in Developing Countries: Agricultural Education Conference I.* Working Paper. New York: Rockefeller Foundation, 1974.
Golden, William G., Jr. "The Minikit and Production Kit Programs." Paper presented at the Workshop on IADS Approaches to Accelerating Agricultural Development, June 26–July 1, 1977, Airlie House, Virginia. Mimeographed.
Golden, William G., Jr. "Sri Lanka's Agricultural Extension Service." In *Strategies for Agricultural Education in Developing Countries: Agricultural Education Conference I.* Working Paper. New York: Rockefeller Foundation, 1974.
"The Highest Contribution," *Ceres* 10 (1977): 6.
Nickel, John L. "Makerere University, Uganda: Agricultural Research and Educational Programs." In *Strategies for Agricultural Education in Developing Countries: Agricultural Education Conference I.* Working Paper. New York: Rockefeller Foundation, 1974.
Pal, B. P. "The Indian Agricultural Research Institute, The Indian Council of Agricultural Research, and the All-India Coordinated Agricultural Research Program." In *Strategies for Agricultural Education in Developing Countries: Agricultural Education Conference I.* Working Paper. New York: Rockefeller Foundation, 1974.
Patel, A. U., and Olayide, S. O. *The Bedeku Expanded Pilot Project on Rural Development.* Paper prepared for presentation at a seminar on Accelerating National Agricultural and Rural Development, 1976, University of Reading, England. Mimeographed.
Ross, Vernon E. "Historical Development of the IRRI-NFAC Cooperative Rainfed and Upland Rice Applied Research Project." In *Strategies for Agricultural Education in Developing Countries: Agricultural Education Conference I.* Working Paper. New York: Rockefeller Foundation, 1974.
Saguiguit, Gil. "Questions/Comments on Dale Smeltzer, 'Farm Practice Training for College Students.'" In *Strategies for Agricultural Education in Developing Countries: Agricultural Education Conference II.* Working Paper. New York: Rockefeller Foundation, 1976.

Smeltzer, Dale G. "Corn Production Training." In *Strategies for Agricultural Education in Developing Countries: Agricultural Education Conference II.* Working Paper. New York: Rockefeller Foundation, 1976.

Taylor, Ajibola. "Plant Sciences Curricula." In *Strategies for Agricultural Education in Developing Countries: Agricultural Education Conference II.* Working Paper. New York: Rockefeller Foundation, 1976.

Implications for the
assistance community

Toward more effective assistance

Introduction

THE WORLD HAS entered a new era of agricultural development, one marked by the desire of developing countries to force the pace of development by quickly bringing the agricultural revolution to large numbers of farmers even in remote areas. Many nations, some of which must double food availability in less than 15 years (Table 15.1), realize that they must take extraordinary, emergency measures.

There is a danger, however, that assistance organizations and institutions in developed countries will be unprepared to help design and implement programs that sufficiently accelerate agricultural development. The purpose of this chapter is to describe several ways that outside organizations can assist the low-income countries speed agricultural development.

Basic considerations

Attempts to deal with the food-poverty-population problem are hampered by both its invisibility and its complexity. The problem is invisible in the sense that many impoverished, undernourished people in remote areas of agrarian countries have been out of sight even of their own governments and urban dwellers. Moreover, the difficulties of distant, poorer countries are still little known and poorly understood in the legislative halls and by the people of the affluent, technically advanced nations.

The complexity of the problem is greatly underestimated. Many people still mistakenly assume that the solution is simply to produce more food, wherever and however that can be done most efficiently. And the seemingly infinite variety of agricultural systems and economic and ideological conditions makes articulation of a logical and understandable strategy for national and international action difficult.

Table 15.1. Estimated number of years in which food production in selected countries would need to double to meet projected consumption requirements

Country	Doubling time (years)	Country	Doubling time (years)
Asia		Liberia	12
Bangladesh	13	Malagasy	18
Burma	22	Malawi	18
Taiwan	7	Mali	12
India	18	Mozambique	18
Indonesia	17	Niger	13
Korea (Republic)	12	Nigeria	13
Malaysia	11	Rhodesia	19
Nepal	25	Rwanda	15
Pakistan	16	Senegal	11
Philippines	12	Sierra Leone	14
Sri Lanka	8	Somalia	10
Thailand	a	Tanzania	13
North Africa/Mideast		Uganda	16
Afghanistan	15	Upper Volta	15
Algeria	7	Zaire	13
Cyprus	9	Zambia	17
Egypt	14	**Latin America**	
Iran	11	Argentina	a
Iraq	11	Bolivia	10
Jordan	7	Brazil	19
Lebanon	7	Chile	14
Libya	7	Colombia	13
Morocco	14	Costa Rica	8
Saudi Arabia	7	Dominican Republic	7
Sudan	11	Ecuador	10
Syria	11	El Salvador	12
Tunisia	9	Guatemala	14
Turkey	20	Guyana	34
Yemen (P.D.R.)	8	Haiti	11
Sub-Saharan Africa		Honduras	12
Angola	13	Jamaica	7
Benin	17	Mexico	15
Burundi	19	Nicaragua	14
Cameroon	18	Panama	11
Chad	14	Paraguay	20
Ethiopia	17	Peru	10
Gambia	10	Surinam	a
Ghana	17	Trinidad & Tobago	7
Guinea	13	Uruguay	a
Ivory Coast	15	Venezuela	b
Kenya	15		

Source: From highest requirement growth rates calculated by the International Food Policy Research Institute, *Food Needs of Developing Countries: Projections of Production and Consumption to 1990.*
[a] No serious pressure to meet domestic requirements.
[b] Less than 7 years.

Nevertheless, a consensus seems to be emerging from the experience of recent decades. In reviewing ways to further improve assistance to nations, several basic considerations must be kept in mind: (1) the need for action is urgent; (2) politicians and professional agriculturists, while they approach the problem from different perspectives, both have important roles; (3) the intellectual leadership in development thought resides increasingly in the developing countries; (4) the primary solution for the food-poverty-population problem is known; (5) the strategy to achieve that solution consists of complementary implementation of national commodity programs, defined-area campaigns, and reorientation and synchronization of basic services; and (6) the primary responsibility for action rests with the governments of the developing countries—external agencies can only assist.

URGENCY

The burgeoning food deficits, particularly in the poorer countries, are ominous (Chapter 2) and must not be overlooked during periods of temporary surplus. There is an urgent need for poorer countries to speed agricultural development—for humanitarian, economic, and security reasons.

In developing countries, the low level and uneven distribution of purchasing power, which determine the distribution of food, are as much a problem as availability of total food. Increased agricultural productivity and rural prosperity are central to expansion of employment in the rural areas, both on farms and in rural trade centers, and to development of domestic markets for products of urban industry. Unless the rural populations participate in economic growth, unrest in the countrysides promises to challenge many governments. It is politically important to many governments that their nations be self-sufficient in food supplies or nearly so, and that they be insulated from international uncertainties. Given the scarcity and high costs of food in international markets in the early 1970s, government leaders increasingly feel that their best protection lies in encouraging production by their own farmers.

For the industrial countries the need for fast progress worldwide is equally urgent. Unless the developing countries are able to produce considerably more of their basic food requirements, world food supplies can be expected to be increasingly tight (with substantial year-to-year fluctuations associated with weather) and food prices higher. Unless poor countries advance economically, the long-term growth of world trade for both agricultural and industrial products will be stifled, bringing adverse economic effects to the industrial countries themselves. And unless some basic requirements—food, health care, housing, education—are met quickly, rural people will be susceptible to ideologies which promise to meet these needs at the cost of severe regimentation. For these reasons the affluent nations must take agricultural assistance to poor countries much more seriously. And they must greatly increase the effectiveness of bilateral and multilateral aid.

POLITICS AND PROFESSIONALISM

Too many political figures at high levels of national governments and international agencies fail to understand the requirements for accelerating agricultural development and the penalties for inaction. Too often their interest is immediate political advantage.

But political leaders have been inadequately helped by professionals such as biological scientists and agricultural economists in developing agenda for action. Few general economists or financiers have a command of the technical and operational aspects of the agricultural development process, which their plans too often reveal, and agriculturists are only beginning to emerge as leaders in strategic thinking about development.

In spite of the shortcomings of politicians and scientists both have important contributions to make in identifying strategies for accelerating development. Political leaders must recognize that the scientific and technical complexity of agricultural development is no less than that of a space or medical program; they must choose their advisors with commensurate care and arrange for long-term support of development activity. Scientists in turn must devise sound strategies which address the problems of the nation, then make them known in political and financial circles in understandable language.

INTELLECTUAL LEADERSHIP

Since the mid-1960s, leadership in strategic thinking about accelerated agricultural development has been shifting to developing countries. Large numbers of scientists and administrators of developing countries, many of whom have been trained in industrialized countries, were thrust into positions of national responsibility while young. They now have greater perspective on and experience in efforts to step up the pace of agricultural development than their former teachers in the developed countries. Authorities from developing countries sometimes remark that too often the personnel of European and North American universities, assistance agencies, and foundations have little experience that is relevant to current conditions in the developing world and, unfortunately, do not realize it.

The shift is particularly evident in fields associated with policy and organization. Most recent experience with fast-moving commodity production programs, with development of defined regions, and with synchronizing and reorienting government services has occurred in low-income countries.

This growth in intellectual leadership, still an incipient one, deserves to be fostered. New mechanisms are needed to help developing nations exchange information, materials, and views about agricultural research and strategies for rapid agricultural advance. The developing countries will increasingly learn from each other rather than from persons and institutions in the high-income countries.

Universities in the industrialized countries need to identify new ways to keep abreast of fast-moving developments in the low-income countries, for such knowledge will improve the quality and relevance of their advanced education. And agricultural research organizations in the developed countries should seek to cooperate more substantially in world networks of scientific activity because the level and quality of investigations in developing regions are improving rapidly.

THE PRIMARY SOLUTION

The primary solution to the food-poverty-population problem in the agrarian countries is known. It is to increase basic food production in these countries, and simultaneously to increase productivity and incomes of large numbers of rural people, by whatever means is feasible—agriculture, manufacturing, rural works, tourism, or extractive industry—to allow them to purchase food and other goods.

THE STRATEGY: THREE COMPLEMENTARY APPROACHES

There are three necessary, complementary (essentially co-equal) approaches to accelerated agricultural and rural development. For maximum progress at lowest cost and in minimum time, all three must be used to the extent possible:

- Organization of science-based, market-oriented commodity production systems for each significant crop and animal species. Authorities of each national commodity program should be in touch with foreign centers of science and development to ensure that advances, wherever they occur, are promptly used locally. These programs permit maximum gains in output per unit of investment while directly supporting defined-area development.[1]
- Development of defined areas with initial emphasis on increasing productivity and incomes of large numbers of rural people (often by giving priority to raising the productivity of the food crops that support most farm families). This approach, if good commodity-support sys-

[1] Floyd Williams (in a letter to the authors) suggests that "the primary purpose of a commodity program (from a developmental viewpoint), is not the immediate farm production achieved. The commodity program is a convenient (or even essential) vehicle to introduce, test, and prove the institutional changes needed to *continue* to increase productivity."

tems exist, is the quickest, least costly way to achieve widespread and reasonably equitable increases in purchasing power among the poor.

• Reorientation and synchronization of basic services—roads, communication systems, markets, input supply, banking, credit, research, and extension—locality by locality.

WHERE RESPONSIBILITY RESTS

A national government must set goals, establish policies, and take actions considered to be in the interests of its own people. Therefore, the single most important factor in the success of accelerated agricultural programs will be the willingness of governments:

• to commit funds and people to ambitious programs, and to sustain that support long enough to permit progress;

• to arrange for government agencies—agriculture, industry or commerce, planning, finance, education, public works, transportation, communications, and even foreign affairs—to work in concert toward established goals, overcoming entrenched interests where necessary; and

• to encourage business and industry to make the contributions that can best be handled by the private sector.

The government, by its own action or inaction, will shape the country's agricultural progress. Governments that plead that other requirements for funds will not permit large investment in rural programs are in fact according lower priority to those rural efforts. Success or failure in agricultural development in any country is largely a matter of choice for the government, not one of external entities.

External agencies should help those governments which have the will to help themselves. Since it is in the interest of each nation that others advance economically and socially, the affluent countries must make available capital, technical, research, and training assistance, for no other sources of these essential contributions are adequate.

Improving official assistance to individual countries

The assistance community, in cooperation with those governments willing to press for acceleration of agricultural development, could greatly improve the effectiveness of aid to individual countries in several ways.

STRATEGIC, COUNTRY-WIDE PLANNING

As a first step, the government of each developing country, aided by the major external agencies working with it, should identify long-term goals (up to 20 years) and plans of action.

Assistance versus cooperation

In 1966 David Bell pointed out that a foreign-aid program must be a partnership. Aid is not something a donor does *for* or *to* a recipient; rather, it should be *with* a recipient. This concept of cooperation appears to be replacing an earlier sense of "assistance" (with its implication of charity), in part because of the recognition of the mutual benefits of joint efforts to increase food supplies and to spur economic and social progress. Seemingly it is in identifying and facilitating new forms of cooperation—among disciplines, among agencies within developing countries, among the governments of developing countries and donors, among developing countries, among scientific groups wherever they are, and among the assistance agencies or donors themselves—that the greatest opportunities exist for improving the effectiveness of joint agricultural and rural development efforts.

The goals should reflect how demand will be influenced by growth in population, increases in affluence, and change in both the industrial and agricultural sectors. Goals should be accepted as estimates, at best, expressed as orders of magnitude and used as guidelines for action. Planning groups must not lavish time on detailed calculations or elaborate explanations which political leaders and agencies will not have time to read or which attempt levels of precision which the quality of basic data will not justify.

Broad plans of action should be prepared for the major components of the rural program—implementation of commodity production programs, development of defined areas, synchronization of basic service organizations—and all should be related to the long-term goals.

Planning should go well beyond design of specific projects to consideration of economic policies. The need for farmers to realize economic gain from their labor to justify production for sale in the market often conflicts with government policies aimed at generating revenues or holding down food prices in urban areas. Some observers believe that widespread distortions in prices are the primary barrier to the improvement of agriculture, to gains in prosperity in rural areas, and to general economic advance.

To be credible, planning should be conducted by qualified persons representing diverse areas of expertise and agencies of government. For design of commodity or defined-area programs, foreign advisors may be required, as is the case for other high-technology activities.

Planning is a continuous process. Properly implemented, it will bring together government officials, business administrators, scientists, financiers, and political leaders. Development of long-term plans will reveal both needs and opportunities for synchronizing the efforts of all con-

"Many LDC's [less-developed countries] perversely manipulate the market against their own agriculture. In 1975 the United States Department of Agriculture in a survey of 50 LDC's found that 38 countries in various stages of development controlled producer prices, typically holding them down; 35 countries also controlled consumer prices, typically holding them low; 26 countries practiced government procurement of food crops (requisitioned at fixed, low prices, typically enforced by heavy penalties); 22 countries levied export taxes on farm products often in ways exploitative of agriculture; and so on."

Charles M. Hardin
"Agricultural Price Policy in the United States"

cerned. Foreign agencies will then have a logical framework within which projects of narrower focus or short duration are likely to be reinforcing. If probable requirements are stated, priorities determined, and plans established by competent authorities, both the government and the assistance agencies will be better able to assess investment priorities.

NATIONAL COMMODITY PRODUCTION PROGRAMS

Few assistance agencies support direct national efforts to increase production of specific major basic food crops and animal species and to improve related marketing systems in the poorer countries. Clearly, support of campaigns to improve output of basic food commodities, if oriented to small farmers, contributes to improvement in the well-being of great numbers of the rural poor. Such action would both support and provide time for organization of efforts to develop rural areas, region by region.

Bilateral and multilateral agencies should provide financial and technical support for development of high-priority commodity production and marketing systems in each country, including the critical commodity research and training programs, and should insist that governments commit resources to these activities, set prices at levels which will allow farmers to participate profitably, and establish other policies necessary to success (Chapters 10 and 12).

AREA-DEVELOPMENT CAMPAIGNS

The number of agricultural development campaigns in localities or regions of developing countries has increased substantially since 1965 as interest in small farmers and other rural dwellers has grown. Bilateral and multilateral agencies, foundations, and private organizations should continue their support to these efforts (Chapter 10).

Systematic analyses, or comparisons, could improve the effectiveness of area-development campaigns. Exchanges of information at three levels should be encouraged. First, project leaders within a country should meet periodically to review progress, problems, and means of mutually reinforcing their projects. Second, projects in different countries within a region should be reviewed, as has been done in recent years in Southeast Asia. Third (and less frequently), interregional workshops or symposia should be organized to provide the project leaders and policymakers a broader range of experiences. External agencies can be particularly helpful in sponsoring regional and interregional comparative analyses.

INVOLVING COLLEGES AND UNIVERSITIES

A valuable change which could be made in some developing countries would be to enable colleges of agriculture to participate directly in research and development in partnership with other institutions and agencies in the national system (Chapter 14).

Too frequently, colleges are centers of dissent and agitation. However, many universities and colleges are making major contributions and are leaders in innovation. Means should be sought to make such advances known to authorities of other countries through preparation of case studies, symposia, and support of task forces with the mandate to describe strategies for university and college development.

CONCERTED, SUSTAINED SUPPORT

Most developing countries have numerous scattered schemes involving irrigation, forestry, plantation crops, livestock, credit, or integrated rural development. One country reported having over 150 projects involving more than 50 external assistance organizations, but there was little synchronization of activities either among donors or between donors and national agencies.

The presence of many projects in a country indicates the willingness of assistance agencies and the government to collaborate. The projects are evidence that professional and political people in governments are anxious to improve both strategies and operations. But if only short-term or isolated projects exist, agricultural development is unlikely to accelerate.

Large numbers of independent projects in a country result from several factors. For example:

- The leaders of local agencies may be changing frequently, with each new leader having a new set of priorities.
- Representatives of an assistance organization may encourage local agencies to undertake activities which it has the funds to finance or capabilities to implement, which are of short duration to avoid commitments that might go beyond its authority to implement alone, and which are simple enough to be easily understood by the head office.
- The recipient country may lack personnel who can orchestrate the

diverse activities of the many assistance agencies. Projects are approved which seem meritorious and which do not place excessive demands on local human or financial resources; then they are implemented in geographical or administrative isolation from others.

- Assistance organizations may be unwilling to accept coordination of their efforts with other bilateral or multilateral agencies in a country.
- Some recipient governments may not want the assistance community to cooperate, preferring instead to play each aid organization against the others in efforts to obtain the best deals possible.

The remedy may involve three related actions. First, the capabilities of national agencies to manage comprehensive development efforts and to negotiate with assistance organizations should be strengthened. This can be accomplished by training local personnel or by lending expatriate authorities to work *for* national agencies in negotiations with outside agencies.

Second, consultation among donors and assistance organizations on technical and financial support to the country should be continual (in collaboration with local authorities) to ensure that priority needs are met.[2]

Third, flexible and sustained grant support for planning, research, training, supplies and equipment, and outside expertise should be given to complement the support for discrete projects.

The home offices of assistance agencies may have to encourage their local representatives to work in concert with other foreign agencies. In each country a mechanism will be required for pooling some funds and personnel to supplement and complement work in the various projects negotiated by governments and individual aid agencies.

The world system: Opportunities for advance

Assistance agencies can also take several broader actions to improve the effectiveness of aid.

ACCOMMODATING POLITICAL CONSTRAINTS

The actions of most bilateral assistance agencies are influenced by year-to-year variations in political relations between donor and recipient, as well as by political and economic conditions within the aid-giving

[2] The World Bank sponsors periodic consultations of major assistance agencies for several large developing countries (Chapter 6).

country. This instability works against provision of the sustained help needed for agricultural development. New forms of cooperation are needed which accommodate political realities but which allow long-term and flexible support for agriculture. The Consultative Group for International Agricultural Research (Chapter 6) is one new mechanism of this type.

JOINT ACTION ON LARGE PROJECTS

Some development projects are so large that they may have to be implemented in phases spread over many years. They may cross national borders and they may require several assistance agencies and governments to pool their expertise and financial resources. Examples of such large undertakings within countries are the harnessing of the immense hydroelectric resources of Nepal and the development of 80 million hectares in southern Sudan. Examples of massive international projects are the efforts of the Club des Amis du Sahel in Africa and the Indus Basin Development Program in India. In *Development at a Crossroads: Present Problems, Future Prospects,* David Hopper explores the requirements for implementing such very large programs.

Large-scale projects often profoundly improve the climate for agricultural development. There is, however, no implicit reason that the farming operations within the project area should be large-scale and dependent on heavy machinery. Farm enterprises should be family owned and family operated unless there are clear-cut reasons for other systems (Chapter 11).

TECHNICAL SUPPORT TO SMALL POOR COUNTRIES

Most small poor countries must rely on outside institutions for agricultural research of the strategic and supporting types described in Chapter 12, for help in organizing programs for accelerated development, and for specialized training of their young people. The assistance community has responded to these needs in part by sponsoring the network of international agricultural research institutes (Chapter 6). Still, for many crops (vegetables, fruits, oilseeds, to name a few categories) and animal species, developing countries cannot readily find high-quality technical help and training. New ways are needed to facilitate the access of each country to research information and materials from other developing countries and to allow personnel to be trained at universities or institutes elsewhere in developing regions. Establishment of a nonpolitical and highly professional mechanism to link and strengthen national agricultural research and development systems could bridge important international scientific and technological gaps and greatly speed the progress of the countries concerned.

TERMS OF AID

One problem associated with loans or grants is that many assistance organizations have targets for commitment of funds by country or by sector (of which agriculture is one). As the *Asian Agricultural Survey 1976* notes: "One of the main performance criteria by which the agencies are judged within their home governments (bilateral agencies) or by their member governments (multilateral agencies) is the level of commitments made in any one budget year." The developing countries often do not generate enough good proposals. The agencies' own shortages of agricultural specialists preclude them from preparing small projects. In consequence, assistance agencies are tempted to look for easy ways to meet the targets. Large loans or grants may be favored because of the lighter workload per dollar of aid, while important but relatively inexpensive activities may be neglected. Or projects submitted by developing countries to donor-country embassies that have no agricultural staff (but that are still under pressure to meet commitment targets in agriculture) are transmitted through foreign-service channels to headquarters. By the time the proposals reach the assistance agency for review, the embassy may be committed to support, leaving the assistance agency little choice but to fund the projects, even if they are poorly conceived.

Another problem is that aid funds are commonly restricted to financing foreign-exchange requirements. This policy favors projects requiring large amounts of imported equipment or substantial numbers of foreign personnel over projects that are labor intensive or that rely on local talent. Bilateral-aid funds "tied" to procurement of equipment or personnel in the donor country restrict the ability of the recipient to shop for the best buy. And if operating funds are tied to use of assistance personnel solely from the donor country, the recipient country may be unable to obtain the best technical assistance (which is increasingly available from other developing countries).

A third problem is that the processing time for loans or grants often stretches to months or years. Some delays are caused by the indecision of agencies of recipient governments.

Experienced administrators in most agencies are aware of these shortcomings of aid and are relaxing rules and improving procedures as their adverse aspects are understood.

IMPROVING TECHNICAL ASSISTANCE

Developed nations have few agriculturists (with either natural or social science backgrounds) who are experienced in planning and implementing *accelerated* agricultural efforts. Agricultural advisors must have a good background in agriculture, knowledge of economics, experience, creativity in tailoring programs to meet local goals, and the ability to write proposals which can be funded and implemented.

Two main problems exist in preparing these individuals. First, the scientific and technical base for establishing high-yield agricultural production programs in the tropics and subtropics is still weak. Much agricultural technology, especially the biological and social components, is location specific—knowledge gained in temperate-climate countries cannot be directly transferred to tropical regions. Second, skills in planning and implementing accelerated agricultural efforts are learned most effectively through participation in intensive field programs. In the past, personnel from developed countries have acquired these skills by going abroad early in their careers in intern-like arrangements. Opportunities for young technicians to gain experience have decreased recently because of shortages of funds of donor agencies and the reluctance of the developing countries to accept advisors who lack substantial experience.

Some bilateral agencies are relying increasingly on universities and private institutions for expertise. At least in the U.S., however, the universities face a dilemma. On the one hand, U.S. universities recognize the serious needs of developing countries, they recognize that their staff members can help alleviate food problems and can benefit professionally from experience abroad, and they recognize that some lessons learned abroad may have relevance at home. On the other hand, their primary responsibilities, the duties for which they receive public support, are to serve their own states, so overseas work is usually difficult to justify. Their agricultural courses and research programs are becoming more narrowly specialized to serve the advanced agricultural systems of the U.S. Consequently, universities have fewer agricultural strategists and they are producing few of the broadly trained agronomists or animal production specialists developing countries need. In order to train personnel in these areas while carrying on their regular programs, the universities feel they must overstaff, which is difficult without long-term financial support. In addition, frequent overseas assignments interfere with professors' abilities to guide research programs at home, to produce publishable results as required for advancement, and to supervise graduate students.[3]

The number of agriculturists working in development can be expanded, and the quality of their contribution improved, in the following ways:

• Assistance agencies should explore means to increase professionally rewarding career opportunities in agricultural development, including assignment of technically competent agriculturists to high levels in assistance agencies.
• Universities and other agricultural institutions should receive long-term

[3] Title XII of the International Development and Food Assistance Act of 1975 is the latest U.S. effort to strengthen the capability of the U.S. universities to participate in international agricultural development.

government financial support to improve their knowledge of tropical agriculture and of strategies for rapid development.

• Opportunities should be sought for young professionals to work with more experienced persons on problems in developing countries.

• Biological scientists, economists, and others should be able to meet frequently to study and debate rapid-development strategies and techniques. Workshops, using case studies and participated in by authorities from both developing countries and assistance organizations, can be helpful.

DEEMPHASIZING BENEFIT-COST ANALYSES

The process of carrying out benefit-cost analysis—the discipline imposed by having to consider the different aspects of the project which may contribute to costs and benefits—can be instructive. However, preoccupation with deriving precise numbers can take the element of vision out of the development process. Use of benefit-cost analysis as the major tool to guide investments of talent and money may cause investments to flow to narrow, short-term projects in which costs and benefits can reasonably be calculated rather than to more flexible, sustained, and comprehensive programs for which benefits might be huge but quantitatively unmeasurable. If a good case for an investment can be demonstrated via benefit-cost analysis, that investment may well be of relatively low priority.

STRENGTHENING DEVELOPMENT-ORIENTED INFORMATION

A vast amount of literature on agricultural science and development is being produced for specialists or for popular audiences. Information on a crop or other topic is often highly technical and scattered through a wide array of scientific journals. Articles in the popular press are often so general as to be valueless for agricultural policymakers. Many of these articles are misleading, if not inaccurate.

Few publications exist which help individuals understand the basis for organizing national commodity research and production programs and the world research system on which nations can draw.[4] Nor are there enough short, readable, and credible statements on what is known and not known about implementing effective programs in land tenure, rural credit, processing, storage, marketing, or related matters. Most persons responsible for development programs in most countries are not trained in either agriculture or economics. Publications communicating the con-

[4] Over 300 agricultural commodities are produced in developing countries. FAO reports production data on about 100 of these. The international research centers are working with only about 25 commodities. Some, such as rice, wheat, maize, and sorghum, are of great and widespread importance, but many of the others, still neglected, are significant somewhere and important to the livelihood of many people.

cepts, principles, and strategies for accelerating agricultural development in understandable language are urgently needed.

VOLUME OF AID

Financial assistance for the agricultural development of low-income countries has been growing. However:

- Inflation has significantly reduced the "real" contribution of the aid.
- Probably less than two-thirds of the commitments for agricultural activities are related to food production.
- Not all of the additional food produced from the activities to which assistance is provided benefits the poor or malnourished.
- The indebtedness of the developing countries is growing rapidly, increasing the burden of interest repayment.
- Tariff barriers to imports from the developing countries remain high, inhibiting the ability of the low-income countries to generate financial resources through expanded trade.

In relation to the needs of the recipients or the resources of the donors, the level of financial assistance by developed countries is small. All sources of financial assistance in agriculture amount to less than a dollar a person annually in the developing countries. A constituency must be built up to support increased economic and technical assistance to the developing world.

FOOD AID AND FOOD RESERVES

Two controversial subjects in the assistance field have centered on provision of food to deficit-countries: food aid and the accumulation of grain reserves to stabilize fluctuations in prices and availabilities.

Food aid. For many years food commodities have been made available to developing countries as grants (gifts) or through concessional sales (Chapter 5). There is widespread support of emergency food aid for any nation hit by natural disaster or for the innocent victims of civil or international conflict. Likewise there is general support for food aid to supplement the nutrition of particularly vulnerable groups such as lactating mothers and very young children. While much more effort must go into making these programs work better, they generally are not an issue.

However, the case for food aid to contribute to the economic development efforts of low-income countries is not so clear. On the positive side, food aid can buffer shocks to the economic progress of countries which are subject to severe weather fluctuations. The poor, who spend most of their income on food, can benefit substantially if food prices do not rise abruptly. Food aid can also be used to employ the rural poor in labor-intensive construction of roads, markets, and water supplies, which form vital parts of a productive agricultural infrastructure. The fact is that, for internal political reasons, commodity aid costs donor countries less than direct financial aid. Prices and availability in the international grain markets change sharply over short periods.

Often, however, developed countries have used food aid as a foreign-policy tool. Because of short-term interpretations of "security interests," food aid has been available irregularly to some countries, and that has hurt their ability to use food aid effectively as development assistance.

Food aid should be planned and implemented so that it does not cause disincentives for food production in recipient countries. It should not be used as a means for lowering prices that farmers in developing nations receive. It must not encourage governments to neglect their agricultural sectors.

Food reserves. There never has been a "world food reserve" as such. Stocks have been held by some nations to meet possible year-to-year deficits, or to be released when prices climb during seasonal shortages, or in anticipation of war needs. And a number of exporting countries have accumulated surpluses for export or aid.

Considering the growing imports by developed and developing countries and the recent variations in weather, many informed observers expect wide fluctuations in future availability of food stocks, with even wider swings in prices. Some system of reserve stocks and related protective measures may be needed. It might have four elements, of which a "world" reserve is only one.

First, each developing country must be responsible for its own national reserves. Most will not wish to be dependent on others in a period of unpredictable supplies and prices. Nations that face periodic food deficits might be assisted by loans from international banks or bilateral-assistance agencies to establish storage facilities and to begin acquiring inventories of grain, flour, or other products which can be stored for long periods. While richer nations might provide some initial inventories on a concessional or grant basis, most supplies should be sold by exporters at market prices to avoid stifling the recipient nation's agriculture and its economic advance, or creating the undesirable dependence of any recipient on any donor.

Second, arrangements for mutual assistance among nations (food treaties) in the event of food shortages should be sought.

Third, stocks should be maintained in exporting countries. Individual exporters must be in a position to fulfill sales agreements if they are to retain shares of the world market. In the U.S., Canada, and perhaps other countries, farm storage adds resiliency to the world system while protecting the farmer against the necessity to sell at harvest time if prices are low. Governments, either by holding supplies directly or by facilitating storage by farmers and cooperatives, supplement the storage efforts of private business firms.

Fourth, creation of a world reserve stock should continue to be explored. Agreement must be reached on who would finance the reserves and in what proportions and on who would authorize their release and under what circumstances.

While reserve stocks are being organized, every possible effort should be made to raise food production and lower population growth rates wherever a food-population problem exists. The greatest food reserve is the world's underdeveloped capacity to raise yields.

Broadening private participation

As suggested in Chapters 3 and 8, increases in agricultural production by farmers, wherever they have occurred, have been aided significantly by

- advances in basic, supporting and strategic research by both the public and private research communities;
- innovation in marketing of products, manufacture and supply of inputs, organization of enterprises, and financing of agriculturally related activities, largely by private companies; and
- government policies which not only permit but encourage innovation and investment by private groups, adoption of productive and profitable systems by farmers and other rural people, and the synchronization of public and private activity.

Nevertheless, the crucial role of business and industry in accelerating agricultural development is still widely misunderstood.

BUSINESS AND INDUSTRY

Some leaders and citizens in developing countries believe the business world is made up of greedy organizations which are interested in quick profits (to be shipped out of the country in the case of multinationals) and which are indifferent to adverse effects on local people. Some industry executives counter that governments make conditions for profitable involvement difficult or risky, and have little regard for business's need to provide shareholders a fair return on investment in the investor's currency. However, rapid progress clearly will occur in most countries only if the private sector is directly and substantially involved.

The potential contributions of industry to agricultural advance are many. First, at substantial research and development cost, private companies are contributing a wide range of products, methods, and expertise for development of roads, transport, communications, irrigation, and power systems—all of which are essential to expansion of market-oriented agriculture in rural areas. Much of the research and development has been done in the industrial countries, and a high proportion of this technology, being nonbiological, can readily be transferred or adapted to developing countries. It is important, however, that future construction of road, power, and irrigation systems be coordinated with programs to strengthen agricultural production practices, input supply and marketing systems, and assistance to farmers.

Second, the private banks are experienced in mobilizing financial resources, nationally or internationally, and in administering credit systems. Credit must be extended to family farms and small rural businesses quickly, wherever other requisites for agricultural advance are in place. Particular attention must be given to financing the sale of large landholdings to family farmers and to the reinvestment of the proceeds in rural and urban industries. National and international private banks might contribute more effectively to national development as well as to their own business interests by hiring personnel who understand rapid agricultural development and can contribute unique insights to the design of strategies and more effective services.

Third, some private companies which specialize in the production, processing, storage, and marketing of specific commodities have access to major world markets. To acquire such expertise and to be able to compete in international markets, governments should seek out companies that are willing to participate in joint ventures. Attention should be given especially to arrangements for family-farm production of commodities for sale under contract to companies which will establish processing, handling, and marketing facilities.[5] This would allow rural people the benefits of land ownership yet provide for the integration of production, processing, and marketing.

Fourth, private producers and distributors of inputs such as seed, vaccines, or fertilizers are generally more efficient in their operations and more effective in getting farmers to use these critical products than are public agencies. They have the financial incentives to deliver quality products on time and at reasonable prices. Their distributors have an incentive to help farmers try new practices: they want to ensure payoff from use of the products and thereby foster repeat sales.

[5] Such arrangements are not without problems, however. In a review of the subject Maureen Mackintosh notes a trend toward establishment by multinational companies of small-grower schemes in developing countries, often with aid-agency collaboration. She cautions that through control of virtually all farm operations the small-grower may be unduly exploited. Such activities could become "as detrimental in their effects on rural areas as the much criticized plantations."

Fifth, much of the world's farm-machinery design and manufacturing skill resides in industry. Innovative small- and medium-scale machinery has been designed in some parts of the world. If world agriculture is to develop at a rapid pace and to benefit increasing numbers of rural people, small, inexpensive machinery must be provided together with manufacturing and repair facilities in the developing countries, as has occurred in Taiwan and Japan.

Opportunities exist for much more cooperation among private companies to foster rapid development of agriculture in developing countries and thereby to expand the world market economy. Local industrialists could organize to help the public sector advance as well as to promote private enterprise. For example, in the Dominican Republic the Association for Development, an organization of a dozen leading Dominican industrialists, has launched a major private bank, a savings and loan association to provide mortgage funds for middle-income people, and a college of agriculture which specializes in training young people for agribusiness careers.

"Industry," a vast complex of companies with diverse interests, is difficult for nonindustry people to comprehend. Industry must make more vigorous efforts to contribute to the implementation of strategies such as those described in this book. A few already exist:

- The International Executive Service Corps, an organization of retired business executives and other specialists from industry, headquartered in New York, provides assistance to companies in developing countries.
- The Latin American Association for Development, launched by a consortium of U.S. business firms, is helping small businesses in Latin America and the Caribbean.
- The Industry Cooperative Program of FAO has consisted of a number of major international firms which joined in efforts to accelerate development.
- In the U.S., the Agri-Business Council assists American corporations and companies or government agencies in developing countries to identify mutually beneficial investment opportunities and then to organize cooperative ventures.

"NONGOVERNMENT" ORGANIZATIONS

The numerous voluntary organizations that participate in agricultural and rural development provide clear evidence of the widespread desire of private citizens to help those less fortunate than themselves. These organizations vary in effectiveness, size, scope of activity, and sponsorship. Generally their staffs are dedicated and willing to work at the village level, even in difficult areas. Most deserve continuing financial support.

One frequent weakness of voluntary organizations is that the head-quarters personnel do not understand the agricultural development process and do not recognize the need for field people to have technical agricultural knowledge as well as farming skills. Such organizations should review the competency of their headquarters and field staffs to determine if they possess the necessary agricultural and technical background. Assistance agencies might consider financial support to enable organizations to strengthen their technical capabilities.

Implications for the U.S.

In this chapter we have spoken generally about the ways in which outside organizations can assist the low-income countries in their agricultural development efforts. However, we, the authors, while concerned about the world system, are citizens of a single country, the U.S. We have several recommendations which, if implemented, might greatly strengthen the contribution of the U.S. A number of these recommendations are applicable to other countries as well.

The U.S. has capable public institutions, industries, and individuals in agriculture, but they have been able to give only limited support to developing countries because of several handicaps. The first, primarily a political one, has largely been overcome. Until 1969, U.S. foreign-assistance agencies were reluctant to support programs to increase productivity of the basic food crops, particularly the cereal grains (Chapter 5).

Second, U.S. assistance efforts have been heavily influenced by short-term political considerations. Annual U.S. economic assistance to low-income countries totals only US$4,000 million, of which almost $1,500 million is in food aid. Over 40 percent of the rest goes to two countries, Egypt and Israel, leaving relatively little for the great numbers of other countries needing help. U.S. priorities need reexamination.

A third handicap is that most U.S. institutions and individuals have little experience in organizing fast-moving agricultural development campaigns. For 30 years, U.S. problems have involved overproduction.

Finally, neither the importance of U.S. involvement in agricultural development abroad nor a clear-cut strategy for U.S. participation appears to be understood at the higher levels of government. U.S. national science agencies are dominated by physical scientists, many of them carry-overs from the space program. There is little evidence that these people, by and large, understand the development of systems involving variables which are largely biological and social. In recent years the U.S. Agency for International Development has reduced the number of agricultural

Public support for foreign aid

In the wake of substantial publicity surrounding the 1974 World Food Conference, *The Christian Science Monitor* of January 22, 1975, reported substantial popular U.S. support for assistance to poorer countries. A poll indicated that 65.3 percent of Americans would "support long-term aid to other nations to help them to grow more food on their own"—even if it means "their taxes would rise"; only 16.6 percent were opposed, while 18.1 percent gave no response.

scientists on its staff, so its ability to handle agricultural programs has been seriously weakened.

It is time for the U.S. to redirect and strengthen its assistance to foreign agricultural development. It has much to gain by doing so.

First, U.S. policy must reflect the fact that increased food production alone—in the U.S. or elsewhere—represents only half of the solution to the food problem. The other half is lifting the incomes of the poor; this is the only way for most to gain access to food as well as to other necessities.

Second, the U.S. needs a clear strategy for its own long-term efforts to stimulate the agricultural and general economic development of scores of nations. That technology-led strategy must promote labor-intensive agricultural systems, industries, and public works, especially in densely settled, largely agrarian nations. The participation of U.S. citizens and institutions should be tailored to those needs.

Third, the U.S. should maintain a much stronger bilateral technical assistance program. The activities of the international banks and international assistance agencies are improving and deserve continuing and expanded U.S. support. However, there is great strength in complementary efforts.

Fourth, assistance for agricultural and rural development should be placed under the guidance of the most knowledgeable and experienced people in the country. For the same reason that agriculturists should not be put in charge of a space or energy program, agricultural and rural development efforts should not be entrusted primarily to political or physical scientists, or to individuals without experience in accelerated development abroad.

Fifth, a permanent organization is needed to develop and pursue a national strategy for all U.S. agricultural assistance—financial, technical, research, training, and food assistance. The organization should have the funds to implement the strategy and should be able to involve universities, government agencies, industry, and voluntary organizations in a concerted effort. Such an organization should be insulated from varying political objectives and divorced from military assistance.

Sixth, a federally supported "war college" for development should be created. At this research and study center, U.S. personnel and students from abroad could work together on strategies and techniques for rapid agricultural and rural development. The center would have an experienced full-time staff. Faculty members of the nation's universities could participate from time to time for a semester or a year. Participating for a semester, students from the U.S. or abroad could study the development process and learn how to manage its components. Credit for courses could be granted by the cooperating universities. Through involvement of its faculty and students in activities at such a center, the effectiveness of each university's international program could be upgraded.

These suggestions, when combined with the more general observations of the previous two sections, might provide a basis for a new, more effective U.S. agricultural assistance program.

Concluding comments

It may now be realistic to hope that much of the world's hunger and poverty can be alleviated within the next generation. Progress will be uneven, because advances must occur nation by nation, and their governments vary in commitment to action.

IMPORTANCE OF VISION

The environment for payoff in agricultural development is of central concern to officials of assistance agencies. As David Hopper ("Investment in Agriculture: The Essentials for Payoff") remarked in 1968:

I have met only a few government officials in developing countries who have a clear vision of what is and what will be needed to modernize national agriculture. The absence of such a vision is perhaps the single most serious impediment to developing action strategies for rural economic advancement. In some countries rigid bureaucratic plans for orderly development are used as substitutes for management based on clear vision; the result need not be discussed here, for it is a depressing topic. In other countries development is left to the free play of economic and social forces, and little attempt is made to provide direction or to focus on the components of growth; this is a solution that saves trouble but does nothing to promote change. Still other countries rely on outside, usually short-term, experts, who often have little vision and seldom possess more than a superficial understanding of the agriculture of the country. Yet unless government leadership has a vision that is rich with understanding, the ebb and flow of development will be viewed with consternation, opportunities will be missed, and the weather-induced vagaries in national output will induce alternate periods of depression and self-congratulation.

"Man has become the potential master of his own fate in his struggles for subsistence. Thanks to science and technology, he has the means to restrict his numbers simply and humanely and to increase his food supplies quickly and substantially. But to become actual master of his fate, he must have the will and wisdom to utilize fully his present means and the wit to devise better ones for the future."

> E. C. Stakman
> "Education: Needs and Virtues, Crimes and Misdemeanors"

But men of vision, if found, must be supported by the concerted actions of government agencies if their visions are to be translated into realities. Responsibility for planning and implementing action is typically sunk in a morass of confused lines of authority, split among overlapping agencies that separate related functions and group separate functions, surrounded by petty bureaucracies that place a higher premium on self-preservation and enhancement than on performance, subject to irresolute leadership in administration, and hampered by staff policies that provide few rewards for effective performance and even fewer methods for punishing and removing delinquents.

Although I have painted a dark picture of government impotency, it is my belief that once agriculture gathers momentum, the political initiative for sustaining the forward motion will be seized by farmers pressing demands for advancements in technology, for more input supplies, and for remunerative prices. In the face of these demands, few governments can remain unresponsive. A shifting of political initiative from urban elites to rural spokesmen is already evident in some developing nations, and while farmers, politicians, and bureaucrats may make strange companions in the quest for mutual enlightenment, the search, once begun, cannot be halted.

Men of vision are emerging in governments, in assistance organizations, in academia, and in industry. Were it not so, the networks of financial, technical, research, and training assistance would not exist, those governments now taking action would still be ignoring their opportunities, and the strategies for rapid development could not be emerging. Nevertheless, men of vision—strategic thinkers—are still in extremely short supply.

NEED FOR STRATEGIES

What are needed now are strategies for action, country by country and globally, to guide the many partners whose futures are intertwined and at stake.

We have attempted to outline a general strategy. It is obviously based on our own interpretation of evidence and experience. Others with different experience will probably be able to present and defend other, perhaps better, approaches. That should be encouraged in and for each developing country, in each bilateral- or multilateral-assistance agency, in each university, and by industrial groups. While much work remains to be done on individual pieces of the strategy (for example, research and extension systems, decentralized marketing and input supply systems, farm enterprise options, strategies for individual farming districts), comprehensive or overall strategies should receive the attention of individuals or groups capable of describing what to do and how to do it, in language that is understandable to educated people of diverse interests. Are there alternatives to the three-component approach we have described which would result in faster progress at lower cost to the countries in difficulty?

TIME FOR ACTION, NOT DESPAIR

Many weaknesses remain in the world's assistance efforts. However, in recalling that the seriousness and complexity of the world food-poverty-population problem was not generally recognized until the mid-1960s, one might say that progress has been remarkable. As strategies are understood, tested, and perfected, as we expect they will be, progress should become more rapid. As assistance organizations demonstrate that they are in command of a realistic strategy, as they find new ways to cooperate, and as they staff their organizations with competent and experienced persons, public support of their efforts should grow.

This is a time not for despair, but for a renewed commitment characterized by confidence, competence, and increasing cooperation.

References

INTRODUCTION

International Food Policy Research Institute. *Food Needs of Developing Countries: Projections of Production and Consumption to 1990.* Research Report No. 3. Washington, D.C.: International Food Policy Research Institute, 1977.

BASIC CONSIDERATIONS

Hopper, W. David. *The Politics of Food.* Ottawa: International Development Research Centre, 1977.

IMPROVING OFFICIAL ASSISTANCE TO INDIVIDUAL COUNTRIES

Bell, David E. "The Quality of Aid." *Foreign Affairs* 44 (1966): 601–7.

THE WORLD SYSTEM: OPPORTUNITIES FOR ADVANCE

American Council of Voluntary Agencies for Foreign Service. Technical Assistance Information Clearing House. *U.S. Non-Profit Organizations in Development Assistance Abroad.* New York: American Council of Voluntary Agencies for Foreign Service, 1971.

Asian Development Bank. *Asian Agricultural Survey 1976.* Manila: Asian Development Bank, 1977.

Brookings Institution. *Toward the Integration of World Agriculture.* Washington, D.C.: Brookings Institution, 1973.

Hardin, Charles M. "Agricultural Price Policy in the United States: The Political Feasibility of a Market-Oriented Policy." Mimeographed. Davis: University of California, 1977.

Hopper, W. David. *Development at a Crossroads: Present Problems, Future Prospects.* Ottawa: International Development Research Centre, 1977.

Partners in Development: Report of the Commission on International Development, Lester B. Pearson, chairman. New York: Praeger, 1969.

U.S. Department of Agriculture, Economics, Statistics, and Cooperatives Service. *International Food Policy Issues: A Proceedings.* Foreign Agricultural Economic Report No. 143. Washington, D.C.: U.S. Department of Agriculture, 1978.

Williams, Maurice J. *Development Cooperation: Efforts and Policies of the Members of the Development Assistance Committee—1976 Review.* Paris: Organisation for Economic Cooperation and Development, 1976.

BROADENING PRIVATE PARTICIPATION

Brandow, G. E. "The Place of U.S. Food in Eliminating World Hunger." *Annals of the American Academy of Political and Social Science* 429 (1977): 1–11.

Mackintosh, Maureen. "Fruits and Vegetables as an International Commodity." *Food Policy* 2 (1977): 227–92.

IMPLICATIONS FOR THE U.S.

McCormick, Lynde. "How to Help World Hunger." *Christian Science Monitor,* January 22, 1975, p. 5.

Poats, Rutherford M. *Technology for Developing Nations.* Washington, D.C.: Brookings Institution, 1972.

U.S. President's Science Advisory Committee. *The World Food Problem,* vol. 1. Washington, D.C.: U.S. Government Printing Office, 1967.

Wortman, Sterling. *The World Food Situation: A New Initiative.* Working Paper. New York: Rockefeller Foundation, 1975.

CONCLUDING COMMENTS

Hopper, W. David. "Investment in Agriculture: The Essentials for Payoff." In *Strategy for the Conquest of Hunger: Proceedings of a Symposium.* New York: Rockefeller Foundation, 1968.

Stakman, E. D. "Education: Needs and Virtues, Crimes and Misdemeanors." In *New Concepts in Agricultural Education,* edited by A. S. Atwal. Ludhiana, India: Punjab Agricultural University Press, 1969.

Corn. *See* Maize
Cost-benefit studies, 294
Cowpeas, 171; cooperative yield trials on, 171; diseases of, 172
Credit: agricultural, 8, 9, 118, 333, 361–65; rates of, 361
Crookes, Sir William, 84
Crop campaigns: in India, 10, 11; in Kenya, 10; in the Philippines, 11; in Turkey, 11. *See also* Chapter 8.
Crop domestication, centers of, 36 (Fig. 3.1)
Crops: improvement of, 43; neglected, 178; rotation of, 37; varieties of, 8; yields of, 147
CRRI. *See* Central Rice Research Institute, India
Cyperus rotundus. See Sedge

de Datta, S. K., 152n
Default, 363
Defined-area campaigns, 10, 219–24, 249, 252–58; payoff from, 293, 294; production and training centers for, 331, 33; staffing of, 330
Defined-area research systems, 329
Department of Agriculture and Natural Resources, Philippines, 217
Developing countries, 17 and n, 122; characteristics of, 4, 123
Developing market economy countries, 1n, 30
Development, 97, 98, 415; agricultural (*see* Agricultural development); area campaigns for, 412, 413; economic, 4, 229, 265; information on, 419; institutional, 11; orientation of, 399; rural, 3, 117n, 251
Development Assistance Committee, OECD, 114 and n
Diaz-Cisneros, Heliodoro, 221n, 223
Dioscorea spp. See Yams
DMCS. *See* Developing Member Countries of the Asian Development Bank
Domesticated plants, 36 (Fig. 3.1)
Drainage, 354–57
Drilon, J. D., 217
Drought, 20; in Argentina, 20; in China, 20; in India, 20, 23, 25, 90; in Pakistan, 20, 23; in Sahel, 20
Dry beans. *See* Beans

East Coast fever, 66, 181
Economic Research Service, USDA, 85
EMBRAPA. *See* Brazilian Corporation for Agricultural Research
Energy, 72, 73; nonrenewable, 73, 74; use of, 73

Environment, and agriculture, 63
Erisyphe graminis. See Barley, diseases of
Erlich, Paul, 84
Escuela Agricola Pan-America, Honduras, 392
Esman, Milton J., 220
Euroconsult, the Netherlands, 127
European assistance programs, 114
European Development Fund, 119
Ewell, Raymond, 70n
Extension services, 9, 190, 312 and n, 313–15, 391, 395, 396; in Japan, 194

Factors of production, 38
Family farm, commercial, as a national objective, 278, 279
FAO. *See* Food and Agriculture Organization, UN
Farm credit. *See* Credit
Farm enterprises, 271–89; allocation of labor in, 41; associations of family farms, 277, 278; corporate, 275; family, 276, 277; group, 275, 276; latifundia, 278; minifundia, 278; state, 275, 276
Farmers: instruction of, 237, 330; participation of, 8, 262; programs for, 8, 102, 103, 104, 239–41, 312, 362; rationality of, 40, 42; small, 8, 102–4; small, bias against, 362; status of, 42
Farming: diversified intensive, 48, 49; modern, 358, 359
Farming systems: development of local, 39, 298, 299; improved, 8, 236, 237, 329, 333; input availability and distribution in, 343; profitable, 3; subsistence, 7; traditional, 2, 7, 38, 39
Farm production, increasing, 7, 8; and on-farm trials, 328, 329
Farm size, in selected Asian countries, 103
Feasibility studies, 262
Feedgrain production, 23
Fertilizer, 37, 44, 67, 145, 188, 227, 344–49; consumption of, 45, 67; distribution of, to the farmer, 348; estimating demand for, 347, 348 and n; nitrogen, 70; organic, 69; phosphate, 70; potash, 70; pricing of, 347; production of, 69, 187; recommendations for use of, 344; testing of, 333
Field station system, 335
Fish, 74–77; protein concentrate from, 97
Fishing: financial of, 118; international understanding on, 76; management of, 76

Library of Congress Cataloging in Publication Data

Wortman, Sterling, 1923–
  To feed this world.

  Includes bibliographies and index.
    1. Food supply. 2. Underdeveloped areas—Food supply. 3. Underdeveloped
areas—Agriculture. I. Cummings, Ralph Waldo, joint author. II. Title.
HD9000.6.W64   338.1'9   78-8478

ISBN 0-8018-2136-3   ISBN 0-8018-2137-1 pbk.